Dire Wolf Project:

Creating an Extraordinary Dog Breed

Jennifer Stoeckl

Forward by Lois E Schwarz

DireWolf Publishing

Hunters, Washington

LIMIT OF LIABILITY/DISCLAIMER OF WAARANTY: This publication is designed to provide accurate and authoritative information in regard to the subject matter covered. Some names and identifying details of people described in this book have been altered to protect their privacy. It is sold with the understanding that neither the author nor the publisher is engaged in rendering professional services. While the publisher and author have used their best efforts in preparing this book, they make no representations or warranties with respect to the accuracy or completeness of the contents of this book and specifically disclaim any implied warranties of merchantability or fitness for a particular purpose. No warranty may be created or extended by sales representatives or written sales materials. The advice and strategies contained herein may not be suitable for your situation. You should consult with a professional when appropriate. Neither the publisher nor the author shall be liable for any loss of profit or any other commercial damages, including but not limited to special, incidental, consequential, personal, or other damages. This book presents the research and ideas of its author and a great breadth of professionals. It is not intended as a substitute for consultation with a veterinary professional, geneticist, or other professional in animal husbandry who is familiar with the latest advances in the field. The author and the publisher disclaim responsibility for any adverse effects resulting directly or indirectly from information contained in this book.

DIRE WOLF PROJECT: CREATING AN EXTRAORDINARY DOG BREED

Traveling from purebred to strongbred on the road to healthy, long-lived dogs

By Jennifer Stoeckl

1. Science : Zoology - Mammals 2. Biological Sciences : Zoology : Mammals 3. Animal Care & Pets : Dogs – Breeds

Library of Congress Cataloguing-in-Publication Data is available.
ASIN: B07M6H8YM8 (Kindle eBook)
ISBN: 978-1-950333-01-1 (Paperback)

Cover design by Jennifer Stoeckl, Edited by DireWolf Publishing

Printed in the United States of America

DireWolf Publishing, 5502 Highway 25 South, Fruitland, WA 99129.

www.direwolfpublishing.com, www.direwolfdogs.com, www.direwolfproject.com

For Lois E Schwarz - mother, mentor, and Master of Nothing from the University of Zilch.

Table of Contents

Silver River (Harpo/Aspen), 2019

Acknowledgements

First of all, I would like to thank those members of the Friends of Pedigree Dogs Exposed Facebook group for their generously unrelenting questions and unrestrained accusations. It was truly a pleasure debating and discussing the differences of the majority's accepted way of breeding from the Dire Wolf Project's way of breeding. Indeed, the endless poking and prodding at the very foundation of why and how the Dire Wolf Project chooses to breed gave rise to the idea for this book. It was the repeated accusations that the Dire Wolf Project is unscientific and unethical in its approach that started the incessant nagging in the back of this author's mind that a comprehensive book housing the scientific background and code of ethics with which Dire Wolf Project breeders strictly adhere was sorely needed.

I would also like to thank the administrative team behind the Friends of Pedigree Dogs Exposed Facebook group for their ability to see that the debates were productive in their content and therefore did not need to be squelched or silenced. Although the interchanges were at times emotional, those who participated were mostly willing to politely respond to someone with a different view. My only regret was that I invariably left so many questions unanswered. The pace of the debates were exceedingly swift and I was not able to see each question at the time it was posted and as a result many questions slipped by without a reply. I know that some people were frustrated that not all of their questions were answered and perhaps the fast-paced, all-against-one feel of the interchange on Facebook is not the best approach to understanding the differences between us. In any respect, this is one of the reasons I felt a strong need for this book.

One particular person, Carol Nicheli, was extremely instrumental in my understanding of the need for this book. I would personally like to acknowledge the gratitude I have for her unyielding desire to spread how wrong it is to breed as shall be described in this book. Ms. Nicheli's vast knowledge of the right way to breed created a vessel for which I became increasingly dedicated to challenging those strong and deeply held beliefs about what is right and what is wrong when it comes to sustaining and maintaining a healthy, long-lived and stable-tempered dog breed. Ms. Nicheli was always kind in spirit and respectful in her debate when speaking about her understanding of dog breeding and for her ability to challenge with respectful dignity I tip my hat. It is my hope that those who may not agree with the Dire Wolf Project's views may be as spirited and yet also as respectful as she. It is my belief that respectful debates surrounding dog breeding should occur. To challenge each other in our disagreements can bring us to better ideas and give rise to better lives for our most cherished of pets. Thank you, Ms. Nicheli, for your willingness to stand up for what you believe is right and not back down when you easily could have. Your thoughtful challenging retorts have earned this author's deepest respect and my gratitude for your ability to debate on such a level strengthens my love for humanity.

I would also like to deeply thank the founder of the Dire Wolf Project, Lois Schwarz, for her ability to face outright disgust and hate for her breeding practices without losing her unyielding focus. If what Fortune 500 consultant and author Dave Yoho says is correct, "The power of any idea is measured by the resistance it attracts," then Lois Schwarz has been able to put together the greatest dog breeding regime that has ever existed. The opposition she receives is unrelenting, vulgar, spiteful, hateful, and ever watchful to catch her in the slightest mishap. But, throughout the years of opposition, Lois has remained steadfast, devoting her entire life to this pursuit. By being the massively strong person she is, Lois Schwarz has influenced a new generation of breeders who can look beyond the majority's rhetoric and seek what is true, no matter what consequences arise. Lois Schwarz is a fierce warrior for truth, but she is also a person who does not dictate what others should do or how they should be. She has a passion for what she does and her unwavering, stoic dedication to her passion is one of the most endearing aspects of who she is. When this author first became interested in this breeding project, there were so many questions flying around. Lois not only answered them, but then gently stated, "If you don't believe me, go look it up." She never once tried to influence me to think one way or another. When the research began, it was a certainty that she was wrong. After all, how could the majority be wrong and this unknown person without credentials or influence of any kind have more understanding about breeding than so many others claiming the exact opposite of her own approach? However, with each question that was posed, the research proved Lois correct time and time again. After ten years of questions and researching, I finally realized that Lois was not wrong in her way of breeding and that, in fact, her breeding practices made a lot of sense and could be backed up by solid evidence. It was then that this author chose to join her in her quest to create a dog breed unlike any other: a modern breed for a modern age.

My endearing gratitude for my husband Jay who chose to put up with the countless hours of research throughout the years and ultimately came to the conclusion that this "hobby" was much more than he ever thought, giving all of his support. He has helped me through so many writing dilemmas that I could not have resolved on my own. Thank you to my dearest friend.

Furthermore, I would like to thank Shawna Davies for her willingness to accept our disheveled and humble beginnings and ride along with us as the Dire Wolf Project progressed in its ability to openly share how and why we operate. She has endured the test of time and hasn't given up on the future she saw for the people who clung to the ideals in this book. She deserves a most hardy thank you for her encouragement to pursue this writing and for her steadfast friendship throughout these years.

A big thank you to Dave for the care and feeding of my DireWolf Dogs for an entire summer so that this author had the chance to spend the time necessary to lay down the majority of the content in this book. The many hot days that he toiled away in the sun in order to make life a better place on our land are sincerely appreciated. Without his support when my husband was away for extended periods of time, this book would not have been written.

It is with great esteem that I acknowledge the generosity of Pete Puleo. He helped to fact-check several of the most technical chapters to keep me on the path of truth. His ability to check my math and help me see the broader perspective was invaluable. His support of the Dire Wolf Project gives hope that this work will one day be welcomed by those much smarter than myself.

A warm and heartfelt thank you to all of the dedicated American Alsatian owners who have stood by the Dire Wolf Project through thick and thin. The gratitude that we feel for our cohesive owner's group is beyond measure and it is with deep conviction that we keep seeking knowledge together. Each American Alsatian owner knowingly enters into a family of believers in a new way of sustaining an entire dog breed over the long term, where attention to health and longevity come first and temperament is honored above the outward appearance of the dog. If this book could hold the number of pages, I would list you all by name.

Forward by Lois E. Schwarz

Jennifer Stoeckl is my natural born first child of Anthony George Mezey Jr and was with me in my life for the first 10 years of her life. These were very impressionable years in her life as she learned all she could from me as a mother and teacher to her. After having my two other children and then leaving an abusive relationship, Jennifer went to live with my mom and dad so that she could grow up in a secure world; one that I could not give her. During this time, I got back on my feet and delved more into the canine world than I had ever been, owning many dogs and many dog grooming/training and boarding shops. During this time I gathered information for many books I had planned to write, started up the many different mix breedings, as well as developed my own style of breeding when I put together the new breed of dog that I called the 'Shepalute'.

Though Jennifer was not with me through all of this intense study, breeding, and caring for these dogs, she was into her studies in school getting top grades and credits that would take her off into the direction of "teacher." My mom and dad had given her the stability and devotion to her trainings that I could have never given her for my struggle was in a different area. I do believe this was all for the good of our family and our lives.

When she did visit she didn't have a clue what was going on within my complex mind. All she knew was that her mother was into her dogs and her work. Jennifer saw me not as a mom so much, but as a dog breeder, trainer, shop owner, groomer and I am sure she thought me a bit "touched." My life was chaotic in comparison to her wonderfully stable life with my mom and dad and her piano lessons after school.

It was not until I lost everything and traveled up to see my folks that my first born and I would spend more time together. Though she was off to school studying to be the best teacher she could be and into her own life and relationships, we began gaining back some kind of a relationship that I felt was not as a mother and daughter, but more of friends. It was not a fast, "okay, you are my mom and I will respect you" kind of a relationship, it was more of a "you're a crazy person and you are my mom, but I am not a child and let's see how this goes" kind of a relationship.

After Jennifer got married to Jay Stoeckl we had more time to chat over the phone or over the internet and she began to ask me about my dogs. She knew I was still breeding my dogs and she had visited my web sites but she thought I was simply a great salesperson and laughed at me many times. She had a few of my dogs and had seen some of them but she had no real clue as to what it was I was doing. "Who is my mother?" was more like how it was.

In the 1990s, I had given her one of my dogs back in which she named Sophie. She really liked this dog, but I had co-owned it with her and I needed Sophie to come back to the Ojai Ranch for breeding. While at the ranch Sophie suddenly died. All I could think is that she died of a broken heart as she passed in the morning while I was gone to the Grooming Shop. I am sure this event affected her greatly. She never had another of my dogs until 2008 when I began breeding a few up in Southern Oregon at her grandmother's home. My dad had died and I stayed with my mom to help her out. I brought a few dogs up with me and had a couple of litters. Jen and Jay came by and said they wanted to have a pup that they could train for search and rescue. I discussed the temperaments of a litter and chose an independent pup for her and Jay. I told her the reason why this pup was better for her and that I did not desire independent pups in my breeding program. I think she investigated everything I ever told her about my breeding ideas, but I had no clue she thought that I did not know what I was doing. Lol… I really did think she knew that I knew a lot about dogs. What I did not know was that she thought I was just the world's best salesperson. Haha. I will NEVER forget the day she gave me a plaque stating I was the world's best person at knowing nothing.

She did start looking into the things I was telling her and that's when her study began in earnest. Besides training her dog for search and rescue, she and I now had a multitude of things to discuss over the phone and internet because she was now in the field for which I was so deeply involved. And so, she continued researching everything I was telling her. That is when she began to put what I was saying into perspective and it all came together for her that her mother was actually brilliant and a genius. Lol! I remember one day she told me that she looked up the word "hybrid vigor" and wondered how the heck I knew anything about that!

Jennifer has been doing what Jennifer does best. She studies. She uses her mind and she delves into what she loves and believes in. She owes the government hundreds of dollars in school loans for all that education and knowledge she gained to become a teacher and she dropped out of teaching. The love the beliefs that she and Jay hold in their hearts. Beliefs for liberty and justice of the American people, freedom, and TRUTH; for knowing life and education had been politically sacrificed so much that teaching was no longer done in earnest and there were far too many demands and rules against teachers and their ability to share their classrooms in the way these two knew it should be done. Teaching today was not as they believed it should be. Teaching was more of a strenuous demanding job without the dedication of great people standing behind teachers as support. There was nothing that could be done but to continue to teach with their hands tied behind their backs and that was not acceptable to these folks that would give their all to teach in the ways that they felt would best benefit our children. So they left the teaching field to give their time and life to what they believed in; that which would benefit more of Gods children of the earth - breeding the best companion dogs ever!

At first I did not know if they could do this. It takes dedication and a strong will, along with a strong heart to breed dogs and then to breed them my way. These two folks were very companionate and loved life and nature, almost to the point of being what I called "tree hugger." I felt that a few dead puppies and they would be out of the business of breeding my dogs. But, I am a person that can sit back and wait, watch, and listen. I gave them a few dogs and conditions and they both got through it all. Many phone calls and emails and chatting. Many of my writings to her, my thoughts, my words of wisdom and knowledge she took to heart and studied, researched, and proved. See we are not people that take the words of another and just "believe" them. We are people that challenge and research and discuss things, and so she did. And each time I talked with her, she went on the Internet and challenged my positions. Always she came back astonished that I knew anything at all about what I had been doing all my life. How did her mother know such things?

What she has learned, what she has written, what she has grown into, I am very proud to say, is her. She can and does take my meanings and write them so that the more educated can "see" what I am saying. I am not a college educated gal. I am an "earth mother." I am nature and my words are simple. I strive to communicate to the basic human beings in small easy colorful ways, so that many can "hear me" or "see" what it is I am saying. Jennifer understands me and can take what I am saying and put it in a different way; can compare my ways to the ways of another world of which I am no part of.

I am excited to see all she has learned, all she has to say. I am glad that this girl is in this world and happy that she has the love of God's children in her heart. I love you Jennifer Stoeckl. You go girl!

Introduction

I suddenly felt extremely uncomfortable, that kind of feeling you get in the pit of your stomach just before you know something bad is about to happen.

Two of the world's most prominent dog breeders, each with their own highly passionate but opposing views, clenched their fists and glared at one another, gearing up for a turbulent verbal debate. Unfortunately, I sat between them. Furthermore, I loved them both since the two rivals were my mother and her sister.

I was born into a dog family. You know how some people are born into a wealthy family, poor family, nomadic family, artistic family, or some other type of family. Well, I was born into a dog family. My mother, her two sisters, her brother, and her parents are not only passionate about the love they share for man's best friend, but they are also deeply entrenched in the all-encompassing dog breeding, showing, and training game for their favorite breed. My aunt in Florida breeds and shows Irish Wolfhounds with a keen eye for beautiful conformation. She is on the road to American Kennel Club (AKC) judgeship and will likely become a judge for the Irish Wolfhound breed in the near future. My other aunt in northern California owns an organic dairy farm. She trains livestock guardian dogs, mostly the Great Pyrenees, for farm work. Not only has she professionally shown the English Cocker Spaniel and the German Shepherd Dog through AKC, but has also successfully trained many Border Collies and Farm Shepherds to do what they love, herd on the farm. My mother's oldest brother in Las Vegas is a highly dedicated purebred dog owner, representative of the average dog owner around the country. He and his wife have always had two or three dogs in their home and are never without them. Their dogs are their furry children and are raised as any other human member of the family. My mother's parents, who raised me from five years old onward, always kept dogs in the house. They bred their dogs from time to time and sold the puppies to local families around southern California. You could say they were the epitome of the backyard breeder. But, it is my mother, Lois Schwarz, someone I had always sought to know more intimately, who unwittingly influenced me to follow in my family's passion for dogs. Always the black sheep in a soft, grassy meadow of white ones, my mother took a completely different path. You see, my mother is the founder of an entirely new breed, the American Alsatian dog, bred specifically for a new purpose in order to advance the evolution of our furry companions to fit within our rapidly shifting modern western society.

Many truly dedicated dog people have a certain way about them and my family is no exception. We tend to be highly passionate people with an even deeper passion for the knowledge we have learned about the four-legged creatures we love. The trouble is that each of my family members has come to a different understanding about dogs. When it comes to training, showing, and living with dogs, there are so many different opinions out there. My family is the perfect microcosm of the larger dog world and so each has a different way of training and breeding, with a different eye for beauty. Needless to say, it is oftentimes difficult for my family to get together at one table and share openly about their lives. Too much tension quickly arises because the most passionate topic for all of my family inevitably gets broached. So, talking about dogs has become taboo and mostly we each go our separate ways with very little interaction from one another.

In this rarer moment of family bonding, the founder of an entirely new dog breed and a very well-respected Irish Wolfhound breeder and future AKC judge sat on either side of me as the tension mounted. "If you breed one of your Irish Wolfhounds to a M'loot Alaskan Malamute, your puppies would have better health and longevity." And the battle began.

Explaining the reason these two very knowledgeable and passionate minds have come to completely different conclusions regarding dog breeding is the very purpose of this book. My aunt is of the strong majority opinion that dog breeding should adhere to the long established breeding practices of the purebred world. When we look at the purebred dog and genetic health issues that have proven to be on the rise, one has to wonder what it is that has occurred to change these once thriving dog breeds toward a now uncertain future.

Conversely, through trial and error, Lois, ever the non-conformist, found the old way, nature's way, and through her work she has revitalized this long forgotten breeding path.

As you will come to understand through reading this book, I have found, through long and arduous study, that my mother holds the key to the future of dog breeding; a future where genetic disease is nearly eliminated and genetic diversity remains high resulting in healthy, long-lived dog breeds, and thus the very breeds we cherish so much are preserved -- no longer pure of breeding, but strong in breeding.

The methods established by the founder of the Dire Wolf Project, Lois Schwarz, are different in so many ways to that of the majority's prescribed breeding practices. In fact, in many cases, the methods used by the Dire Wolf Project are the exact opposite from those of the majority. We make no apology for our approach. Instead, we wholeheartedly embrace the practices established by our founder and hope that more breeds will choose to utilize some, many, or all of our methods for the betterment of their own breeds. With that being said, we do not claim to know all there is to know about breeding. We leave that to God's all-knowing understanding of what should be and why when it comes to breeding for the best health and longevity in the canid. We have, instead, been sharp observers of what God has created and the rules by which nature breeds so that we can employ them as much as humanly possible in our breed.

Many of those who do not understand (or are unwilling to understand) have ridiculed and defamed our breeding practices, labeling us as "worse than a backyard breeder." This unfair and hypocritical analysis of our work is one of the reasons it has been necessary to put all of our research and understanding inside one volume. This book has, as a result, been designed to establish a sort of burden of proof for our claims. It has taken over ten years of research, study, breeding experience, and founder questioning to write the contents written herein. Extreme care has been taken to not only be exactingly true to the founder's practices, but also to interpret her methods with clarity. Research and keen scientific observation has been the bedrock and foundation of this breed and this book. Throughout every chapter, it has been the sole intention to make sure that the research used is solid, reproducible, and without bias and that the arguments are logical and do not contain fallacy. Here, in this book, is what Lois has been working on since the beginnings of the breed and what we in the Dire Wolf Project believe to be a better way of breeding the domesticated dog. It is this author's intention to present the facts, backed by solid research and explained through experience.

In chapter one, we will immerse ourselves deeply in the most common logical fallacies that people insist upon using when debating their understanding of the most prominent dog breeding practices. Without a firm grasp of how we can get off track in our thinking, we cannot hope to fully understand our own mind without blending it with thoughts that derail us.

In chapter two, we will look at the different approaches people can take when reading this book. We will acknowledge the mind of the skeptic versus one seeking truth without opinion versus a completely open-minded individual. We will learn why it is important to reject the view of the skeptic and read this book with at least neutrality.

Thereafter, each chapter will address the different facets of the breeding practices employed by Dire Wolf Project breeders. At this point, there is no need to read the chapters in the order in which they were written. These chapters are meant to be a thorough review of each topic and are written with a mind to preserve our practices for those who come after us.

It is only through further study and research that the dog breeding community as a whole will come to a better way of breeding man's best friend and the Dire Wolf Project is no exception. In general, it is this author's opinion that today's current breeding practices simply cannot continue as they are without dire consequences to those dogs we love so much. It is hoped that the Dire Wolf Project will continue to utilize solid research to ever improve the lives of the beautiful animals we breed. As more and more breeders hope to join our ranks, this book will become a necessity for study.

With this book, we establish a new way of breeding that challenges others to look at maintaining the long-term health and longevity of the domesticated dog from an entirely different perspective. We anticipate that there will be many skeptics who oppose our views and disbelieve the facts presented here, as indeed, they already exist in number. We welcome them to the debate and hope for a true discussion on the subject of breeding dogs. It is our belief that through logical and serious debate real and lasting change for our beloved pets will come no matter who breeds them.

In the fall of 2006, before I had completely resigned myself to becoming a certified breeder of the American Alsatian dog, under strict guidance from the founder, I bred a crossbreed litter with a beautiful black-tipped cream colored dog named Don Juan to an American Alsatian dog named Sooner. Five beautiful puppies emerged, one with a gorgeous dominant black wolf coloring. As usual, Lois chose a black/tan puppy with the best temperament in the litter over the beautiful wolf-like colors from the rest of the litter. Her strict adherence to her conviction of breeding for temperament over looks surprised me as it was the first time I had truly realized just how steadfast she was. My admiration grew considerably at that moment.

Since my breeding business had yet to be established, I did not have a significant list of families lined up for puppies so I advertised the puppies locally. Each puppy eventually found great homes in the surrounding area, but one particular family made the difference in my mind as to whether I would fully embrace the life of a dog breeder or continue working as a special education teacher in the public school system.

Ed lived in a beautiful home just outside of the town of Durango, Colorado where he refurbished classic cars in his retirement. Before choosing a puppy, Ed spoke of his last dog that died and how great this dog was. Ed's moistened eyes sparkled as he described the love he shared for a dog that passed on much too soon. He described how he could never hope to obtain another dog as great as that one, but perhaps a puppy would fill his heart once more. After comparing the puppies from our litter, he chose a beautiful silver wolf gray pup that he later named Sarah. She grew to be a hundred pound silver female with bright yellow eyes. A true beauty.

Ed was the only family who stayed in contact with us after the purchase. Within the first week and the weeks that followed, he often called my husband and me to let us know how special Sarah was and how much he loved her. He told us that she was such a fast learner and knew even within the first few days that she was not to go into the kitchen, but wait on the carpet nearby. She followed him everywhere and waited for him to return if he was away. Sarah's devotion to Ed showed him that his heart could mend and that the unconditional love of a special dog was a rare gift that he had somehow found once again in his life.

It was in those moments, listening to Ed describe what a precious dog he had found in Sarah that my heart and soul finally came to understand what my mother had been working so diligently all of my childhood to accomplish: to create a large dog breed that could mold itself to our modern human lives in such a way as to make an impact in them and give them peace and love without the added burden of working dog traits that sometimes get in the way of enjoying what can be so special about owning a dog. That is what the Dire Wolf Project is all about, breeding exceptionally healthy companion dogs that change hearts and minds forever. Welcome to the Dire Wolf Project's strongbred dog breeding story. It is such a pleasure to share this story with you.

Sarah (Don Juan/Sooner)

Chapter 1
Burden of Proof

"I would rather stand for what I believe in and be hated than bow down and be loved."[1] *– Dave Rubin*

The year was two thousand four and I was newly married. My husband, Jay, and I moved out from the rainy Pacific Northwest to sunny southwestern Colorado near the Four Corners to live in the beautiful Rocky Mountains, a dream we never thought we would realize so quickly. The penetrating elation we felt for our new found freedom overwhelmed us many times. Our new life away from the trappings of extended family and the familiar roles into which we had placed ourselves seemed bounding with endless possibilities. Jay and I felt a real sense of freedom; a beautiful beginning to our marriage which had the potential to define our recently joined paths for the next moments of our life. We clung to our love for one another and hoped for the promise of peace a mountain life could bring to our souls.

It is ironic, then, that it was only through this physical separation from my family that I actually came to understand the many family dynamics that had been invisible to me before. Because my family is not an outwardly emotional one and can appear unfeeling and uncaring to those on the outside, I never knew how to make a connection to my mother, who I so often misunderstood. Throughout my years growing up with my grandmother, I had

1

no idea what made my mother remain so steadfastly convicted to her work - breeding, selling and training dogs. Why did she labor so hard for animals and not as hard for a connection to her oldest daughter? Why did she seem to cling to such an arduously physical life that demanded so much of her time? I always longed to know her better and to feel her love for me, but those times always seemed to me so few in number. Her mind was filled with so many unspoken dreams. I look back now and wish she had shared them with me. Her real dreams. The ones that she only shared in notebooks and on planners. But, then, perhaps I would have been a different person if she had.

As I sat in front of an old Dell computer with its cream colored mega tower to the right of its large, imposing monitor, an expansive length of land lie between Colorado where I lived and southern Oregon where my mother had settled. In those days, I still had dial-up Internet service, but compelled by an ever deepening desire to learn exactly what motivated my mother, I found myself corresponding with her each week on a forum she had created for her followers. Why did she have followers anyway? She was only breeding mutts of no consequence, after all. What could my mother know that would prompt anyone to follow her and listen to what she had to say? The questions plagued me each time I read a post from her. Thus, I unknowingly embarked on a quest. A journey that was initially undefined, but that would take me to a new understanding that great love demands great sacrifice.

Those first few years of my life in Colorado were not easy. My husband and I struggled to find adequate work and pay the bills that surrounded us each month like an ever-tightening noose. At one point, broken and destitute, I hung my head and shamefully opened the heavy glass doors to the welfare office. Despite the difficulty of that time, I found my mother's regular correspondence in the forum comforting. Somehow, there was a foothold to stand on so that the noose didn't seem so tight and suffocating, even though she was not always writing to me in particular. I had begun to realize that enjoying a true relationship with my mother meant I must enter her strange and unfamiliar world and find out, once and for all, the answers to my long-plaguing questions.

One day, my mother posted about breeding female dogs on the first heat. Knowing nothing about this topic, I did a search on the Internet for some possible articles to understand the issues behind breeding a female dog on its first heat. The Internet was not like it is today, Siri or Alexa answering every question as if the smartest person in the world were right there in the room with you. It was a pretty slow process of weeding through all of the webpages on the subject to find the ones that were the most relevant. And a dial up connection meant page loading took several minutes at the very least. Nonetheless, I came across a bunch of sites, some very well respected, which claimed a breeder should wait until the female was at least two years old before breeding her. Surely my mother had to be wrong about her idea that breeding a female on her first heat is not only acceptable, but may even be good for the bitch in the long run if she is to continue to be a mother at another time. I presented her with my contradictory findings and she quickly dismissed them without explanation. "Wrong!" was her stark answer. I was immediately crest-fallen at such a curt response to my time-consuming inquiry, but not broken, so I read her next post which was, "Read Leon Whitney's book and you will see." It took her seconds to type her reply to me; a stark contrast to the hours of research I had done in order to write my dissenting remarks.

Beyond a doubt, my mother's challenging claims went against the status quo. The vast array of websites and breeders that I eventually found to support "waiting to breed a female dog until she is at least two years old" surely had to have some merit. Should it not be my mother's non-conformist views that place the responsibility to prove her claims on her own shoulders? Why should I do all the work? I found myself thinking something very similar to what Carl Sagan, the famous astrophysicist said, "Extraordinary claims require extraordinary evidence." Well, what evidence did my mother have to support this outlandish claim? One book written half a century ago?

Going against the grain of a long held belief is not easy. It takes time and consistency of message to change a disbelieving majority's tightly held opinions because disbelievers have already decided on which side the truth lies. Take the historic example of those who believed the earth was flat. When I was young, it was taught to me in school that the majority of western civilization around the time of Christopher Columbus believed that the earth was flat. Indeed, it was taught that the very reason for Ferdinand Magellan's travels by ship was to find a western route to the Spice Islands, thus proving once and for all that the earth was spherical in nature. Today, there is a significantly growing number of people who state that the majority of western civilization believed no such thing and according to Stephen Jay Gould, an American paleontologist, evolutionary biologist, and science historian, "there never was a period of 'flat Earth darkness' among scholars (regardless of how the public at large may have conceptualized our planet both then and now). Greek knowledge of sphericity never faded, and all major medieval scholars accepted the Earth's roundness as an established fact of cosmology."[2]

Nonetheless, school-aged children all across our great country in the late seventies and early eighties were taught that much of western civilization in the fourteenth century believed the earth was flat. Was the flat earth story simply a myth perpetuated by those with an agenda? Which perspective is true and which perspective is not?

The difficulty when speaking of historical events and processes that take experience and time to fully understand is sifting through the arguments and claims to find out what is true and what is not true in order to come to a conclusion that the information presented is generally to be believed. There are three different ways through which a person can seek his/her ultimate determination: skepticism, neutrality, and credulity. Depending upon which of these approaches a person chooses determines how willing and open they are to hear what is shared.

When one speaks of whether to believe someone based on information that he/she presents, one can begin as a skeptic and ride along the well-established road of cynicism, which defines a person as guilty until proven innocent. Proof in the form of facts must accompany everything in order for the pessimistic listener to shift his/her thinking. Reason is rarely considered and if there is one aspect of the presenter's logic out of line then the entire discourse comes crumbling down. A skeptic looks to prove others wrong in order to continue to operate within their narrowly defined worldview. A person who doubts everything has to start with the premise that a presenter is automatically incorrect because if the presenter were to be correct, the skeptic would have to completely change his/her entire understanding of the world in order to accommodate the new information. A cynic picks out those things that are flawed no matter how much is actually true because the doubter already believes the presenter is wrong. The problem is that skeptics need so much proof that they, themselves, could not even prove their own position. They do not hold themselves to the same level of validation.

Since the beginnings of the breed, skeptics have held the Dire Wolf Project to an exorbitant standard. One such cynic stated that Dire Wolf Project breeders should not breed dogs until they are eight to ten years old in order to establish longevity in the breed. If we do not wait to breed to this degree then, it is presumed, we have not done our due diligence to find out if our breed truly possesses a long life as we claim. Therefore, the entire Dire Wolf Project is deemed to be false. No need for further investigation because if this one breeding practice is false, everything else with which we adhere is also false. Who came up with that idea? A skeptic did. And so, it is a skeptic's world view that says, "They don't have enough proof. They aren't doing it right." The truth is that no one in the dog breeding world, mixed or purebred, could live up to such a standard.

On the other end of the spectrum is credulity, which defines a person as believing until convinced otherwise. Richard Sweinberg, Emeritus Professor of Philosophy from the University of Oxford, put it this way, "We should believe what others tell us, unless there is good evidence to think otherwise." This may be a good place to start if one is on a jury in a court of law since we want to always think well of our fellow man until we can prove that all is not well. But, sometimes, a credulous person can believe in something so blindly that any contradictory facts never enter into the equation. These are the groupies; the cult followers that stick their head in the sand when their most cherished belief turns out to be false. They easily refuse to believe the plain facts staring them in the face because to acknowledge them would require a change of belief. When a person comes to a claim with credulity, that person chooses to believe the claims as correct without concern for the facts and only irrefutable facts will change their mind.

Then there is a place in the middle called neutrality. It is in between skepticism and credulity. A neutral person is open-minded, but will check the facts and let the truth speak for itself. If the facts lead one to the understanding that most aspects of the presenter's logic are not true, then the neutral individual shifts his/her thinking toward skepticism and begins to believe that the presenter is not trustworthy. But, if the facts presented hold true and over time more and more facts are seen to be true, it will lead one toward the side of credulity.

It is impossible to corroborate everything that happened in the past. For example, it is impossible to assert after thirty years that the American Alsatian dog pedigree is completely true and without error. One cannot travel back thirty years to physically see exactly what happened in order to determine if Lois told the truth or not when she wrote down her pedigree information. Although one cannot verify everything in the American Alsatian dog pedigree, there are some details that one can confirm. For example, one could perform a DNA test on one of the dogs within the project. If the physical evidence shows what the pedigree says it should and other DNA tests reveal the same then, the more positive results, the more one can believe the overall claim regarding the entire pedigree. So, if the details one checks out are factual, then the rest of the document should earn what is called the benefit of the doubt or a general assumption of reliability. If the evidence reveals random parts of the pedigree to be true then one can say that the entire pedigree is generally reliable.

An assumption of reliability dictates that if a general reliability is established in several different lesser areas then the whole is factual unless there is good reason to think otherwise. If all of the ideas presented are true time and time again, the presenter eventually earns credulity. At the same time, the claims that one cannot verify earn the benefit of the doubt, which, in turn, earns the reader's trust. If the presenter has earned the reader's trust, a historically favorable presumption prevails. The writer must be shown to be generally reliable in order to satisfy the burden of proof. Once the requirement for proof has been met, then any skeptic remaining must prove why they disagree. One of the main purposes of this book is to establish that the Dire Wolf Project is generally reliable. Therefore, this book is our proof.

Every person reading this book must make a choice. Does one begin with skepticism, believing from the beginning that everything Lois says and does is automatically false until or unless there is enough evidence to prove otherwise? Does one begin with credulity believing that everything she says and does is true until there is overwhelming evidence to show information is generally not true? Or does one begin in the middle with neutrality, a sort of agnostic approach, neither believing everything is false nor believing everything is true, but suspending belief and disbelief, as well as checking the facts along the way to determine if the information is generally correct or not. Yes. One must make a choice, but it is impossible to go back in time to be in the room with her those years ago and enter Lois's mind to know if her intentions were truthful and that what she states is correct.

My dear readers, you have already chosen whether to believe, disbelieve, or be open-minded regarding the writing presented in this book. If you have already chosen to completely disregard everything written here as false until you are shown enough evidence to convince you otherwise, you will be sorely disappointed because this author knows that there will never be enough proof for a skeptic. A cynic has already determined what is true and what is not. If you find yourself in this category, you already have established what you believe and because your beliefs do not follow with the Dire Wolf Project's ways, the project most undoubtedly will be determined to be false no matter what is presented herein. There is no room for any deviation from your own worldview. Therefore, this book is not written for you.

However, if you have come to this book with at least a neutral viewpoint and an open mind, we hope that this book will help you understand the very well-established and researched reasons for the work that we do. Whether you ultimately agree with our practices or not, at least you will be able to understand that we do not come by our breeding practices without carefully considering all of the facts and have made a conscious decision to breed as we do. We believe wholeheartedly in the practices presented in this book and hopefully by reading further, you will be able to fully understand those beliefs and why we cling to them so fervently.

What I did not know when first entering my mother's world all those years ago, and which took me over ten years to fully understand, was that I had been committing the logical fallacy of appeal to the majority. Instead of finding legitimate scientific research, fully all of my resources were from those espousing opinions, including professors of universities, prominent breeders, kennel club rules, laws in other countries, scientists, veterinarians, and animal advocates. None of my so-called research actually showed any actual tests proving that it was harmful to a female or her puppies for her to be bred on the first heat. I could produce hundreds of sources of material, but none equaled the one source from Leon Whitney's book which actually reveals true research done on female dogs over time comparing those bred on the first heat to those that waited to breed. To be sure, if such research were to be performed today, I believe the researcher would be ostracized from the dog community at the very least and maybe even prosecuted for animal abuse crimes. As it turned out, my mother, in her outwardly abrasive way, taught me that truth doesn't have to be overwhelming to be powerful. One can find the truth in the most unexpected places and even a person without credentials and accolades from prominent figures in our day can hold the truth so deeply that no matter who may come along to uproot them, the truth remains. My mother presented me with her proof, as humble as it was, I simply had to have the open-mindedness to take hold of it and learn.

Cindy (Skipper/Anastasia) at 4 months old 2019

Chapter 2

Logical Fallacies

Over the next couple of years while the beauty of Colorado still remained new and exciting, Jay and I embarked on a mission to save up enough money to put a down payment on our first house - a cabin in the woods on the edge of the largest wilderness in Colorado. For me, that meant walking several miles to and from work to save on not having to buy a second car, even in the winter when the snow accumulated. During this time, internet correspondence with my mother became a regular part of my day. She drew me in with each new outrageous claim so that I had no recourse but to follow up and find out for myself whether she was correct in her thinking or completely out of her mind.

Little did I know that throughout this hopeful time in our lives I would enter through the front doors of a school for which I did not apply, I did not pay, and I would never graduate. Nonetheless, this school taught me more about life than all of the formal education I had received acquiring my master's degree and further certifications. My mother's world seemed to lie within my grasp as now daily I eagerly reached into her mind to find out more about what it was that made her so steadfast in her convictions throughout her life.

Lois was extremely generous with her time and although she never handed me a cup runneth over with all the answers, she lead me to the well where I could drink from the water that held the knowledge I needed. She never made me drink, but through her prompting, I always understood that I had the choice to plunge in deeper or back away to leave her world without a second glance. I always chose to drink and the more I did, the more surprised I was that my mother may have actually been right all along. Lois has a phrase that she uses to sum it all up, "You should believe your mother because she is always right. If she is ever wrong you can write it on the calendar as a special day of celebration." Indeed, I have found that throughout the years of being in my mother's world, it is few and far between when she is flat-out wrong regarding something related to dogs.

Let me take you back into one of the many moments in time when I thought I had caught her advocating for irresponsible breeding and, as usual, it turned out that I was the one who had fallen onto the slippery slope of illogical thought.

The topic of the day at our online meeting was formal hip and elbow testing. Again, I knew very little about the reasons for formal health testing, but on the surface, it seemed plain to me that a truly responsible breeder would choose to use all of the formal testing available to them to breed the healthiest dogs that they could. Many breeders revere the Orthopedic Foundation of Animals (OFA) as the authority on canine hip dysplasia. Then, as now, fully all dog forums have dog breeding advocates that proudly exclaim that only irresponsible breeders fail to use OFA to prove that their dogs are clear of canine hip and elbow dysplasia. Along with that claim, they assert that OFA requires a dog to be two years old before a full-scale evaluation can be reached. Therefore, the argument proceeds, it is also an irresponsible breeder who breeds a dog before it is two years old and is able to be completely evaluated through OFA.

Not wanting to fall back into the trap of believing the majority without checking the facts, I went to the OFA website to read up on the research for myself. As plain as day, there was a link to OFA's preliminary hip and elbow testing. I was surprised to find out that OFA does indeed test dogs earlier than two years old. On that page describing the preliminary testing, it clearly states that although young dogs are able to be hip and elbow tested, the accuracy does diminish as the dog's age decreases. For example, a dog that is thirteen months old has a ninety-eight percent accuracy rating. Wait. What was that? Yes, you read that correctly. If the thirteen month old dog receives a good or excellent rating from OFA preliminaries, there is a ninety-eight percent OFA assurance that the dog will not be dysplastic at two years old - a full year before the Holy Grail of responsible dog breeding. This means that a breeder would only need to skip a large breed female's first heat around nine or ten months old allowing the breeder to be able to breed the dog on its second heat around fifteen or sixteen months of age. The loud speakers on every dog forum of which I have had the privilege of frequenting over the years echoed back their two year sentiment, but now, my trust in their collective voices waned considerably. If they had conveniently left out this interesting bit of information in order to promote their hate for breeders who did not wait until a female was at least two years old before breeding, what else were they hiding?

Over time, I also found out the history of the OFA and in the chapter on responsible breeders I go into much more detail about OFA and its sordid past. It is amazing what one finds out just by doing a bit of research instead of automatically believing the assertions of the majority.

My education from Lois's school of breeding was beginning to take shape and I began feeling more comfortable speaking with others about the information I now understood. More and more frequently, I entered dog breeding forums to debate these ideas with others willing to engage. Most often I found the participants to be unified in their condemnation for any argument but the ones to which they clung so passionately. Their collective voices reverberated off of the forum walls, each of them echoing the sentiments of the others.

One night, as Jay lie sleeping and the dark room lit by the faint blue glow of the computer screen deepened, I sat on the swivel chair hunched over waiting for the next reply. I now found myself locked into a battle of wits with a young woman from England. It was the morning for her and late in the evening for me and likely everyone else on the forum was sleeping or working, so we had the entire forum to ourselves. Through questioning, I found that this young lady adamantly believed that formal health testing is the only way to determine whether a dog is healthy or not, much like my own thoughts before my lessons with Lois. The more she wrote her explanations for her conclusions, the more I realized that she ultimately proposed that a dog, without formal health testing to prove its superior health, must automatically be assumed to be riddled with disease. I quickly determined that this person operates within a skeptic's worldview, which contends that something is to be disbelieved until there is enough evidence to warrant otherwise, formal health testing being that evidence.

Finally, I had a skeptic all to myself without any other skeptic for back-up. I asked myself, "Could I guide this person to think logically through her thoughts to ultimately come to a reasonably logical argument for what she believed?" I wasn't initially seeking to change her opinion. Instead, I wanted to push her to find a logical conclusion to her own understanding. Could it be logical to assume that all or even a majority of dogs that are not formally health tested are ultimately hiding terrible genetic deformities or deleterious genetic traits to be potentially passed on to their offspring, thereby creating further horrors? Could simply not using formal health testing be the determining factor for whether a dog was free of health issues or not? The debate continued.

My fellow challenger graciously followed me and surprisingly she continued to reply to my questioning in a civil and respectful manner. This propelled me to continue writing back to her. Eventually, through our discourse, I found that I had inadvertently lead her to a dead end in her thinking for which she could not reconcile her own deeply held beliefs. The conundrum she felt of the possibility of true health regardless of whether a dog had been tested or not versus a test's results began to break down. Remarkably, she eventually agreed with me that a dog could be healthy even though it was not tested. Ultimately, she also agreed with me that a dog could be unhealthy even though it tested healthy for the formal health tests that are available. But, when putting these two ideas together, she refused to agree with me that a dog could be said to be healthy without formal health testing. My opponent quickly realized that she had to shift her thinking a bit in order to remain logical in her conclusions and once she felt cornered to make that next logical leap, which went against her original premise, she became extremely violent in her language and refused to speak with me further that night.

The next day, after a night of unsettled sleep replaying the discussion in my mind, I returned to the forum to answer more questions from others, like an addict lighting up another cigarette in anticipation of a long day ahead. After each one of my replies, my former well-mannered adversary from the night before turned into a vicious and hateful villain shedding all logical thought for a torrential rant of fallacies. "This breed is the worst kind of inbred, unhealthy mongrels I have ever seen!" she replied; each response disintegrating further into more illogical thought and hateful rhetoric. "Irresponsible and extremely unethical breeders of the worst kind!" she persisted.

What had happened? My head reeled to find an explanation for her abrupt and undeserving change in attitude. Had I said something to offend her? I went back through the conversation from the night before and everything looked to me to be a kind and supportive exchange of ideas; perhaps even a productive one. But, the next day, among her cynical comrades, it was as if our polite conversation had never happened. Or worse, she had decided that the conversation had somehow been mean and hateful, which somehow justified her to retaliate in this most egregious way. Not surprisingly, there was no way to find out the true reason behind her switch, but I did ultimately find a common tendency of others who cannot sustain a logical thought process to turn to logical fallacies to bolster their arguments and sway an unsuspecting audience.

Assertion vs Argument

First of all, there is a vast difference between an assertion and an argument when it comes to logical thinking. An assertion is a confidently held point of view or a forcefully made statement, regardless of whether there is or is not solid reason behind it. An argument, in the academic sense of the word, takes the assertion and rests it upon adequate reasons and facts, backing up the claim with scientific and/or logical truths. As I hope to show in this book, Dire Wolf Project breeding practices are based on solid evidence; scientific, researched, and experiential, that have shown lasting results in health, longevity, and temperament throughout the thirty years that the project has been in existence. In fact, many of these same breeding practices have been successfully used throughout history by breeders around the globe breeding all kinds of domesticated animals in all walks of life. Unfortunately, many people insist that a particular, narrow way of breeding is the only legitimate way to breed without any good reason behind these beliefs other than a generic claim that any other way is unethical. It is very rare indeed when one finds an opponent who can transcend this basic assertion and cross over into a logical and well-established argument. An even more disturbing modern trend is to pass laws based solely on these assertions, which then prohibit others from breeding outside of these very narrow and in many cases possibly harmful breeding practices.

When people utilize unsupported assertions, they oftentimes assume that everyone agrees with them so there is no real need to back up their point of view with any evidence. Unfortunately, many of the accepted breeding practices of today do indeed have a majority group of dog breeding enthusiasts who claim expertise in the dog breeding realm. These obnoxiously persistent so-called breeding experts single out certain breeders crowning some as practicing the gold standard in ethics and responsibility while completely shunning and even slandering breeders who do not conform to the same practices.

These self-proclaimed breeding experts have a loud, demanding and confident voice that convinces unsuspecting multitudes without having the background knowledge to understand the intricacies of the art and science of breeding dogs. To oppose the so-called breeding expert instantly places a permanent negative label on the dissenter from the loudest of those participating in the so-called breeding expert's viewpoint. The newly labeled one is then ostracized from any further conversation as their future involvement is now seen as completely unworthy of the so-called breeding expert's proud heritage of superior thought. However, as we shall see below, just because a group states an assertion loudly and profusely, it does not mean that the group's viewpoint is the most ethical or correct way. Dire Wolf Project breeders stand up against some of the most deep-rooted notions in dog breeding and we do so with firm conviction and dedication because the health and longevity of our beloved furry companions is more important to us than remaining in good standing with the so-called breeding expert collective. For the sake of our beloved animals, we cannot afford to compromise on these practices. If that means we must endure blatant hateful criticism and complete dismissal, then we will stand alone, but we will stand firm and upright backed by our logical, well-researched, and experienced beliefs. We must strictly strive for the best interest of the animals we have been graced with knowing and loving.

Breeders working within the confines of Dire Wolf Project breeding practices must understand the background behind why our breeding practices were developed the way they were. The founder of this project learned her craft in the school of hard knocks. She passionately researched the truths behind dog breeding; what works and what does not, without an initial bias blocking the study of what she ultimately found to be fundamentally true. When we peer through the knothole of what actually occurs in dogs by breeding without having to conform to the so-called breeding expert's established rules, a long history of successful dog breeding that goes back to the very moment man decided to domesticate the wolf starts to come into focus. In fact, as you shall see, the so-called breeding expert's current rules on dog breeding have only more recently been brought into effect and the results of their adherence to these rules has been devastating to dog breeds around the world in a very short amount of time. It is only by looking to the past, carefully including new scientific research without throwing well-tested methods to the wayside, and remembering that we are not God and cannot ever pretend to play God's role that we will have the knowledge to bring *Canis familiaris* well into the future with renewed health and superior longevity.

The truth is that when so-called breeding experts, acting solely on assertions, bully their opposition into submission it should be considered tyranny. When dog breeders practicing outside of what is now considered the "correct" way to breed dogs are deliberately targeted by the so-called breeding expert acting through the democratic process, it is time to take a stand to save ourselves from any future oppression.

As you read this book, please understand that we are not stating that our way of breeding is the only way and everyone must think and conform to what we do, but we do hope to show that there can be legitimate alternatives to breeding as the majority dictates that do not warrant targeted, hateful dismissal or even worse, legislation to ban any of the breeding practices we have come to view as viable options to healthy, long-lived dogs. If we do not stand up for the right to breed a different, and even possibly more ethical, way, especially when it secures the healthful future of our beloved pets, we will lose the right to do so altogether in the very near future. Time is urgent because this battle has unfortunately already begun and the narrow-minded rule establishers have quickly gained a lot of ground as no one has stood in open defiance to their claims. With that said, the Dire Wolf Project formally rises up to continue to take a different path and secure our freedom to breed dogs in a different way;

one of fierce determination to focus only on securing the healthy future of our most loved of all God's creatures, the dog.

If you have found yourself believing any of the so-called breeding expert's assertions laid out in this book, we do not fault you. Many people have been duped into believing this "correct" and "responsible" way to breed. After reading this book you will have a much better arsenal at your fingertips to combat the incessant blather that constantly rings out in every dog forum in existence. I, for one, would urge you to also stand up with us for the freedom and ability to breed dogs without tyranny and oppression. It is only when breeders who have had enough of the bullying and constant targeting rear up and take a stand that we can keep what is being threatened; our freedom to breed healthy, long-lived, stable-tempered dogs.

Logical Fallacies

Before we examine the intricacies of the Dire Wolf Project's breeding program, we should address some generic smears that often arise. Doing so would allow them to continue to voice these flaws in reasoning unchallenged. Continuing to allow the community to wallow in the illogical thought processes on which they have come to rely further establishes their firm convictions that they are right and you are wrong. The most insidious consequence of an exchange without an insistence that the group refrain from logical fallacies is that those bystanders listening to (or reading) the conversation may indeed be swayed into believing a flawed conclusion which could have been completely avoided had the conversation moved to a productive exchange of ideas. Lastly, the most unfortunate aspect of a biased debate is that it turns an important conversation about how best to breed for health and longevity into a completely unproductive one thereby eliminating the chance for a real look at needed change in the dog breeding world.

When someone uses a flawed conclusion in argumentation that seeks to negatively undermine another who is arguing, that person, whether realizing it or not, is being dishonest. The very reason for this book is to begin to move the conversation about dog breeding for health and longevity from a laborious exercise in trudging through the muck of dishonest thinking to a productive dialogue so that the dogs themselves will benefit from our collective human intellects. It is only when the condemnation stops and a spirit of understanding our differences begins that we will be able to realize comprehensive and lasting change for our most cherished pets. I propose that the vast majority within the dog breeding community begin to look outside their high walled box and consider another way, especially if those different practices produce real results in overall health and longevity.

15

These flawed and oftentimes irrelevant arguments from those who seek knowingly or unknowingly to undermine a productive conversation about breeding for health and longevity come in many different forms. The hasty generalization seeks to brush away the disagreement with an easy wave of the hand. The strawman seeks to make the argument from the opponent seem weak and easy to knock down. Stacking the Deck seeks to make the opponent's conclusions seem irrelevant by completely disregarding or ignoring them altogether. Many times, those operating in the logical fallacy category do not have a deep grasp of the knowledge and practices they preach and so they unknowingly turn to a vast array of illogical appeals in an attempt to quickly shut down the conversation or get the other person to become frustrated and leave.

It is truly unfortunate that formal education on logical thinking skills as well as how to spot illogical thought processes are no longer being taught in many schools today. Mathematics concepts are quite often presented without any knowledge or acknowledgement of its fundamental purpose. As a result, many unknowing spectators peering into a conversation surrounding dog breeding are easily swayed by the sheer number of people proclaiming what should and should not determine a reputable breeder. And indeed, this has been the case for decades. Books published by well-respected dog breeders in the 1930s attest to the frustration of dealing with those without the experience to back up their redundant and incorrect claims. As Leon Whitney points out in his book entitled How to Breed Dogs, "Whenever the question comes up in a group discussion someone says, 'Well, it wouldn't be right for a 13-year-old girl to have a baby.' This is a case of anthropomorphizing the dog. There is no basis for comparison; the 13-year-old child is nowhere near grown when she first menstruates, and a bitch is almost always full grown when she first comes in heat."[1] As it turns out, those very same claims continue to exist today. This book will look at each one in turn and provide the reader with the solid evidence to refute the claims and argue that there can be other ways of breeding that are equally correct and perhaps even more ethical than the currently accepted way that unfortunately is being pushed through legislation.

As early as Aristotle, sometime after 384 BC, flawed arguments were recognized and categorized. Fallacies in thinking have been listed in many different ways since that time, but many now generally accept four basic categories of logical fallacies: fallacies of relevance, component fallacies, fallacies of ambiguity, and fallacies of omission. First of all, when a person chooses to introduce a statement that is completely irrelevant to the conversation and makes absolutely no productive contribution to the topic at hand, that person commits the fallacy of relevance. It is a way to undermine the other's viewpoint and discredit them quickly without further conversation. On the other hand, if the person errs in their deductive and inductive reasoning it is considered a component fallacy. Logical reasoning should flow easily from one thought to the next without gaps or missing components. When something just seems to be wrong in the logic used, it may be considered an error in the very components of the logic itself. However, when a person shifts another's words around, changes meaning or skews the original idea so that the idea seems much less important than it initially could have, this is considered a fallacy of ambiguity. The person hopes to undermine the opposing viewpoints and ideas by interpreting them in a way not originally meant thus hoping to sway the opinions of others. Lastly, if the person leaves out important or relevant information that might hurt their case, this is considered the fallacy of omission.[1a]

When one wants to get at the truth, all of the facts are important to consider and leaving them out or hiding them is dishonest. All of these four types of argumentative fallacies stop any real conversation from happening and may easily sway an unsuspecting audience from giving any real credit to the one posing the challenge to the group. Let us eliminate them here and now so that we can begin to look into the breeding world of the Dire Wolf Project with an open mind that seeks the truth.

Throughout each chapter, my promise to you is that I will refrain from using logical fallacies in the arguments presented. In turn, I hope that you, the reader, will leave any logical fallacies by the wayside as you enter the chapters to follow.

So, let us start by taking a brief look at the different illogical arguments that some choose to present in order to quickly quell any productive conversation and afterwards we will move on to the heart of the matter; how the Dire Wolf Project increases overall health and longevity for the dogs within its breeding program. For your convenience, a list of typical logical fallacy arguments has been provided in Appendix A. A brief discussion of each one follows as a reference for speaking with others about the Dire Wolf Project and its breeding practices. Feel free to reference this list at any time during the book.

Confirmation and Disconfirmation Bias

Sometimes, in an effort to persuade others, a person seeks out and presents only the research that confirms their beliefs, especially when a person's beliefs represent a highly charged emotional response. The tendency to search for, interpret, favor, and recall information in a way that confirms one's preexisting beliefs or hypotheses is called confirmation bias. It is a type of cognitive bias and a systematic error in inductive reasoning. People display this bias when they gather or remember information selectively, or when they interpret it in a biased way. Emotionally charged issues or deeply entrenched beliefs elicit a higher tendency toward the use of confirmation bias.

Not only are people apt to readily accept what they believe is confirming evidence, but they may also unconsciously set a higher standard of evidence for hypotheses that go against their strong beliefs. The tendency to subject disconfirming evidence to more critical evaluation is known as disconfirmation bias.[2]

As Francis Bacon put it in his Latin work entitled "new instrument of science" in 1621, "The human understanding, when any proposition has been once laid down... forces everything else to add fresh support and confirmation: and although most cogent and abundant instances may exist to the contrary, yet either does not observe, or despises them, or it gets rid of or rejects them by some distinction, with violent and injurious prejudice, rather than sacrifice the authority of its first conclusions."[3]

According to many following an unwritten consensus for ethical breeding practices, the non-conforming ideals of the Dire Wolf Project are automatically assumed to be unethical and are regularly ridiculed. As a result, the Dire Wolf Project is actively shunned from formal breeding practice discussion. One such person decided that Dire Wolf Project breeders shall remain unethical until and unless all of the dogs within the project live to be sixteen years old and have absolutely no ill health except for normal aging. Then, this person stated that she might, perhaps, consider us ethical. Because she fundamentally disagreed with how we breed based on her own deeply held beliefs regarding dog breeding, she could not accept any logical conclusive arguments to the contrary. Furthermore, in order to prove that the Dire Wolf Project operates in an unethical manner, she suggested that we would have to achieve a much higher standard than any other dog breed in existence in order to prove our worth to her. No other dog breeding group would be able to achieve her demands. Therefore, in her mind we remain unethical and she does not have to do any difficult thinking which may ultimately challenge her deepest convictions and shatter her entire worldview. She can continue to live in her well-ordered world where anyone who deviates from the norm in dog breeding is unethical.

Unfortunately, this is more the case than not. You see, the Dire Wolf Project does not conform to the norms established by either the purebred dog enthusiast or the animal breeding activist. The sad part of it is that the Dire Wolf Project justifiably poses a threat to each group's distinct ways of thinking. This threat undermines the flaws in their own logic and if they were to seriously look at their own beliefs they might have to acknowledge that some of them are faulty and/or out of date. It is much easier to state that someone else's thinking is wrong simply because it does not conform to a majority's established beliefs than to think through the problems in their own logical thinking. So, group think begins to emerge and any research that even slightly suggests that the group think is correct is reposted, linked, and referenced. The research that goes against their thinking is then deemed as somehow flawed in its execution or conclusions.

Quickly, let's make a clear distinction about what is meant by the term "research." There are two kinds of research: primary and secondary. Because the term, "research," is used interchangeably for each, it can be confusing about which type is being discussed and which is not. There is a difference between research based on a wide review of previous studies and original research where strict scientific methods are employed. Primary research is oftentimes more expensive and time consuming, so much of the time secondary research, also called "desk research," is used instead. While primary research is highly accurate, original, and relevant to the topic being studied, secondary research can be advantageous when a comprehensive review of all of the research studies conducted on a specific topic are discussed without bias. Secondary research may help solidify various ideas and come to understand numerous conclusions in a more broad and sweeping way. But without strict attention to include all of the research on the subject, there is always a risk for confirmation bias, so we must remember to establish a well-rounded review of all of the research on a topic no matter what the outcome. Certainly, we should not extrapolate one piece of the research that fits our worldview and disregard the rest.

A great example of research confirmation bias is the interpretation of a detailed research study from the University of California, Davis published in 2013 comparing the diseases found in 27,254 dogs, both purebred and mixed breed. The fifteen year study found that purebred dogs have higher incidents of ill-health in ten out of the twenty-seven identified genetic diseases while mixed breed dogs show a significant increased incidence rate for one disease, ruptured cranial cruciate ligament.[4] Many purebred dog enthusiasts decided that because the mixed breed dog group was found to have a much higher incidence rate with regard to one particular health issue, the lesser yet more abundant health offenses seen in purebred dogs could be dismissed and/or completely ignored. Furthermore, many specifically noted one statistic that over half of the diseases in the study showed no significant difference between purebred and mixed breed, disregarding the unseemly damning evidence that did not fit their agenda. Susi Szeremy, writing for AKC, shows her confirmation bias by stating, "...a 2013 study conducted at the University of California, Davis... found that more than half of the genetic disorders included in the study were prevalent in about same number of mix-breed dogs as in their purebred counterparts. Another study, this one on hip dysplasia, revealed no statistical difference in the prevalence of hip dysplasia between purebred dogs and mix-breeds*. In the final analysis, these studies have concluded that purebred dogs are no more prone to genetic disorders than are mix-breeds, and to suggest otherwise is misguided."[5] However, as prominent vertebrate biologist and founder of the Institute of Canine Biology, Carol Beuchat, explains, "This study found that purebred dogs have a significantly greater risk of developing many of the hereditary disorders examined in this study. No, mixed breed dogs are not ALWAYS healthier than purebreds; and also, purebreds are not '*as healthy*' as mixed breed dogs."[6] Selecting only the information from a study that confirms one's bias and/or disregarding the information from a study that disconfirms one's beliefs is intellectually dishonest.

Intellectual dishonesty is a type of close-mindedness that involves reasoning processes that fail to think rationally to independent thought, usually by obscuring the fact that the speaker has a hidden agenda and the "reasoning" is really just a rationalization for unreasonable beliefs. Thus, simply put, the speaker can be said to be intentionally lying. Tim House, a database application developer for a non-for-profit agency explains it this way, "People advocating for a cause tend to distort the truth, and tend to believe that it is perfectly permissible to do so. Many of the same people who think it's morally wrong to lie to a loved one in order to avoid incurring that person's wrath do not think it is morally wrong to distort truth before an audience in order to convince the audience to adopt their position. Both are forms of dishonesty. The former is almost universally deplored. The latter is almost universally accepted."[6a]

Relativism

Purebred dog breeding advocates believe that promoting and securing the integrity of each individual dog breed is essential to the meticulous breeding and distinguished legacy that comes with owning a purebred dog. The official AKC objectives for 2017 are to "advance the study, breeding, exhibiting, running and maintenance of purebred dogs." Purebred dogs offer predictability, health, community and legacy according to AKC blog contributor, Susi Szeremy.[7]

On the other side of the coin, mixed-breed dog breeding advocates believe that superior health and longevity is more important than the prestige and predictability of owning a purebred dog breed. As Dr. Patty Khuly, VMD explains, "To the annoyance of most purebred breeders, most of us [veterinarians] tend to side with the mixes (and, no, we don't consider hybrids, like Labradoodles, exempt from the purebred designation). Mutts mostly win out for their sheer hardiness, thriftiness and longevity, due to their lower incidence of genetic disease."[8] Although Dr. Khuly acknowledges that purebred dogs have their strengths, she ultimately concludes, "It's a DNA crapshoot, this game of genetics. Some win, some lose. Similarly, nature will always prevail. Whenever humans tinker with creatures to our own specifications, we end up with a more expedient animal in some ways but an inferior one in others. With purebreds, the benefits we gain in form and function are inevitably coupled with side effects we're not always capable of offsetting. Does this mean I'm anti-purebred? No way! Purebreds will always have their place. But I will admit to a significant cautious response to them, given the health issues I so often see. Can you blame me?"

So is there an underlying absolute truth to the purebred vs mixed-breed dog breeding controversy? The Dire Wolf Project believes that there is and that the truth lies in the middle between purebred and mixed. The amazing fundamental truth is that both claims can be right. When dog breeders from both sides of the breeding equation come together to share their most valued breeding practices, they will finally come understand how it is that the Dire Wolf Project never fit in either camp. Not a purebred dog. Not a mutt. But, a new kind of dog sharing the best of both worlds: a strongbred dog. Now let's enter our journey together and spend some time engaging our minds to the real possibility of lasting change in the dog breeding world that may just bring our best animal friends to wholeness and healthfulness again.

Buck (Boss/Bellatrix) at one year old 2018

Chapter 3
The Responsible Breeder

Here was my chance. Finally, I could directly participate in my mother's life. I decided to embrace dog breeding and help Lois in her cause to produce the world's first large breed companion dog. As an enthusiastic new dog breeder, I possessed an excessive energy and commitment with an inexperienced, youthful exuberance that comes from an overwhelming knowledge that a great responsibility has just been placed on one's shoulders. I felt a sincere need to accomplish only what was acceptable and proper in order to not foul up Lois's entire life's work.

I began my initial zeal to be an integral part of the process by following Lois's desire to breed the best sire in the Dire Wolf Project at the time, Zorro, to a third generation silver beauty named Nadine. Zorro was large and imposing with an impeccably gentle, yet solidly confident, temperament. He had yellow eyes, erect ears, and the most beautiful wolf gray coat. He had sired many litters before and had produced a plethora of gorgeous puppies with no health issues. Certainly, he would be the ultimate sire for my first stud dog. Equally as impressive, Nadine was a beautiful silver wolf gray color with erect ears and a sweet, loving temperament. She had returned to Lois after almost dying when a pack of German Shepherd Dogs attacked her, ripping her neck open to the bone and permanently damaging one ear. After her full recovery, Nadine went on to whelp many healthy and beautiful puppies for the breed. Most assuredly, she would be the perfect dam for my first stud dog. Two great dogs in health, temperament and beauty joined together to whelp the ultimate litter. I rubbed my hands together in a gesture of anticipation bordering on greed. With this breeding, I could finally acquire a silver male puppy with striking yellow eyes that would surely become the best foundation stock male for my new breeding program.

Nadine brought five amazing puppies into the world on April 22, 2012; four males and one female. The joy I felt at that time was immeasurable. Each puppy received constant devotion and attention. As a result, I knew each one intimately. Although all of the puppies had a solid, stable, sweet, gentle, loving, and calm temperament, two males were particularly nice; a gold and a silver. All things being equal, I chose the large silver male with yellow eyes. I named him Aslan and to this very day, he remains the best dog I have ever owned.

In Aslan lie all of my excited hopes for the future of the breed. But, as any new responsible breeder would do, I wanted to make sure that this dog was as great as he promised to be before breeding him. I plunged into any information that could describe all of the most important responsibilities of a dedicated breeder and vowed to follow them all. In my lustful desire to not mess up what had previously been so carefully laid down, I wanted to be crowned the most conscientious and responsible of breeders so that it would be said that if I did fail in some way, I did the best I could with what I had been given. I certainly did not want anything negative to befall the breed at my own hands. Even the thought of it made me shudder.

But, what exactly makes the best and most responsible breeder? What criteria formulates one who has done all that can be done to make sure the dogs one breeds are the healthiest, best-tempered, and sound dogs one can? How should one go about evaluating their own dogs to make sure what they breed is truly producing great puppies with no health issues?

According to the so-called breeding experts on many of the dog forums in which I frequented, a very specific list of responsible breeding practices can be developed. Here is what I found them to unanimously expound:

1. Dogs should not be bred until after two years old.
2. Dogs should be formally health tested for hip/elbow dysplasia.
3. Dogs should be DNA tested.
4. Only dogs that conform perfectly to the standards of the breed should be bred.
5. The coefficient of inbreeding (COI) should never reach above 7%.

6. COI should be calculated on no less than a ten generation pedigree, although calculating as far back as possible within the pedigree is the ideal, otherwise a genetic COI should be used.
7. Puppies should be raised in the home and not outside in a kennel facility.
8. A waiting list of serious potential owners should be established before breeding.
9. Only one male should be bred to a female during each breeding in order to be sure that each puppy's sire is fully known.

Furthermore, I found that according to the American Society for the Prevention of Cruelty to Animals [ASPCA]:[1] responsible breeding requires adherence to the following best practices:

1. Screen for heritable diseases.
2. Remove unhealthy animals by way of spay/neuter.
3. Never breed a dog with a genetic health condition.
4. Do not breed extremely young or old dogs.
5. Avoid inbreeding.
6. Breed dogs in the home.

The American Kennel Club (AKC) also weighed in on what it takes to be a responsible breeder:[2]

1. Perform pre-breeding health checks.
2. Do not breed a bitch at the first heat.
3. Do not breed a bitch on consecutive heats.
4. Keep dogs inside.
5. Raise puppies with lots of socialization before the sale.

And finally, the Kennel Club [KC] in the United Kingdom has been authorized to officially standardize dog breeding for their entire country. As such, the Kennel Club General Committee will not accept an application to register a litter when:[3]

1. The dam has already whelped four litters.
2. The dam is older than eight years at the date of whelping.
3. The dam was under one year at the time of mating.
4. The offspring are the result of any mating between father and daughter, mother and son or brother and sister.

It is further recommended, but not expressly mandated, that bitches should not be allowed to produce more than one litter within a twelve month period or on consecutive seasons and never without veterinary guidance.

Even WikiHow explains that responsible breeders should:[4]

1. Never breed dogs with conditions that might be inherited.

2. Don't breed dogs if their medical condition is not known.

WikiHow also clearly states that dogs can begin mating between twelve and twenty-four months. It seems, instead of accurately reporting that dogs can come into heat at six months old, the contributors of this WikiHow article chose instead to bypass the argument completely and simply imply that it is physically impossible for a female to begin mating any earlier than twelve months old.

The clouds parted and a perfect glowing path became illuminated in front of me. I could do all of the above and breed with the integrity and confidence that I had done everything possible to secure a great future for the American Alsatian dog breed. Certainly that would attain a degree of accomplishment for me. With fervor, I launched into performing all of the activities that a responsible breeder should do.

OFA preliminarily evaluated Aslan's hips and elbows at thirteen months old. It was determined that he was free of elbow dysplasia and received a fair score for clear hips. Not satisfied with those scores, I retested Aslan through OFA for his full scale report where it was found that he now received a good score for clear hips. Great. An unbiased, third-party had clearly determined that he was free of canine hip and elbow dysplasia. I could now check that one off of the responsible dog breeder list.

Furthermore, DNA testing revealed that Aslan was clear and not a carrier of any of the 165 genetic diseases tested for through Embark Veterinary Services. This DNA test includes genetic hypothyroidism, degenerative myelopathy among so many others. Awesome. Another unbiased, third party now agreed with my assessment that Aslan was perfectly healthy.

Lest I be accused of skirting my duties as a responsible breeder, I also had Aslan's sperm tested by a local veterinarian's office, which found that his swimmers were plentiful and vibrant. The veterinarian also checked Aslan's heart and eyes, which were perfectly normal. Nice. Aslan would surely be the greatest foundation stock dog in the history of new dog breeders.

I evaluated Aslan's temperament through a standardized system of measurement created by the founder of the breed in order to come ever closer to her lofty temperament goals. Aslan measured up perfectly to the breed's ideal inherited temperament. Brilliant. It appeared as though I had found the crown jewel of stud dogs. Excitement and anticipation grew.

In order to prove his ability to learn new tasks with ease, Aslan attended dog training classes and learned all of the skills to pass the Canine Good Citizen test with flying colors. Excellent. Aslan was a well-mannered, beautiful boy that would accept a friendly stranger with ease and loved to do all that I asked and be an excellent example of the breed.

Aslan at one and a half years old.

Not only was Aslan proven to be superior in health and temperament, but he had a lovely silver wolf gray coat with a long mane and golden amber colored eyes. He had extra-large feet and dark black pigmentation. He was broad and heavy with a massive head and thick bone structure. Apart from being shorter than breed standards, he was adored by all for his stunning beauty.

As I looked through Aslan's pedigree and his DNA scores, I realized, to my dismay, that Aslan was extremely inbred at 54%. A blinking red light accompanied by a loud warning buzzer exploded in my mind. "All hands on deck!" a frantic thought shouted at me. Like you perhaps, my mind reeled in disbelief at why Lois had allowed such a highly inbred match. A dog forum member blared, "Aslan is more inbred than any purebred dog, ever!" As it turns out, according to current Embark DNA sample data including tens of thousands of dogs, purebred dogs are seen to rise upwards of 70% COI, so he was not quite at the top of the inbreeding scale, although certainly greater than most. While his inbreeding was shockingly high, I reasoned that this also meant that he could only produce exactly what he was and certainly it would be a good thing to have more Aslan's in the world, especially if I could significantly reduce the inbreeding coefficient in his puppies without losing too many of his great qualities. I knew that I would have to choose his mate carefully.

The female chosen for Aslan, Gemma, was a first generation from a completely unrelated German Shepherd Dog named Bear... a drastic reduction in inbreeding would be the result, leaving the inbreeding danger zone of death and entering into a much more manageable level. According to pedigree calculations going back ten generations and accounting for Aslan's known COI, the puppies from this match would drop down to 25% COI, within the range where most purebred dogs fall on Embark's collective purebred dog inbreeding scale. Some of you who strictly adhere to the responsible breeder ideals mentioned above may believe 25% is still way too high and wish to admonish me for my poor lack of judgment, but at this time, this was my best option to significantly reduce inbreeding. (For a more in-depth look at inbreeding, please refer to the inbreeding chapter in this book.) That being said, my immediate plan was to continue to decrease inbreeding even further in the next generations, attaining 7% COI or below; the sweet spot touted by so many of those so-called breeding experts. I vowed that no incoming missiles would strike down this ship before it entered the secure waters of adequate genetic diversity.

I waited to breed Gemma until her second heat, skipping her first to give her enough time to fully mature. In the meantime, she was evaluated through OFA and found to possess normal elbows and good hip scores. She was sweet and loving, albeit less confident than wanted, but I felt I could improve that fault by coupling her with Aslan's superior confidence. She would be bred one time only to Aslan and then be spayed, returning to her permanent home in eastern Arizona. A picture of near perfect responsible dog breeding became etched on a golden plaque above my head as I took the helm to steer the highly inbred ship to safety.

But, in the back of my mind questions began to bubble up from the clear, still waters of responsible breeding. Where did these breeding rules come from, anyway? Who decided what makes a responsible breeder and what does not? When did these rules come about? Would it be possible for a breeder to perform all of the rules above perfectly and still not attain responsible breeder status? Can someone consciously choose to go against these rules for any reason and ultimately still be considered a responsible breeder?

I reasoned that if someone could perform all of these rules and yet still breed irresponsibly, then these rules were insufficient at best or not meaningful at worst. Furthermore, if someone who chooses not to perform all of these rules has solid reasons for not conforming and produces dogs that are fit, healthy, and live average to above average ages, then these rules may even be arbitrarily compiled by people who may think they have all of the answers to dog breeding ethics when, in fact, they do not.

Let's return to Aslan, but jump into the realm of the hypothetical for a moment. I had performed all of the so-called "responsible breeder" tasks. No one came down from their lofty throne to formally dub me a responsible breeder, but by their own rules, I had mastered the game. Would it now be possible for me, a new member of the elite responsible breeder club, to cheat the system in some dastardly way; outwardly appearing to be a responsible breeder on all accounts, but secretly choosing to be an irresponsible breeder of the worst sort? Yes. In fact, it would be very easy for me to have done just that. Here's how.

First, I would place all of the formally gathered health, temperament and conformation information onto Aslan's web page. I would add a live link to each formal health test so that anyone could easily verify that I stated the truth regarding his health and training credentials. Professional quality photos of Aslan would show him to be perfect in stance and structure. In fact, many people I knew did want a puppy from him, but there was one fundamental flaw... he developed both hypothyroidism and a serious lung condition, COPD, at three years old; one full year after his second birthday. Now, remember, his DNA test revealed negative for genetic hypothyroidism and there is no formal test for lung health.

Now, I could do one of four things. I could simply not tell anyone of these new health developments since his formal testing data shows perfection. Then, continue to breed him. I could flat out deny that Aslan had genetic hypothyroidism, as the DNA test clearly revealed that he did not have a genetic version. Then, continue to breed him. If I wanted to, I could truthfully reveal that he did develop hypothyroidism, but that he did not have the genetic version only a type of hypothyroidism that occurred due to the ingredients in his food. I could further justify breeding him because canine hypothyroidism is actually on the rise and being diagnosed at a much higher rate than previously. I could argue that so many unsuspecting vets are actually misdiagnosing hypothyroidism when, in fact, these dogs may simply have low T4 counts, but their TSH counts are normal. I could blather on about this or that cause and how it is anything but genetic and therefore I am still justified in breeding him. Then, I could continue to breed him. Or, I could simply tell the truth and forgo breeding the best dog I have ever owned. In my mind, there is only one option in order to remain ethical and continue to hold on to that responsible breeder title.

Fortunately for everyone, I only bred Aslan one time before his disease developed, keeping no puppies from him to further the lines in the breed. Unlike an irresponsible or unethical breeder who may think of nothing else but the profit Aslan could bring from his looks alone, I told the truth about Aslan's hypothyroidism and his COPD. I informed all owners of his one litter as well as the entire American Alsatian dog community about the issues that arose for Aslan and I never bred him again. Tragically, he died two years later much too young at five years old from complications of COPD.

Aslan after hypothyroidism developed and just before medication.

Through reasoning based on my own experience I realized that no amount of formal health or temperament testing can make a breeder legitimate, responsible, or ethical. This is because there will always be genetic health issues that do not possess formal tests with which one can align their breeding programs just as there will always be people willing to exploit the health testing system. Performing a certain "correct" number of health tests, then, does not mean a dog is healthy. There are many prominent canine diseases that do not currently have formal tests: epilepsy, panosteitis, arthritis, certain cases of hypothyroidism and many others. No one can test for perfect health. One can only test for disease. Therefore, any number of health tests can never tell you if your dog is genetically healthy.

At the same time, there are many people willing to perform all of the same tasks I did and still fail to disclose the true genetic health of their breeding stock. People lie. People cheat. People claim things they ought not to claim. In fact, one can seriously argue that being brutally open and honest about all of the ill-health that resides in a prominent breeder's dog breed would be the exception, not the norm. After all, even I can attest to the fact that losing an almost perfect stud dog from a breeding program is a huge loss and the temptation to keep the genetic secret is overwhelming, not to mention easy to do. One cheap small pill a day and Aslan never looked better. Who would know?

I further understood that no amount of time lying in wait for ill health to appear before breeding a dog would ever be enough to make sure that the dog does not develop a late onset health issue. Dogs can develop genetic health issues at any point in their lives, which no one can predict. My American Alsatian dog, Odessa, developed COPD at ten years old. Aslan's father developed bladder stones when he was nine years old. Severe arthritis does not generally appear until a dog is aged. So, should we follow the skeptic earlier in this book and wait to breed dogs until they are eight to ten years old? The truth is that it would not matter if I did wait to breed a dog until eight years old. That same dog could develop a genetic health disease at ten, eleven, or twelve.

So, if a person can perform every task above to secure their responsible breeder title and yet still have the ability to breed unhealthy dogs riddled with health issues only to die much too young, then the initial definition of "responsible breeder" is seriously lacking and may even be said to be outright meaningless. The mark of a truly responsible breeder is not that one performs this or that genetic health test, but instead that one owns up to the health issues that do arise, all of them, publicly tracking all health issues that have been reported, because genetic health issues inevitably will exist, regardless of if there are genetic health tests to root them out or not. Furthermore, when a health issue does rear up, an ethical breeder would have an extensive health guarantee placed in the contract to back up the buyer so that he/she can receive support if a genetic health issue should arise, no matter at what age, and the breeder would consistently honor that guarantee should it be needed.

But, disclosing all genetic health issues and guaranteeing the lifelong genetic health of all dogs bred within a person's breeding program is not currently the definition of a "responsible breeder." Could it even succeed as a legitimate definition? Where are the multitudes espousing this logical type of responsible breeder? Crickets play their gentle tune as the silence from the so-called breeding experts deepens. They would rather strictly dictate exactly what tasks should be performed to reach the golden cup of breeder titles, regardless of if those tasks actually produce someone who is responsible. The power one receives by wielding the sharp-edged sword of ridicule toward anyone who does not conform is so very tempting. And if one can secure his/her power by legislating these arbitrary breeding rules onto all those who dare to breed for a living, well, so much the better.

So if a fundamental change to the currently accepted definition of responsible breeder is necessary, that leaves only one other question. Can a person consciously breed outside of these responsible breeder rules and still produce healthy, long-lived dogs with solid temperaments? In the chapters that remain, we will work tirelessly to answer this question. We will go into depth to find out if it is possible for a person to outright reject these responsible breeding rules and still produce sound dogs in both health and temperament. In fact, we will explore ideas on how it may be possible to breed for superior heath and a specific companion dog temperament. We will turn to wild breeding practices and ask ourselves, could breeding practices that have sustained wild species over tens of thousands of years wield a responsible breeder title? Just exactly what breeding practices naturally occur in the wild? The white-tailed doe, for example. Would she allow multiple males to breed her or does she choose only the strongest male based on who wins a deadly fight? Does she breed at first estrus, or does she wait to breed until a certain maturity level is achieved? How often do other animals allow multiple sire matings and do they breed on their first heats? What formal health tests do wild animals choose to perform before they breed?

Aslan's death reminded me that truth is hard won. It is far easier to lie than it is to face the humility of difficult facts with dignity and confidence. But, without seeking the raw honest truth regarding the genetic health and temperament of one's favorite dog breed and instead following those with the loudest voice, we just might lose the right altogether to responsibly breed man's best friend. Pretending to know all that is right can only harm the furry ones we love.

We must not give in to the rhetoric that many proclaim from on high that responsible dog breeders must perform this or that genetic health test or be shunned, ridiculed, slandered, or persecuted for being different. Instead, we must find the true reasons why a breeder would be considered responsible and honor those who are.

Chapter 4
The Founder is Bonkers

"All we have in the world to give is ourselves. All we have is TIME... it's all we are." - Lois Schwarz, 2017

Ten brass buttons cascading down either side of her pressed red jacket sparkled in the morning sun. The polished black leather strap sat in perfect position on her chin holding up the tall red furred hat as she stared calmly forward at a fixed point in the distance on the football field at Port Hueneme High School. A single wispy white feather blew gently in the breeze. Her hands lie stiff and motionless at her side beneath bright white gloves. Lois stood in rigid attention awaiting the signal to begin. In a silent moment of anticipation, she inhaled. Eight years of dedication playing the flute for the band had prepared her for this day. This was her year, her senior year. She had anticipated this moment all summer and now it was time. Her bright red cape caught a slight breeze and fluttered in the silence. She exhaled. The judge nodded and right on cue Lois snapped her head to the left, lifting her knees and baton in unified step to the familiar band music in her mind; every movement made with perfect command. Her body became a machine of precise motion, marching forward as she imagined leading the band through its formation. She knew every twist and turn that guided the band as the crucial responsibility of drum major took hold; her tall, thin frame a beacon for all others to follow.

As the last note trailed into the distance, Lois stood in rigid measure. Facing the judges, she ended her routine with a slow, methodical military style salute; a sign of respect and honor acknowledging those of authority. The two outside judges leaned toward the large, forbidding man in the middle. He folded his arms and listened to his counselors as he stared down at Lois in quiet resolve. His head slowly nodded as Lois took her leave. Surely her many years of unwavering dedication to the marching band would be a feather in her cap. This would be her last chance to become the leader she always knew she was. She walked briskly to the bleachers as she unstrapped her hat and sat down next to her best friend, Debbie.

Popping up from the seats behind her, a skinny, bubbly young girl in a frilly short skirt and tall white leather boots giggled sweetly. On the breeze created from the girl's carefree flight down the stairs, Lois smelled a hint of roses as the girl flicked her long dark brown curls behind her and adjusted the strap on her chin. Her velvet red skirt lie atop folds of white ruffled tulle that bounced as she floated by; her silky olive skin contrasting perfectly with her honey brown eyes. Upon reaching the grassy field, the young beauty turned in one elegant motion and bowed low to the judges with one hand outstretched and a sweet smile on her pink lips. Lois snickered under her breath and rolled her eyes. What a showboat. Over the next few minutes, the girl twirled and danced to the silent rhythm of a cantata only she could hear. "There was no question she could dance and she certainly had some beautiful movements, but a drum major must lead and she clearly was not capable of that," Lois thought. Lois leaned over to Debbie to find out more about the tiny dancer on the field. It turned out that this senior girl, Suzie, had never been in the band before and could not play an instrument. Surely, that alone would disqualify her. Lois ignored the giddy laughter as she bounded back up the stairs to sit back down with her cheering friends.

After a few agonizing minutes, the large band conductor in the middle stood up from his perch on the field and waddled down the stairs, shifting side to side as he held tight to the railing. Someone handed him a microphone while he surveyed the small group of students waiting in anticipation on the bleachers. He cleared his throat and wiped his sweaty brow with a handkerchief. "Thank you all for coming this morning. It was a great pleasure to see the dedication to the band from our students." The band conductor licked his lips and smiled broadly at the dark beauty smiling down at him from above. "It is with great pleasure that I announce that Miss Suzie Tandem will be our next drum majorette." And with that, Lois's entire world shattered as unwanted tears of disbelief began to pool under her eyes. She walked back to the girl's locker room in despair as Suzie and her friends laughed and giggled behind her, obviously possessing absolutely no understanding of the honor she had just received. To Suzie, becoming the leader of the band was simply another fun activity to add to her list. To Lois, becoming bandmaster was a privilege to be performed with dedication and hard work. In that one crestfallen moment, Lois finally grasped a fundamental truth that would shape the rest of her years; most people do not care about heart and internal commitment; they care about outward appearance and how something makes them feel. Lois had everything it took to be the best bandmaster, including raw passion and dedication, but she had misunderstood the desires of shallow, worldly people. These judges didn't want a bandmaster, they wanted flash that could thrill and dazzle the audience.

As it turned out, Suzie was given a triangle to tap which fulfilled the requirements that the bandmaster must play in the band. Having no experience in the band whatsoever, Suzie took charge of the band members, many of whom were Lois's long-time friends, as Lois sunk further into disillusionment. Without the band's practice sessions to motivate her an hour early, Lois often arrived late to school, skipping first period all together. She grew impatient and bored with her schoolwork and failed her first period class, which meant she could not graduate with her classmates.

Lois's high school graduation picture

35

Only at her mother's strong insistence did Lois finally complete her studies at summer school and earn her high school diploma. Her diploma arrived in the mail without pomp or circumstance, but no piece of paper signed by some dignitary would ever mean anything to her again. When the undeserved could rise to fame and prestige based upon an arbitrary acknowledgement from someone in authority, while the truly passionate were ignored and often ridiculed, Lois decided to travel a different path; one that often challenged the status quo.

A perfect example of Lois's steadfast willfulness to confront an established irrational pattern happened a few years later at an American Kennel Club (AKC) sanctioned dog show. The AKC's own mission statement declares "The American Kennel Club is dedicated to upholding the integrity of its Registry, promoting the sport of purebred dogs and breeding for type and function..."[1] Lois believed that statement. She believed she was giving her honor and dedication to the cause. But, the American Cocker Spaniel's function of flushing out birds, especially the American woodcock, would no longer apply today due to the spaniel's excessive cottony coat. The officially approved 2018 AKC standard for the Cocker Spaniel reads, "Coat: On the head, short and fine; on the body, medium length, with enough undercoating to give protection. The ears, chest, abdomen and legs are well feathered, but not so excessively as to hide the Cocker Spaniel's true lines and movement or affect his appearance and function as a moderately coated sporting dog. The texture is most important. The coat is silky, flat or slightly wavy and of a texture which permits easy care. Excessive coat or curly or cottony textured coat shall be severely penalized. Use of electric clippers on the back coat is not desirable. Trimming to enhance the dog's true lines should be done to appear as natural as possible." Yet, the American Cocker Spaniel today looks nothing like it did just fifty years ago.

High-pitched barking came from the Yorkshire Terriers three rows over to the left. Last minute primping for a standard poodle two stations over to the right. People and their dogs pranced by as their number was called to return to the ring. Nearby, the hunting dogs geared up for their scheduled time in front of a judge. The smell of shampoo and perfume filled the air. Emotions ran high with nervous optimism. A few more minutes and the American Cocker Spaniels would be presented.

Lois calmly led her shiny solid black colored American Cocker Spaniel, Black Satin, out of her crate and placed her on the folding table. She brushed her out one last time making sure her coat was clean and in place. Satin stood perfectly still as Lois combed out the final touches. Satin's coat was somewhat thick and course, but long and fluffy. The excessive feathering on her feet created a dark flow of cascading fur that swayed with each touch of the brush. Lois wiped the inside of Satin's long ears with a cotton swab and patted the inside of Satin's eyes to make sure no moisture was present. Satin's tongue flicked out to touch Lois's arm as it passed by. One spritz of perfume and Satin was ready. Lois waited for her breed to be announced over the loud speaker.

First, the male Cocker Spaniels entered the ring. Each one had been stripped of the long coat on its back and forehead using a special bladed comb that took hours of delicate work to accomplish to the degree exhibited as the dog glided around the ring. Each feathered foot had been meticulously scissored to rounded perfection as the handlers picked up each foot and placed it in position to be judged. Lois looked down at Satin. She had purposely not stripped Missy's coat or scissored her feet, choosing instead to keep her naturally coated, although clean and brushed. The long-flowing feathery coat of each male dog passing by one after the other caused the dog to look as if it were gliding over ice by wearing a full skirt of long fur, not a hair out of place. A flashy party colored male won the dog class. He stood with perfectly positioned pride on the platform for pictures.

Next, it would be the bitch class. Lois stood up and lifted the show lead. Satin dutifully followed beside her, Satin's long thick brown coat swishing about her as she glided by. The handler behind her gave a snort, but Lois pretended not to hear. All the people around her began to whisper in hushed tones. Lois wanted to find out just what would happen if an AKC judge was presented with a fully registered AKC bitch with an impeccable build, but without the carefully crafted trimmed look that was the hallmark of the show Cocker Spaniel and as usual, everyone around her thought she was nuts.

Lois bravely stepped into the ring in line with the other handlers and bitches. Satin pranced perfectly beside her, stopped and positioned herself in a beautiful stack. The judge took one look at Satin, pointed with stoic impertinence and declared with indignation, "Disqualified" and the steward escorted Lois out of the ring. The handlers around her smiled broadly and watched her walk out.

Lois and her Cocker Spaniels

Lois's experiment had abruptly come to an end, but her hypothesis proved true. Indeed, just as the bandmaster try-outs had shown, the unspoken standard required to conform to a particular outward presentation was more important than truly finding the most superior specimen that matched the standards of the breed, which certainly did not have anything to do with how well one could trim and primp a dog's coat. So much for the Cocker Spaniel's written ideal that the moderately feathered coat was "not so [excessive] as to hide the Cocker Spaniel's true lines and movement or affect his appearance and function as a moderately coated sporting dog." Lois concluded that AKC did not necessarily judge based on its standards, but on the perceived ideal of the day for each breed. If they had, Satin would never have been disqualified because she was simply clipped incorrectly, but judged based on her "type and function," as AKC clearly states in their mission statement. In this moment of full understanding, Lois vowed to leave all superficial dog shows behind and venture into finding out just what exactly was most important in order to produce a healthy, long-lived, stable-tempered dog breed that the public would be proud to own.

After formally leaving the AKC, Lois bred Cocker Spaniels for her own knowledge of dog coat color genetics, registering them through the United Kennel Club. She bred her Cocker Spaniels to the standard in body type and function, but she wanted to know more about what coat colors would appear in the dogs as she continued her lines. It was at this time that she began to formulate her idea of a genetic sliding scale. She began her research by working with coat color intensity and progressive greying. All of her original cockers were deep solid black except one dog that had a slight red tint just under the coat. Over time, she developed her ability to see very minute shades of lighter and lighter black until one day Lois found that she had bred solid chocolate dogs without changing the black pigmentation. She also bred livers and blondes in her quest to learn more about dog coat color genetics.

Because she had recently separated from an abusive relationship and did not yet have a job, she had to find a way to make money to survive. She began to formulate ideas for how she could make money using her passion for dogs. That is when she began Bozeman's Barnyard Kennel where she started dog training classes and learned her initial grooming techniques practicing on her cocker spaniels. At this time, she also bred chickens for increased egg production. She learned that her white Cornish hens produced more eggs per week then the Rhode Island Red. Lois also bred guinea pigs, parakeets, love birds, goats, and many other barnyard animals.

When Lois was able to get back on her feet and continue her quest for true beauty married to form and function, Lois took out a business loan, using credit card, to begin her first business called the K-9 Emporium where everything dog could be found. Not only did she sell dog food and supplies, but she groomed and trained dogs of all sorts. After having dabbled in electronics, a short military career, modeling, long haul truck driving, and security dog work, she had finally found her passion in life.

She rented a large thousand foot space in a building on the west side of town in between two naval bases. Next to her shop to the right was a Mexican bar, named the Bull Ring, closed during the day, and next to the bar was a small Hispanic-run convenience store selling the largest, spiciest pickles one has ever seen. There was an open parking area in front of the shop which Lois planned to occasionally block off for dog training classes. She proudly hung her hand-painted sign and opened her doors for business. Lois bought a copy machine and began making flyers and advertising herself. She pulled her kids in a wagon to hand flyers out door to door. At the fourth of July, Lois went to the beach where everyone was gathered and placed flyers on each parked car. She also went to supermarkets to put flyers on cars. Her favorite song was, "I Walk the Line" by Johnny Cash. She did everything and anything to make a penny.

People began to respect her hard work. One person said that she saw Lois and the kids and admired her hard work so she came into the shop. Soon, people began to frequent her business. Regulars brought in their dogs every week to keep a well-maintained manageable coat. Lois found helping others with their dogs an easy task that she greatly enjoyed.

A few months later, a soft bell jingled as the windowed door flew open to the shop and a large German Shepherd Dog strained on its leash to get inside. Behind the dog braced a young woman with splotchy red eyes and a forlorn despair upon her face. She tried to tug the dog back, but the hairy beast jumped onto the front counter, sloppy wet paws splattering water all over the paperwork lying there. The lady apologized and yanked the dog back in exasperated desperation as Lois shuffled her papers out of the way.   "Please,"   the woman pleaded. "I can't handle it anymore. I have tried everything. Please, will you help me? I don't know where else to turn. She barks at everything, chases our cats, digs giant holes in the backyard, won't heel, and now she's started to snap at me. We can't take her anywhere and I am afraid for my new baby. Can you please take her?" Lois saw the weariness in the woman's tear-stained eyes and knew she was at her wit's end. Obviously, the woman would not be emotionally able to consider other options and this dog certainly needed a better life. Lois walked around the side of the counter, quietly took the leash and led the dog into the back kennel. Before she closed the gate enclosing the dog, she heard the soft ring of the front door bell and knew the woman had gone.

This story happened many times in different ways over the years at the shop. Lois learned throughout her time as a dog shop owner that hundreds, if not thousands, of people around the city found themselves in desperate situations with the dogs they owned. "Maybe they need someone to guide them." Lois reasoned. After all, the unruly German Shepherd Dog was able to settle down with a bit of manners training. Lois began dog training classes on Saturdays at local parks around town to help those owners who needed more instruction. Her beginning obedience classes were always full. I, myself, attended many of these classes in order to help set up and take down as well as train my own party-colored English Cocker Spaniel named Bonnie. Many people found relief through her teaching, but, still people would come and go from her shop with dogs that obviously did not suit them.

The front doors had been closed and locked hours ago, but in the back of the shop behind a large partition, a small dim lamp glowed atop a worn brown desk which obviously had been painted many times as patches of different colors peeked through the scratches. A single mattress lay on the floor beside the desk adorned with freshly laundered blankets and pillows. Snuggled underneath the layers, a ten year old child with dark hair covering her face lay sleeping, my sister, Amey. The gentle scratching of pen to paper was the only sound apart from the faint muffled Mariachi music from the Mexican bar next door.

Lois sat alone on a gray folding chair, hunched over a school-ruled notebook, writing dutifully. A thick reference book on dog breeds lie dormant next to her on the desk. She often stayed awake many quiet hours into the night to write out her thoughts from the day. The all-caps heading at the top of the page read, "Traits People Look for in a Dog." Underneath the title, in neat bullet-pointed rows, Lois wrote out the characteristics of the ideal dog based on her clients' complaints. Dogs that needed to work a behavior over and over many times in order to learn a new task were frustrating to many owners, so she added "intelligent" to the list. Dogs that learned obsessive behaviors, such as constant barking and wall jumping, created from being cramped in a small backyard for too many hours/days/months without exercise drove many families to despair, so she added "calm" to the list. She continued down her list until she exhausted all the complaints she had heard and written all the desired traits that would counter the issues families faced with the dogs they owned. Her list included: smart, calm, quiet, gentle, sweet, loving, aloof, stable-tempered, good with children, good with cats, good with other dogs, remain close to home, easy to train, easy to groom, healthy, long-lived, manageable coat, large in size, beautiful with deterrent features, and on and on the list continued.

Then, Lois turned her thoughts to the owners, themselves. Most people now lived in cities and suburbs, no longer on farms and ranches. What were the average lifestyles like for these dog owners and what were their needs? She flipped the page and entitled the next list, "City/Urban Folks and Their Needs." She noted that many families now had two working parents with children of varying ages. They typically lived away from their extended families. These were people who did not have a lot of experience with animals apart from the occasional family dog or cat or sometimes a bird. The families she saw in her surrounding area were very busy and did not have much time to devote to training a dog. They had smaller backyards and modest houses and did not have a lot of money to spend on added health care issues for their family pets. Yet, they were devoted to their animals as if they were human children. Lois saw the love they had for their beloved furry companions. People wanted their animals to return this love with as much loyalty as Lassie and as much devotion as Rin

Tin Tin.

She opened the dog breed book and looked through each breed's description. She wrote down the issues which she saw owners face with each dog breed. A picture of an ideal dog began to formulate in her mind. In Lois's book, The American Alsatian, written in 2001, she recalls, "For the public to be able to train this dog, the dog itself would have to be attentive, watchful and not bounce all over the place. I found that too many dogs were taken to the pound because new owners could not devote the time necessary to train their animals to stop digging or barking. These were unwanted traits. I knew that this new breed could be selectively bred not to dig or bark."[2]

The muffled sounds of the Mariachi music next door subsided as closing time came and went. In the now silent stillness of the night, with the steady glow of the lamp beside her, Lois looked down at her list on the desk. A whisper reached her ears as her mind protested, "You can do this." She placed her hands on her hips and closed her eyes as if her eyelids created an impenetrable barrier between the words she had written and her future. Time stood still and in that decisive moment, a flash of future events scrolled across the recesses of her mind. She saw the difficult path forward, imagined the dog breeds she would have to acquire, and realized the unwavering devotion she would have to give. In that moment, she knew that if she took on this task there would be no turning back.

She opened her eyes and turned toward her daughter sleeping peacefully nearby. Amey's long brown hair flowed softly over the pillow as her chest rose and fell in a deep, gentle rhythm. "What kind of life would this be for my children?" she pondered. "They will learn to honor truth and follow their dreams with unyielding passion," came the quiet reply. "Where will I find the resources that will be needed?" she questioned, not yet convinced that she had the strength to endure the hardships she foresaw. The voice remained calm and confident, "The resources will come when they are needed. Be at peace." Her mind reeled. "I do not have the credentials," she countered. "You have all you need." There was a simple answer to every question she posed until her mind became still.

She reached over the list on her desk, turned off the lamp, and crawled into bed next to her daughter, draping her arm around Amey's small frame. As she closed her eyes, she saw herself running down a steep grassy hill with a pack of large wolves moving as one around her, their fur brushing against her thighs as they passed. She knew each one intimately and felt at peace in their presence as she drifted off to sleep.

As Shaun Ellis, the man who lives with wolves, recalls, "When you are living with wolves, all that matters is staying alive and protecting the pack; days slip into weeks, weeks into years. Time, as we know, has no relevance."[3]

Lois was most at peace in her life at the Los Padres National Forest amidst nature and her dogs where her husband worked as a caretaker for an apple orchard an hour from her dog shop in the city. The naturally easy way that all of life seemed to be at harmony in the face of both suffering and renewal spoke to her own heart's desires. She was closest to God walking among His creation without the trappings of busy city life. In this quiet forest setting, Lois was drawn to Nature's way. She patiently observed its cycles, making notes as she watched life unfold around her. In nature, there was no rush to accomplish this or that goal, but simply a desire to breathe and live each moment as it came. She came to understand that struggle and hardship were a natural part of life which taught her to cherish the peaceful moments when cares seemed to disappear.

Lois spent countless hours at the ranch studying and observing her dogs. She read books and walked the rocky fields behind her cabin accompanied by the dogs she loved. But, life at the ranch always ended on Monday when she would rise long before the sun, hop into her white cargo van, and head back down the mountain to the city and her shop. Years passed as thousands of dogs and the countless people received help from Lois at her shop. Lois bred, bought, and sold hundreds of dogs in many different breeds and spent hours training unruly dogs for others.

Her experience and dedication to her craft went beyond mere enjoyment, to a lust for knowledge that ended relationships and estranged her from her children and family. But, still she could not give up on her passion. Despite the pain and heartache from outside and inside, she kept going, kept seeking, kept learning, and kept breeding.

She made all of the mistakes. She experienced all of the trauma and tragedy of puppies dying, births going poorly, health issues claiming entire litters, picketers protesting what they perceived as unethical behavior, complaining neighbors, death threats, etc. to arrive where she is today. It could not have been about the money, since she has never had much in her life and what she had went straight back into the dogs. It could not have been about prestige, since the path she chose was a path in which both sides were against her; the purebred and the activist. Her complete and utter devotion to her passion was what propelled her throughout the years. She has made it her life's work to be the best at what she does. And she has come to know valuable information that one cannot find or understand simply by reading or staring at it from afar. Without actually being accepted into Nature's pack; without the harsh experiences of being bitten, growled at, intimidated, and starved by those who hate what she stands for; without a great amount of personal sacrifice, her passion would have long ago ended.

Lois preferred to "do" the work, rather than only read about what others had done. After she became resolved to pursue the ultimate companion in a large wolf-looking dog, she did not waste any time. She understood that time was all she had to give to this life and she feared there wasn't enough of it to complete what she had begun. She vigorously studied books and research spending many nights with a few hours of sleep only to wake again to open the shop and help more people with their dogs. Her passion consumed her day and night. She wanted to do the work; see the results for herself; study the actual temperament and see if she could alter it. She desired nothing more than to roll up her sleeves and find out the answers to her questions about breeding and genetics. She did not seek accolades from others, but quietly pursued knowledge for knowledge's sake. She did not write academically because she never understood the academic language. She spoke the language of individuality and blunt reality without frills or showmanship. She came up with terms and ideas on her own based on the successfulness of the breedings themselves. But, her vast performance experience is what makes her ideas so grand.

Dyslexia

Lois is dyslexic. She will often say that she is simply lazy and does not take the time to fix her spelling mistakes and adamantly denies this claim, but those who know and love her understand that not only does she show a lack of understanding for basic spelling and grammar rules, but she often misspeaks, using similar sounding words that mean something other than what she hopes to convey. She has significant difficulty reading names or words that are not familiar to her. But the most incredible piece of Lois's dyslexia is that she thinks visually using a big picture mindset to bring concepts together in fundamental ways.

The official definition of dyslexia from the International Dyslexia Association (IDA) is, "Dyslexia is a specific learning disability that is neurobiological in origin. It is characterized by difficulties with accurate and/or fluent word recognition and by poor spelling and decoding abilities. These difficulties typically result from a deficit in the phonological component of language that is often unexpected in relation to other cognitive abilities and the provision of effective classroom instruction. Secondary consequences may include problems in reading comprehension and reduced reading experience that can impede growth of vocabulary and background knowledge."[4] This Definition is also used by the National Institute of Child Health and Human Development (NICHD). Many state education codes, including New Jersey, Ohio and Utah, have adopted this definition, as well.

That being said, dyslexia does not impede one's intelligence. Quite the contrary, actually. Being a special education teacher in both elementary and high school for over eleven years, I knew many children struggling to learn to read who greatly excelled in other areas of academics when appropriate accommodations were put in place for their success. The IDA further explains, "Research indicates that dyslexia has no relationship to intelligence. Individuals with dyslexia are neither more nor less intelligent than the general population. But some say the way individuals with dyslexia think can actually be an asset in achieving success."[5]

Jim Rokos, an expert on dyslexia, understands the baffling language phenomenon this way, "Dyslexia is not a disability – it is an alternative brain structure, which creates a processing difference and so brings alternative aptitudes. One could equally label someone as disabled if they were not good at visual thinking, but we would not do that, because most people are not strong visual thinkers. It would not make sense to regard a majority of people as disabled. Diversity is advantageous in groups of people."[6] Jim Rokos, as well as a growing number of professionals, believes that people who are dyslexic are primarily visual thinkers, whereas the majority of the population is verbal thinkers. As Ray Davis and Suzanne Hailey explain, "Dyslexics are primarily picture thinkers. Rather than using self-talk (words, sentences, or internal dialogue), they specialize in mental or sensory imagery. This method of thinking is subliminal.[7]

This fundamental difference in thinking structure produces a group of individuals who can shift and change images easily just by using their minds. They can "see" what an object would look like upside down or backwards or even inside out. And, indeed, Lois has mentioned that when she was young, she was asked to take a test (likely an intelligence test) in which one task asked her to look at objects and point to pictures of the objects in various rotated states. She describes how easily she could do this and scored exceptionally high in this area. Because she was young, she does not remember the name of the test or even what she was there for, particularly. In Lois's youth, dyslexia was only beginning to become acknowledged and most people experiencing trouble in school were labeled as trouble-makers or stupid. Lois describes school in very much this same way.

Since dyslexics think in pictures or imagery, they tend to use global logic and reasoning strategies. They look at the big picture to understand the world around them.

Dyslexics tend to excel in areas such as:

Strategizing

Creative endeavors

Hands-on activities

Solving real world objective problems

They tend to have difficulties in areas such as:

- Word-based thinking
- Sequential, linear, step-by-step reasoning

Thinking primarily with images, dyslexics also tend to develop very strong imaginations. They use a picture or feeling based reasoning process to solve problems rather than a verbal one. If they are at first confused (or intrigued), they will mentally move around an object and look at it from different viewpoints or angles. From this thought process, they develop many unique abilities and talents in areas such as:

- Reading people
- Strategic planning
- Music/dancing
- Engineering
- Manual skills
- Artistic ability
- Building
- Piloting vehicles
- Designing
- Mechanical arts
- Drama/role playing
- Athletic ability
- Inventing
- Storytelling

When disoriented, someone with dyslexia will experience their own mental images as reality. A dyslexic disorients on a daily basis as a reaction to confusion. Disorientation is what occurs when the dyslexic is using their natural problem solving skills. Dyslexics tend to have difficulty with unreal (two-dimensional) and symbolic objects, such as letters and numerals. Many dyslexics commonly garble or mishear words or the sequence of words in sentences. Their internal sense of time can also become distorted and their motor coordination can appear delayed or clumsy.

As Fernette Eide, MD, founder and CEO of Dyslexic Advantage, explained in a Wired interview with Danielle Venton, "One of the biggest misconceptions is that dyslexic brains differ only in the ways they process printed symbols, when in reality they show an alternative pattern of processing that affects the way they process information across the board. Dyslexic brains are organized in a way that maximizes strength in making big picture connections at the expense of weaknesses in processing fine details."[8]

This is exactly what is seen in Lois's case. Yes, Lois has difficulty with spelling and grammar, but she also understands words in a different way than is typical. The following quote, taken directly from Lois's website, has been used numerous times by skeptics. Let's take a look at it and break it down to understand her meaning. When Lois states,

"As far as breeding 8 mo old dogs, I don't breed them, they do it themselves. My dogs live on five acres of farmland in a pack and breed whenever GOD decides that it is time. What I do is to make sure that the right dog is in the right place when the time comes. Nature knows better than you do that's for sure. Please don't give me this cr_p about breeding an 11 yr old human child either as that would just emphasis the fact that you talk like so many others who know nothing. I have been breeding animals and living in nature for over 50 yrs and I have not just been spouting off and talking from the couch. I got involved in breeding all kinds of animals and keeping records of the genetics of the prodigy around the age of 7 yrs old. I am not talking one or two generations either. Neither do I purchase several 18 generations solidly bred animals and breed one time and say, 'oh my look what I have created, arnt [sic] I smart' as some breeders do. That is not breeding, that is stealing or using anothers [sic] breeding stock.

Breeding animals is an art. There are many folks who do things, but to do things proper and to the best of ones abilities takes devotion and yrs and yrs........ of education on the matter." – Lois Schwarz

That is what she says. Now someone with ill intentions can take what she says and grossly misrepresent her if they take her words out of context or only take one part of her statement in order to make it seem like she means something other than she does. Taking only parts of what Lois writes in a way that fundamentally alters her intentions for the express purpose of using it against her to discredit her is seriously intellectually dishonest. In one instance, someone quoted this from Lois statement above, "As far as breeding 8 month old puppies, I don't breed them, they do it themselves. My dogs live on five acres of farmland in a pack and breed whenever GOD decides that it is time." Without the other part of the quote, people interpret this statement to mean that Lois places all of her dogs into one large pen and the dogs breed as they will without any involvement from Lois, herself. But in the very next sentence, which is oftentimes not quoted, Lois explains that she places the correct dogs in the correct place, thus selective breeding. Doing this in order to discredit her is slander and unlawful.

However, when one actually uses their mind to understand exactly what Lois is trying to convey, instead of using their mind to find ways to undermine her, a clearer picture of what she means comes into focus. For example, here is my interpretation of what she means:

As far as breeding dogs on their first heat, I do not make dogs breed. I could never make dogs breed. Dogs have natural and instinctual urges that I could never alter. Furthermore, I do not artificially inseminate or force dogs to breed. Breeding is a natural event. Feral dogs, such as those living in New York, do not think to themselves, "Are we old enough yet? I think we should wait before breeding. Maybe we should wait until we are two years old just to make sure this is the right thing to do." Instead, the natural way a dog would breed is superior to human interference. Nature is created by God and the way that nature selects for health first and function second is superior to any way that humans could come up with as a way to breed. It then becomes simply that we, humans, should work to mimic nature as much as we

48

humanely can. Of course, I make a conscious decision after looking at health issues (or lack thereof), temperament scores, pedigrees, and structural needs to place the dogs that will advance the breed in health, temperament and/or a closer bone/body structure toward the Dire Wolf... in that order. But, I have a lifetime of experience breeding dogs and I believe it is stealing to claim credit for breeding one dog to another unless one has personally bred much of the line. It is not worth my time to talk with someone who does not have the experience, thus the education, to understand. – Lois Schwarz, interpreted by Jennifer Stoeckl

She could have spelled it all out and explained all of the aspects of what she does, taking the time to truly detail her beliefs in a way that makes others feel better about her, but she does not care what others think. I suspect that there is even a small part of Lois that wants to weed out those people who cannot think for themselves and who blindly follow what others say without trying to get to the truth. Lois understands that not everyone will take the time to understand her meaning or read through her other pages to compile the information she presents into an overall picture of her work.

To be sure, it has taken this author over ten years to fully gain an understanding of what Lois has described over the years. In many ways, this book was written in order to put all of the pieces of her way of breeding together in a way in which others can fully understand. In a very real sense, this book is an interpretation of Lois's life's work. All of the ideas are hers. Lois is the originator who found a way to meld current science together with practical breeding strategies in a way that puts breeding healthy, long-lived animals into perspective; to reveal the big picture, so to speak. Sometimes her ideas may seem extremely controversial, but by being open-minded and understanding the thinking and experience behind the ideas that follow from her, perhaps one just may come to appreciate Lois for the fiercely passionate, strong-minded, and deeply loving, salt-of-the-earth type of person that Lois is.

Twice Exceptional

Lois may very well have been considered twice exceptional if she had been a child in today's world. Not only does Lois show significant regression in her ability to use and manipulate words and grammar as well as a difference in thought processes, but Lois also excels significantly in art and design. As the National Association for Gifted Children explains, "Like other gifted learners, 2e [twice exceptional] students are highly knowledgeable and talented in at least one particular domain. However, their giftedness is often overshadowed by their disabilities, or these students may be able to mask or hide their learning deficits by using their talents to compensate. Sometimes a twice-exceptional child's special education needs are overlooked until adolescence or later, or are never identified through his or her life."[9]

Lois and her artwork 2017

Lois has a keen sense of color and can see even very minor differences or shifts in color and texture. Although she has never taken any art classes, her paintings are very detailed and accurate to life. But, just as with so many aspects of her life, Lois does not paint in the same way that other painters would. Her approach is always different, even though the result is usually stunning. Here's an example. Lois often paints using water colors, but instead of using water, she dry brushes the canvas using much more color than water. As a result, her water painted works look much more like very thin acrylic painting would. She has dabbled in China painting, as well.

For several years, she attended an annual China painting seminar. She signed up for classes, but ended up never using the same technique the teacher recommended. After years of attending this same seminar, she finally stopped attending classes and chose to sit outside the classroom and paint her own versions, using her own techniques. Her works are masterpieces in their own right, but not in any way produced as would be recommended. Instead of painting with delicate strokes and spending lots of time on the finer details, Lois paints using more paint than is recommended and wiping off the excess paint to the desired degree. She has described her style of China painting as "painting the negative space." Her eye sees the space between the colors and she finds that more effective than painting the colors directly. Lois's ability to see the empty space in a painting and use that to create her works of art is not an approach that many can master, but her mind allows her to see differently and exceptionally.

Lois is also a person who can think very broadly and with a completely different focus or approach. As with her China painting techniques, she does not like to be placed inside narrow parameters, preferring instead to let go of all barriers to any thinking and come at a problem or situation by being able to look at all aspects before making to a decision on which way to take. In grade school, she often recalls, she was a very curious child and asked lots of questions, looking for reasonable answers to be able to relate to her way of thinking in order to learn and remember. She wanted to put together the big picture to the learning puzzle of school in which she found herself. Unfortunately, her teachers did not appreciate her incessant questioning and viewed them as defiance instead of merely her mind's curiosity. As a result, many times during her childhood she felt alienated and unappreciated. She was scolded by the staff for being disruptive and argumentative, even though she was far from wanting to cause the trouble in which she frequently found herself.

The International Dyslexia Association explains a lot of the features that also describe Lois. "Parents and teachers may fail to notice both giftedness and dyslexia. Dyslexia may mask giftedness, and giftedness may mask dyslexia. Some common characteristics of 2e individuals follow:

- Superior oral vocabulary
- Advanced ideas and opinions
- High levels of creativity and problem-solving ability
- Extremely curious, imaginative, and questioning
- Discrepant verbal and performance skills

- Clear peaks and valleys in cognitive test profile
- Wide range of interests not related to school
- Specific talent or consuming interest area
- Sophisticated sense of humor"[10]

Lois has always had advanced ideas and opinions. She possesses high levels of creativity and problem-solving abilities. She has always been extremely curious, imaginative, and questioning. She certainly had a wide range of interests not related to school clearly developed a specific talent and a consuming interest area. She shows a sophisticated sense of humor which most people do not fully understand or grasp and it is for this reason that it is hard to know when she is joking or not.

Lois was also a very emotional child, wanting approval in a desperate sort of way, but never receiving it to her satisfaction. She ached for others to like her and want to be her friend. Her naive understanding of the world left her powerless to understand just how manipulative some people could be. When she was in the second grade, a janitor befriended her and because she was so desperate for approval, she immediately liked the janitor and trusted him to be her friend. However, in this sick and twisted man's mind, Lois was an easy target and he took advantage of her at the end of school by asking her to come with him to the outside janitor's closet. She was so ashamed of this that she did not speak of it to anyone until she was an adult.

Several times as a young child, she found herself packing a few belongings and running away from home, seeking a better life than the one she knew. But stepping away from her family, she always felt afraid to venture out too far from what was familiar and she would return home again vowing to try harder to be a child who could please the adults who she respected. Eventually, as she grew older, she found that she was never able to try hard enough to be that good child she wanted so much to be and lost much trust and respect for people as a result.

During these most difficult times in her childhood, Lois found peace and solace in animals. She was always happiest when she could be around the fish, ducks, geese, chickens, and dogs that her father loved to bring home for the family to enjoy. She often went to the library to study about animals and had an interest early on regarding genetics and how breeding worked.

One time, Lois recalls that she had been observing a pregnant fish. She was always curious about how the world worked and wondered why this fish had not given birth yet. She wanted to know what it was like for a fish to give birth, but the fish was not yet ready to release her babies. Lois, ever wondering, decided to find out, so she captured the mother fish and gently squeezed its belly releasing all of those tiny squirming bodies. She quickly found out that nature does not take kindly to meddling unnecessarily, and all of the baby fish as well as the mother died. It was a very heartbreaking lesson on letting nature take its course and to not be in a hurry. She would carry this lesson with her throughout her life.

At the time she turned eighteen, the early 70s had arrived and many other young people had already decided to rebel against society and what had been considered the norm or what should be. This fit with Lois's own understanding of out of the box thinking and she entered her adult years with a sense of defiance and willfulness. Never being able to conform to society's expectations as a child, Lois found herself selling drugs and meeting men who would give her the attention and recognition she had always sought. Life was very hard during this time for her. Lois entered the dark world of sex and drugs, which taught her to be hard and mistrusting of her fellow man. Outside of her mother's arms, she began to find that many people were only out to use and abuse her. Learning about life from the school of hard knocks taught her to "live life like a warrior," as she is fond of saying. She had truly become the black sheep in her family and her four other siblings quickly dismissed her as a degenerate.

One of the wonders about Lois, though, is that she never lost her own sense of worth. She somehow knew that she was not at fault, but that the system just was not able to accommodate her. She never knew why she was different, but she was able to embrace her differences internally and keep her self-esteem intact.

It is interesting that Lois never stopped believing in herself and her abilities. She decided early on that teachers at school did not understand her because they were not as intelligent, so instead of developing a self-loathing of her lack of abilities in school, she chose to develop an attitude that others were beneath her and she was the one with the superior intelligence. She continues to believe this about herself to this day and will find ways to show that she is smarter or more knowledgeable than any other person. This type of attitude does indeed get her in trouble, but she also makes it a point to speak her words precisely and she expects others around her to interpret her precisely as she has spoken. She is often misunderstood, however. Here is an example. One time, probably around 2004, on a forum when she was speaking with others about her dogs, she told another person that they were ignorant. The other person immediately took great offense and claimed that Lois was name calling. However, Lois chose her words on purpose to convey the word "ignorant" as meaning severely uninformed regarding the topic. She did not mean that the person was stupid or dumb, but instead meant that the person did not know what she was talking about and therefore beneath even a conversation between them.

Throughout Lois's entire career, she has always worked to be clear and concise, not mincing words or causing confusion. But, Lois understands the world so differently than most people that it can be difficult to understand her meaning if not taken at face value.

Lois is exceptionally kind-hearted and generous, as well as soft at heart and very emotional. She cries for each lost life and hurts deeply when her family alienates or sees her as less knowledgeable because of her differences. But, she has also built an icy northern wall of protection around herself and, therefore, she can seem callous and unbending to a casual onlooker. If one does not take the time to get to know Lois, one may go away with disdain, thinking that she is a mean-spirited, heartless kind of person. To be truthful, Lois wants this to happen. When those people who browse her website find that her way of bluntly speaking is too crass or brazen, she eliminates those people who cannot take a deeper look at her words and see the person she is behind them. This way only those select few who can look past her harsh exterior will penetrate her icy wall and move into her heart. Her many close friends will certainly attest to this.

Chapter 5
God's Breeding Plan

"Evolution is not separate from Creation. Creation is evolution. Creation was the beginning of evolution." - Lois Schwarz written for the Dire Wolf Project Breeder's Association Facebook Group, February 14, 2018.

I drove as fast as I could down the highway to get home to my husband, Jay, who had just informed me that one of our dogs, Tina, was in labor. According to my calculations, Tina had two more days before she was due. We were caught unaware and birth waits for no man, so Jay delivered the first puppies as he waited from my arrival. I still had a six hour drive from Portland to our new property overlooking Lake Roosevelt. Time seemed to meander slowly by as I coached my frantic husband through the first puppy births. The mile markers flew by in a blinking blur as my heart raced and my mind cried out in hopes that everything would be okay.

When I returned, I hopped out of the car and climbed the steps to the RV as quickly as possible. I immediately saw that Tina was noticeably uncomfortable and not very responsive. The worst of my fears were upon us. One puppy had died on my way home and the other four puppies were trying to suckle as Tina moaned in distress. I immediately took her temperature and found that it was elevated. This was a vet emergency if ever there was one. With no time to spare, we scooped Tina up along with her puppies and headed out into the chilly night straight to the emergency vet clinic an hour's drive south, frantically calling them as we raced down the road.

Upon arrival, the emergency technician team gathered outside for us. They hurriedly carried Tina in on a stretcher and set up an incubator for her puppies. I breathed a silent sigh of relief. Surely, now that we were at the vet's office, everything would be alright. The veterinarian induced labor using oxytocin and Tina was able to have all six of her remaining puppies through natural birth. The veterinarians worked through the night to help Tina. The medical team found that the new mother was dehydrated so they set up an intravenous tube and gave Tina the life-giving water she needed, which allowed her to look much better.

The emergency medical team x-rayed Tina's abdomen after the last birth and found no more puppies. They gave us some medication for our new mother and we placed all ten puppies in a basket which I carried on my lap. Tina hobbled to the car and we helped her into the back seat. Surely she would feel better soon since her pregnancy ordeal had now ended. When we arrived home, we placed Tina and her puppies in the whelping pen and Jay and I fell exhausted into bed.

The next day, Tina did not seem any better and still would not eat or drink. Since it was during the day, we called our regular veterinarian in Colville and she wanted to see Tina right away. Off we went, back to the veterinarian's office with Tina and all of her puppies. Tina looked miserable as her puppies squirmed in the box in which we had set them.

We had the x-rays from the night before sent over to Colville for assessment. It just so happened, that when the new veterinarian reviewed the x-rays, she saw a little piece of Tina's intestine which did not look right. The veterinarian wanted another set of x-rays to see farther up her abdomen. Those new x-rays revealed that Tina hadn't suffered because of her pregnancy, as everyone had assumed, but instead a large unidentified obstruction in her small intestine revealed the reason for Tina's tortured distress. The vet quickly informed us Tina would need immediate surgery.

Once the surgical team looked inside Tina's abdomen to see just what damage had occurred, they found that she had unknowingly swallowed a large piece of rope toy that had blocked the passageway between her stomach and small intestine. "No wonder she did not touch her food or water," I thought. Wringing my hands nervously as I waited to hear about the next steps, the vet sank into a low voice. My heart skipped a beat as she tragically informed us that Tina's small intestine was so mangled that parts of the intestine had died and were no longer functioning. It was likely that Tina would not survive the operation. It was one of the most devastating moments of my dog breeding career. As tears flowed helplessly down my cheeks, Tina passed away quietly on the operating table and my heart sank into despair. God, if you are out there, please hear my prayer.

Tina Turner (Hammer/River) 10/2015 – 07/2017

However, unbeknownst to me, the hardest times were yet to come. How were we going to raise nine puppies without a mother? We couldn't even begin to know. When we returned home, I mixed up a batch of generic puppy formula according to the package directions and began feeding the puppies one by one using a bottle specifically made for puppies that we had purchased at Walmart. The puppies drank heartily, but still did not seem to be thriving. Then, without warning, two puppies took their final breaths. Our hearts, reeling from Tina's passing, now seemed as though they would burst. I called the vet back with a lump in my throat and tears flowing endlessly. Why all of this suffering? Where are you, God?

The vet's office was extremely sympathetic and got us in right away. On our way to the vet's office with the remaining seven puppies huddled in a basket, one of the puppies seized dramatically and then stopped breathing. We could not save it. Uncontrollable sobs emerged as my heart finally gave out and my mind became numb.

Through the emptiness, I clearly heard a still, small voice say, "Cry as hard as you want to, but when you stop crying, make sure you never cry for the same reason again." It was a hard and unsympathetic sentence. Actually, I remember feeling resentment at the thought of it. I couldn't believe it had been thought, but there it was; too prominent to ignore and too difficult to reflect upon. Without a way to escape the thought, however, my only recourse was to try to understand what the sentence had meant. After some thought, my only conclusion was that it was okay to feel powerless and empty, but through the pain and agony, one must fight for the living, not dwell on the dead. Renewed strength and passion emboldened me and I vowed right then and there to figure out how to do what Tina would have naturally been able to do, no matter how hard it would be, to save the rest of these puppies from death.

When we arrived at the vet's office, one more puppy seized and the veterinarian humanely ended its misery. With four puppies left, the vet showed Jay and I how to drive a large needle under each puppy's skin on the back of their neck in order to hydrate them. They were severely dehydrated due to the lack of hydration given to them by their mother when she was not able to eat or drink. In fact, these puppies were so dehydrated that their mouths were completely dry. They needed immediate attention and continued hydration therapy for the next five days, twice a day. Imagine having to hold a tiny screaming newborn puppy as a large needle is thrust through the delicate skin producing a large bubble of water creating a hunchback of hydration. I can tell you that it is not easy, physically or emotionally.

Armed with our supplies, Jay and I piled back into the car with our four remaining puppies. In desperation, I searched for how to naturally create puppy milk replacer that would be able to help these puppies retain their water and give them the nourishment they needed. As if on cue, I found a page from Leerburg's site where Ed Frawley describes exactly the same situation we had gone through with distressed and dehydrated puppies. He generously gives the ingredients to an all-natural puppy milk replacement formula, so we headed directly to the store to pick up the supplies.

All through the day and all through the night, Jay and I took turns mixing the formula, feeding the puppies, inducing bowel movements and heating rice bags to keep the puppies warm. We laid the puppies in a long, narrow plastic bin that we placed in between us on the bed so that we could attend to them each hour. Twice a day the puppies received their daily agony of hydration therapy. One week slowly passed as the puppies finally began to grow and gain in weight. I will be forever grateful for Leerburg's in depth public account of how they saved their puppies from death when they lost their mother dog as well.

The Survival Litter inside the heated plastic tub 2017

Red-eyed and exhausted, Jay and I finally found some semblance of a routine. We were able to move the puppies out to the living room on the second week as they became more and more able to sleep longer during the night. At the end of the second week, the puppies had outgrown their initial plastic whelping bin and now could move to the official whelping box that previously had been set up for Tina and her puppies. Everything seemed promising as the storm clouds began to lift from our minds and hearts.

We named the puppies after Gilligan's Island since they were the survivors of a major twist of fate. There was MaryAnn, Ginger, Lovie, and Skipper. Four beautiful puppies were now normal weight and continuing to gain. They each enjoyed snuggling and being close as they ate with their human parents. They looked forward to their meal times and interacting with their people.

But, the peace was short-lived as one day in the later part of the second week, just as the puppies were beginning to open their eyes and start to walk, I woke up to find that one of the smallest puppies, MaryAnn, was not able to use her left front leg. I gently moved it around, manipulated it up and down, and looked for any injury or trauma. Nothing seemed to jump out at me. That day, I waited to see if it would get better, but by the next day, two of her feet were not working and now she screamed in pain whenever I touched her joints. Not only that, but Ginger, also, began showing signs of these same symptoms.

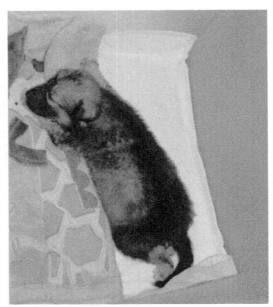

MaryAnn separated from the litter to heal 2017

I spent my time researching the symptoms online only to find that all of the symptoms suggested that a virus had attacked the puppies. Without their mother's initial colostrum, the puppies never had the opportunity to acquire the immunity they needed to overcome a virus, should it attack. We called the vet again and back we went. They took x-rays of Ginger and MaryAnn's legs and found small fractures lacing their limbs. Apparently, as they had begun to stand, their bones were too brittle to hold their frame, so their bones broke and the result was a painful healing process just at the time they were working on learning to stand and walk by themselves. Just to be safe, the veterinarian went ahead and checked for distemper, which thankfully turned out to be negative. To this day, the vets at the Colville Animal Hospital scratch their heads in bewilderment as to what occurred with these pups and cannot explain the pup's initial brittle bones and resulting fractures.

The only puppy that did not seem to be affected by this apparent virus's ability to soften the bone structure of these developing babies was Skipper. He never cried out in pain and never had any difficulties walking or moving. It was then that I knew, Skipper must be the only puppy to be kept in the breed to further the lines. He had, for whatever reason, been able to fend off the virus without any noticeable symptoms. Later on, after we received the DNA test from this litter, Skipper was the only puppy to have acquired "high diversity" in immunity, but I already knew that, didn't I?

The Survival Litter 2017

The Problem of Evil

The problem of evil, especially natural evil, has been said to be the greatest obstacle to a belief in God. After all, why would an all-knowing, all-powerful, all-good God allow such seemingly needless suffering? Certainly, if we, humans, were to take on God's role, we would not allow suffering to exist to the extent we see on earth. William Rowe, a prominent atheist philosopher, describes the argument as follows,

"There exist instances of intense suffering which an omnipotent, omniscient being could have prevented without thereby losing some greater good or permitting some evil equally bad or worse. An omniscient, wholly good being would prevent the occurrence of any intense suffering it could, unless it could not do so without thereby losing some greater good or permitting some evil equally bad or worse. There does not exist an omnipotent, omniscient, wholly good being."[1]

But, how do we know that there are some evils that do not ultimately serve a good end? With my limited finite mind, I can think of a few ways that goodness prevailed after the seemingly unnecessary and tragic evil of losing Tina, losing six of her babies, and going through the turmoil and pain of a virus all because of the fluke event of swallowing a large chunk of rope toy. As a result of these horrific experiences, I definitely became a stronger individual, I learned a great deal about caring for young puppies, I was able to see the puppy with the highest diversity in immunity which lead me to choose him to go on in the breed rather than one of his siblings, and my bank account became so drained due to all of the vet costs that I needed to learn how to fit our budget into a smaller platform and begin to manage our money within a much tighter playing field. I also learned to rely not only on my own desires, but to take things as they come, one step at a time, and weather the storms of life with my head held high. Now, was it necessary to endure this much suffering and experience the loss of a great dog in order to attain this knowledge? Well, I certainly would not know how much it takes to raise a puppy without a mother unless I actually had to experience it.

Do not get me wrong. It was the most horrific experience of my breeding career and I almost left dog breeding because of it. Perhaps another person may have done just that. But, when a person can learn from the suffering in life, one's character improves. One's ability to understand another's suffering improves. One's convictions about dealing with the tragedies and consequences of being alive improve. In fact, I have come to believe that those who have not endured significant struggles and experienced tragic evils in life are the ones at a disadvantage. As a result of their lack of experience, they have a much more difficult time relating to the tragedy that others face and do not have as much ability to understand another's loss and mourning.

In fact, many of the virtues that make the world a better place are practiced in response to some kind of evil. Take, for example, the courage to do what is right in the face of danger. The compassion to suffer alongside someone else. The love of putting another person's needs ahead of one's own. I would strongly argue that these human traits would be infinitely more difficult to attain without the suffering that can accompany our lives.

So what about natural evils that do not seem to make any difference in the lives of any human being, such as a maddening flash flood lifting whole trees only to bash a young, innocent and unsuspecting fawn just waking from a night's rest. Surely allowing that type of suffering is needless and cruel. But, the type of suffering we see all of the time in the wild may just be a consequence of living in a world governed by natural laws; laws that do not require intervention from a creator. Water that eliminates our thirst and is essential to life can also kill when a flash flood rages down a narrow ravine unless God always intervenes miraculously when water becomes too violent. But, God allows suffering to play out each and every day on our planet.

Over time, paleontologists and anthropologists have discovered just how prevalent suffering, death and eventual extinction were with many of our planet's animal ancestors. Take, as an obvious example, the Dire Wolf, the most densely populated species of animal found to have repeatedly suffered an agonizingly slow death inside the thick black ooze of La Brea Tar Pits. God did not intervene the countless times when what looks like entire packs of wolves became entrapped by the sudden collapse of land beneath them. Surely, it took time to descend into the earth's belly as well as time to succumb to the eventual realization of inevitable death. The screams of animals still clinging to life, fighting to stay alive, must have been ear-shattering. And still, God did not intervene. But, does this prove God does not exist simply because he allows natural law to prevail, which also allows suffering to exist?

As we shall explore in this chapter, perhaps there is an essential good that comes about as a direct result of allowing natural laws to dominate this earth without constant intervention from an all knowing, all powerful, all good God. As Barbara E Royal, DVM put it in her contribution to the journal, the Huffington Post, "Animals in their natural surroundings are healthy — chronically healthy. While walking in a forest teeming with robust species, I never ask myself, where are all the aging ravens with their pill boxes? Or the diabetic robins tucking syringes in their nests? Where are the arthritic squirrels, the obese rabbits, and the deer taking puffs from their inhalers? Yes, survival of the fittest and predation may take the weak and the diseased. But this doesn't fully account for the vigor of the remaining animals. Nature effortlessly propagates health..."[2]

The truth is that suffering exists. It is a part of being alive on this earth and no human being can escape it, no matter how much money we own or how much protection and padding we try to accumulate. Without searching for the goodness amidst the tragedies, the suffering that accompanies all of life may indeed seem hopelessly unnecessary and all-consuming. It is my belief that true goodness can only be seen through the veil of suffering, if one has eyes to see. Through all of the tragedy and sorrow Jay and I faced with the Survival Litter, we chose to look toward the good that has come from this horrible ordeal in our lives as without it, life simply makes no sense at all.

Does God breed our dogs?

What about the suffering that is caused by human beings? If we cannot eliminate all suffering from life, perhaps we can at least work to eliminate any suffering caused by our own human weaknesses. For example, can human beings, in all of our wisdom and knowledge, end suffering for the animals and people we love? Surely dog breeders have the awe-inspiring responsibility to intervene and alleviate the pain and suffering that can occur in our beloved pets. But, can we? Or rather, should we? That might sound crass and unfeeling, but again, suffering allows us to see and face our own human weaknesses and shape ourselves, altering and changing our wrongs to mold and conform to better examples of kindness and goodness. It is only through truly looking at the suffering that we work to improve the lives of those around us, especially our furry companions. It could even be said that a breakdown of our society has much to do with the belief that we must end all suffering wherever it occurs. This creates an unnatural sense of entitlement as well as a constant disappointment whenever suffering occurs.

Breeders who believe it is their duty to eliminate suffering at all costs in their animals may find themselves unknowingly increasing the suffering in their animals over time. For example, if I had ignored the suffering from the brittle bones from the survival litter, I would have chosen the gorgeous MaryAnn instead of her brother, Skipper. Everyone I knew wanted me to choose her since her ears rose early and would give the breed more of a chance for erect ears. But, would choosing her have perpetuated something genetically worse, such as no immune diversity, thereby significantly decreasing the immune strength in our breed? "MaryAnn is fine," I could rationalize. She endured the virus, is no longer suffering, and will pass on her immunity to her offspring, thereby eliminating future suffering.

MaryAnn at 4 weeks old

These same breeders scorn Lois and the breed for her strong belief that God can and does intervene in the work of breeding the American Alsatian dog. After all, isn't it the job of the breeder, not God, to shape and mold the animals in our care? Surely after fifty years of breeding animals, Lois should at least have the knowledge, herself, without needing to rely on some arbitrary intervention from a God that allows natural law to take over. Some people ridicule or laugh while others are simply appalled at this quote from Lois on her website, "Our dogs breed as God chooses." Perhaps they assume that Lois places all of the dogs into one pen and leaves them there to breed randomly, which is absolutely untrue. But, the founder of this dog breed does believe in one all-knowing God who plays an active role in deciding which puppies will be kept in the breed for future endeavors and which will not. As we shall see, these beliefs and why they are fundamental to the work that certified breeders do within the Dire Wolf Project is one of the most important features to our breeding program and without it, no American Alsatian Dog breeder can hope to succeed for long.

When breeding dogs, one often finds oneself pouring over pedigrees, endlessly calculating inbreeding coefficients, comparing the traits of one to another, and diligently planning for future matches. Then, there are the physical designs for how to house and care for the animals that are acquired. Many times one's schemes are fulfilled without a hitch; however, there are also times when one's carefully laid plans fall through unexpectedly.

Why do some ideas happen to come to fruition and others not? Some would say that the fault lies with the person. Perhaps the one in charge did not plan as well as he/she could have. Perhaps a mistake was made in the calculations. Maybe there were fewer funds than anticipated. The excuses and finger pointing can pour down like a heavy monsoon rain. But, whatever the reasons one finds, the truth remains; sometimes, despite one's mistakes, some plans are completed perfectly and yet even with the most carefully designed intentions some are washed away in the flash flood of human creativity.

If one takes on the belief that he/she alone has all the knowledge, wisdom and capability to perfectly execute the tasks needed for procuring a well-run, successfully thriving breeding business, this person will be missing a fundamental element in their program; the unforeseen disaster. Times of trouble and woe can come unsuspectingly, gripping the very detailed planner like a vice. It is what happens in these moments of devastation that one must come to terms with a force in the universe that is greater than one's self.

A dark whisper is heard carried on a chilling breeze that humans are the highest life form on our planet and we alone have the introspection to plan and reason; there is no thing greater than the human mind. Yes, indeed, the human mind has brought cell phones, satellites into orbit, Martian landings locating water on Mars, and piecing together our earth's prehistoric past among so many other amazing accomplishments. Yet, in all of our human wisdom, we have yet to be able to calm the storm, bring back the dead, or cure the common cold. Human beings are not all-knowing and all-powerful nor will they ever be. We live in a finite world in mortal bodies in which we know not the hour of our death. We make mistakes. We harm one another and ourselves. Some live in the harshest poverty while others bask in the supposed glory of extreme wealth. Human beings have not mastered their fears or brought their fellow man to total enlightenment and peace. No one human community is without its faults. Human kind in all its wisdom, knowledge and power has not eliminated poverty or eradicated injustice. Human perfection simply has not been reached and likely may never be within our grasp. So, what makes one imperfect, mistake-prone person believe that his/her intellect alone will be the answer to bring about better health and/or longevity for his/her chosen dog breed?

The truth is that it is extreme arrogance and folly to believe that one is the perfect, shining example of all of human kind who can break through the veil of other's mistaken tragedies to produce, from one's superior intellect alone, a healthier and longer-lived breed of dog. One may, indeed, produce many great dogs with perfect health, living lives longer than any other. However, not even the most knowledgeable and responsible dog breeder could ever surpass the consistently superior health and longevity that is seen from wild wolves living in captivity when nature's harsh elements have been eliminated.

It has been experienced many times where wild born wolves that have been captured and placed in artificial environments regularly live upwards of seventeen years of age according to PBS in 2012.[4] In fact, according to the Texas Wolf Dog Project, the average lifespan of mid to high content wolf dogs is between twelve to eighteen years old, depending largely on the dog breeds used in the mix.

With this as the measure, how could the intelligence of one human mind compare? Dogs are after all 98% genetically similar to wolves. If wolves can live this long with their large size and experience minimal health issues, should not all of our large breed dogs be as healthy and long lived?

But, humankind did not breed the wolf and we cannot claim the prize for the longest living canids on the planet. In many cases, our breeding interventions have given us much lower average lifespans with many more health issues. In fact, a comprehensive study printed by the American Veterinary Medical Association in 2013 reviewed the medical records of 27,254 cases of inherited disease in dogs, comparing purebred dogs to mixed breed dogs of unknown origin. Purebred dogs showed a significantly higher incidence of ten genetically inherited diseases including: dilated cardiomyopathy, elbow dysplasia, cataracts, and hypothyroidism among others. While mixed breed dogs showed a significant increase in only one area: ruptured cranial cruciate ligament.[5] Many others corroborate this data that genetic health issues in purebred dogs are more prevalent and on the rise. Just one other example, Carol Beuchat, PhD founder of the Institute for Canine Biology writes, "...the list of genetic disorders in dogs continues to get longer and longer."[6]

In the journal, Scientific American, in 2014 Claire Maldarelli explains her reasoning for why diseases plague purebred dogs, "When a male dog wins numerous championships, for instance, he is often bred widely—a practice known as popular sire syndrome—and his genes, healthy or not, then are spread like wildfire throughout the breed. As a result, purebred dogs not only have increased incidences of inherited diseases but also heightened health issues due to their bodily frames and shapes, such as hip dysplasia in large breeds like the German shepherd and the Saint Bernard, and patellar luxation, or persistent dislocation of the kneecap, in toy and miniature breeds."[7]

Let's look more deeply at several purebred dog breeds. For instance, the Irish Wolfhound, an extra-large breed, regularly lives an unnaturally short life only to die most readily from dilated cardiomyopathy and bone cancer between the ages of 4.95 to 8.75 years old. According to a 2007 review of all of the health data researched in the Irish Wolfhound breed over the last one hundred years, "Irish Wolfhounds are subject to a decrease in average lifespan as well as a number of hereditary diseases and diseases with a hereditary component, and that lifespan in the breed has decreased markedly since the 1960s. While this is likely due to a number of concurrent factors, the decrease in selection pressure towards health traits is common to the majority of them."[8]

A young Irish Wolfhound

In a significant study in 2014 by Gretchen Bernardi and backed by the Irish Wolfhound Club of America, it was also found that short lifespans for the Irish Wolfhound have been a consistent trend for over fifty years. "Irish Wolfhounds in the United States from 1966 to 1986 lived to a mean age of 6.47 and they died most frequently of bone cancer."[8a] A common argument from purebred Irish Wolfhound breeders is that the breed is too small in number to effectively increase selection criteria which would eliminate a significant number of dogs from breeding and thus create an effect that reduces genetic diversity as a result. But, according to the 2007 research review above, "the results of the study at hand make it quite clear that, given the apparent lack of inbreeding influence on lifespan as well as the exponential increase in population size over time, the potential for severe health- and vigour-based selection was never as good in the breed as it is at present."[8a] Whatever the case, will the Irish Wolfhound breed survive if breeders continue to ignore these critical suggestions?

A King Charles Spaniel
Photo Credit: Pleple2000 10-18, 5 April 2006 (UTC) [CC BY-SA 3.0
(http://creativecommons.org/licenses/by-sa/3.0/)]

Think for a moment on the fact that, in 2011, a research survey of 555 King Charles Spaniels, reported by their owners as having no clinical signs of the disease, found, using MRI scanning, that 25% of one-year olds and 70% of those six years old or older had developed syringomyelia, where the skull is too small for the brain. In affected dogs, fluid filled cavities (syringes) form within the spinal cord because of a discrepancy between the size and shape of the skull and brain. This condition, in which the back of the skull is less rounded and smaller than would be considered normal in a similar sized dog, is called a Chiari-like malformation.[9] As this dog's brain grows, the pressure on the inside of the skull is too great and the dog suffers horribly before it passes on at an early death. There is no cure for this illness because the issue is caused from the formation of the skull itself, which we know to have been altered to suit our human whims through artificial selection.

An English Bulldog

Another shining example of human intervention gone awry is the English Bulldog. Its body has been so unnaturally changed that it can no longer breed on its own and all English Bulldogs must now be artificially inseminated in order to produce offspring. Furthermore, they cannot give birth naturally and must have a C-section in order to birth their young due to the abnormally large skull size of the breed. That is without even mentioning how the muzzle on the English Bulldog is so short that it oftentimes must undergo surgery in order to open the airways for it to breath without difficulty.

All of this unnecessary suffering seen in our purebred dogs is not the dog's fault, but the fault lies squarely with our own human interference in the ongoing lives of man's best friend. As Shaun Ellis states so eloquently in his book, The Man Who Lives with Wolves, "We have assumed the role of the dominant creature on this earth and yet we have no idea how to manage the creatures under us. We don't know how to maintain the balance that regulates everything--which animals do naturally."[10]

Of course, not every dog has serious health issues with which to contend. There are many purebred dogs that live full and happy lives dying of the inevitable aging process, of which we all have to face someday. According to the Guinness Book of World Records, the greatest reliable age recorded for a dog is twenty-nine years and five months for an Australian cattle-dog named Bluey. Bluey was obtained as a puppy in 1910 and worked among cattle and sheep in Australia for nearly twenty years before being put to sleep in the latter half of 1939.[11] Butch, a Beagle, was once reported by the Guinness Book of World Records to be the longest living dog at twenty-eight years old until his death in 2003. But, these are extreme examples. What about the average lifespans of our purebred dog breeds?

In 2008, Dr. Kelly M. Cassidy compiled numerous longevity studies on domestic dogs to compose a list of the average lifespans by breed group. She compared vet school studies, breed club surveys, and data from two different kennel clubs: the American Kennel Club and the Kennel Club in the United Kingdom. Accounting for sample size and using standard deviation measurements, she found that the reported longevity in purebred dogs ranged from 6.9 in the mastiff group to 12.6 in both the small companion dog group and the Northern sledding dog group.[12]

In 2010, Dr. Vicki J. Adams, a Canadian veterinary epidemiologist, published a report on dog longevity in the Journal of Small Animal Practice entitled "Methods and mortality results of a health survey of purebred dogs in the UK."[13] She found that the median life expectancy in dogs in the United Kingdom ranged from 3.83 in the Dogue de Bordeaux to 14.83 in the Irish Terrier.

Lastly, in 2011, VetCompass completed a surveillance report of United Kingdom dogs sifting through extensive veterinarian data, which also listed crossbred dogs. With a sample size of nearly four to seven times that of purebred dogs, crossbred dogs' median age sits at 13.27, very near the longest living purebred dog breeds.[14]

We have now taken a look at the average longevity of the wild wolf in captivity, the wolf dog, the purebred dog and the crossbred dog, but what of dogs that begin their lives as domesticated companions and over time revert back to a wild existence? How do they compare in their overall health and longevity?

Indian Pariah Dog

The Indian Pariah Dog is an indigenous landrace, meaning that it is a domesticated, locally adapted, variety of dog. This particular type of dog is not believed to have been selectively bred, but domesticated itself through adaptation. This landrace's physical features, mental characteristics, and longevity are the sole result of natural selection. According to INDog, "[The Pariah Dog] has evolved entirely through natural selection, without human interference of any kind. The result is a very hardy dog."[15] INDog cites the average life expectancy of the Indian Pariah Dog to be fifteen years or more under good conditions.

An Australian Dingo
Photo Credit: Kim Navarre from Brooklyn, NY - Dingo, cropped, CC BY-SA 2.0,
https://commons.wikimedia.org/w/index.php/curid=11713886

Another wild domesticated dog, the Australian Dingo most likely came with the ancient boats to Australia and then became wild, intermixing among themselves. As a result, pure Dingoes now have a very similar look and temperament. Although longevity data for the Dingo is rare, there was a significant study completed in 2016 in which scientists tagged and tracked three Dingoes within the isolated Dingo population on Fraser Island. This study suggests that Dingo populations tend to attain average life expectancies of thirteen years and are able to bear young for as long as ten years.[16] Other free-ranging dogs, such as the New Guinea Singing Dog and the Canaan Dog, have similar longevity statistics living an average of thirteen to fifteen years old.

So, if man cannot take the prize for consistently breeding the healthiest and longest living canids, to whom or what should we give the prize? What force caused the circumstances to come together in such a way to produce these superior statistics in the wild wolf that rise far above our own human ones? Some would say that it is the element of nature itself that causes the events that procure superior health and longevity in the dog's wild cousin. So, let us turn to science, that great observer of natural events, for some possible answers. Science reveals to us what is called the law of causality, or the law of cause and effect, which says that every material effect must have an adequate antecedent or simultaneous cause. (Miller, 2011) In 1934, professor of philosophy at Princeton University, W.T. Stace, wrote in *A Critical History of Greek Philosophy* concerning causality: "[E]verything which has a beginning also has a cause" (1934, p.6) Alexander Spirkin, a Russian philosopher, wrote in his piece entitled *Dialectical Materialism* in 1975, "Causality is universal. Nowhere in the world can there be any phenomena that do not give rise to certain consequences and have not been caused by other phenomena."[17]

Because our planet had a beginning, nature on this planet also had a beginning. As there was a beginning, there must also have been a cause. So, what caused the elements in nature to come about in just the right way to produce the perfect conditions in which wolves develop their superior health and longevity?

Perhaps we can say that adaptation through evolution caused the element of nature which caused the wolf's superior health and longevity. But, what caused evolution? Maybe the passage of earthly time, itself, caused evolution to occur, which then caused the element of nature to exist in just such a way which caused the wolf's superior health and longevity. But then, what caused the passage of time to exist here on earth? Perhaps we can say that the earth revolving around the sun caused time to exist for our planet. But, what caused the earth to revolve around the sun? Perhaps some scientists are correct and the earth is a particle that spewed forth from the sun which just happened to have enough mass to be pulled into orbit at the exact location which was needed for life to thrive. But what caused the sun to spew forth particles? Perhaps the sun's own evolution caused the particles to spew forth. But then, what caused the sun to come into existence and begin to evolve? Perhaps it came from the growing universe. So, what caused the universe to grow? If multiple universes really do exist, perhaps our universe came from a series of other universes all growing and dying in their time. But, what caused these multi-universes to form? Perhaps the expansion from the Big Bang where nothing suddenly became everything. So, what caused something to come from nothing?

Well, as we said above, something cannot come from nothing. If there was nothing, absolutely <u>no thing</u>, the cause of this something would have to, itself, not be caused. It could not have mass or be made of any 'thing,' but rather be a force that could act outside of time (because time is some 'thing'), be all knowing (in order to be able to create something from nothing), all powerful (to be able to force something to come from nothing) and eternal (to not exist at any time would mean it would have had a cause). This force is what some call "God." Lois is fond of saying, "God wiggled His big toe and caused the Big Bang." Of course, God cannot have a literal big toe, but the point is clear. Lois believes that God caused the Big Bang, which in turn caused all the rest to occur.

What is the cause?

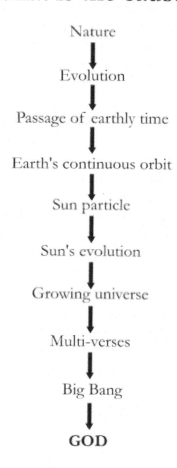

Nature

↓

Evolution

↓

Passage of earthly time

↓

Earth's continuous orbit

↓

Sun particle

↓

Sun's evolution

↓

Growing universe

↓

Multi-verses

↓

Big Bang

↓

GOD

So, if we reason through sound logic, as our founder has, that God set everything in motion which caused the perfect circumstances that came together in just such a way to produce the formula in which wild canids living in captivity remain consistently healthier and longer lived than their domesticated cousins, we can legitimately surmise that God created a breeding plan for the wild canid (and consequently many other animals, which is beyond the scope of this book). God's Breeding Plan, as Lois describes it, can be scientifically studied by observation and the information gathered in detail. Below is a list of some of the areas about which we might study in order to come to a deeper understanding of just exactly what this plan or formula is that produces such great results for the wolf. Many of these areas have already been studied by prominent scientists and so we can turn to their work to help us understand this plan that God so carefully engineered all those millennia ago when he wiggled His big toe and set everything in motion which caused something to appear from nothing.

Nature Uses God's Breeding Plan
<u>Natural Selection</u>

The definition of natural selection from Dictionary.com is "noun 1. the process by which forms of life having traits that better enable them to adapt to specific environmental pressures, as predators, changes in climate, or competition for food or mates, will tend to survive and reproduce in greater numbers than others of their kind, thus ensuring the perpetuation of those favorable traits in succeeding generations."

Another term quite often used interchangeably with natural selection is "survival of the fittest." Herbert Spencer first used the phrase "Survival of the Fittest" in his book, <u>Principles of Biology</u>, in 1864, which can best be understood as "Survival of the form that will leave the most copies of itself in successive generations" or "Survivors survive, reproduce and therefore propagate any heritable characters which have affected their survival and reproductive success." However, "Survival of the Fittest" is not a term that most modern biologists use because it implies a tautology, such as "survivors survive." Well, of course they do, but it is only through those that survive that have the heritable characteristics which allow it to survive which go on to produce more of its kind.

Natural selection can also be analyzed by identifying what attributes among animals survive to give their traits to succeeding generations. These traits have evolved for millennia to procure a place in their role in an animal's overall health and longevity. In the wild wolf, we have identified the following aspects of natural selection which play a significantly important role in the continued survival and adaptiveness of the wild wolf:

1. Ability to adapt to different environments around the globe
   a. seasonal shedding
   b. ranges in size between wolf types
   c. range of coat coloration
   d. pack structure and pack communication
2. Ebb and Flow between inbreeding/outcrossing
3. Analysis of wild type predator phenotype features needed for survival
   a. erect ears
   b. medium double coat
   c. agouti coloration
   d. dark pigmentation
   e. tail length
   f. slanted eyes
   g. yellow (or light colored) eyes
   h. long mane on males
   i. no excessive feathering or long coats
   j. short hair around the face
   k. large paws
   l. large heads
   m. leg positioning adapted for easy travel
   n. slope of back can have some rise in the hips, not sloped like shepherd, but straight backs is more natural
   o. short necks
   p. holding head at level, not held high
   q. ears coming off the side of the head, not top of the head
   r. black nails
   s. puppies are born dark and lighten over time (especially if they are born in the dark)
4. Inherited temperament which allows for survival

How the Dire Wolf Project uses God's Breeding Plan

The Dire Wolf Project uses the term "God's Breeding Plan" to describe a way of breeding through artificial selection that is fashioned after Charles Darwin's idea of Natural Selection as described above. Natural variation regularly occurs in individuals of any species. Many of these traits do not affect one individual's survival (such as eye color), but some of these variations do make a big difference in an animal's chance of survival in its natural environment. For example, the peppered moth's ability to blend in with its environment and pass on its color traits to its offspring increases the chances that any one peppered moth will survive to reproduce and allow its species to grow.

Although American Alsatian breeders cannot utilize natural selection, it is possible to mimic this natural genetic event when selecting individual dogs for breeding. When choosing specific traits to improve the American Alsatian dog breed, the American Alsatian certified breeder must be able to select dogs that, if in the wild, would naturally be the ones to continue production and exclude dogs that, if in the wild, may have naturally perished or not been allowed to reproduce. God's Breeding Plan means then that humans breed with a plan that mimics the natural selection that would occur in the wild as it pertains to the conformation and health of each puppy.

While American Alsatian breeders regularly practice God's Breeding Plan, it is necessary to differentiate between natural selection for health that would occur in the wild and natural selection for temperament that would be detrimental to most in our current lifestyle. The temperament needed for carnivores to survive in the wild is not beneficial to average families living today. Therefore, we do not use God's Breeding Plan to select for a wild type temperament. The American Alsatian breeder must think of the companion temperament traits that would be selected for life in our modern world. Those would include: quietness, calmness, aloofness, confidence, friendly when approached, etc.

Furthermore, we do not mimic all of the aspects of the wild wolf living in the wilderness. That would simply be an impossibility for animal husbandry. For example, we cannot mimic the wolf's need to roam long distances each day or the wolf's exact eating habits such as the alpha wolf eating the most choice portions of the kill and the beta wolf eating the remains. Also, we cannot reproduce the mating practices of the wild wolf, as the domesticated dog has been fundamentally altered through domestication, which happens to be one of the main aspects that is used to determine whether a dog that looks like a wolf

77

has any significant wolf blood in it. Furthermore, we cannot replicate the wolf's social circles or pack dynamics, as that, too, has been fundamentally altered in the domesticated dog.

We can, however, mimic the reasons for why a wolf perishes due to genetic conditions in the wild. For example, if a wolf were to die during childbirth, of which there is only one recorded occurrence in the wild wolf, due to any number of reasons; a uterus constriction, a stuck puppy, or any number of other birth-related reasons in the domesticated dog, we can eliminate that dog from furthering the lines by spaying the female when it is safe to do so and not breeding any of her offspring, thereby closing her entire lineage from the breed.

In the case of the Survival litter described at the beginning of this chapter, I could have kept any of the other puppies in the litter, especially Mary Ann who had the closest look toward our standards, but the virus that the litter contracted allowed for a clear conclusion based on the use of God's Breeding Plan. Accounting for the fact that Tina, the mother, died of a non-genetic cause, the puppies that were affected by the virus in such a way as to not be able to walk would have naturally perished in the wild. Only one puppy would have survived the virus attack, Skipper. I was able to utilize God's Breeding Plan by choosing the puppy in the litter that showed no affect toward the virus, thereby securing a high immune diversity within his line.

Skipper (Grinch/Tina) 2017

The Morality of God's Breeding Plan

Is it even moral to consider breeding in this way? Nature is unfeeling and inconsiderate regarding pain, suffering, and death. Sometimes the end to an animal's life can be described as cruel and unscrupulously brutal. Although Disney paints a picture of the beauty of the circle of life, the truth is much more violent and foreboding.

Even though it is necessary to be dutifully steadfast when deciding to spay/neuter a dog that should not pass on its genetics, we do not brutally harm dogs in the process. We simply spay/neuter and/or find them a great home. It is offensive to even suggest we mean otherwise. Once we know a dog should not go on to breed, decisions are certainly quick. Breeders cannot let their feelings for a dog stand in the way of breeding for health first, but George R.R. Martin's character, Ramsay Bolton, in a Song of Ice and Fire series should not come to mind when someone thinks of how one can successfully employ God's Breeding Plan. Making sure to breed from only those dogs that will improve the breed in either health or temperament is not the same thing as brutally torturing animals for the sake of mimicking death in nature. I hope that is obvious.

Nonetheless, sometimes it is necessary to achieve a small sacrifice in order to secure a larger gain. A particularly relevant example that is seen currently in the breed is Canine Multifocal Retinopathy (CMR1). CMR1 is a genetic eye disease that causes a small permanent spot to form in the eye at a young age. In extremely rare cases, the spot manifests in such a way that it can cause blindness. No current breeding dogs are affected by this eye disease, but several breeding dogs have been identified as carriers. It is the only known genetic condition detected through DNA in the breed at this time. Rather than eliminate the carriers of this disease, we choose to breed them. We work to breed non-carriers to carriers in the hopes of eliminating the disease completely from the breed in the coming generations. But the chances of an affected dog showing blindness are so rare that it may actually be worth breeding two carriers if not doing so would otherwise harm the breed. A smaller sacrifice now for an ultimately larger gain later is an acceptable reason.

Also, God's Breeding Plan demands that we not cower from death. Instead, we must accept death as a natural part of life. After all, everything living must eventually die. So, when death does appear, we do not panic. We give all of our sorrow and pain to that precious soul and honor the life it was able to live. We cherish life enough to not prolong death because we feel deep sorrow. For this reason, we do not save puppies who are dying due to natural causes. As senior writer for LiveScience magazine, Rachael Rettner, defines, "In simple terms, natural causes refer to internal factors – like a medical condition or a disease – as opposed to external factors, like trauma from an accident. In other words, natural causes could be anything from cancer to heart disease to diabetes."[18]

When a puppy is stillborn, we can perform basic actions to clear the airway and stimulate the heart, but we never rush to the vet to save a pup that would otherwise die naturally from internal causes. That is not nature's way. Instead, we cry and mourn the little life keeping it comfortable until natural death arrives.

It is not easy to speak of these emotional moments of breeding animals, but we know that saving the life at all costs only harms a breed in the long run. It is our goal to produce the healthiest dogs and that sometimes means allowing the weak to perish as they naturally would. It is weakness and emotional cowardice to believe that all life must be saved at all costs. When one chooses to bring more animals into the world, that person must be responsible for each and every life that arrives as a result of their actions. No one else should bear the burden that is squarely placed on the breeder's shoulders. No one else chose to live the life of a breeder. Therefore, a breeder should never expect others to bear the responsibility of taking care of a sick animal that the breeder caused to come into this world. Saving a life that was meant to die and then passing that burden onto the public so that the breeder can feel morally superior and then continue to produce more dogs with health issues is definitely immoral in this author's view.

The wolf living in the wild sometimes fights to the death or near death when males challenge one another for the rights to breed a particular female. Some have speculated that God's Breeding Plan, therefore, means that Dire Wolf Project breeders must keep all of the dogs together in one pack and allow them to breed at random, living as wolves would in the wild. This is not the case, nor do we advocate for such a thing. While we would not mind if our dogs lived in as natural a setting as possible, with running streams, enough space to run around and play in a beautiful forest setting, living in rock dens deep in the ground where it does not freeze or become too hot from the summer sun, etc., it does not mean that we must therefore also place two intact males together to fight it out for their right to breed. Of course we do not allow our dogs to harm one another and dogs are paired and separated based on how they interact with one another, just like in any other dog breeding facility. It certainly would not be advantageous to have the best males harmed for the sake of "breeding like the wild."

Also, it would not be selective breeding if one did not actually make informed breeding decisions based on the need of the breed at the time. A breeder should never force any dog to breed and we take into consideration that a female may not accept a particular male no matter what plans were prepared. That being said, we also refuse to artificially inseminate, choosing instead to allow the dogs to naturally cover. This makes sure that the physical aspects of breeding can actually be performed by the breeding pair. It also makes sure that dogs who cannot perform are not inadvertently used to perpetuate the issue further.

Lastly, if the wild breeding model, or God's Breeding Plan, does indeed produce healthier and longer-lived animals, why should anyone settle for less? Who has the right to impose one's moral rule on another simply because a group of people dislike how something is accomplished. If the dogs are not being physically or emotionally harmed, if the breed as a whole is healthy and vibrant, if the dogs within the breed live long and happy lives in great homes, if the goal of the program is to improve health and longevity and the method does not harm, who should be allowed to claim that God's Breeding Plan is immoral or in some other way wrong? As long as the United States remains free and the government does not impede a breeder's right to do what is necessary to breed happy, healthy, loving, long-lived dogs, then the Dire Wolf Project will continue to test the merits of God's Breeding Plan. And if it can, at some point, show an increase in improved health and longevity for our beloved furry pets, it is hoped that others will consider it as a viable method to improve other dog breeds.

God Sends a Message

When someone believes in a personal God who is active in our world and sustains life from day to day, holding existence in the palm of His hands, that person believes that God has a purpose for every one of us and is willing to communicate it. However, it is unlikely that very many of us respond, even though His words may be clear. While there have been many people throughout history who possess the wealth, education and talent to achieve great accomplishments, God also calls the child, the outcast, the poor, the disabled, or the homeless to share a fundamental truth to the world. Oftentimes the outcast, the ones fully discredited by the elite and educated, produce some of the most revolutionary ideas.

Although Lois does not have framed credentials from prominent universities and other prestigious institutions, she has the steadfast dedication to carefully and persistently study how the seasons of life ebb and flow. Through her years of reading books and research in the field as well as devoting her life to experiential learning, she has the conviction to live Nature's way and the heart to love all of life; the joy and the pain.

1. God spoke to an insignificant flawed human being; someone with no formal education or training; someone open and humble enough to receive the message clearly without altering it.

2. Lois heard, recognized, and followed the message faithfully. She was exceedingly and steadfastly dedicated to the point of losing her family in many different ways because of her convictions.

3. In 2004, Lois's daughter finally noticed her unwavering pursuit of a seemingly insignificant endeavor and although it was still very confusing, she worked to understand Lois's actions and reasoning.

4. Through unending research and discussion with Lois, it eventually became clear that Lois could not write down what she knew in a way that others could clearly understand, so her daughter became the interpreter of the message of God's Breeding Plan for the world.

Chapter 6
Inbreeding

"Important principles may and must be inflexible." - *Abraham Lincoln*

Lois looked around her empty corner house. She did not have much time before the heavy doors on this part of her life would close with permanent resound. Even now, all these years later, the effects of this difficult time still echo with a faint quiver. For over twenty years Lois had worked in southern California to help dogs and their people in need and now it quickly faded. With a nervous suspicion and a foreboding sensation that someone was watching her, she quickly scanned the living room where she had lived for the last five years. Something caught her eye in the corner to the left of the large brick fireplace. A metal pen cap glistened in the sunlight pouring through the front window as Lois stole a last few moments to recall the many hours she sat on her bed in this room writing out her breeding plans. Years ago she had repurposed the living room as her bedroom when she had turned each of the two bedrooms and the extra room adjacent to the house into halfway residences for three recovering drug and alcohol addicts. Each person had been drawn to Lois through dogs and each one's lives changed drastically as a result.

The older woman, Teresa, who lived in the bedroom to the left had been with Lois the longest. She had been a talented groomer in Lois's shop for several years. Although she smoked like a chimney and was tiny and frail, she groomed dogs with talent and dedication. However, working for Lois turned out to be much more than just another job. As the days came and went, Lois began to know her grooming colleague more and more and eventually realized that this woman sought a way out of the six foot deep hole she had been creating for herself from a serious alcohol addiction. That was the first time Lois gave up her bedroom for someone in need. Teresa took the bedroom on the left as Lois moved into the smaller bedroom on the right.

An unkempt gentleman with unruly greasy hair and a large gut named Mack then came to Lois seeking work as a groomer. He had worked all over town and could not find a way to settle down into a routine. Lois hired him to give him a leg up, but quickly learned that he had a serious heroin addiction on top of his alcoholism. She did not want to give up on him when he swore to her that he wanted to change his life around for the better. Perhaps he would have a chance to pull himself out of the black abyss if she could give him a place away from the friends who constantly dragged him back into the dark world of drugs. She agreed that he could work for her as a groomer in part to pay for his rent at the corner house. This was the second time Lois gave up her bedroom for someone in need. She then moved into the large empty room annexed to the house.

Not shortly afterwards, Lois met a beautiful young woman in her twenties, Mikki, looking for answers to the severe depression she felt without a clear direction in her life. Lois taught her the finer points of grooming dogs as Mikki had just graduated from grooming school through a work program for recovering drug addicts and for the third time, Lois gave up her bedroom for someone in need. That is when Lois finally moved into the living room. Lois created strict rules for life in the house, including curfews and cleanliness policies, hoping that some order and routine would help each of them find peace.

At this time, the American Alsatian dog breed, then called the North American Shepalute, was nearly twelve years old and Lois had several different lines to maintain. After her divorce to her husband, Gary, she no longer had the ability to use the large isolated land in Los Padres National Forest where Gary worked as a caretaker on a thirty acre apple orchard, so she kept some of her dogs in the backyard of the little house on the corner. She housed others at her grooming shop and still others were co-owned to families in the area. Although her dogs had everything they needed, a retired school teacher next door to Lois's corner house loathed the daily commotion Lois's life provided to an otherwise quiet street. As if obsessed, she felt compelled to investigate all that was going on at Lois's house. One day, with a particularly heightened indignant resolve, she contacted animal control and accused Lois of severely abusing her dogs by not providing food, water, or adequate shelter. Animal control was so convinced by the neighbor's testimony that eight armed officials completely blocked off two side streets running adjacent to Lois's house with four fully-loaded control units, sirens blaring and lights flashing. The uniformed officers drew their weapons and approached the little house on the corner with steadfast discipline. As it happened, Lois was not home. Undeterred from their mission, they entered the backyard and scanned for any signs of animal abuse. Everything seemed to be in order, except no one noticed the automatic water lick attached to the faucet at the very back of the yard near the alley for the dogs to drink at will. They wrote out a citation and pinned it to the door explaining that Lois needed to provide adequate water for the dogs and that they would be back soon to check on the improvements. The spectacle then quietly departed as the neighbor's drapes rustled shut.

The next Saturday morning, a chill settled upon the little corner house as Lois's teenage daughter, Amey, wondered why she hadn't seen Mikki in a while. She called Mikki's number. No answer. She called Lois at the grooming shop. No one had seen her. A panicked ache seized Amey's mind as she became more and more worried that something terrible had happened. Amey knocked on Mikki's door. No reply. The curtains blocked any view into the room so she called out, but again, only silence. An unshakeable terror took over as she ran into the main house and shook me awake from my dreams. In a desperate voice, she relayed her fears and we both agreed that the situation was such that we needed to break the side window to Mikki's room and open her door to see if she was there.

It turned out that the side window to the annex was unlocked and so we slid it open and unbolted the door. Darkness permeated the room, but when the morning light from the door streamed in we could just make out the silhouette of a large lump draped onto the side of the bed in the middle of the room. My hands shook as I turned on the light and our worse fears were realized. Mikki's body sat motionless on the floor with her right arm folded on the bed and her head resting on her arm with her eyes closed as if she were sleeping. Amey stayed by the door as I went over to Mikki to see if she would wake. It was clear upon touching her cold body that she would no longer be able to ever wake again. Mikki's overdose, as we later found out, had been the direct result of heroine she had acquired from Mack living in the room on the right. This tragic accident ultimately became the catalyst that initiated the darkest period of

Lois's life. That time in one's life when a person seriously wonders for what purpose we are here. The moment that either beats you down completely or builds you up and makes you stronger through its intense suffering. No one purposefully seeks to go through such a time, but without it, one cannot become the strong person he/she would be today.

Not long after Mikki was laid to rest, Teresa passed away quietly in her sleep and Mack stopped paying his rent. Sadness lingered over the little house on the corner like a thick fog and after months of excuses from Mack, Lois finally had to haul him to court to get him evicted. Upon court order, Mack finally packed up his belongings and disappeared, but without the money that was owed her, Lois found that she had to sell many of her possessions so that she could pay her own mortgage, which included some of her breeding dogs. The other tenants that came afterwards also eventually refused to pay and Lois found that she had to bring each one of them to court to hold them accountable for their rent. Not long after the animal control incident, picketers began to appear in front of the little house on the corner at all hours of the day and night. Their signs read "Animal Abuser" and they targeted Lois for the dogs she kept in her backyard and at the grooming shop. Lois made the local news as rumors began to flutter that a dog had died in her shop from being overheated by the drying fan. Her file began to grow at the local police and animal control as her neighbor continued to complain. She sold a few more of her dogs to pay for the growing court fees, and the monthly mortgage.

Lois felt pelted from all sides as a strong depression settled around her. The dark cloud thickened as she once again knocked on one of her tenant's doors to ask them to leave after not receiving several month's rent.

The brawny woman flatly refused with an indignant tone which made Lois's blood boil. Lois gently placed her hand on the woman's shoulder as she reiterated her firm request for the woman to leave - an almost fatal mistake. The woman's fist sent a loud crack as Lois's head suddenly reeled backwards. The enraged woman grabbed Lois's shoulders with unbridled vengeance and kicked her in the stomach sending shooting pain up her spine.

Lois knew this would be the end if she did not act quickly. As another strong blow sent a flash of white light to her eyes, Lois grabbed the closest thing she could find, a lamp near the door, and flung it as hard as she could at the woman's face.

The woman hesitated slightly, then her face scowled with fierce hatred as she drew back for another powerful thrust. Just as her fist connected for the third time to Lois's face, a friend of Lois's heard the commotion and ran forward to pull the inflamed woman away. Screaming obscenities, the woman retreated into her room and slammed the door as Lois fell bleeding and beaten onto the cold concrete below.

Her friend helped her to the hospital where it was found that Lois had sustained whiplash-like symptoms among her many bruises and cuts. Now, Lois could not walk anywhere in the city without anxiously looking over her shoulder to make sure no one was there. Her eyes saw shadows moving in the darkness and people lurking behind corners and doors. Post-Traumatic Stress Disorder [PTSD] had now set in.

As if cursed, only a few weeks passed when two police officers knocked on her door to serve her an official court documented eviction notice from her mortgage company. Stunned, Lois searched her memory for any instance in which she had failed to pay her mortgage. With confusion and worry plastered on her recently battered visage, she quickly called the company. The operator revealed that they had no record of Lois ever having paid them. Eventually, Lois discovered that the woman who gratefully accepted her mortgage check each month had cashed the money and neglected to give it to the company.

Unfettered disbelief and exhaustion washed over Lois and her knees weakened as she sank slowly onto the edge of her bed in the living room. She gently wiped a tear from her cheek as she read the notice. She had thirty days to gather her things and vacate the premises. After several quiet minutes, she sighed heavily and called a lawyer who was able to convince the judge to allow Lois one year to inform the tenants, gather her belongings, and ready the little corner house for resale. Bankruptcy shortly followed.

As soon as Lois knew that she would lose her little house on the corner, she developed a plan to secure the diverse genetics within her various Shepalute lines. She bred her co-owned second generation English Mastiff male, Rasmussen, to the only female she had available to her that did not contain her other line, a loving Golden Retriever mix named Girl. Bach, a sweet-tempered and beautiful cream colored male kept from this crossbred litter, grew up securely at Lois's long-time friend's house, Darlene. As the six month mark loomed over her and time began to run out, Lois now felt a strong push to secure this crossbred line before she no longer had a home or a way to breed. So, she bred Bach to her last Shepalute female, Betty Boop, to birth one final litter before Betty left for her new home. The two puppies Lois chose to keep from this match now waited for her at Darlene's house.

Lois bent down to pick up the metal pen cap in the corner by the fireplace and put it in her pocket. In the silence of the now empty house on the corner, she wept. So many hopes had been violently dashed away. So many laborious hours giving all she could now seemed to be wasted. Her servant's heart had no more service to give.

As she locked the door to the little corner house, she turned with quiet, sober steps to her truck and camper. Her last male, Packer, sat in the passenger's seat panting softly in concealed anticipation. He could not know the overwhelming despair Lois felt in that moment as she realized she had lost it all: her friends, her business, her home, her belongings, and most of all, so many of her precious Shepalute dogs.

Packer, alone, held all of the genetic components she had diligently developed throughout the last twelve years. Out of all of the dogs she had bred to develop her Shepalute dogs, she selected Packer as her one true genetic link back to all that had come before. She knew that within Packer lie the key to continuing what she had so meticulously established and now had to leave behind.

Lois climbed into the driver's seat and headed north to her loyal friend, Darlene's, house to collect the two crossbred female puppies, Patty and Polly, waiting for her. The three dogs rested beside her as she wondered just where her life would take her next. She drove around aimlessly for a few miles when suddenly a thought popped into her head; she could simply move away from southern California. She had never even considered such a thing before, but now, with all of her belongings packed in her truck and camper, this new idea grew. But, where would she go, exactly? Gary had moved back to South Dakota and she had heard that Montana was a beautiful state. Perhaps she would go north.

As she worked her way up Interstate 5, her spirit lifted with each mile. She stopped at a pay phone and called her parents in southern Oregon. They asked her to stop by on her way north and so a plan began to take shape. She would stay a few months with her folks, gather her wits about her, save up a few dollars, and eventually head farther north to Montana where she could begin again. But, shortly after she arrived at her parent's house her father succumbed to his battle with congestive heart failure and passed away. Her mother then asked her to stay and take care of her in her last years left on earth in exchange for the house and property, so she did and to this very day, Lois lives with her aging mother and many of the breed's most beautiful dogs.

But how did those three remaining dogs in 1999 formulate an entire breed without losing the valuable work that had come before? The answer is through Inbreeding... significant inbreeding.

Calculating Inbreeding

Today, inbreeding is likened to a dirty word and many may have a strong desire to stop reading further because their deep disgust toward inbreeding may be such that it does not allow them to wade through a well thought out and logical case for an action that they deem unethical. But remember our initial discussion in the logical fallacies chapter, relying on emotions to state one's case does not actually prove that inbreeding cannot be beneficial to sustaining a healthy, long-lived breed over time. If one has an open mind, one just may come to understand through this chapter the very real reasons that inbreeding can be beneficial and may even ultimately be essential to managing our most beloved of all pets, the dog. So let's explore the different ways a breed can inbreed in order to achieve sustainable healthy, long-lived dogs.

Sewall Wright, 1965

Inbreeding is generally defined as the practice of mating closely related individuals through common ancestry. Throughout dog breeding history, accurately maintained pedigrees that list the same ancestor(s) on the mother's side as on the father's side are considered inbred. The closer the relation to the common ancestor, the more inbred. Inbreeding levels also increase the higher the number of common ancestors reside within the ancestry of the offspring. Dr. Sewall Wright, an evolutionary geneticist working for the Bureau of Animal Industry in the United States Department of Agriculture in 1922 saw the mathematical relationship between common ancestors in a pedigree and established a formula for creating the coefficient of inbreeding that gives a number from 0, no inbreeding whatsoever, to 1, completely inbred. Dr. Wright's method has been the sole preferred means of determining the inbreeding coefficient of an individual and is still in wide use today, however, in 2005 geneticists developed the first comparative genetic map of the dog and now inbreeding can be determined genetically as well.

After the ability for DNA sequencing became available, the way one thinks of inbreeding shifted dramatically as a result. Instead of simply looking at common ancestry via a pedigree as a means for determining inbreeding, now geneticists find that inbreeding "mean[s] that your dog inherited the same piece of DNA (identical by descent) at that place in their genome from both parents." as the International Society of Genetic Genealogy defines.[1]

Today, a swab from a dog's cheek can be analyzed to see just how much of your dog's genes have been identically received from both the mother and father, regardless of what is revealed on a pedigree. When a matching segment of DNA on the paternal and maternal chromosomes is identical it is now referred to as inbreeding. Calculating how much of a dog's chromosomes are identical determines a genetic coefficient of inbreeding. As Dr. Kate Robinson, a geneticist for Embark Veterinary, states, "The COI is the proportion of the genome that falls within these homozygous regions. This is by far the most accurate way to compute COI."[2] Jemima Harrison, the producer of the highly acclaimed documentary, Pedigree Dogs Exposed, explains in her article, *A Beginners Guide to COI*, on the Dog Breed Health website, "The more gene-pairs that are homozygous = less diversity. The more gene-pairs that are heterozygous = more diversity."[3]

Note: Many times the notion has come to this author's mind that with this new genetic method of calculating the coefficient of inbreeding perhaps the breeding community should begin to consistently utilize a more accurate term than simply continuing to describe inherited diversity, or lack of, as inbreeding. Inbreeding has generally implied a related pedigree to most while calculating the coefficient of inbreeding by DNA analysis can include quite a diverse range of parentage for the same identically inherited chromosome segments. Calculating the inbreeding of a dog using pedigree data may give one a general idea of risk, but showing the exact percentage of identically inherited portions on a dog's chromosomes may be better served by simply describing exactly what it measures: genetic diversity. Using the term genetic diversity to describe the inherited diversity of an individual is straight forward and cannot be confused with a coefficient of inbreeding calculated by pedigree. But, it has been found that many researchers continue to use the term inbreeding as a way to describe what they ultimately mean to be genetic diversity. Since many seem to randomly switch between the two terms inbreeding and genetic diversity, for

90

the purposes of the information presented below, I have tried to make sure that the different methods of calculating inbreeding are clearly defined.

No Need for Inbreeding?

Forty-two years before the most recent advancements in gene mapping technology, W.V. Soman pointed out in his 1963 book entitled <u>The Indian Dog</u> "in-breeding followed by line-breeding of good stock, associated with the usual elimination of the unwanted, may be practiced for many generations without any undesirable consequences till one achieves one's goal."[4] With the large advances in the genetics related to dogs, now Soman's book may appear quite dated and many may argue that so much more is known about genetics and inheritance that there is no longer any suitable reason to inbreed. But is that statement accurate? Has the science of genetics truly revealed to the world that inbreeding is no longer needed to sustain a healthy, long-lived breed?

In light of recent genetic advancements, those who passionately argue against inbreeding as a viable means of improving and maintaining a dog breed assert that setting breed traits is simply a matter of achieving homozygosity, regardless of parentage. Therefore, they reason, because DNA sequencing identifies whether certain traits are homozygous or heterozygous, inbreeding is not needed. For instance, when a particular desired trait, such as wolf gray coat coloring, is the only color that a dog can give to its offspring, then that trait is said to be "set" and homozygosity is achieved for that trait, no matter if the parents were actually related. Systematically breeding for all of the wanted homozygous traits in a breed, they maintain, will allow purity without ever resulting in inbreeding.

No-inbreeding-ever argument:
Setting breed traits is attained through homozygosity.
Homozygosity does not depend on inbreeding.
Therefore, inbreeding is not needed to set breed traits.

Indeed, doing exactly this would be easy if each of the thousands of possible inherited traits could be hand-picked by the breeder as if one could choose each trait while walking the aisles at the grocery store. If that were the case, it would not take any effort or time whatsoever to create a new dog breed. Unfortunately, working with only five heterozygous traits such as: masked/no masked, agouti/tan points, non-dilute/dilute, furnishings/clean, short/long coat would produce 25 different phenotypic combination options from each parent, which in turn produces 1024 different inherited trait possibilities in the offspring. If we assume an average of five puppies in each litter, to obtain the exact combination of those five traits that one desires may take breeding 205 litters from just one breeding pair.

But a breeder does not improve only five traits at one time. What if a breeder worked with all of the 20 known appearance traits that have been identified by DNA? That would amount to 1,048,576 different combinations possible in each offspring. Now we're talking about the potential of 209,715 litters to obtain the one perfect combination of traits from a particular match.

But, a breeder does not simply work with a DNA test's genetically identified traits. Instead, a breeder must manage hundreds of inherited traits all at one time, including all aspects of a dog's temperament and all polygenic inherited health and appearance traits which are not yet fully identified through DNA testing. Relevant examples include: epilepsy, panosteitis, masticatory muscle myositis, yellow eye color, erect ears, large feet, or a very specific range of height and weight dimensions. That equates to a novemdecillion (10 followed by 60 zeros) different trait combination possibilities every time a litter is born.

Number of Possible Trait Combinations

# of traits (n)	# of phenotype options from each parent (2^n)	# of combined possibilities $(2^n)^2$
5	32	1024
7	128	16,384
20	1,048,576	1,099,511,627,776
100	1,267,650,600,228,229, 401,496,703,205,376	1,606,938,044,258,990,275,541, 962,092,341,162,602,522,202, 993,782,792,835,301,376

The entirety of the domesticated dog's diverse health, temperament, and appearance is certainly vast and perplexing. According to the National Institutes of Health, "The dog genome is similar in size to the genomes of humans and other mammals, containing approximately 2.5 billion DNA base pairs."[5] When beginning a new breed of dog, one works with multiple breeds of diverse origins to tease out the specific ideal traits that match the founder's map, or standards of the breed. It is not just a matter of matching the twenty known appearance genes to create a homozygous masterpiece.

Having said that, even if every genetically inherited health, temperament, and appearance trait became identified through DNA sequencing, it would still not negate the benefits inbreeding affords to a developing breed. That is because when one solidifies a desired trait through homozygosity, that trait must be maintained while working on the others. But many desired traits in a particular dog breed, such as yellow eyes in the American Alsatian dog's case, are recessive and are often masked by the more prevalent brown color that is specifically prized in most purebred dog breeds.

Setting traits in a dog breed can be compared to solving a completely mixed up Rubik's cube. Solving one side of the Rubik's cube puzzle is relatively easy when compared to working the entire puzzle. Many people can achieve it. However, once all of the colors match on that one side, the most difficult challenges in the puzzle remain. It temporarily becomes necessary to lose some of the gains achieved on the solid colored side in order to progress further to solve the other sides. Furthermore, each color has a particular space and in order to solve the entire puzzle matching all of the colors correctly, each piece of the puzzle must be in its proper place. Just like the Rubik's Cube, when several traits within a dog breed have become set, or homozygous, it oftentimes becomes necessary to lose homozygosity temporarily while working on other bringing in other traits which also must be set.

Ideal Appearance Traits in the American Alsatian Dog:

Coat Color
- wolf gray [agouti]
- brindle*
- no mask
- dominant black
- progressive graying*

Coat Type
- wiry/harsh*
- seasonal shedding
- undercoat thickness - medium*
- straight

Coat Length
- medium*
- long mane/cape*
- no furnishings

Eye Shape
- almond*
- small*

Eye Color
- yellow*
- yellow-green*

Skeletal Structure
- wide skull*
- muzzle length-medium*
- slight stop*
- tail length to hock*
- straight back*
- longer than tall*
- no cowhock*
- no pidgeon toe*
- adequate angulation*
- large feet*
- large bone thickness*
- straight back*
- straight tail, no curve*

Skin Pigmentation
- deep black*
- no risidual white*
- no piebald*
- no Irish spotting*

Body Size
- large in five known traits
- consistent 31 inch height*
- consistent 120-150 lbs*

Ear Size and Carriage
- small*
- erect*
- carried low*
- angled forward*

* not yet identified by DNA testing

When one works to create a new breed using both known and unknown single-gene and polygenic inherited traits coming from several distinctly different purebred dog breeds, such as is the case in the Dire Wolf Project, the extensive temperament and appearance diversity between these separate breeds must eventually be decreased until the dogs within the new breed begin to share consistency of type. Hundreds of different phenotypic traits must then be systematically pared down to only those that matter to the new breed.

In fact, the very definition of a breed, according to the Food and Agriculture Organization of the United Nations (FAO) is, "Breed: either a sub-specific group of domestic livestock with definable and identifiable external characteristics that enable it to be separated by visual appraisal from other similarly defined groups within the same species, or a group for which geographical and/or cultural separation from phenotypically similar groups has led to acceptance of its separate identity."[6] However, once consistency within the new breed has been achieved, one just may find that some of the ideal breed traits one had solidified initially have now gone missing in the course of achieving consistency and it becomes necessary to once again bring them back.

When a person assumes that solidifying all of the new trait combinations in a new breed is simply a matter of matching homozygous traits one after the other they are grossly oversimplifying a complex and comprehensive task. When a person believes that modern science automatically has the answers that negates any use of inbreeding because so much more is known about genetics than ever before without explaining how it is possible, that person is relying on the logical fallacy of Appeal to Novelty.

No Inbreeding Ever

Recently, I debated a few so-called breeding experts who insisted that a breeder should never inbreed ever and that all inbreeding is bad at any time. Before we move on from this idea, let us take a moment to really allow that statement to sink in to the very core. If one never inbred ever to any degree, what would that look like? Let's put on our hypothetical rose colored glasses for a moment and imagine what dog breeding would be like if breeders never inbred at any time in order to maintain a coefficient of inbreeding of 0%.

First of all, in order to find out where to begin we would need to initially determine which dog breed had the most genetic diversity to begin our quest of not resorting to any degree of inbreeding. Unfortunately for us, during the time that purebred dog breeding began in earnest around the late Victorian era, inbreeding was recognized as a valuable and highly desired way to solidify the look and temperament of a dog breed. As Stephen Budiansky, a prominent history and science writer, states "Only with the establishment of breed clubs in the late nineteenth century did [dog breeding] begin to change dramatically. In the name of developing and maintaining 'purebred' animals, the kennel clubs in Britain and the United States set up closed breeding books... eugenics was the intellectual fad of the early year of the twentieth century, and its scientific trappings gave it considerable influence in everything from criminology to dog breeding."[7]

It appears that finding a pure breed of dog that has any significant number of unrelated lines might be a bit of a challenge. Luckily for us, in 2016, a significant research study by Dreger et al. calculated the genetic inbreeding of 111 distinct breeds of dog. Perhaps we can find a purebred breed that will be diverse enough with which to begin our journey to the hypothetical ideal of never inbreeding. As it turns out, genetic research found that there was "... a range of 0.179 (Papillon) to 0.536 (Basenji)..." degree of inbreeding among those breeds tested using single-nucleotide polymorphism (SNP) genotyping.[8] Basically, no breed tested had an inbreeding level lower than what would be the result of mating first cousins. In fact, only around twenty breeds turned out to have less than 25% inbreeding which would be the result of a full sibling match. All of the other ninety-one breeds showed average genetically calculated inbreeding percentages at greater than 25%. One Norwegian Lundehund tested using whole gene sequencing (WGS) even topped the charts at 80% inbreeding. This means that out of the thousands of dogs within a single purebred breed, crossing any two from within the breed at random would result in a significantly greater than 0% inbreeding.

The study further revealed that most breeds now consist of only a few genetically diverse lines of dogs. According to DNA analysis, "the Nova Scotia Duck Tolling Retriever displays the lowest amount of genetic diversity of all the pedigree breeds [4.9 effective ancestors], whereas the Papillon shows the highest [51.4 effective ancestors]."[8] With only a few genetically separate lines from the breed with the most diversity, the Papillon, it appears that no current pure breed would be a good contender for this plan of no inbreeding ever.

Perhaps we should scrap the idea of choosing one purebred dog breed for our thought experiment, since they do not afford us the overall genetic diversity we need to begin with the inbreeding coefficient at zero. In order to make sure that inbreeding remains at zero percent even from the very beginning, let's just start over and create a brand new breed of dog that, from the onset, works to maintain a zero percent inbreeding coefficient at all times.

For the purposes of our mind challenge, the ideal would be to keep our new breed absolutely free of inbreeding throughout the entire lifetime of the breed's existence. Some breeders use a five generation pedigree to track coefficient of inbreeding (COI). Others insist on utilizing at least a ten generation pedigree. While still others maintain that one must reach at least twenty to thirty generations with the goal of including all of the ancestry in order to obtain as accurate a COI as possible. Sewall Wright, the inventor of the calculations used to obtain a COI by pedigree puts it this way, "By tracing the pedigrees back to the beginning of the herd book, the coefficients of inbreeding are slightly increased." There appears to be a distance within the pedigree at which common ancestors have little effect. Sewall Wright continues, "Remote common ancestors in general have little effect on the coefficient."[9] Carol Beuchat, a prominent biologist and founder of the Institute of Canine Biology, concludes her discussion on how many generations of pedigree data are the most accurate with a question, "Does it matter how many generations you use when calculating COI? Yes. How many generations should you use? As many as you can."[10] It appears that we should strive for as many generations as we can, but to keep our time reasonable, we will work to achieve at least ten generations at a minimum.

What if we started with a large number of founding dogs, say 154, all of them from different breeds of known origin that have no common ancestors as far back as the pedigree can reach? According to the Fédération Cynologique Internationale (FCI), the world governing body of dog breeds, sometimes known as the World Canine Organization, there are about 340 recognized breeds.[11]

Utilizing 154 different dog breeds would effectively include 45% of the dog breeds recognized all over the world, but we shouldn't be daunted by that. Producing the best dogs we can by never inbreeding to any degree is more important than preserving individual dog breeds with their outrageous level of inbreeding, right?

So, why choose 154 dog breeds? Why not utilize all 340 recognized dog breeds in order to obtain the most diversity possible? I suppose we could. But, for the purposes of this challenge, let's include a lower number of dog breeds while striving for the highest number of possible generations. After all, the entire point of creating a uniform dog breed instead of a random mix of breeds is to be able to somewhat predict the health, temperament and conformation of the puppies. By only including 45% of the recognized breeds around the world, we can already begin to select for the traits we want. After all, our task is to create a breed of dog, not just a random mix to traits.

So, with our 154 dog breeds in hand, it is important to remember that we need an equal number of female dogs as we do male dogs, since we do need to breed them together, so, that leaves us with 77 females and 77 males. When we pair the initial dogs together we will begin to establish separate lines of dogs within our hopeful new breed. To keep out the inbreeding, we must keep those lines from ever crossing so that no ancestry will ever be seen on both sides of the pedigree we are beginning to establish. Breeding those 154 initial dogs together now leaves us with 77 completely unrelated lines. Not allowing for any inbreeding whatsoever effectively cut our diverse population of dogs in half within one generation.

It is important to note that 77 litters would probably take a large team to monitor and care for the pups and their parents in their homes and infinite funds to make sure they were always healthy and safe. But, again, the fun thing about dreaming is that we can also add in unlimited resources. For the purposes of this game of thought, let's assume that each litter had an average of 5 puppies. That would give us somewhere in the ballpark of 385 puppies. But keep in mind that we plan to never cross related individuals, so no matter how many of the 385 puppies we keep, there are only 77 distinct lines from which to choose our next generation. To make it easier, since we are not going to inbreed ever for any reason, let's just imagine keeping one dog from any one litter.

For the second generation, we now split our 77 crossbred dogs into half females and half males and are left with 38 completely unrelated dogs in our second generation with an extra dog lying in wait. Again, we have halved our genetically diverse population size to 39 dogs, but it is still a lot more than many breeds began, so we still look pretty good on this high road to no inbred dogs.

Again we separate our dogs into males and females for a total of 19 in each category. When we breed those dogs together, we now have 19 puppies that are completely unrelated to one another and again one odd dog out. Presumably, we could match the second extra dog to the other dog that we left out previously, for a total of 20 completely unrelated litters in our third generation.

We now combine 10 males and 10 females for our fourth generation.

We now have 5 opportunities to continue our purposeful no-inbreeding-ever plan. When we match the males to the females, we have a total of 5 completely unrelated litters of puppies. This, then, is our fifth generation.

Now, we match up our remaining 5 lines, male and female, for a total of 2 new completely unrelated litters and once again an odd dog out. As always, we halved the number of unrelated lines, leaving us with 3 lines of completely unrelated dogs. This is now our sixth generation.

Continuing on, undeterred, we take a male and a female from those two remaining litters so that we now have one solid litter of puppies with a coefficient of inbreeding of zero percent which can be matched with the extra line that we previously put aside. This is our seventh generation.

We can now match the last line with the extra line we saved out from previously for one last breeding, which achieves our eighth generation.

Congratulations, we have successfully eliminated 154 different breeds of dog and are left with only one.

Generation	Total # of Dogs	Males/Females
Foundation	154	77/77
F-1	77	38/38 + 1
F-2	39	19/19 + 1
F-3	20	10/10
F-4	10	5/5
F-5	5	2/2 + 1
F-6	3	1/1 + 1
F-7	2	1/1
F-8	1	
F-9		

So now, where does this theoretical breed go from here? We have not yet achieved our desired ten generations. We have one dog left in our breed that holds the genetics we chose to keep from the original 154 dog breeds. Hopefully, many of the traits we wanted to set are now homozygous and we have achieved what no purebred dog has ever embodied before; one dog that breeds pure yet is completely void of any inbreeding. Unfortunately, we have no other dog within our program with which to continue to breed. The only way to continue without inbreeding from this point is to significantly crossbreed once again, since we have exhausted all of our initial ancestry. But, that would mean that our one dog with the established traits we desired would now be mixed with the myriad of other genetic traits that exist in any crossbreed we chose. In order to be true to the ideal of no inbreeding ever, we must make sure that we do not include any dog from any of the 154 breeds with which we began our no-inbreeding-ever process.

Let's say we do crossbreed. As before, we must take a completely unrelated dog from a completely different unrelated breed as our initial dogs in order to breed that dog with the last remaining dog from our eight generations of zero inbreeding. Hopefully that crossbreed has many of the genetic features we have been working to solidify in our own breed or we will once again introduce genetic variants that will ultimately need to be bred out. However, that would achieve the ninth generation. From here, we would need to introduce one more unrelated dog breed in order to reach our minimum goal of ten generations. Would we now be safe enough to once again use any of the founding breeds without introducing any significant degree of inbreeding? Interestingly, some may still say no.

By the way, in order to achieve all ten generations without resorting to crossbreeding at the end, as we have just been forced to do, we would have had to begin with 514 different dog breeds, over one and a half times the number of FCI officially recognized dog breeds. Also, in order to achieve nine generations without crossbreeding, we would have needed to include 258 dog breeds at the beginning of our thought experiment, almost 76% of FCI recognized dog breeds. The very lowest number of dog breeds we could use to achieve eight generations without crossbreeding is 100. Any fewer than that and only seven generations would be able to be achieved without inbreeding.

At this point in our no-inbreeding-ever experiment, we have three choices left: completely replenish our breeding stock and once again obtain 154 dogs from completely different breeds, breed one litter and one crossbreed at a time, or simply stop breeding altogether.

But, what does our new breed look like? With 45% of dog breeds being initially represented, we surely began with extra-large dogs as well as miniature dogs. We must have had either long and short coated dogs or dogs with long drooping ears and short erect ears. Presumably, we have chosen the puppy that fit closest to our ideal from each litter, but, those initial 154 breeds were so completely diverse from one another could we theoretically attain a consistent look throughout our entire new breed of dog within these first seven generations?

For the purposes of our thought experiment, let's say we were able to achieve this with the aid of DNA testing to help point out the appearance genotype of each of our dogs. We could breed for or against curly coats, recessive black coat coloring, blue eyes, or rear dewclaws. Even though, geneticists have yet to reveal a gene responsible for the curled tail or whether a dog's ears will stand erect or flop down and genetic testing cannot predict how long the tail or muzzle will be or whether a particular dog will have white spotting or develop the Dalmatian's black spots, we can at least obtain homozygosity in the twenty appearance traits that have a clear genetic identity. And besides, does it really matter what our dogs look like as long as they maintain a zero degree of inbreeding and no identified genetic diseases?

But then what does our new breed act like? With absolutely no science to reveal genetically testable inherited temperament traits, I suppose we would just have to leave much of the temperament in our hypothetical breed completely to chance. Managing the inherited temperament diversity of all 154 different dog breeds would include dogs in each of the seven identified dog groups: the terrier group, the toy group, the hound group, the herding group, the working group, the sporting group, and the non-sporting group. But, perhaps our selective breeding could at least eliminate excessive aggression and fear, since we are only dreaming.

I once heard a proponent of no-inbreeding-ever state, "Inbreeding is a lazy man's way to solidify the traits within a dog breed." I can only assume this person meant that a breeder can solidify the traits within a dog breed by never inbreeding to any degree just as well as a breeder can solidify the traits within a dog breed through inbreeding, although admittedly over a longer period of time. What do you think? Are you convinced that this would be the case after reading our theoretical zero inbred dog breed thought experiment?

It is this author's strong belief that those who believe in the no-inbreeding-ever model may in fact have an alternative agenda, because they easily and viciously criticize and ridicule any breeder openly defending inbreeding. They very well may not even be breeders themselves, but individuals working toward total elimination of pet breeding and ownership. It appears to me to be the only logical answer, since taking their no-inbreeding-ever scenario to its final conclusion means that eventually there will be nowhere to go except to stop breeding. As we have seen, by using all of the available lines of recognized purebred dogs in the world, one would not even be able to achieve ten generations without inbreeding.

Inbreeding Depression

In stark contrast, when one looks outside of the sometimes highly controversial dog breeding realm, one clearly hears a much different answer. In a collaborative effort through the diverse members of the Livestock Conservancy, which has emerged as a globally respected source for information and procedures concerning rare breed conservation, the authors conclude that "[t]argeted close linebreeding or inbreeding is an effective strategy that can correct the under-representation of the genetic influence of rare bloodlines, or specific founders of rare breeds."[12] As renowned vertebrate biologist, Carol Beuchat PhD, explained in 2017 even in light of all the modern genetic advancements in dogs, "Inbreeding is part of the process of breed formation in domestic animals and is used to produce homozygosity in the genes most responsible for type and breed-typical traits."[13]

So what is the real controversy regarding inbreeding? If inbreeding is necessary for securing breed formation, why the horror-filled shrieks from so many when someone mentions a match between a father and his daughter? Why has the first organized purebred dog breeding club in the world, the Kennel Club in the United Kingdom, decided the following: "To help reduce the highest degrees of inbreeding, the Kennel Club does not register puppies produced from a mating between father and daughter, mother and son, or brother and sister, save in rare exceptional circumstances for scientifically proven welfare reasons."[14] The answer lies with a very well-established phenomenon called inbreeding depression that reduces the biological fitness in a given population as a result of inbreeding. Charles Darwin, an English naturalist whose scientific theory of evolution by natural selection became the foundation of modern evolutionary studies, published a book in 1876 entitled, <u>The Effects of Cross and Self Fertilization in the Vegetable Kingdom</u>, which was the first published source to realize "that cross-fertilization is generally beneficial and self-fertilization injurious to the offspring."[15]

Since Darwin's time, the science of genetics has blossomed and we now know that inbreeding depression, or loss of reproductive fitness, occurs in both domesticated as well as wild animal species. As the comprehensive online guide to genetic health in dog breeds, Dog Breed Health, points out, "Many pedigree breeds are already highly homozygous, i.e. many of their alleles contain only a single gene type. This means that the characteristics that these genes produce will be the same in all puppies, regardless of which parents from the breed are used (i.e. no breed diversity)."[16] Furthermore, the highly referenced textbook used at Cambridge and elsewhere as an introduction to conservation

Charles Darwin, 1868

genetics states, "There is now clear evidence that inbreeding adversely affects most wild populations."[17].

This same textbook clearly defines the symptoms of inbreeding depression this way, "Inbreeding has been shown to adversely affect all aspects of reproductive fitness, including offspring numbers, juvenile survival, longevity, interbirth interval, mating ability, sperm quantity and quality, maternal ability, competitive ability, developmental time, immune response and disease resistance in animals."[18] In fact, severe inbreeding can lead to a phenomenon called an extinction vortex where a small, closed population results in greater and greater degrees of inbreeding which eventually results in a higher and higher infant mortality rate eventually decreasing the population to an unsustainable level.[19]

Inbreeding Levels

That brings us to a very important question. If inbreeding is part of the process of breed formation and yet inbreeding also presents highly undeniable and significant health issues leading to increased risk of early death and eventual extinction, what degree of inbreeding can be considered safe in order to maintain a healthy, long-lived dog breed? Let's take a look at some prominent studies using various animals including purebred dog breeds to give us a well-rounded look at the levels of reproductive fitness at varying degrees of inbreeding.

Lobund-Wistar Rat

Dr. Helen Dean King, an American biologist working for the Wistar Institute in 1919 developed an entire purebred strain of albino rats that are still predominantly in use as laboratory rats today. In her meticulous research, she initially bred fifteen generations of brother/sister matings and "concluded that the closest form of inbreeding in mammals is not necessarily inimical to body growth, fertility, or constitutional vigor, provided that one selects the best animals from a large population to breed." Astonishingly, Dr. King went on to breed over fifty generations of brother/sister matings of her Wistar rats without any reported decline in fertility, growth size, and longevity.[20]

Today, the descendants of the Wistar Institute's albino rat population from 1919 still play a significant role in laboratory rat production. Slc:Wistar outbred rats along with the genetically similar F344 inbred rats show an 89% genetic inbreeding with 32 fixed loci out of 36. The 2015 genetic study revealing the extremely low diversity among laboratory rats "demonstrates the importance of characterizing outbred rats and the need to pay ample attention to the genetic characteristics the Slc:Wistar rats for their proper use."[21]

Leon F Whitney, DVM describes a brother/sister inbreeding experiment he completed with his Pointers in the 1930s. He bred brother to sister together for five generations noting that litter size decreased steadily in each generation until only one 5th generation offspring was able to breed successfully.[22] Using a five generation pedigree with the assumption that the founding dogs were unrelated, that would equate to a 46.875% COI at which point Dr. Whitney ended his experiment.

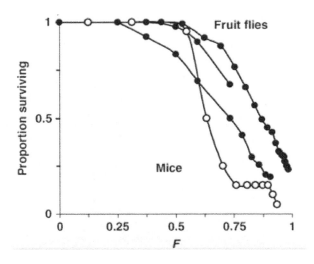

In an inbreeding and extinction study by Richard Frankham in 1995 using mice, fruit fly, and house fly populations it was shown that, "Extinction risks in rapidly inbred populations of mice and fruit flies increased markedly at F = 0.5 [50% COI] and beyond, and F values for the housefly populations at extinction lay within a similar range (0.38-0.66) [38-66% COI]."[23]

Bouvier Belge Des Flandres

A 1992 study calculated the coefficient of inbreeding using Wright's pedigree calculations of 168 Bouvier Belge Des Flandres with osteochondrosis, food allergy, autoimmune disease, neoplasm, or hypoplastic trachea. The inbreeding levels of these diseased dogs were then compared to a random control population of 123 of the same breed born within the same time period. The control group was found to have inbreeding coefficients ranging from 0.0 to 0.406. The diseased study group were consistently found to have higher inbreeding coefficients than the control group.[24] From this, we can ascertain that inbreeding coefficients higher than 40% began to see increases in various genetic diseases within this breed.

As we noted earlier in this chapter, the highly endangered purebred dog breed, the Norwegian Lundehund, was shown through whole gene sequencing to sustain a coefficient of inbreeding of over 80%. As a study by Anne Kettunen et. al. in 2017 regarding the medium-sized Norwegian puffin hunter explains, "Reduced litter size has been suggested as a sign of inbreeding depression in the Lundehund. Currently, the Norwegian Lundehund club reports average litter sizes of 2.8. Low

Norwegian Lundehund
Photo credit: Томасина - Own work, CC BY-SA 3.0,
https://commons.wikimedia.org/w/index.php/cu rid=29848807

average litter size is a reflection of a high proportion of one-puppy litters and near complete absence of litters with six or more puppies. Moreover, breeders have reported problems relative to fertility, such as "invisible" heat, behavioural problems when mating, both in males and females, and low sperm quality. Overall, reduced litter size most likely reflects inbreeding depression in several traits, both physiological and behavioural, as well as a high frequency of non-viable embryos due to lethal alleles."[25]

As with the Wistar rats, maintaining an 80% level of inbreeding generation after generation shows significant inbreeding depression concern within a closed breed. We will learn more about most recent efforts to diversify this unique breed in the crossbreeding chapter.

In March 2015, the French Kennel Club performed an extensive inbreeding study on seven different purebred dogs from 1990 to 2012. It was found that "for litters with an inbreeding coefficient of 25% (equivalent to a mating between full siblings), a reduction of 0.65 puppies per litter on average in comparison with non-inbred litters. Females with this inbreeding coefficient could be expected to produce 0.5 puppies fewer per litter in comparison with non-inbred females."[26] It appears that this level of inbreeding begins to show a reduced litter size by a small, but measurable, way.

Standard Poodle
Photo Credit: Inbalsigal – Own work, CC BY 3.0,
https://commons.wikimedia.org/w/index.php?curid=15025833

John B. Armstrong, PhD from the Department of Biology at the University of Ottawa in Canada performed a comprehensive longevity study with Standard Poodles in 1999. Using the data collected from 627 Standard Poodles and calculating inbreeding using a ten generation pedigree, he found that increased inbreeding levels decreased overall longevity at a predictable rate. The 32 poodles with a lower than 6.25% inbreeding lived on average to fourteen years, while the 71 Standard Poodles with a higher than 25% inbreeding lived on average 11.5 years of age. According to the author, the data in the 6.25% inbreeding group most closely resembled that of the non-inbred population.[27] In this study we learn that a 6.25% inbreeding level is very similar to non-inbred levels, but as the inbreeding increases from there, inbreeding depression symptoms begin to appear. At a 25% inbreeding level, a consistently shorter lifespan appeared.

When we combine these statistics, inbreeding limitations begin to come into focus. Albino Slc:Wistar and F344 inbred rats, descendants from the original Wistar Institute in 1919 maintain an 89% genetic similarity with a very cautious warning to be extremely mindful when breeding them to other lines. 80% inbreeding definitely shows significant inbreeding depression symptoms throughout the endangered Norwegian Lundehund dog breed. 50% inbreeding in fruit flies and mice begins to plummet toward an extinction vortex. 46.875% inbreeding definitely caused Whitney's Pointers to show serious fertility issues. Above 40.6% showed a higher incidence of health issues in the Bouvier Belge des Fladres. Between 38-66% inbreeding caused severe inbreeding depression symptoms for the house fly. A 25% inbreeding showed a marked decrease in litter size in the French Kennel Club study. In the Standard Poodle study, a 6.25% most closely resembled the non-inbred population data with 25% inbreeding showing a four year lifespan decrease.

Overall, inbreeding levels from 0% to 6.25% strongly suggest no measurable inbreeding depression symptoms either individually or breed-wide. Low levels of inbreeding depression symptoms begin to emerge in managed populations sometime shortly after 6.25% and are shown to increase slightly thereafter in correlation to inbreeding percentages. The greater the overall inbreeding throughout a closed population, the more inbreeding depression symptoms begin to appear throughout a breed. A 25% or higher inbreeding level across a closed population shows a proportional decrease in litter size and lifespan. Although it appears from many of the studies above that a higher rate of inbreeding (>25%) can be individually tolerated in genetically healthy animals without too much health risk to the individual or the population as a whole, unchecked breed-wide increases in inbreeding above 25% appear to significantly increase the overall risks of inbreeding depression for a closed population with eventual extinction vortex levels appearing at 50%, especially in smaller populations. Also, it is important to select healthy individuals on which to inbreed because higher inbreeding levels (>40%) tend to identify hidden recessive deleterious alleles, as the Bouvier Belge des Flandres study suggests.

Inbreeding and Inbreeding Depression in Wild Canid Populations

But what about free roaming wild populations? Surely wild animals that have naturally existed for thousands or tens of thousands of years might have something to teach us, especially since nearly 200 years of closed stud book breeding has been shown to adversely affect many of our beloved furry pets. Is inbreeding a practice that happens naturally in wild animal species or is there somehow an innate inbreeding avoidance ability at work? Does inbreeding always negatively affect wild populations or is there sometimes a benefit to inbreeding?

In 1999, scientists compared 169 inbreeding depression fitness estimates within 35 separate species living in the wild to their comparative species living in captivity. It was determined that wild estimates had a substantially higher mean cost of inbreeding than their captive counterparts. "...inbred wild species measured under natural conditions frequently exhibit moderate to high levels of inbreeding depression in fitness traits."[28] Well known conservation geneticists, Richard Frankham, Jon Ballou, and David Briscoe, in their comprehensive work entitled, Introduction to Conservation Genetics, point out, "There is now clear evidence that inbreeding adversely affects most wild populations."[29] There is strong evidence that inbreeding not only occurs in the wild in much of the animal kingdom, but also significant inbreeding to the point of showing inbreeding depression symptoms is regularly seen. Is it possible to conclude from these natural breeding practices which have sustained wild species for thousands or tens of thousands of years that a certain tolerance toward inbreeding depression symptoms may be necessary to sustain a vibrant wild species long term? It might not be all of the story, but let's find out if it is part of the story to sustaining a healthy, long-lived breed.

African Wild Dog

From 1997 to 2006, twenty African Wild Dogs from various locations were reintroduced to the KZN province in South Africa for the purposes of intensive demographic and behavioral monitoring. Over the seven year study, the population of African Wild Dogs grew steadily comprising a total of 257 identified individuals. A genetic analysis of 113 of the KZN wild dogs was conducted in 2010 revealing that the mean internal relatedness of each parent was 39% across all loci. In addition, the range of genetic internal relatedness was shown to be quite wide extending from 10% to 90%. Furthermore, the research team was able to establish two to three generation pedigrees for 181 KZN wild dogs. Assuming no degree of initial inbreeding between the twenty founding dogs, the researchers observed that after seven years, 37.5% of the wild dogs had a higher than 0% coefficient of inbreeding. The researchers concluded that "the small effective population size and the observed, occasional incestuous matings had not yet occurred at sufficient frequencies to create a signature of reduced genome-wide heterozygosity detectable by our markers and sample size."[30] This study suggests that, although inbreeding occasionally occurs in the wild, there may be an inbreeding avoidance factor allowing naturally breeding African Wild Dog populations to effectively manage inbreeding.

Two years later, in a separate but related study conducted by the same team members, it was concluded that inbreeding was rare in natal packs (0.8%), after reproductive vacancies (12.5%), and between sibling cohorts (3.8%). "Only one of the six (16.7%) breeding pairs confirmed as third-order (or closer) kin consisted of animals that were familiar with each other, while no other paired individuals had any prior association."

Applying this data, the South African wild dog conservation team used computer simulation to predict inbreeding depression and eventual extinction. When inbreeding was allowed at any level, the computer simulated population never went extinct throughout the hundred year timespan. When inbreeding avoidance was measured at varying degrees, the simulation always led to eventual extinction for the population. "Computer-simulated populations allowed to experience inbreeding had only a 1.6% probability of extinction within 100 years, whereas all populations avoiding incestuous matings became extinct due to the absence of unrelated mates." Populations that avoided mating with aunts or uncles or any closer relation became extinct after 63 years. Populations that avoided mating with half-siblings or any closer relation became extinct after 37 years. Populations that avoided mating with parents and full siblings became extinct after 19 years. "Although stronger inbreeding avoidance maintains significantly more genetic variation, our results demonstrate the potentially severe demographic impacts of reduced numbers of suitable mates on the future viability of small, isolated wild dog populations. The rapid rate of population decline suggests that extinction may occur before inbreeding depression is observed."[31]

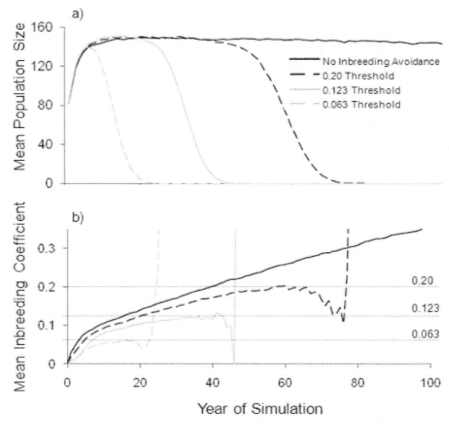

Inbreeding Avoidance Influences the Viability of Reintroduced Populations of African Wild Dogs (Lycaon pictus) - Scientific Figure on ResearchGate. Available from: https://www.researchgate.net/figure/Projections-with-and-without-avoidance-Mean-projected-population-size-a-and-mean_fig5_225030176 [accessed 21 Feb, 2019]

The research team came to realize that without allowing for significant inbreeding, suitable mates would quickly fail to be available and extinction was inevitable. Allowing for significant Inbreeding was the key to eliminating the possibility of extinction well beyond 100 years. Although the actual population of African Wild Dogs that were part of the study did not generally experience significantly close inbreeding levels, the dogs naturally did show a degree of inbreeding suggesting a more sustainable population over time.

Inbreeding is a well-established aspect of the breeding behavior in wolves, however, a strong tendency in wolves toward inbreeding avoidance has also been suggested in recent years. American wolf research scientist, David Mech, and conservation biologist and animal ecologist, Luigi Boitani, pieced together a comprehensive review in 2003 of all of the statistics and observation data on wolf behavior and ecology throughout the last eighty years in one expansive volume entitled, Wolves: Behavior, Ecology, and Conservation. These wildlife biologists maintain that "neighboring wolf packs tend to be genetically related. The closer one pack lives to another, the greater its chance of being related to the other. This tendency results from the budding and splitting processes constantly under way in a vigorous population, as well as from attempts by dispersed offspring to fill in interstices among pack territories."[32]

Isle Royale Wolf

They further submit that while inbreeding occurs, "[n]evertheless, the constant churning of the population resulting from strong competition and intraspecific strife, as well as from the immigration of dispersers from distant populations, continues to ensure a certain level of unrelatedness."[33]

In 2011, a separate research team confirmed the idea that both Gray Wolves and Arctic Foxes in neighboring packs show higher degrees of relatedness. For the Arctic Fox, the team compared the breeding preferences of the outbred fox populations in Iceland to the breeding preferences of the inbred fox populations in Scandinavia. For the Gray wolf, they compared the breeding preferences of the outbred wolf populations in Denali National Park in Alaska and Superior National Forest in Minnesota to the breeding preferences of the inbred wolf population in Isle Royale National Park in Michigan. Surprisingly, they found that inbreeding avoidance was not a significant means of mate selection when the mate came from outside the pack.

At the same time, it appears that wolves and foxes do exhibit a preference for unrelated mates when choosing potential breeding partners from inside the pack. "We compared kin encounter rate and the proportion of related breeding pairs in noninbred and highly inbred canid populations. The chance of randomly encountering a full sib ranged between 1–8% and 20–22% in noninbred and inbred canid populations, respectively. We show that regardless of encounter rate, outside natal groups mates were selected independent of relatedness. Within natal groups, there was a significant avoidance of mating with a relative. Lack of discrimination against mating with close relatives outside packs suggests that the rate of inbreeding in canids is related to the proximity of close relatives, which could explain the high degree of inbreeding depression observed in some populations"[34] Because of the lone wolf's tendency to disperse and then crisscross throughout territories until they find their mate and produce pups, this may allow specific inbred pockets to formulate, regardless of population size.

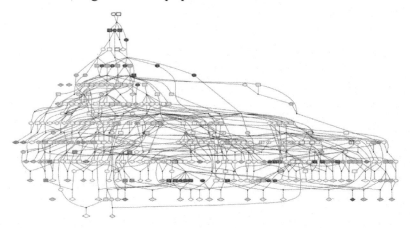

Pedigree of breeding Scandinavian wolves from 1983 to 2012. Ellipses are females, rectangles are males, and diamonds represent litters where no offspring has yet entered the breeding population. The colours represent the inbreeding coefficient f of the individuals and litters (dark blue: $0 \leq f < 0.1$, light blue: $0.1 \leq f < 0.2$, yellow: $0.2 \leq f < 0.3$, orange: $0.3 \leq f < 0.4$, red: $0.4 \leq f < 0.5$, grey: unknown f). Founders, assumed to be nonrelated and thus their offspring $f = 0$, are nonfilled symbols with a blue frame. The pedigree also contains the identity (numbers) of the 28 wolves (Table S3, Supporting information) included in the 14 target pairs.

However, somehow even small populations of wolves with few founders find themselves able to maintain lower levels of homozygosity through DNA testing than expected through pedigree analysis. A group of scientists were quite perplexed when they found in 2006 that the endangered Scandinavian Gray Wolf showed significantly more heterozygosity than the pedigrees foretold. "Recent analyses have questioned the usefulness of heterozygosity estimates as measures of the inbreeding coefficient (f), a finding that may have dramatic consequences for the management of endangered populations. We confirm that f and heterozygosity is poorly correlated in a wild and highly inbred wolf population. Yet, our data show that for each level of "f," it was the most heterozygous wolves that established themselves as breeders, a selection process that seems to have decelerated the loss of heterozygosity in the population despite a steady increase of "f.""[35]

This finding is significant because it reveals that although a coefficient of inbreeding calculated from a known pedigree may suggest a certain estimated level of inbreeding, the actual inheritance of matched alleles from each inbred parent can differ significantly. It was shown in this population of inbred wolves that wolves with more genetic diversity tended to become breeders regardless of relatedness, lessening the effects of overall inbreeding by a measurable degree.

However, inbreeding depression symptoms are frequently shown in wild animal populations around the world. A research review of inbreeding depression symptoms in the wild by Peter Crnokrak, a biologist and agricultural scientist, and Derek Roff, professor of Biology at the University of California, found that "inbred wild species measured under natural conditions frequently exhibit moderate to high levels of inbreeding depression in fitness traits."[36] Clearly, inbreeding regularly plays a part in wild canid breeding practices to the point that inbreeding depression symptoms can be measured at moderate to high levels.

Inbreeding to Manage Inbreeding

So if wild animals regularly show higher levels of inbreeding and inbreeding depression symptoms, how do they keep from going extinct? As we have seen, there is some evidence of inbreeding avoidance by wild canids and heterozygosity tends to be retained at a higher rate than expected, despite relatedness, but there is another significant breeding practice that naturally occurs in the wild that uses inbreeding to lower overall species level inbreeding.

Etienne Joly, a biomedical expert in Immunology and Molecular Biology & Genetics in France, explains how inbreeding within a geographically close ancestral population creates inbred pockets that develop specific traits over time. "...one cannot dispute that speciation occurs, i.e. the fact that, starting from an ancestral population, some groups of animals will start breeding more among one another than with the rest of the population, and will progressively acquire a range of characters that sets them apart from the original group. This, in fact, happens everywhere and all the time around us, in wild and domestic species and is the reason for the appearance of particular characters, or traits, that lead to the definition of subtypes, morphotypes, races, varieties, subspecies, species...."[37]

So, groups that maintain a degree of inbreeding over several generations begin to concentrate their genes diversifying themselves from other inbred groups. When animals from one inbred group disperse to surrounding regions and infiltrate other inbred groups, regular outcrossing is

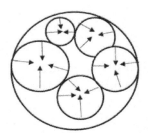

Inbreeding in different directions can keep more genetic diversity in a breed. (from Sponenberg & Bixby 2007)

the result. Small pockets of inbreeding that then occasionally mix with other small inbred pockets appear to create a very sustainable means of survival for the species over time. The Introduction to Conservation Genetics textbook confirms this occurrence in many naturally breeding animals. "[P]opulations of bighorn sheep, gray wolves and bears in North America all show increasing differentiation with geographical distance. Similarly, the red-cockaded woodpecker and the northern spotted owl show relationships between genetic and geographic distances, as do many other species."[38] The Livestock Conservancy group agrees, "Specific strengths and uses for inbred animals include using them for outcrossing to other lines in an effort to balance genetic founders within a breed or herd, to increase vigor and vitality, or to reap the benefits of some specific trait in a given line."[39]

Inbreeding for Better Health

There are only two ways to reduce the effects of genetic health issues in a population. Since it is known that most all negative health issues are recessive in nature, the first way is to mix up the genes within a population so that only the dominantly healthy genes are expressed. This can be accomplished by maintaining a low level of inbreeding and a high degree of genetic diversity within a large population. This type of breeding is often used today and is the most accepted way to approach good health in our dog breeds. However, this breeding technique cannot eliminate health issues from a breed. It can only lessen the degree of its occurrence by reducing the chances for any one dog within the population to inherit the specific combination of traits that will express its effects.

The other way to reduce the overall effect of genetic health issues in a population is to identify the disease by pinpointing exactly where it is located. Only known health issues can be completely eliminated from a breed through selective breeding. Additionally, there are only two ways to find out where a deleterious recessive allele is hiding; either through DNA testing or by test mating, a specific use of inbreeding.

As of this writing, Embark geneticists have identified over 172 genetic diseases in dogs through DNA. More diseases are identified all of the time and genetic testing for pets is expanding rapidly. As Ian J. Seath, Chairman of the Dachshund Breed Council UK and contributing writer for Dog-ED magazine in the United Kingdom recently wrote, "There are over 700 inherited disorders and traits in dogs, of which around 300 have a genetically simple mode of inheritance and around 150 available DNA tests."[39a] DNA testing can greatly aid a breeder by significantly decreasing the amount of time needed to strike out a monogenic disease from the lines. Simply swab a dog's cheek, send off the saliva to the genetic facility, wait a few weeks for the results, and any identified recessive genetic health mutations can be known, including any hidden carriers.

The Dire Wolf Project DNA tests breeding dogs through Embark Veterinary specifically to identify any known deleterious genetic health issues in our lines. With over fifty dogs now tested, only one genetically identified disease is currently carried in the American Alsatian dog breed, canine multifocal retinopathy (CMR1). Furthermore, two of the tested dogs were identified with two copies of the CMR1 gene, but neither showed symptoms of the disease.

Some caution should be noted when utilizing DNA testing to make major life-altering decisions, though. Hundreds of thousands of dogs have now been genetically screened, but the science behind DNA testing is still very new. According to three geneticists, Lisa Moses, Steve Niemi, and Elinor Karlsson, in an opinion article they wrote for Nature, an international science journal, in July 2018, "Most of these tests are based on small, underpowered studies. Neither their accuracy nor their ability to predict health outcomes has been validated."[40]

It appears that mass disease identification through DNA testing has its limits. Even though the tendency in DNA testing facilities is to list all of the known disease alleles on a large list, many of the genetically identified diseases are breed specific and may not affect different breeds in the same way. As Angela Hughes, veterinary genetics research manager with the Mars Wisdom

Panel, said in a Washington Post article, "This panel has a lot of benefits, but it has to be used with caution. We may know of a mutation in Dobermans, and then we see it in Dachshunds, then we have to do clinical validation studies to follow up and investigate that. What does the mutation actually do in Dachshunds? So, we flag it for the Dachshund owners and very clearly state what is a known problem in a breed and what is a potential concern that we are investigating with additional studies."[41]

It appears that genetic mapping can be pretty difficult. Most dog genetic tests are based on studies of candidate genes, but as the three geneticists who challenge the current trend of dog DNA testing state in the Nature article, "In humans, fewer than 2% of candidate-gene studies have stood up to further investigations using more-advanced methods, such as genome-wide association studies."[42] Adam Boyko, chief science officer of canine genetics at Cornell University, agrees, "As you get more genetic information, there are more opportunities to misinterpret it. Dog breeders, when they started testing and there were one and two mutations, that wasn't so bad. But when you're testing for 50 or 60 mutations, you have to understand that it's not always deleterious."[43]

With DNA testing becoming such a popular addition to dog health, it is important to keep two important aspects in mind. The science behind DNA testing is not yet completely reliable and there are many more genetic health diseases that remain unknown through DNA such as: panosteitis, epilepsy, urinary bladder stones, and heart disease, to name a few. In light of this, breeders have an obligation to continue to breed out genetic diseases within their lines using the only other known method of disease elimination, inbreeding through the use of test mating.

According to renowned professor of pathology at Michigan State University and one of the world's most celebrated researchers on the subject of canine genetic diseases, George A Padgett, DVM, "There is no subject in canine genetics that is more misunderstood by geneticists and breeders alike than test-mating (T-M)."[44] The National Rat Terrier Association describes testing mating this way, "test mating is done to a dog that is affected with the genetic problem (resulting usually in puppies that are both affected and non-affected carriers) or by inbreeding to a related dog that also doesn't show the signs of being affected (usually littermates are used) this will usually result in some puppies free of the problem, some puppies as carriers, and some puppies affected."

Three prominent arguments against its use are:
1. Too many matings are wasted searching for dogs that might have a deleterious recessive gene.
2. It takes too long.
3. It costs too much.
4. Test mating produces an increase of genetic disease.

However, without test mating, there is no other way to allow a hidden recessive to rise to the surface so that its position within the breed can be identified and removed. Apart from the few diseases identified through DNA that we discussed, a breeder generally becomes aware of genetic disease when one or more of the offspring that he/she produces develops a defect. It is at this point that test mating can greatly aid in understanding the nature of the defect for the benefit of all dogs within the breed. Once the genetic disease is identified, it can be cleansed from the line. Test mating requires a certain degree of inbreeding to purposefully test whether the resulting offspring will produce the disease. There are some very important rules to follow when utilizing this inbreeding strategy:
1. Do not test-mate a dog unless it has a higher risk of carrying the negative health issue than the general population of the breed.
2. A breeder is obligated to tell any purchaser of any puppy from a test-mating exactly what risk the puppy has to develop a genetic disease or to be a carrier of that defect.
3. Never breed an animal that is of lesser quality than what a breeder would normally breed simply because of a test-mating.
4. Test-mating is generally reserved for severe, debilitating diseases that are expensive to diagnose and treat.

Unfortunately, almost no breeder or breed group talks openly about genetic disease in their dogs. Mostly, dogs that are affected by disease are swept under the rug and never outwardly identified. That is one of the main reasons why it is so very difficult to obtain a reasonable idea of how much disease is within any one dog breed. But, the Dire Wolf Project is different. We pride ourselves on openly sharing any and all potential genetic diseases within our dog breed in an extensive health database. This helps us analyze when a potential test mating would be needed within the breed. It keeps us accountable and it also assures owners that they are getting exactly what we have described. Inbreeding can be used as a tool to root out severe health issues that plague a breed so that they can be completely eliminated, not just simply suppressed.

In Summary

Natalie Green Tessier, independent writer and editing professional who attained a Bachelor's of Fine Arts degree from Cornell University and is a contributing editor at BetterBred, LLC which analyzes the genetic diversity of purebred dog breeds that have been DNA tested through University of California, Davis, summed it all up superbly in her response to an inbreeding debate on the Friends of Pedigree Dogs Exposed Facebook group in 2018,

> "Folks, inbreeding in and of itself is not the issue. Inbreeding across a population, especially in closed gene pools, is the big problem. This happens as we all know, when there are few founders and/or popular sires, or catastrophes like wars and famines.

> "Dog breeders have exploited natural defenses against the deleterious effects of inbreeding to create breeds and to develop populations with very consistent phenotype. This very often leads to population wide inbreeding - where all the individuals or most of them are quite related. Inbreeding can be withstood due to various natural buffers, but for only a certain number of generations and thereafter the effects of that inbreeding are left on the population. In the wild, animals have instincts that minimize actual genomic inbreeding - meaning they choose mates that are least like themselves by instinct - AND, importantly, are subject to natural selection so any individuals with vulnerabilities are much less likely to reproduce. Humans do not replicate those conditions - they inbreed the wrong animals and they make sure all the offspring survive at all costs - especially when they prefer their appearance.

> "How many dog breeders look at their long lived inbred dogs and say "What's wrong with this?" without looking at the larger context?

> "If you are going to inbreed regularly, you had better be prepared not to save weak offspring, and to cull (neuter/spay) them along the way when necessary. You had better be ready for some puppies to come back to you, or break someone's heart, or suffer. To minimize that though, you could instead be open to analyzing the genetic state of your breed, and be prepared to outcross to a different breed if your breed has lost too much diversity. You ought never to insist on a mating the dogs don't want to complete on their own. Otherwise you won't maintain the breed with its original vigor and specific traits indefinitely and you'll pass the problem on to people down the road and the dogs will suffer." – Natalie Green Tessier, 2018

Bravo. The Dire Wolf Project completely agrees. Inbreeding is not a practice to be thrown around without regard, but it is a very effective tool that is occasionally used to search out and eliminate hidden diseases, to solidify or "set" genetic traits, and to create specific related lines within the breed that can be used as outcrosses with other lines to maintain a healthy, long-lived dog breed over time. It is not the only tool, but it is a very important one that should be understood and used with full knowledge and commitment.

Genetic Rescue after a Bottleneck Event

With her one male, Packer, and her two crossbred females, Patty and Polly, Lois had a very steep uphill climb from the bottleneck she now found herself facing. With such a tiny representation of the breed left and much work still to be done to reestablish a viable population to secure the future of the breed, anyone else in her position could have easily chosen to simply stop breeding all together and end the work to establish the first large breed companion dog bred specifically for the modern family. Still another person may have chosen to significantly outcross thereby losing the breed's most defining trait, its calm and loving companion dog temperament. But, Lois does not waiver in the face of adversity. She does not shy away from taking the road less traveled, but embraces the hardships that she may need to face in order to do what must be done for the benefit of the dogs she loves. Lois recognized that within Packer's genes resided her original ideal vision for health, temperament, and appearance in its entirety and she knew a way to keep the hard-fought genetic development she had established. Instead of losing it all or beginning again, she chose to utilize a controversial conservation process called genetic rescue.

Genetic rescue is a mitigation strategy both to restore fitness through genetic diversity without instigating outbreeding depression and to reduce extinction risks in small, isolated, and frequently inbred populations. In order to successfully achieve genetic rescue, one must add individuals to the population in an effort to prevent its potential extinction. Unfortunately, when an endangered population is extremely small in size, it becomes very difficult to add individuals without initiating another documented issue called outbreeding depression, which we will discuss further in the chapter on crossbreeding. When no others are available for breeding, the way in which one adds individuals to the population is by breeding to a cross species/breed and then breeding back to the original pure strain for multiple generations until the population and the original pure individuals' gene contributions increases. As the Livestock Conservancy explains, "The key to success with this strategy is to use it only as a rescue strategy for a rare blood-line, or to limit it to truly outstanding individuals. If used on weak or average individuals, the risks of inbreeding depression outweigh the potential benefits of salvaging the genetic material."[45] When comparing the suggested rescue strategy from the Livestock Conservancy to the process Lois used in 1999 to increase the valuable health and temperament traits she saw in Packer, a very similar breeding pattern can be seen.

The Dire Wolf Project does not adhere to the no-inbreeding-ever model and believes that striving to maintain a no-inbreeding policy would be detrimental to long-term sustained breed management. As an organization dedicated to creating and maintaining an entire healthy, long-lived breed of dog, it is highly beneficial to use inbreeding to keep inbreeding from becoming out of control. Inbreeding is also necessary in order to manage over a quadrillion complex, polygenic health, temperament and appearance traits. And lastly, significant inbreeding was successfully used as a genetic rescue program when an extinction bottleneck occurred in 1999. It

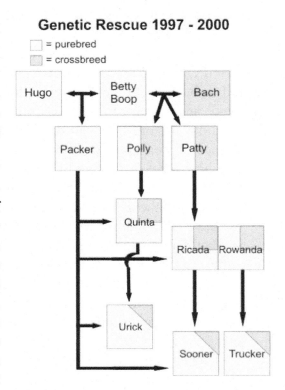

appears that individual inbreeding levels in specific dogs can reach 25-35% without significant individual health risk or breed-wide inbreeding depression deterioration, with a 6.25% or lower breed-wide average level of inbreeding in a population of at least one hundred breeding dogs as the ideal for long-term sustainability and maintenance. For these reasons, we believe that inbreeding is a vital tool that aids in maintaining healthy, long-lived dogs. But, inbreeding must be managed. We strive to keep breed-wide inbreeding as low as possible and retain as much genetic diversity in the breed as we can while at the same time working toward solidifying and setting important traits that set our large breed companion dog apart from other large breeds.

Lois used her one purebred male, Packer, and those two first generation crossbred females to reestablish a population large enough in which she could once again crossbreed without losing the healthy, gentle, sweet-tempered genetic base she had so diligently established throughout the previous twelve years. As illustrated in the 1999 Bottleneck Inbreeding graphic, she bred Packer to both Patty and Polly and kept three females from these litters... a silver, a gold, and a black and tan: Quinta, Rwanda, and Ricotta. She bred those females back to their father, Packer, in order to significantly decrease the crossbred genes and proportionately increase the probability of strengthening the genetic material coming from Packer, her one full link back to the past. Then slowly Lois began to separate the breed into different lines by keeping one male and one female from Rwanda, one male from Quinta, and one female from Ricotta. Now she had four excellent dogs that she mixed and matched in an array of different combinations seeking to increase the overall population while keeping the genetics tight. After three more generations, and more selecting for continued superior health and correct temperament, Lois now had a collection of five dogs that produced exactly what they were in health, temperament and conformation. She went from one to five solid purebred specimens with which to begin the next phase of her mission, to increase the genetic diversity that disappeared from the necessary close inbreeding.

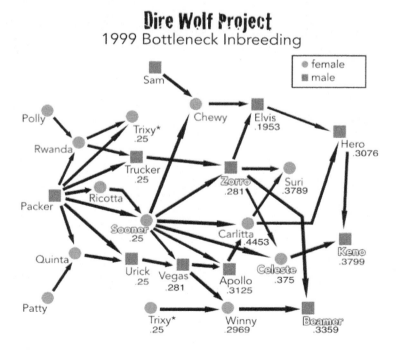

Dire Wolf Project
1999 Bottleneck Inbreeding

American Alsatian puppy at 7 weeks old

Chapter 7
Crossbreeding

Have you ever experienced the intense adrenaline-laced thumping in your heart that accompanies the realization that you just barely escaped death and if one small event had gone differently, you may not now be alive today? Well, that feeling encapsulated the breed in 2003 when Zorro was born. Prior to his birth, all of Lois's efforts to produce a large breed of dog that fit perfectly with modern city life dangled precariously in the balance between whether the breed was going to completely die out or continue to cling to life. Lois used all of her breeding prowess to continue the lines she had developed, but as a result, the breed lost much of its genetic diversity and Zorro, Apollo, and three females were her sole link back to all of the years before. Lois knew that with these five dogs that represented all that was good about her work she could move forward, but not for very long. You see, finally all of her dogs now had the exact temperament she had been aiming to achieve. Each of them bred true to type and consistently produced a similar temperament and look. But yet, there were still two small problems for her to overcome. First of all, her dogs did not completely look like her ideal and certainly did not match the Dire Wolf's bone and body structure. But, more importantly, she had a very small population size that did not equate to continued growth and viability. Without introducing unrelated dogs, Zorro and his companions would be the last of their kind. Crossbreeding was inevitable if the breed was going to continue. But, would introducing other breeds ultimately cause her to lose the temperament she had so diligently developed? Furthermore, could she maintain the great health and longevity for which her dogs were known? Crossbreeding is definitely not an easy task, but without using this breeding tactic, her breed could not hope to endure.

The sun's morning light through the kitchen window illuminated the few dust particles gently meandering about as Lois yawned awake to another day. Five years had passed since her exodus from Southern California and she now woke peacefully without the constant pressures she had felt living in the city. Country life agreed with Lois as she rubbed the sleep from her eyes and pulled on her slippers. Her mom would be awake soon, so she walked into the kitchen and turned on the coffee maker for a fresh brew. Lois made her way over to the back window and peered out. Her five dogs still lay curled up in their wooden dens that her father had made for his English Cocker Spaniels several years before he passed away. The giant elm tree swayed in the gentle spring breeze as the birds fluttered around the main bird feeders chirping their happy songs. A new day had begun on the small farm in southern Oregon surrounded by the beautiful Cascade Mountains and a strong sigh left her as her mind began once again to think about her dogs... her deepest passion.

Her thoughts took her back to the search she had been engaged in for the last year. Lois turned around, poured herself a cup of coffee and walked into the enclosed porch where she kept her computer. She set up her office in this room because the windows on the porch looked directly out to her dogs and she could watch them as she researched and wrote about them. Nothing excited her more than thinking about her favorite topic. With a flick of a switch, the computer screen glowed blue, the main tower beeped its approval, and the dial-up Internet began its connection routine. The pleasant humming sounds of the inner workings of the computer lulled her mind toward the various dog breeds she had been exploring to add to her still tiny, but steadily growing, breed.

The temperament of the puppies in each litter was now exactly where she wanted it: sweet, loving, gentle, extremely calm, smart, easy to train, submissive, reserved but not shy, devoted, and loyal. Her dogs were healthy and solid in appearance and their puppies were easy to raise with no underlying health issues to cause weakness. Owners were very happy and began to dialogue with her regularly on a new online forum she had created to keep in touch. Consistency in health and temperament now defined her once highly diverse mixed breed. For the first time in eighteen years she finally felt that she could concentrate on some of the more trivial appearance traits that she never allowed herself to notice before.

Once the dial-up completed its electrical churning, she sipped her coffee and opened the Internet browser to continue her search for an unrelated dog that would launch the next phase of her project; the bone and body structure of the extinct, prehistoric Dire Wolf. Today, as she felt a particular peace wash over her, the search for a large-boned, heavy dog with slanted eyes and a somewhat more wolfish appearance came to an end. There, right in front of her, unfolded a website describing a completely different type of Alaskan Malamute that she had never seen before; the M'loot Alaskan Malamute. These Malamutes were said to come from the original dogs bred by the Inuits in Alaska and although pure of breeding, did not adhere to AKC's Alaskan Malamute standards in size and weight. One of the only breeders responsible for maintaining this larger type of Alaskan Malamute, Marlene Ross, explains that "Wakon Giant Alaskan Malamutes are pure-bred descendants of the pure M'Loot type of Malamute that lived with the ancient Inuit peoples in the high Arctic, hundreds of years ago."[1]

Marlene's giant Alaskan Malamutes look very different from the Kotzebue or Hinman strains of Alaskan Malamutes that are mostly used in the AKC show rings today. The M'loot type is taller, heavier, and has a larger bone structure. To Lois's surprise, these Malamutes also had highly slanted yellow eyes as well as a short tail and a large head with small erect ears. Now that Lois had set the gentle, mellow temperament of the American Alsatian, she was finally ready to begin to focus on the outward appearance goals of the Dire Wolf Project as well as to improve the genetic diversity that had been lost in her dogs through her work setting the temperament and reestablishing a larger population after the bottleneck. The M'loot Alaskan Malamute seemed to be the perfect crossbreed.

Lois smiled contentedly as she picked up the phone to place an inquiry call. Marlene's voice pleasantly surprised Lois and through their conversation Marlene revealed that she did not have puppies available at this time, but she had an older male named Mount Rainier that was available for purchase. Lois's heart beat faster and she stood up in excitement as she learned from Marlene that her Wakon kennels were in Washington State, only eight hours north. Lois held her breath as she realized that she could drive there and back in one day. Her voice quickened as she let Marlene know she was on her way. Lois began planning her trip even before she hung up the phone. Her years of searching for just the right animal to bring into the lines had practically fallen into her lap.

She shook her head in disbelief as she wrote out a note for her mom, grabbed the keys to her Suburban, and rushed out the door.

When Lois turned onto the dirt driveway at Wakon Kennels, the green carpeted arms of lush evergreen trees beckoned her forward. Still reeling from her amazing find, Lois parked her SUV and walked out to meet another well-seasoned breeder singlehandedly holding together a rare dog type. Marlene led Lois through the large barn-like facility where all of her many giant Alaskan Malamutes lived. Each one of Marlene's dogs were large-boned, tall and heavy with large heads, small, erect ears and light colored eyes. Lois could hardly believe her luck. She knew it was not easy to keep size and girth over time in a group of dogs and marveled at the years of hard work to which Marlene must have dedicated herself.

In a small pen toward the back, Lois set eyes on Mount Rainier. He was a humongous silver color with a shorter coat, highly slanted yellow eyes, and a massive head. He stood just over thirty-eight inches tall at the shoulders and easily reached the top of the kennel fencing when he stood up to greet her. These were the features Lois needed to improve the size and overall appearance of her own dogs. Mount Rainier was

Wakon Kennel puppies, 2011

friendly and sweet as she led him out of the pen to take a better look at him. He did not hesitate to come with her. Lois noticed that he had very little angulation in the knees of his back legs, but his gate was great and his hip movement gave no indication that he had trouble in that regard. His ears had never risen, but they were small in size and thick leathered. He was a bit goofy and very confident, but sweet-natured and not overly hyper. Apart from his knee joints at the back legs, which she knew that she would need to quickly breed out, he was ideal for her needs. Marlene showed Lois his pedigree and they talked as old friends about the many dogs Marlene had loved throughout the years. When it came time to depart, Rainier jumped into the back of her SUV without difficulty or hesitation and Lois waved good-bye to a fellow breed warden.

126

As Lois drove home, she allowed her mind to dream of her next tasks with breeding Rainier into her lines. She did not have a great idea of Rainier's temperament quite yet, but regardless she would need to select for her ideal temperament while working to keep the improved size that this crossbreed would ultimately bring to her lines. If everything worked out as she imagined, Rainier would

Mount Rainier, 2011

consistently produce his size and weight which was a real asset for Lois in this stage of the breed.

Isn't Crossbreeding Just Breeding Mutts?

A mutt is generally a term to describe a dog of unknown origin or a dog without a pedigree. The word mutt has a derogatory slant to it, as if dogs of unknown origin are less worthy of admiration than a dog that can be defined by its parentage in a pedigree, especially if the pedigree includes ancestry with significant awards or recognitions. The Merriam-Webster dictionary definition of the word mutt states, "a mongrel dog: cur" Merriam-Webster then defines mongrel as, "an individual resulting from the interbreeding of diverse breeds or strains, *especially*: one of unknown ancestry" and cur as, "a mongrel or inferior dog." Vocabulary.com defines the term as, "Dogs called *crossbreeds* are deliberately bred to combine characteristics of two or more recognized breeds, while mutts — also known as *mongrels* — are the result of accidental mixing of breeds." However, the word mutt is also sometimes used to describe any crossbred dog, especially when the person wielding the term does not agree with the crossbred breed in some way. There is now evidence in some dictionaries that the word mutt has shifted to a more general definition. The Cambridge Dictionary describes mutt as "a mongrel" which in turn is defined as "a dog of mixed breed."

However, crossbreeding is now being successfully used in a few purebred dog breeding programs as a means to increase genetic diversity as well as increase healthy alleles that have been lost within the breed over time. As we shall explore, these goal-oriented crossbreeding programs within purebred dog breeds bring vitality to closed breeding systems that otherwise show significant increases of inbreeding depression symptoms. Since the very beginnings of the breed, the Dire Wolf Project maintains that systematic and regulated crossbreeding within an otherwise isolated breed is one important tool to maintain healthy, long-lived dogs over the lifetime of a breed.

Types of Breeding

highly uniform

Inbreeding

Inbreeding - breeding close or first degree relatives

Linebreeding - breeding slightly removed or second degree relatives

Backcrossing - breeding a crossbreed back to its parent or equivalent

Outbreeding

Linecrossing - breeding two line-bred dogs of different lines

Outcrossing - breeding unrelated dogs within the same breed

Close crossbreeding - breeding unrelated dogs of similar breeds

Crossbreeding - breeding unrelated dogs of diverse breeds

highly variable

Crossbreeding vs. Outbreeding

Crossbreeding is actually a special type of outbreeding. Outbreeding is the general term used to describe the breeding for parents not closely related to one another. Since inbreeding is breeding to relatives that are related to one another, outbreeding is inbreeding's opposite. A different way to look at it is that outbreeding is any type of breeding strategy that seeks to increase genetic diversity and decrease the coefficient of inbreeding by pedigree, in turn decreasing any inbreeding depression symptoms that may have crept into a population. Whereas inbreeding decreases diversity; outbreeding increases

128

diversity. So let's explore the many different ways a breed can outbreed in order to achieve sustainable healthy, long-lived dogs.

There are four different types of outbreeding that one might employ: linecrossing, outcrossing, close crossbreeding, and crossbreeding. The closest type of outbreeding is called linecrossing, which is shown by breeding two inbred or line-bred dogs within the same breed that have diverse ancestry. This is also referred to as cluster breeding. The parents may look very similar to one another and have many of the same features, but some genetic drift has occurred by keeping the lines separate over a period of time which allows for the lines to achieve a degree of diversity. As we saw in the chapter on inbreeding, when inbreeding is employed responsibly to produce distinct lines of dogs within a breed, linecrossing can then be used to bring down the inbreeding levels within each line and enhance the diversity that each line brings to the breed.

A bit more diverse is the breeding practice of outcrossing, which is when two completely unrelated dogs within the same breed, showing as little inbreeding as possible as far back as the pedigree will allow, are bred together. Breeders generally try to go back at least ten generations for a true picture of outcrossing. The deliberate practice of line-breeding or inbreeding is not required in this type of breeding. It is simply the lack of relation to another dog within the same breed that is sought.

Two Types of Crossbreeding

Even a more diverse for of outbreeding is the practice of crossbreeding. There are two types of crossbreeding. Close crossbreeding is when two unrelated, but very similar, breeds are used for breeding, such as the Irish Wolfhound and the Scottish Deerhound. Although these two breeds have many similar features, they also have quite significant differences between them and they have been maintained as separate breeds with different goals and original purpose for an extended period of time.

Irish Wolfhound   Scottish Deerhound
Photo Credit: Lilly M [CC BY-SA 3.0
(http://creativecommons.org/licenses/by-sa 3.0)]

The Scottish Deerhound and the Irish Wolfhound have these similarities:

1. Both are coursing dogs.
2. Both have a similar shape to the body overall.
3. Both have a wiry coat.
4. Both have similar color choices.
5. Both have furnishings, which are longer hairs on the muzzle and forehead.
6. Both have long tails.
7. Both have drop ears.
8. Both have dark brown eyes.
9. Both have longer muzzles.
10. Both shed moderately.

The Scottish Deerhound and the Irish Wolfhound have these differences:

1. The Irish Wolfhound is taller and has an overall larger build, which equates to a heavier weight.
2. Originally, the Irish Wolfhound was bred to hunt wolves and the Scottish Deerhound was bred to hunt deer therefore there is some difference in overall inherited temperament.
3. The Irish Wolfhound's tail curves slightly whereas the Scottish Deerhound's tail hangs straight.
4. The Scottish Deerhound shows slightly more hound features than the Irish Wolfhound.
5. The Scottish Deerhound shows an ear that sets back slightly and the Irish Wolfhound shows a hanging ear.

The second form of crossbreeding, crossbreeding itself, is when two highly diverse dog breeds are bred together, such as the English Mastiff and the German Shepherd Dog. In 2017, a beautiful and very detailed genetic map of the different dog breeds and their relation to one another was created. Elaine Ostrander and Heidi Parker, geneticists at the National Human Genome Research Institute in Bethesda, Maryland, and their colleagues spent 20 years collecting DNA samples from all over the world to reveal just how dogs developed. Their research includes 1346 dogs representing 161 breeds. By comparing the differences at 150,000 spots on each dog's genome, they built a family tree of the most well-known domesticated dog breeds.[2] When comparing the English Mastiff breed to the German Shepherd Dog on this map, one can see that the breeds are not only distant in relation to one another, but their degree of separation from each other compared to other breeds is also quite large. That being said, it is easy to see by their appearance and behavior alone that each of these dog breeds is extremely diverse in their genetic make-up.

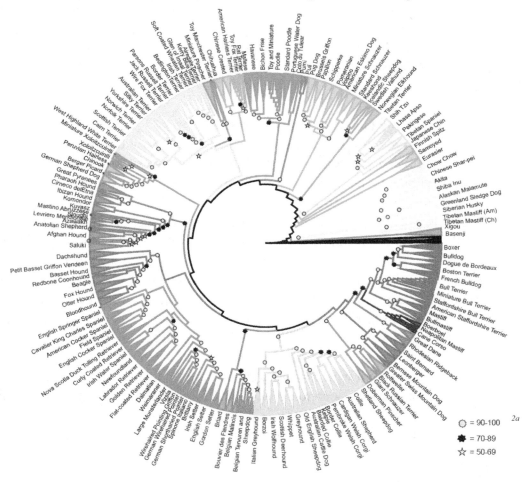

131

Crossbreeding History

Humans have been breeding dogs for thousands of years and throughout this time dogs were mostly bred for function rather than form and pedigree. As Live Science contributor, Remy Melina, explains "When ancient humans bred dogs for features such as a louder bark (for added protection of their owner's property) or a docile temperament (so it would be less likely to lash out at its owner), they were actually already tinkering with the selection of dog genes."[3] Specific dog breeds were not well established, but defined as functional types, races, or strains with an overall similar look or style without a written ancestry. Dr. Johannes Caius created a list of Tudor dog types in 1570 classifying them by function rather than appearance. Dr. Caius recognized sixteen varieties including, "Terrare, Harier, Bludhunde, Gasehunde, Setter, Water Spainel or Fynder, Spainel-gentle or Comforter, Shepherd's Dog, Mastive or Bande-Dog, Wappe, Turnspit, Dancer."[4] A farmer's manual in the late seventeenth century described many of the same breed types, "Grey-hound, Blood Hound, Rach, Sluth Hound, Tumbler, Tarier or Harier, Leviner, Beagle, Spannel, BanDog, and Field-Dog."[5]

Outbreeding for Healthy, Long-lived Dogs

Each type of outbreeding aids a breeder in maintaining a larger degree of genetic diversity within a breed while also allowing for a way back to the established breed type. Generally, the more diverse the dogs are to one another, the more diversity within the litter will be seen. The mark of an exceptional breeder is one who can crossbreed using highly diverse breeds and eventually be able to return to a standard approved consistency of type without losing the genetic diversity advantage that has been gained by originally introducing the crossbreed in the first place. As the Introduction of Conservation Genetics textbook reveals, "[R]ecombination in outbreeding sexual populations allows natural selection to more effectively oppose fixation of deleterious alleles, as some progeny have higher reproductive fitness than that of their parents."[6] This added diversity can be a benefit to a breeder when the trait selection has diminished to a point where many great qualities in health, temperament and/or conformation are now seen to be lacking. Crossbreeding benefits a population in three ways:

- reintroducing a greater availability of selection to a population

- providing a renewed ability to reduce any health, temperament or conformation issues that existed in the breed before the cross
- significantly increasing the overall diversity of traits that are not needed to secure the desired type

The vast majority of dog breeding history relied on personal performance assessment, word of mouth, or informal local or regional trial tests to determine a dog's worthiness. A dog owner of a prestigious herding dog seeking to produce other superior herding dogs, for example, might be inclined to breed to distinguished herding dogs in the area, regardless of known ancestry. Without the availability of modern transportation and easy access to breeding specimens living long distances, most lineages tended to be regional in scope and inbreeding occurred just as naturally as crossbreeding, depending on the superiority of the offspring's abilities. In 1986, Harriet Ritvo, a prolific author and professor of British, environmental, natural, and animal history at the Massachusetts Institute of Technology, wrote, "Before the eighteenth century, domestic animals in England varied greatly within their respective species, but not according to the kind of consistent and intentionally produced distinctions represented by modern breeds. Instead, there were many regional strains, the results of fairly random inbreeding among semi-isolated populations of sheep, cattle, horses, pigs, and dogs. Such animals, as the late eighteenth-century Board of Agriculture noted in its country-by-country surveys of British husbandry, were likely to be hardy, but scraggly and inefficient. Most farm animals continued to be produced in this rather haphazard fashion well into the nineteenth century."[7]

Just before the Victorian age was in full swing, dog breeding was much more open to diversity in appearance in order to more readily focus on the effectiveness of the functionality of each dog within the race. Both the aristocracy and the middle class of the Victorian age promoted the idea of breed purity and the closed stud book with the developing prestige of pedigreed ancestry and the eventual establishment of kennel clubs to manage the growing prominence of pedigreed dogs.

When Inbreeding Goes Too Far

Modern science now confirms that inbreeding rose steadily as a direct result of the rise of purebred dog breeds in the Victorian Age. According to an extensive research study in 2016 by Greger et. al. revealing the genetic diversity within purebred dog breeds today, "all analyzed pedigrees showed a peak in inbreeding post-AKC recognition, although the time required to reach that peak ranges from 9 (Labrador Retriever) to 69 (Papillon) years."[8] When a relatively small group of founding dogs becomes the only accepted ancestry from which to breed and the breed's population exponentially increases for over one hundred fifty years, things can go wrong. Until recently, if a breeder wanted to breed a standard Poodle, he/she could only breed from dogs descended from that original list of ancestors. If someone bred in a similar dog with unknown ancestry or even if the pedigree was known but included dogs of mixed origin, their offspring were considered mutts, mongrels, or curs and could not be competitively shown - even if the offspring looked exactly like a purebred.

Permanently closing a studbook and forever restricting the genetics within a breed to only the few founding animals is like stranding a dog breed on a small island surrounded by shark infested waters. In this case, the confines of the purebred pedigree are the vessels that landed the isolated purebred population on the island in the first place and the sharks are the purists keeping any dogs from swimming on or off the island. This is exactly what occurred for the Isle Royale Gray Wolf population in Michigan and it hasn't gone well for them. In the 60 years of this long-term wolf study, fifty wolves, their highest recorded population number, dropped to only one confirmed wolf in December 2018. The rapid recent decline in population size was likely due to increased inbreeding depression symptoms recorded by those involved in the study which eventually plummeted the isolated wolves toward an extinction vortex.

Many of the island's wolves suffered from deformities and other severe inbreeding depression symptoms as well as a significant decrease in population size in a short period of time.[9] Perhaps a little too late, but as of June 7, 2018, researchers approved the addition of twenty to thirty unknown wolves onto the island to aid in the repopulation of Isle Royale wolves after it was shown that a somewhat overwhelming population increase of moose on the island seems to be having serious effect on the island's flora.[10] As the Introduction to Conservation Genetics textbook teaches, "Genetic diversity is generally lower in small populations than in large populations."[11] The Conservation Genetics textbook further explains, "Loss of genetic diversity would not be of great concern if it were regenerated rapidly by mutation. However, times to regenerate genetic diversity are very long, as mutation rates are low... Clearly, we cannot rely on mutation to regenerate genetic diversity in threatened species, at least in time spans of conservation concern. The implication is that every effort must be made to prevent loss of current genetic diversity in the first place."[12] Sadly, conservationists have observed the Isle Royale gray wolf's story in numerous other small and isolated populations of animals all around the world and many are working to prevent the same bitter end. Several domesticated dog breeds could be said to be riding down the same extinction path and alarm bells have begun ringing out as a result.

The Rise of the Designer Dog

As we explored in the chapter on inbreeding, high levels of inbreeding can cause serious adverse consequences to a population of animals. Many have suggested that inbreeding levels within the purebred dog have become so outrageously high in many breeds due to bottleneck events and popular sire syndrome that perhaps mixed breed dogs are better able to withstand the effects of genetic disease. Is it true that designer dogs, also called crossbred dogs, are overall healthier than purebred dogs? This has been the fundamental question in the dog world for at least the last forty years. As we have now discussed, purebred dogs have dominated the prestige of dog ownership for over a hundred and fifty years. However, in the 1980s, many people began to seriously question the vitality of purebred dogs. In 1948, geneticist James F. Crow explained that, "Hybrid vigor has been observed for centuries but explanations in terms of Mendelian heredity have, of course, been formulated only recently. The word heterosis was proposed by Shull (1914) for this increase in vigor following the union of dissimilar gametes and has come into general use."[13]

Trickling down to the mainstream, this notion of hybrid vigor, or heterosis, began to be widely known as news of significant increased yields for hybrid maize reached the public's ear. Many people began developing the idea that pedigreed dogs experience an increase in health issues while the scientifically observed occurrence of hybrid vigor began to take hold in the broader community. The atmosphere was ripe for the designer dog to become a hugely popular breeding phenomenon.

In 1988, Wally Conron, Australian breeding manager for the Royal Guide Dog Association of Australia in Victoria, specifically bred a purebred Labrador Retriever to a purebred standard Poodle in an effort to secure a non-allergenic dog that would be able to successfully work as a service dog for a woman in Hawaii. Wally Conron chose the one puppy from the match, Sultan, who exhibited all of the qualities he needed for this particular task. But he could not find permanent homes for his other crossbred pups. As he explains, "With a three to six-month waiting list for people wishing to foster our pups, I was sure we'd have no problem placing our three new crossbred pups with a family. But again I was wrong: it seemed no-one wanted a crossbred puppy; everyone on the waiting list preferred to wait for a purebred. And time was running out – the pups needed to be placed in homes and socialised; otherwise they would not become guide-dogs. By eight weeks of age, the puppies still hadn't found homes. Frustrated and annoyed with the response to the trio of crossbreeds I had carefully reared, I decided to stop mentioning the word crossbreed and introduced the term labradoodle instead to describe my new allergy-free guide-dog pups. It worked – during the weeks that followed, our switchboard was inundated with calls from other guide-dog centres, vision-impaired people and people allergic to dog hair who wanted to know more about this "wonder dog". My three pups may have been mongrels at heart – but the furore did not abate."[14]

No longer simply seen as a mutt or mixed breed, the designer dog seemed to have the specific advantage of combining the best traits from both purebred parents. It also became associated with first generation hybrid vigor that is frequently observed in the cross pollination of two previously inbred plant species. Although heterosis is only experienced in the first generation, many took the idea of hybrid vigor and began applying it to any type of mix coming from two purebred dog breeds. As fidosavvy.com owner, Sue, rightly explains, "The heritage and ancestry of mix breed puppies is often hazy at best, and most likely of a total unknown quantity. In contrast, the background of designer dog breeds/hybrid dogs,[sic] has a definite structure."[15] Sue goes on to explain the differences between first, second, and third generation crosses as well as backcrossing to one of the founding purebred breeds.

In our time, several different registries have popped up to register designer dog breeds including: American Canine Hybrid Club, Australian Labradoodle Association of America, Designer Breed Registry, and

International Designer Canine Registry. On April 14, 2009, the AKC officially announced a new program specifically for mixed breed dogs where owners of dogs that do not qualify for purebred registration can still participate in many AKC sanctioned events.[16] Similarly, the Kennel Club in the United Kingdom now registers crossbred dog breeds for participation in several Kennel Club licensed events, "The Kennel Club's primary aim is to protect and promote all dogs, and crossbreed dogs, such as 'Labradoodles', 'Puggles' and 'Cockerpoos' etc, may be registered with us on the Activity register."[17]

But the question of whether the crossbred dog is overall healthier than the purebred had been mostly informal speculation until a significant study coming out of the University of California-Davis helped shed some light on the answer. From 1995 to 2010, the researchers from University of California-Davis Veterinary Medical Teaching Hospital studied 27,254 dogs with twenty-four different inherited disorders in five categories. They separated the dogs into two categories: purebred dogs, and mixed breed dogs. Of the twenty-four disorders the researchers monitored, thirteen held nearly the same frequency results for both purebred and mixed breed dogs. Ten inherited disorders were more common in purebred dogs while one disorder was seen to be significantly more common in mixed breed dogs. In summary, it appears that neither the purebred dog nor the mixed breed dog is truly free from inherited disease. In fact, the study suggests that since all genetically tested domesticated dogs originate from six known ancient wolf lineages, haplogroups A-F, that many of the same genetic diseases will likely always remain genetically present in some form throughout the entirety of the dog genome. That is definitely a compelling theory.

But there is no question that certain purebred dog breeds experience a higher number of reported genetic health issues in the canine than others. In 2011, out of 432 separately tracked genetic diseases in purebred dogs and 83 distinct dog breeds represented, the German Shepherd Dog rests in the number one spot for the highest number of genetic diseases reported in the dogs within the study and represents a whopping 89 different diseases. That is a total of almost 21% of the entire list of known genetic diseases in the canine. The American Cocker Spaniel stands at the second spot and represents 73 different inherited canine diseases which is almost a 17% cut of the total list. These two extremely popular dog breeds contrast to other breeds that only show one or two reported genetic diseases, such as: Antarctic Husky, Dutch Shepherd, Harrier, Norwegian Dunkerhound, Polish Greyhound, Scottish Terrier, Sloughi, and Thai Ridgeback. All of the other 78 dog breeds presented in this collection experience a number of genetic diseases that lie somewhere in between.[18]

Clare Maldarelli, a science writer with a B.S. degree in neurobiology, physiology, and behavior from the University of California, Davis, puts it this way, "By age five, for example, half of all Cavaliers will develop mitral valve disease, a serious heart condition that leaves the dogs susceptible to premature death. By the same age, up to 70 percent will suffer from canine syringomyelia, a debilitating neurological disorder in which the brain is too large for the skull, causing severe pain in the neck and shoulders, along with damage to parts of the dog's spinal cord. And although Cavaliers may be a particularly obvious case of purebreds with problems, they aren't alone. Most purebred dogs today are at a high risk for numerous inherited diseases."[19] Although not all purebred dog breeds are riddled with disease, clearly there is much room for improvement in the reduction of canine genetic diseases and increased genetic diversity, especially in highly inbred breeds.

Crossbreeding for Health and Genetic Diversity in Purebred Dogs

It is important to salute a few brave souls who have chanced severe ridicule and potential loss of prestige or continued inclusion within the purebred dog breeding community. These few men and women do what they believe is needed to improve their favorite dog breed regardless of what the majority in their purebred community maintains. The following individuals lay a clear path forward for others to eventually follow. Hopefully their dedication to detail in preserving their unique approaches to increasing genetic diversity will help others to obtain the courage to do the same within their own purebred dog breeds. Here is a list of all of the currently known crossbreeding programs that understand the importance of replenishing the effects of lost genetic diversity as well as diminishing the effects of uncovered recessive deleterious alleles from high inbreeding that plague certain purebred dog breeds.

Dalmatian

<u>Dalmatian BackCross Project</u> - http://www.dalmatianheritage.com/

The Dalmatian Backcross Project began in 1973 when geneticist, Robert Schaible, realized that all Dalmatians that had ever been tested exhibited a metabolic defect that caused them to have abnormally high levels of uric acid in their urine, a condition known as hyperuricosuria (HU). Dogs with this condition are prone to urinary obstruction due to the growth of bladder stones, causing premature death in extreme cases. Knowing that the only way to eliminate the concern was to bring in dogs without the condition, he crossbred his purebred Dalmatians with Pointers. After seven years and five generations later, Dr. Schaible attained a consistent Dalmatian breed type and applied to the AKC for registration. After review, the AKC initially accepted his registration with some notoriety, but when the greater community learned that his mixed dogs had been registered, a disgruntled protest succeeded on placing a hold on any further registration from his lines. It took thirty years before the Dalmatian Club of America finally accepted the ancestors from the Backcross Project. The catalyst for the change of heart was when Danika Bannasch, PhD, DVM identified the genetic mutation causing the condition.[20]

Boxer Dogs (2004)

Bobtail Boxers - http://www.steynmere.co.uk/ARTICLES1.html

This crossbred project began in 1992 by renowned geneticist, Dr. Bruce Cattanatch, in anticipation of a tail docking ban in Britain. Before he began, he informed the Kennel Club in the United Kingdom of his very detailed intentions and kept meticulous notes and pictures of his work. He began his project by crossing one of his purebred Boxer females to a Pembroke Corgi with a dominantly inherited bobtail. Dr. Cattanatch consistently achieved the natural bobtail within the Boxer's body type after four generations. Dr. Cattanatch explains, "The unique Boxer head seems to be the major problem but then, in my experience, this is also the case within the breed."[21] He briefly toyed with the idea of adding the natural erect ear to the Boxer as well, but decided to curtail that project for now. There is some rumbling from a small group who fear that the natural bobtail is actually an unhealthy mutation causing deformed spines when dogs inherit two copies of the gene. Dr. Cattanatch will be working to determine the merits of these claims through breeding. It will be interesting to see how this progresses in the coming years.

Bernese Mountain Dog

Bernese Mountain Dog Vitality Project –
https://www.bmdvitalityproject.org/project/

      The three individuals who began the Bernese Mountain Dog Vitality Project, Anne Nichols, Kathy Berge DVM, and Steve Dudley, explain the very real reasons they initiated this controversial project in 2017, "The present day Bernese Mountain Dog is a breed that is plagued with numerous health issues that are resulting in an abnormally short lifespan. Cancers, immune mediated disease, allergies, digestive issues, degenerative myelopathy, thyroid issues, and widespread reproductive issues are all significantly prevalent in the breed."[22] So far, their website reveals two successful litters. Both litters appear to be first generation crosses. The first litter of puppies stood taller and thinner than a purebred Bernese Mountain Dog, but they do have a road ahead to achieve a look worthy of the standard.[23] Although there is some controversy among purists, there is also enthusiastic support. It will be interesting to watch this project's advancements in the years to come.

Basenji

Basenji Imports – https://www.basenji.org/index.php/sort-by-import-date

The African Basenji originates from the Basankusu area up stream on the Maringa River in the Congo. A particularly dedicated Basenji enthusiast, James E Johannes, periodically travels to the Basenji's original lands to acquire native Basenji pups to include in his Basenji breeding program.[24] According to the Basenji Club of America, nineteen native African Basenji were exported to the United States to increase the limited gene pool around 1990. The AKC again agreed to reopen the Basenji stud book for four years, starting in 2009.[25]

Through DNA analysis, researchers confirm that the addition of African Basenji dogs from the Democratic Republic of Congo aided the breed in maintaining lower inbreeding levels. "We can, however, recognize a distinctive drop in inbreeding values in the Basenji during the late 1980s, corresponding with the time at which new African imports of Basenjis were allowed for registration with the AKC."[26] While not a crossbreeding program as the breed is not crossing to another unrelated breed, it is still an ongoing outbreeding program to regularly improve genetic diversity. Therefore, it is noteworthy that the Basenji Club of America has understood the importance of regular and systematic outbreeding in order to secure the long-term health and longevity of their breed.

Chinook

Chinook Breed Conservation Program –
https://chinook.org/wp-content/uploads/2016/11/Chinook-Breed-Conservation-Program.pdf

      The Chinook dog breed has an interesting breed development story. The Chinook breed began in 1917 by explorer Arthur T. Walden. His Greenland Husky/mastiff-type male stud and lead sled dog, Chinook, formed the basis of his breed. Walden single-handedly developed the breed and kept all breeding within his kennel until he fell on hard times and sold the breed to Julia Lombard. In 1940, Perry Greene and his wife Honey purchased the Chinooks from Lombard. They sold only males or spayed females to keep the breed within the family, but "by 1965 the *Guinness Book of World Records* recorded the Chinook - for the first of three times - as the rarest dog, with only 125 dogs alive and the number dropping rapidly."[27] The Chinook Owner's Association, in partnership with the United Kennel Club, established the Chinook Breed Conservation Program "to maintain a healthy, genetically sustainable Chinook population, with the breed's historical temperament, working ability, structure, and appearance."[28] They aim to expand the gene pool within the breed by introducing crossbreed dogs as new founders to the breed. The application for introducing a new crossbreed is lengthy and all-encompassing. They aim to achieve purebred status for the new crossbred line by the third generation. They allow both purebred and mixed crossbreeds into the program as long as they conform to the program's extensive criteria.[29]

Norwegian Lundehund
Photo credit: Karen Elise Dahlmo

Norwegian Lundehund Genetic Rescue Project –
https://journals.plos.org/plosone/article?id=10.1371/journal.pone.0170039

As we saw in the inbreeding chapter, the Norwegian Lundehund, a special six-toed puffin hunting dog, currently experiences upwards of 80% inbreeding breed-wide. Many also suffer from severe inbreeding depression symptoms and a decreasing population. These extensive issues predict an extinction vortex like situation and many believe the breed's very existence now hangs in the balance. It is for this reason that the Norwegian Lundehund Genetic Rescue Project has begun per the strong suggestion from the genetic researchers who determined the extremely low genetic diversity in the breed. "Our data strongly suggests that crossbred individuals should immediately be accepted as part of the main population and as breeding candidates."[30]

According to the Norwegian Lundehund Club question and answer page updated in 2015, "The [cross] project was initiated as a result of the findings NLK [Norsk Lundehund Klubb] made during the work with the breeding strategy for the "Norsk Lundehund" (RAS) and was included in an Action Plan for NLK after a workshop on RAS at Starum, an open meeting at Øysanden and an open hearing, all in 2013."[31] After an extensive DNA review of several potential crossbreeds, this project has identified three breeds as good candidates for their genetic rescue endeavors: the Buhund, the Icelandic Sheepdog, and the Norrbottenspitz.[32]

The outcross project clearly acknowledges that the identified crossbred breeds are very similar in type and geographic location and so may be related to the Norwegian Lundehund by some degree. However, the Norse Kennel Club replies, "One might argue that we are in fact reintroducing lost genetic variance, as opposed to introducing new breeds."[33] The first litter of the project was born on the 12th of August 2014, between a Buhund female named Tyri and a Norwegian Lundehund male named Casper. It appears that at the beginning of 2017, second generation puppies have now arrived.[34]

Томасина [CC BY-SA 3.0 (https:// www.creativecommons.org/licenses/by-sa/3.0)]

Irish Red and White Setter Outcross Programme – http://www.jbuiten.nl/Ierse_setter/Eindversie%20thesis%20Ierse%20Setter%2 0-%20Iris%20van%20den%20Broek-1.pdf

In a June 2017 Bachelor's thesis conducted by undergraduate Iris van den Broek working under the tutelage of professor Jack Windig from Wageningen University, it was determined that the lesser known Irish Red and White Setter breed does not have enough of a population size to keep from significantly increasing the already elevated breed-wide inbreeding coefficient (19%). Several hypothetical analyses were completed over an imagined one hundred year timeframe to determine the best course of action for the breed. It was ultimately determined that systematically introducing Irish Red Setter crosses into the Irish Red and White Setter breed would not only keep breed-wide inbreeding coefficients from rising exponentially, but would also aid in diversifying the genetic make-up of the breed without straying too far from the breed standards in temperament and conformation.[35]

The Irish Red and White Setter Outcross Programme produced two cross litters in Norway in 2018. "We are motivated to do an outcross because we see the need for new genetic input if the irws [Irish Red and White Setter] are to achieve success for generations to come as a healthy working dog."[36]

145

The Irish Kennel Club fully supports the Irish Red and White Setter outcross program stating, "The Irish Kennel Club has primary responsibility for the well being [sic] health and future of it's [sic] native breeds and takes seriously its responsibility in securing the future of the Irish Red & White Setter in keeping with its proud heritage. It is the expectation of the Irish Kennel Club and also of the Irish Red & White Setter Club that only a small number of breeders nationally and internationally will participate. The programme is sensibly open-ended, not with the objective of stringing the programme out ad infinitum, but to ascertain degree of interest, uptake, outcome, success of outcrosses, and to allow time to determine when and if the objectives of the programme have been achieved."[37] Along with a full set of requirements and procedures for the mating of any outcross dogs, the future of this rare breed looks to be much more secure.

Wetterhoun
23dingenvoormusea [CC BY 3.0
(https://www.creativecommons.org/licenses/by/3.0)]

<u>Wetterhoun Outcross Breeding</u>
- https://www.nvsw.nl/index.php?sp=110

In February 2012, a geneticist and breeding specialist, Ed. J. Gubbels, wrote a comprehensive article entitled, Conservation of the Wetterhoun. In his forthright review, he noted the exceptional and unique qualities of the Wetterhoun in both temperament and conformation, but also called for an expansion of the small gene pool within the breed.[38]
Perhaps in response to Gubbels's writing, a 2012 study conducted within the Wetterhoun breed from 2005 - 2011, showed that 249 mating attempts were reported from 78 males and 183 females resulting in successful litters only 47% of the time. Males attempted mating on average 2.25 times before a successful

litter was experienced and many times males simply did not seem interested in mating at all. This equated to 116 litters in 7 years, or on average 16.57 litters a year.[39] These statistics greatly worried the Wetterhoun breed club in Norway, but the members were split on how to respond. Many breeders' councils were completely opposed to bringing in foreign blood. Some wanted to start with look-a-like crosses. While others petitioned for breeding to completely different breeds.

By March 2012, at the Extraordinary General Member's Meeting, an outcross breeding policy was adopted with a 77 to 44 vote majority. As agreeing member Marjolein Roosendaal explained, "For years there were more and more problems in the breeding of Wetterhoun. Bitches that remained empty, males that did not cover, or did not bother. Immunity problems, heart problems and also some other issues, all of which have repercussions on the health of the breed. The average age drops, and that is a bad sign. Given that there are only around a thousand animals of this beautiful Frisian breed worldwide, it is inevitable that the people who breed these dogs do so by inbreeding. In a closed breed dog population, especially when there are so few animals, there is always inbreeding. That in the long run such a thing has negative consequences is now known. That is why the breed club set up a plan to do something about this after intensive research in collaboration with the universities of Utrecht and Wageningen and with the cooperation of the Rare Pets foundation."[40]

After an extensive review of the genetics behind several different potential outcross breeds at a general meeting in April 2014, the breed club for the Wetterhoun chose to approve the following breeds in their outcross program: Barbet, standard Poodle, Portuguese Water Dog, and Labrador Retriever. They later approved the inclusion of the Sukoku and Airdale Terrier as well. Since that time, the Labrador Retriever, the standard Poodle, and the Airdale Terrier have been established as new outcross lines within the Wetterhoun breed. In 2015, a region-wide search for look-a-like dogs, regardless of breed or mix, was begun with plans to include several of these dogs into the outcross project as well.

Outbreeding Depression

Outbreeding depression is not as widely thought of as inbreeding depression is, but there is a well-documented negative effect of outbreeding that causes a loss of reproductive fitness within a population. Outbreeding depression is defined as the loss of fitness of the offspring resulting from the mating of two dissimilar parents. The most basic example of outbreeding depression can be illustrated by the mule. When a horse and donkey are bred, the resulting offspring, the mule, is sterile and cannot further produce. The complete lack of ability to reproduce is an extreme example of decreased reproductive fitness within a population. This is because without the ability to continually produce offspring, the future of the population can only be extinction.

But the fitness levels in a population can vary depending on the severity of the consequences relating to outbreeding depression. In the Tatra Mountains, the introduction of ibex from the Middle East resulted in hybrids which produced calves at the coldest time of the years.[41] When this occurred, the calves were much more likely to perish as a result of the frosty weather; therefore, the overall fitness of the population declined.

Also, when a rare species suddenly experiences a large dose of outbreeding, the uniqueness of the original species can be lost or masked by the newly introduced population. "Dingos may be wild animals, but they are still dogs and will interbreed with domestic ones. As many as 75% of Dingos in the southeastern forests are now crossbred with domestic dogs. The dingo, isolated in Australia for about 4,000 years became a distinctive subspecies. It is now in danger of being crossbred out of existence."[42]

This experience, especially within endangered populations, is also a reduction in the overall fitness. Over-outbreeding happens both in the wild when a small population size has no other choice but to breed outside of their own strain or race, but it can also occur within domestic populations when humans over-manage endangered animal populations by introducing too many outbred lines at one time. "Many rare species of plants, almond fish and canids are threatened with being 'hybridized out of existence' by crossing with common species. Molecular genetic analyses have shown that critically endangered Ethiopian wolf [simian jackal] is subject to hybridization with local domestic dogs."[43]

The well-established phenomenon of hybrid vigor in the first generation can, in some circumstances, be strong enough to mask the effects of outbreeding depression. A perfect example is when plant breeders create first generation hybrids from purebred strains in order to significantly improve the uniformity and vigor of the offspring. These first generations are then not used for further breeding because of unpredictable phenotypes in their offspring. Unless there is strong selective pressure, outbreeding depression can increase in further generations as co-adapted gene complexes are broken apart without the forging of new co-adapted gene complexes to take their place.

Outbreeding Depression in the American Alsatian Dog

Unbeknownst to Lois, a hidden layer of health concerns lie just underneath that beautiful healthy, giant exterior that Rainier exhibited, including: two copies of the gene for Canine Multifocal Retinopathy (CMR1), double jointed knees in the back legs and innocent heart murmurs. Mount Rainier's first generation puppies were also afraid of heights and had weak stomachs when traveling in the car. All of these aspects brought a reduction in fitness to the breed within this line.

In the subsequent second generation from the original M'loot Alaskan Malamute addition, all but one of the puppies showed an impaired ability to stand at three weeks old. Once they began walking, they initially wobbled and teetered. Each of the puppies were placed in homes that clearly understood the condition and were monitored throughout their lives. The puppies from this litter were seen to be much more prone to joint bruising when any over-exercise occurred prior to achieving their final size. Many puppies easily reached adult weights of 150 pounds or more.

Second Generation (f2) American Alsatian pups (Hammer/Blossom)

Instead of eliminating the new crossbred line from the breed, thereby, also eliminating any increased genetic diversity that occurred, Lois utilized strong selective criteria to significantly reduce the negative aspects that Rainier brought to the breed. This naturally resulted in a lower genetic diversity benefit than had been anticipated. This realization then prompted the need for other distinct crossbred lines to enter the breed's ranks. Each of these crossbreeds were brought into the breed to secure a greater genetic diversity, and increase traits lacking for future progress toward the breed's ultimate health, temperament and appearance goals. The crossbreeds selected for inclusion into the breed were: Irish Wolfhound, German Shepherd Dog, Labrador Retriever, Anatolian/Great Pyrenees, English Mastiff, and another giant Alaskan Malamute. Each new crossbred line initially required differing degrees of selection in order to eliminate introduced health issues, unwanted temperament behaviors, and unneeded appearance traits. The breed is now entering the third and fourth generations from these most recent crossbreeds and is working to keep as much of the increased genetic diversity as possible while also selecting for the desired traits important to the breed.

In our modern age, outcrossing and crossbreeding are all the rage and the real downside to breeding crosses of any type is rarely talked about or shown. Fortunately, all of these issues from Mount Rainier were immediately targeted and bred out. Within a few generations most of these concerns were never seen again from this line, except CMR1 which still remains carried in a few breeding dogs. It is being monitored and will be bred out within the next two years. Indeed, outbreeding depression is real and if one means to improve a breed through outbreeding, it is important to do so with clarity, understanding, and diligent ability to weed out any ill effects of the outcross as soon and as carefully as possible. But, just because outbreeding can be messy at times, it does not mean that it should never be performed. There are important benefits to outbreeding that should not be ignored, especially for the more inbred purebred dog populations.

Maintaining Genetic Diversity without Losing a Breed's Uniqueness

The initial diversity carried within the ancient wolves that began the rising inflation of the entirety of the domesticated dog population on this planet is hidden within every dog in every breed throughout the entire world. A piece of the puzzle that made up those tamer wolves that attracted our kind to theirs remains in each domesticated dog alive today. Overtime, populations of animals held in isolation lose diversity as a direct result of selection pressures. Offspring can carry only half of each parent's genes. Unless a pair of animals produces enough offspring to carry every single scrap of genetic material that resided in the parents and all of the offspring go on to mate and raise young of their own, diversity will inevitably decrease over time. With smaller populations, this process occurs at a much more rapid pace due to the need for inbreeding. Without occasionally crossbreeding to replace the decline in genetic diversity that naturally arises when breeding individual dog breeds, only a decrease in diversity will result.

But, also, one cannot continually outbreed or crossbreed for eternity. For if one does, the original integrity of the breed is quickly lost. Both inbreeding (decreasing diversity) and outbreeding (increasing diversity) are needed to keep the balance scale from tipping too far to one side or the other. This ebb and flow between inbreeding and outbreeding naturally insures the long-term survival of a thriving healthy, long-lived dog breed. We will clearly describe this process in our next chapter presenting a better way forward. Neither purebred nor crossbred, but strongbred.

Lotus (Grinch/Shennara) 2019

Chapter 8
The Strongbred Dog

The twenty-fifth of May is such a great day for a teacher. The classroom is empty and clean. The mountain of paperwork is put away neatly in file cabinets. The summer beckons, just minutes away. I flicked off the florescent lights and closed and locked the heavy classroom door, peering one last time through the double glassed window slit for a swift, but silent, good-bye to another year. I briefly paused to reflect on the last six years I spent teaching and advocating for children with special needs. It was not always easy, but it was always rewarding. As I turned away from the now lifeless room, my eyes brightened and my spirits lifted. The last feeling of obligation left me as I handed my classroom keys to the school secretary. The sun was bright in the sky as I pulled away from the parking lot where only one or two more cars remained representing a few colleagues still making their final preparations. I had almost three months of open-ended, do-whatever-I-wanted, days ahead of me. Oh, the feeling of freedom for a teacher that comes on the twenty-fifth of May!

The first day of summer holds so much promise. The air is pregnant with many thoughts of the activities that can shape each unrestricted day. Finally cleaning out the attic space, planning the summer reads, and doing some hiking and dog training filled my head. But, the number one anticipated project I had in mind for the summer of 2010 was to complete the National American Alsatian Breeder's Association (NAABA) website. I know it is not the first thought that comes to mind when one thinks of a teacher's summer pleasures, but I enjoy planning out pages and researching the information that will fill the contents of an American Alsatian website. I like organizing the structure of how one navigates through the pages and this particular website would surely prove to be a fun project to complete.

As I sat with my laptop on the back porch swing in the backyard of our Colorado mountain cabin, the cool breezes accompanying the end of spring gently brushed my face and my entire body relaxed. I could hear the soft noises of the dogs quietly wrestling in the grass near the back fence and the squirrels rustling in the branches as they ran from limb to limb and tree to tree. A perfect day lie ahead.

As I began the research for the NAABA website, I came across some new information regarding one of my favorite new breeds to track, the Tamaskan Dog. This breed had begun four years prior and in this short amount of time, they now had three breeders in the United States, others in Europe, and more developing in Canada. The seemingly instant success of their breed's endeavors sent my mind reeling, especially since I felt strongly that many parts of the story behind the breed at this time were purposely shrouded in mystery and mistruth. I read on and found that the goal for this new breed was eventually to secure purebred status within the American Kennel Club. I recalled the many times Lois had cautioned me that the American Alsatian dog breed should never seek to secure AKC purebred status as she did not feel this prestigious, world-renowned all breed dog showing club had the best interest of the American Alsatian dog at heart. But, even though her words echoed in my mind, I still could not help but feel insecure about the slow progress of our breed in comparison to the swift advances of this new one.

My mind then leaped to the Shiloh Shepherd dog, created by Tina Barber around the same time that Lois began developing her breed. They had obtained recognition from the American Rare Breed Association in 1991. The Shiloh Shepherd had multiple breeders around the United States and this dog breed was a known household name. "What is taking so long with the American Alsatian dog breed?" I asked myself with a growing feeling of insecurity. "Surely, we should be more well-known by now. Perhaps if we could find a group that would allow us to keep our own registry, but provide the public venue for the American Alsatian dog to be judged, we would grow at a faster rate." I continued to research, now fully distracted from completing the NAABA website.

My fingers flew over the keyboard as I searched through different registries and read through their rules and codes of ethics. Nothing fit. We had strict temperament testing embedded into the judgment system of our breed. No one else allowed that. We wanted to keep control of registering our own dogs. No one else allowed that. We did not want to enter beauty shows to be judged by those who were not part of our breed. No one even addressed that. Each dog group I sifted through mimicked the AKC's rules and regulations in many ways, except one. My hands froze over the keyboard as I clicked over to a newly formed group, the North American Kennel Club (NAKC). This group did not want to register dogs, only show them. I wondered if they would allow us to add temperament testing when judging the best specimens within our breed.

"Ignorance is bliss", I suppose. Or "naivety is the sister of innocence and the cousin of stupid," might be a better way to describe my next actions. In the freshness of the late spring morning with the fullness of the summer ahead, I wrote an email to the president of the North American Kennel Club, John Seibel, NAKC founder, breeder, and judge for over 25 years. A lengthy email.

To Whom It May Concern:

I am the current president of the National American Alsatian Club. The American Alsatian is a rare breed of large companion dog founded in the US in 1988. I was surprised to read that the NAKC is not a registry, but deals with conformation shows only. Our breed club has always shied away from any all-breed shows or registries as we did not wish to bring our breed into the political show ring scene. As a result, we persist in registering our own dogs through the National American Alsatian Registry and will continue to do so well into the future. We have also shown our own dogs through these 22 years as it is our club members who have been the most knowledgeable about our breed. However, after reviewing your website and reading your rules and regulations, our small club is intrigued with the possibility of a recognized rare breed dog showing club without the registry attached. I realize the NAKC would need to approve our breed for admission first, but please allow me to ask a few questions which will help our club decide if we can even consider joining in your noble cause.

1. First of all, would the National American Alsatian Registry be accepted as an approved registry by the NAKC? The NAAR has been in existence since 1988 and maintained by our founder, Lois Schwarz. However, we have never (and will probably never) go to any all-breed registry. We feel strongly that our breed remain in the hands of its members.

2. If our registry cannot be accepted, what would be needed to allow our breed to become a part of the NAKC dog showing community?

3. If the NAKC could possibly approve our registry, who would judge our breed's dogs? Could we, knowledgeable members, judge our own dogs or train judges to judge our dogs appropriately? Our breed has certain requirements that go beyond AKC rules for judging conformation. Our judging guidelines and rules would need to remain intact.

4. Our breed is solely a companion dog in nature. Because all other large dogs are working dogs by history, we needed to define the nature of a large companion dog as there wasn't a clear definition before. Our club has created strict standards and temperament guidelines for what a large companion dog breed should possess. This companion temperament is THE MOST cherished trait within our dogs. How would (or even could) the NAKC be able to judge for this over conformation?

5. If we found that NAKC judges were not placing the correct dogs according to our standards for both conformation and temperament, could we retain the right to leave the NAKC? In other words, what rights do we have as a breed club to protect the integrity of our breed's standards and ultimately our breed?

6. Would we, the NAAC and NAAR, retain all rights to our American Alsatian standards and the American Alsatian name?

We do not mind continuing on our current path of slow growth as we do not want our breed to turn into something is was never intended to be. We also do not mind that our breed is not "recognized" by any other registry but our own. But, we are limited in our ability to provide a venue for dog showing and our members live all over the US and Canada. It would be an added benefit for us to be able to have third party shows as well as many more opportunities for showing events. This may not be the way for us, but we wanted to look into it as an option. Of course, if the NAKC was willing to work with our needs, our breed club would have to be willing to vote to accept this major change in the way we recognized the best of our breed.

I applaud the founders of the NAKC for having the courage to stand up to the political and highly expensive all breed registries. The NAAC and NAAR also cherish family and the idea that it is the <u>dog</u> that wins in the ring, not the dog's pedigree, handler, owner or price.

With all sincerity,
Jennifer Stoeckl, MAT
NAAC President

I hesitated only slightly before pressing send. I probably should have thought this one through a little bit more, but, John Seibel's reply was kind and straightforward and he let me down relatively easy. He suggested that temperament testing in which one produces a startling loud noise would never be allowed in a public arena. Also, he felt that it was impossible for a large breed of dog to be shown as a companion dog. He described how a breed's standards were strictly for how the ideal dog should look and not how one should act. Lastly, he politely disagreed with judges being a part of the breed itself, citing a conflict of interest.

The NAKC president's willingness to take the time to explain his reasoning in a compassionate way made it that much more difficult to swallow. My head sank and a shutter of realization overcame me. I had to accept that the strong beliefs behind the Dire Wolf Project breeding practices and the reasons for what makes us who we are just simply did not fit with any other mainstream establishment. Even though I knew to my very core that temperament testing young puppies was essential to maintain consistency in the truly inherited aspects of a dog's temperament, when a rejection happened from one who has a lot of experience in dogs, even if that person is kind and thoughtful, it still stings. Even though I could see the harm that occurs in a dog breed when judges who do not stick to the standards place the wrong dogs as winners, it still took a small piece from my soul to know that very few others saw it the same way. Even though I knew the value of specifically defining the inherited temperament of a companion dog and that size should not dictate what inherited temperament could be expressed since all dogs belong to the same species, a defeated lonely feeling still permeated through my bones. Even though I understood that temperament was more important than outward appearance, an empty feeling still clung to me when I realized I had to go it alone and almost single-handedly invent the future of the American Alsatian breed from here.

With a heart more broken from a feeling of loneliness than from being rejected, I picked up the cell phone lying on the table next to me and called Lois. She sympathized with me and reminded me that she had been all alone from the very beginning and knew how I was feeling in this moment. We talked for some time about purebred dogs and how many purists could not seem to climb out of their tattered and patched-up box full of arbitrary rules and regulations. We talked a bit more about crossbred dogs and how it took guts to breed generationally, whereas breeding one dog breed to another dog breed simply amounted to riding on the backs of those who came before. Her soothing acknowledgement of what I was going through gave me some hope.

Then it occurred to me. We should not allow others to define what we are. Lois has always stood on her own convictions. Why should I feel the breed could only progress if it eventually conformed? No, we would not conform. We would bring the world something knew, even if no one else stood with us. Even if it took us longer than anyone expected. It was never about notoriety or recognition anyway. It was only about giving the world a beautiful dog that fit a modern lifestyle and did not require a lot of money to maintain health or behavior. I hung up the phone a little more ready to face the world and spent the rest of the day thinking about all the years Lois had endured chasing after this idea all on her own. She had kept an amazing secret throughout this time that I greatly admired.

A Square Peg in a Round Hole

From the very beginning, Lois always intended to design a large breed of dog that could fit easily within modern city life. In her initial research, none of the large purebred dog breeds already in existence exactly fit what owners told her they wanted. It had always been Lois's strong belief that preserving the original integrity of each purebred dog should be the focus of each breed club dedicated to that purpose. As a particularly relevant example, she fundamentally disagreed with breeding mellow, easy-going, non-working German Shepherd Dogs because this breed was specifically created as a high-drive herding and protection dog. So, instead of breeding for traits within a purebred dog that did not fit the standards for which it had been created, she chose, instead, to begin a new breed of dog.

Climbing onto the bandwagon of the designer dog movement, Lois initially sold her first generation puppies as North American Shepalutes - a portmanteau word combining shepherd and malamute. This crossbred combination was hugely popular at the time she began her breed and the Shepalute was featured in the local newspaper, Ventura County Star Free Press's Vista Magazine, and TV news, which brought her new breed some initial notoriety. But, she ultimately knew that her breed was destined for something more.

Once her dogs began to breed true to type in 2005, Lois sought to encourage her new breed's development and advancement as an internationally recognized purebred dog, but her definition of purebred never fit with the overall world view. Instead of defining a purebred dog as simply one with unmixed (pure) decent, she defined a purebred dog as any dog that bred true to type, regardless of ancestry. Another way to understand it is that Lois defined a dog with specifically bred homozygous traits as pure and a dog exhibiting primarily heterozygous traits as not pure. This greatly conflicted with many all-breed dog registries' definitions, which she ultimately could not reconcile. At the same time, she could not conceive of limiting the gene pool indefinitely by permanently closing her stud book and no longer ever allowing crossbreeding to diversify the breed should it need. A new style of breeding continued to take shape in her mind.

Around the year 2006, Lois decidedly realized that her breeding philosophy simply did not agree with what she perceived as an outdated, archaic, and aristocratic idea of what creates a dog breed. But, neither did her breeding philosophy exactly match with the newly identified crossbred dog movement. Although she did not have any issue with breeding crossbred dogs, her ultimate intention was always to produce a dog breed that held to a consistent type in health, temperament and appearance (in that order). Large breed crossbred dogs still held many of the founding dog breed's original working traits, which did not match her desires for a mellow, loving, devoted, easy to train large breed family companion dog. She wanted to fundamentally and selectively alter these established working traits over time to eventually achieve an entirely new and unique companion dog temperament that molded exactly with the needs of our modern lives. Her square peg did not fit in any of the round holes that were available. She simply could not force herself to conform when she knew that both the purebred and the crossbred held a necessary piece to the puzzle of sustaining the long term health and longevity in a uniform dog breed. Therefore, in order to separate her dog breed from both the purebred and crossbred dog breeding circles, in February 2010 she dropped the designer dog connotation that came with the word Shepalute and renamed the breed American Alsatian.

It was not until I faced the world head on by reaching out to the North American Kennel Club in 2010 that Lois's idea finally made complete sense. Just like Lois before me, I, too, now realized that this breed would never fit with the idea of a purebred and was much more than simply a crossbred. We had to find a different way. As I sat back in my porch swing letting the sweet smell of rising sap permeate my senses, a new thought bubbled to the surface of my mind. Lois had been working this entire time to create a healthy, long-lived dog breed with a specific sweet and mellow temperament that would be able to be easily maintained in our modern lives. But, she wanted to do so without severely limiting her gene pool eventually succumbing to a high breed-wide inbreeding dead-end that inevitably results when stud books permanently close. She also reached for a higher ideal of maintaining breed-wide genetic diversity for improved overall health and increased longevity. That way of breeding would produce true strength of health, I thought. My eyes suddenly flew open and I sat straight up pressing my feet firmly to the ground. It was not pure breeding. It was not mixed breeding. It was strong breeding.

Not Pure Breeding, Not Cross Breeding

As we explored in the chapter on crossbreeding, many purebred dog breeders have begun to realize that the only way forward for many highly inbred breeds is to open the stud book to allow periodic and systematic crossbreeding for the renewed health of their dogs. However, it is still a very new and controversial idea for most purebred dog breed enthusiasts. As more and more people have begun to realize that strict purebred dog breeding has its limitations for long term breed sustainability, different types of breeding philosophies have sprung up over the last half a century. Each of these new breeding philosophies hopes to improve upon the original idea of breeding for purity to sustain the integrity of form and function within a dog breed. These new breeding programs recognize that without adding genetic diversity to the lines by periodically crossing with other unrelated breeds, purebred dogs as we have known them may soon become a thing of the past as devastatingly crippling diseases and genetic brick walls stop many of our beloved breeds from moving forward. The steadfast reluctance of purists within the purebred dog breeding scene to demolish the very limiting practice of pure breeding is the very reason why Lois Schwarz created a new way of breeding in 1988 that describes a new type of dog breed.

At the same time, crossbreeding, left unchecked, can have a devastating effect on the long term maintenance of recognizable breeds that are specifically maintained to perfectly perform the duties for which they were originally created. Unbridled crossbreeding can lead to outbreeding depression effects and the ultimate destruction of our most beloved purebred dog breeds. Not only can extensive use of outbreeding completely eliminate any semblance of the population one hopes to conserve, but outbreeding can also introduce unwanted traits that reduce the overall fitness of the breed. For these reasons, responsible inbreeding must be maintained as a viable solution to secure the integrity of a breed. Without it, as we have seen, no breed can survive for long. Inbreeding and maintaining a sustainable population size are also part of the picture for healthy, long-lived dogs.

The Ebb and Flow Breeding Model

The Dire Wolf Project calls this balance between inbreeding and outbreeding the Ebb and Flow Breeding Model. Just like the constant back and forth flow of the tide as it drains away and rises again, a natural, gentle rhythm between inbreeding and outbreeding is required to sustain a thriving population among any animal species. Most of the time, the natural balance between the two breeding properties is gentle and calm without much shift between the two, but when a population suddenly decreases in size due to a catastrophe or unintended isolating event, the pounding rhythm of the waves can become threatening and violent until the storm passes and the species can once again settle into a normal routine. Whatever the case, an equilibrium must always be maintained in order for a species to continue to exist. If the ebb never eventually returns to flow back and ebb again, then the cycle of life will have ended for that species. In other words, extinction is inevitable when either inbreeding or outbreeding is lost.

As the authors of the Livestock Conservancy suggest, "The genetic health of a breed benefits if some breeders are linebreeding and others are linecrossing."[1] Assigning certain breeders to inbreed (linebreed) and outbreed (linecross) ensures that the ebb and flow between your breed will continue. With enough population size and genetic diversity among the breed, this shift between inbreeding and outbreeding can be minimal, striving to keep the inbreeding average for the entire population as low as possible to stave off any inbreeding depression symptoms without compromising on the breed's unique form and function. "Avoiding the inevitability of inbreeding (and the likely depression it brings) can be accomplished by outcrossing occasionally to unrelated animals."[2] The Livestock Conservancy adds. But, if the population dips significantly for any reason or the breed becomes isolated without the opportunity to bring in outcross or close crossbred types, then a larger degree of inbreeding and outbreeding will be necessary until the population returns to a manageable level. In this latter case, high inbreeding levels can rise like a large swell of water and the diversity of a particular cross can crash vigorously onto the shore. Strong selective pressure with a widening population boom will need to occur to achieve equilibrium within the breed once again.

A perfect example of a comeback from extinction using the Ebb and Flow Breeding Model is the story of the Black and White Java Chickens. Black and White Java chickens were hybrids developed by American poultry farmers early in the 19th Century from chickens that once roamed wild in tropical jungles of Southeast Asia. White Javas never became very popular and were seldom seen outside specialty-breed poultry shows. The last flock died out around 1950. Black Javas, however, were one of the most popular and commonly found farmyard chickens through much of the 1800s. Their population began to decline steadily as the large commercial egg and chicken production began to take over the local family farm. Now, however, the commercial chicken is highly inbred; significantly selected for higher egg yield and early maturity for meat production. As a result, the hardy, old stock Black Java Chicken's population dropped to 250 Black Java Chickens worldwide in 1999.

The Garfield Farm Museum in Illinois has been dedicated to reconstituting and preserving this by-gone breed for years, even though there is no commercial value to do so. The museum members understood that with each rare chicken breed that goes extinct, valuable genetic diversity is lost. The genetics that sustain the hardiness that is lacking in the commercial chicken breeds can be a very valuable commodity if anything were to devastate the less environmentally fit inbred strains. Robert Hawes, a University of Maine emeritus professor of poultry science and a leading proponent of maintaining small populations of rare breeds of farm animals as banks of genetic diversity explains, "'There is always the danger that, if we rely on just one variety of any animal in a given market, it may have genetic predisposition to a disease that could wipe out most of the population in one sudden spasm,'"[3]

To combat the loss of genetic diversity in the inbred commercial chicken, the Garfield Farm Museum continues to preserve the lessor known variety of Black Java Chicken. One particular year at the museum, a few off-colored chicks hatched among the black ones. At first no one thought anything about the odd coloration, but it turned out that these two slate-gray colored chicks showed the highly recessive White Java Chicken genes that geneticists thought had gone extinct over fifty years ago. It turns out that the mathematical odds of this color appearing had not even been calculated, but Jerome Johnson, Garfield Farm Museum's director, estimated it to be around one percent. It was later determined that two of the Black Java parents had kept the recessive genes through their ancestry over many generations without anyone's knowledge.

The Science and Industry hatchery became interested in helping the Garfield Farm Museum with their preservation project and the Black and White Java Chicken population again began to rise. Although this strain of chicken remains somewhat obscure, the very act of keeping the Black and now White Java chicken from going extinct will be extremely valuable as a crossbreed if the continued inbreeding of the larger commercial chicken becomes compromised. Inbreeding results in a decrease in diversity, while outbreeding results in increased diversity. If these two opposites are used carefully and consistently, a stable degree of diversity arises. Like the duel necessity of yin and yang, this story illustrates the very important aspects of both inbreeding and outbreeding for breed sustainability.

The Purebred Dog Breeding Model

Today, there is much controversy surrounding the purebred dog concept. With the advent of the widely viewed BBC One investigative video, "Pedigree Dogs Exposed," produced and narrated by Jemima Harrison in 2008, the public at large was able to peer into the inner workings of the highly prized world of the purebred dog. After the program aired, the Kennel Club (KC) in the United Kingdom received severe criticism and various sponsors and trade exhibitors withdrew their support. After forty years of coverage, the large public outcry spurred the BBC to decline to air the top winning KC event for 2009, Crufts, on their network. An agreement could not be reached between the Kennel Club and the BBC, so[4] Crufts is now televised on commercial channel More4 with over 4.5 million viewers.[5] Also, three separate health reports were commissioned as a result of the program. Reports by the Royal Society for the Prevention of Cruelty to Animals, Associate Parliamentary Group for Animal Welfare and Sir Patrick Bateson (funded by the KC and Dogs Trust) concluded that current breeding practices are detrimental to the welfare of pedigree dogs and made various recommendations to improve purebred dog health. Since this time, many more health reports have been completed.[6] The KC's own chairman, Ronnie Irving, noted his thoughts on the Pedigree Dogs Exposed video in his Welsh Kennel Club speech in 2007, "If this programme [Pedigree Dogs Exposed] teaches us anything, I hope it will teach the 'purists' in some breeds that they simply must get a move on and realise that in these politically correct and well informed days, some old attitudes are simply no longer sustainable."[7]

<u>Purebred Dog Definition:</u>
A purebred dog refers to a dog of a modern breed with a documented pedigree in a primarily closed stud book that is registered with one or more breed clubs and may also be part of one or more registries for the purposes of preserving the purity of the breed in both type and function.
The AKC defines a purebred dog as a dog whose sire and dam belong to the same breed and who are themselves of unmixed descent since the recognition of the breed.[8]

The Merriam-Webster dictionary defines a purebred dog as one that is bred from members of a recognized breed, strain, or kind without admixture of other blood over many generations.

<u>A Closed Studbook</u>
Most purebred dog breeders and active club members believe that no outside breeds of any kind should be allowed to enter a purebred breed. As we discussed in the crossbreeding chapter, there are a few breeds that have successfully received permission from their kennel clubs to include crossbreeds into the official ranks of their breed, but for the vast majority of dog breeds this is not possible, and frankly not desired. With a popular dog breed that houses breeding specimens all over the world and many maintain a large variety of differentiated inbred/linebred lines with which to outbreed, a closed studbook does not yet threaten this diverse, but isolated, population. However, not all purebred dog breeds have this privilege. Many rare and endangered breeds are only restricted further by this confining practice, especially if these breeds also experience increased levels of ill health.

<u>One or More Breed Clubs/Registries</u>
The Chinook is a perfect example of what occurs when a purebred dog breed's genetics become broken up by an arbitrary boundary imposed by maintaining a breed in two separate breed clubs and two different registries over a sustained period of time. The Chinook Owners Association is the UKC's (United Kennel Club) official parent club for the Chinook breed and was entered into UKC official breed status in 1991. The Chinook Club of America is the AKC's (American Kennel Club) official parent club and was first entered

into the AKC's Foundation Stock Service ten years later in 2001. This would not be such a problem except the UKC allows significant, albeit highly regulated, crossbreeding through an open studbook, while the AKC maintains a closed studbook for the Chinook breed. Fortunately, the AKC continues to accept UKC registration for the Chinook breed until the year 2023.[9]

Think of the repercussions a duel breed club with different agendas and separate standards has on the integrity of the breed as a whole. Not only that, but when AKC closes the studbook and effectively eliminates all of the related dogs that have not been registered with AKC, genetic diversity is greatly diminished. With one breed club dedicated to increasing genetic diversity by including crossbreeds and the other promoting only a strict adherence to a separate standard, how long will it be before the two Chinook groups permanently part ways and the diversity among them grows larger and larger?

If the Chinook Owners Association and the Chinook Club of America were smart, they would marry their separate ideas for the benefit of the breed's diverse population over the longterm. It was a great idea to allow crossbreeding within this rare breed to increase its genetic diversity [UKC]. It was also a good idea to have separate group maintain breed type by adherence to a standard [AKC]. Both breeding concepts are beneficial to breed maintenance, but the eventual permanent separation means one group maintains the ebb and the other maintains the flow. "However, until the Chinook is granted full recognition by the AKC, the UKC will remain the breed's primary registry. It also remains to be seen what impact AKC registration will have on the cross-breeding program." explains an EasyPetMD article on the Chinook breed.[10] Since 2013, the Chinook Club of America can now proudly proclaim its full recognition to the AKC. "[A]s of January, 2013, when Chinooks were fully recognized by AKC, there were 813 Chinooks registered."[11]

Now that the Chinook is fully registered with the AKC, it remains to be seen how the two different breed clubs maintained by two separate registries handles the split when AKC finally closes its door to any more registrations from the UKC.[12]

UKC	AKC
Chinook Standards - Coat Faults: Long, <u>soft</u>, or thin coat. <u>Lack of double coat in cold climate.</u> Unprotected belly and groin.	Chinook Standards - Coat Faults: Thin, <u>sparse</u>, or <u>excessively short</u> coat, long, <u>rough</u>, or shaggy coat, unprotected belly and/or groin.

The differences in the two standards have been underlined.

The UKC and AKC Chinook standards and visual depictions might not be extremely different from one another at this time, but it has only been eighteen years since the breed clubs separated into two different all-breed registries and the AKC still continues to register Chinook from the UKC. However, over time, these small differences within multiple standards for the same breed make a huge difference.

Here is an example of the German Shepherd Dog maintained by two different registries over the course of at least a hundred years. Both have their own standard and their own ideas of what it means to adhere to their respective documents. Below are pictures of German Shepherd Dogs as they are celebrated by the breed clubs in which they are registered compared to a 1930 champion named Odin.

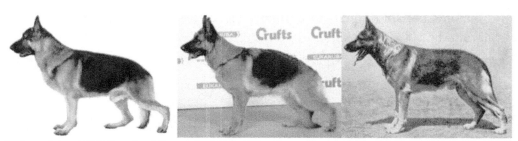

Left to right: AKC Standard Example 2019; KC - Crufts Best of Breed 2016; Odin 1930

In the AKC example, the pasterns are greatly angled, the straighter back is sloped with the back legs reaching way out behind, and the chest juts out considerably. In the KC example, the head is much smaller and the back is roached with a much more dramatic shift downward toward the tail. The back legs are equally as long and reaching, however. In Odin's example, the back legs do not reach as far back to attain a straight hock and the back is not as sloped. Also, the tail more naturally comes off of the top of the back instead of dramatically placed much lower in the more modern examples. Odin looks to be slightly smaller in size with a shallower chest.

The Crossbred (Designer) Dog Breeding Model

In our modern age, crossbred dog breeds have been heralded as generally healthier and more genetically diverse, which allows for an improved ability to manage general diseases and immune issues that might arise. Just as crossbred dogs are highly diverse in their genetics, they are also less predictable in temperament and appearance. Nonetheless, many people hope to capitalize on the good aspects, working with the diversity as they go along. Also, with the advent of the "adopt don't shop" message coupled with the idea that mixed breed dogs are generally healthier, many see shelter dogs as a worthy cause to celebrate.

Crossbred (Designer) Dog Definition:

A crossbred (designer) dog refers to a mixed breed originating from two modern breeds with a documented pedigree in a primarily open studbook that is not regulated by a breed club and is not intentionally bred toward a common standard, but bred instead to take advantage of hybrid vigor and/or increased genetic diversity.

Originating from two modern breeds with a documented pedigree

A crossbred (designer) dog comes from a cross between two purebred dogs. This is significant because the cross utilizes the benefits of the cluster breeding strategy as described in the inbreeding chapter. Two purebred breeds that have been separately maintained for over one hundred fifty years can yield the benefits of hybrid vigor, or heterosis, if both parent dogs are healthy. However, only the first generation of the initial cross receives the benefit from heterosis. Still, many designer dog breeds breed further into the generations.

167

Dire Wolf Project: Creating an Extraordinary Dog Breed

While this limits hybrid vigor, the offspring are still maintained as crossbred dogs when the originating parents are from two modern purebred dogs.

Not regulated by a breed club

A crossbred dog can be obtained from any match between a purebred male of one breed and a purebred female of another breed. There are many breed clubs out there willing to register such matches, but since a specific breed standard cannot generally be established due to the highly diverse range of offspring, it would be difficult for any registry to regulate the health, temperament or conformation aspects of such a cross.

No Common Standard

Because any crossbred dog can take on any number of diverse traits from each parent, a unifying standard is not able to be produced with the same specificity as can be reached in the purebred dog. The traits inherited from the two breeds can be highly diverse as they are mixed and matched depending on the generation from the original cross.

The Strongbred Dog

The strongbred dog marries the idea of sustaining breed consistency achieved through the idea of the purebred dog with the genetic diversity achieved from the idea of the crossbred dog. In an ebb and flow between:

1. breeding within the confines of the breed itself for consistency in form and function until the population of the breed no longer allows for continued maintenance without exponentially increasing inbreeding, thereby decreasing overall breed health within the breed and
2. breeding outside the confines of the breed for renewed genetic diversity at specific and calculated times when the breed requires it due to an inbreeding increase that can be shown to decrease overall breed health,

we can mimic nature's breeding strategy to sustain a vibrant population over time. As the Livestock Conservancy explains, "Breeds need to have enough variability to be healthy while at the same time having enough consistency to be predictable if they are to successfully function as viable populations as well as genetic resources. Only by balancing these two somewhat opposing forces is it possible to ensure that breeds can serve as viable genetic resources."[13]

Strongbred Dog Definition:

A strongbred dog refers to a dog of a modern breed with a documented pedigree in a permanently open studbook that is regulated by unified breed clubs in which all breeders intentionally breed toward a common standard of health, temperament, and sound conformation promoting the strength of the dog species as a whole.

A Permanently Open Studbook

American Alsatian dog breeders and active club members believe that there is strength in openly acknowledging and utilizing regular and specific crossbreeding at exact intervals that will enhance the breed as a whole in vitality, genetic diversity, and vigor. With this responsibility, we believe that crossbreeding should be highly regulated by the breed club as a whole and only introduced within the breed one crossbreed at a time. This then equates to a perpetually open studbook.

Documented Pedigree

American Alsatian dog breeders and active club members agree that a strongbred dog breed is one that has a recorded pedigree. These pedigrees should be openly kept for the general public and truthfully reported and recorded. Each dog documented should include several pictures and registration with the unified breed club. If any pedigree is found to be false, the breed club should perform the research needed to determine the correct lineage.

Regulated By Unified Breed Clubs

American Alsatian dog breeders and active club members agree that only by working together can positive and lasting change happen for the strength of the breed as a whole. All breeders of the American Alsatian dog are organized by a breeder's association that strictly regulates breeding practices based on solid research and evidence of a need for intervention within the breed toward better health, temperament and viable conformation. No breeder may stand alone without the support of the breeder's association and the breed club as a whole. The breed club then has a very important role in the continued development of the breed. All breeders producing puppies within the breed must adhere to these guidelines and play an active role in challenging their breeding practices in order to create a thriving population. A breeding association within a breed club should regularly collect health information, temperament testing results, and openly take an interest in the breed's conformation in order for the breed to perform the duties it was created to perform. The breed club maintains trademarks, certification marks, and service marks to protect their breed's name from ever being divided among other breed clubs.

Intentionally Bred

Each breeding should take place solely for the advancement of the breed toward its common goals in health, temperament and/or viable conformation. The intentionality is evident when breeders follow the guidelines laid out by the breeder's association within a breed club. The guidelines for breeding should be based on solid evidence and research within the breed as a whole to determine the best course of action for the breed at any given time. Again, the entire breed shares a common goal for which individual breeders take responsibility. Instead of breeding for their own kennel's needs, it is a shift in thinking of the entire breed's needs while still maintaining one's own contribution.

Common Standard

With unified breed clubs, there should also be only one common standard for the entire breed world-wide, which should include both temperament and sound conformation. It should be explicit and workable, detailing all of the most important aspects of the dog breed. Specific wording is the hallmark of a strongbred dog breed's standards, leaving little room for misinterpretation or judging based on the popular look of the day. Judges should adhere to these standards or be disciplined and barred from any further judging by the breed club. The American Alsatian dog also has many books and pamphlets from the founder which help correctly interpret the standard. The strongbred dog should not deviate from the original intent of the founder's ideals, lest one creates a completely unintended breed of dog and loses the original breed to the whims of human progress.

Health

American Alsatian dog breeders and active club members agree that health, above all, is the most important aspect of any dog breed. We must breed for health first, no matter the consequences. This is one reason why we allow regulated crossbreeding. But, we must also work toward a longer lifespan within the breed as a whole. Breeders should be rewarded for producing puppies that live longer than the average longevity of the breed. Within this health category, we also give our attention to a sound conformation. We never breed a conformation feature that decreases, or potentially decreases, the breed's overall health. This may include such conformation traits as cow hocks, excessively sloping back, roached back, patella luxation, albino, severe brachycephalic, etc.

Temperament

American Alsatian dog breeders and active club members agree that temperament standards should be added and adhered to in the official standards of the breed. Furthermore, temperament should be tested and scored according to each dog breed's temperament standards and no dog should go on to breed if its genetically inherited temperament is severely faulted. The overall temperament of the breed as a whole should be researched, recorded, openly reported and monitored. Breeding away from temperament faults within the breed should then be regulated according to the needs within the breed at any time.

Sound Conformation

American Alsatian dog breeders and active club members believe that conformation should reflect strength and vitality of the dog breed. Extreme conformation is frowned upon if the result is a dog breed that suffers in health or strength of character or movement. The dog breed should not require human intervention in order to procreate, give birth, walk, trot, run, see, breath, eat, drink, or regulate its bowels.

Strengthening Dogs as a Species

We believe it is the duty of every dog breeder to promote the overall strength and well-being of the dog as a species and not just single-mindedly focus on any one particular breed or specimen. Consistent with our ideals of a permanently open studbook, no breed can be considered in isolation. Rather it is our belief that every breeder must accept the grave responsibility of the role they play in the future of the species.

The Australian Labradoodle: Crossbred, Purebred, or Strongbred?

As we reviewed in the crossbreeding chapter, the Labradoodle began in Australia in 1988 with a first generation cross between a Labrador Retriever and a standard Poodle. In 2004, the Australian Labradoodle Club of America (ALAA) was formed and currently maintains breed-wide pedigree information with 234 certified breeders worldwide. The ALAA seeks "to lobby for international acceptance of the Labradoodle and Australian Labradoodle."[14] The association also works to educate breeders and owners, promote breeder integrity, and sustain and improve dog health.[15] The ALAA has established a breed standard for the Australian Labradoodle and currently registers all generations of Labradoodle, including purebred foundation stock, as long as the dogs seeking registration meet the stringent requirements in health and sufficiently known pedigree. Several certified breeders are now breeding fourth and fifth generation Australian Labradoodles as a result of the efforts of the ALAA. Because of these advancements within the Labradoodle breeding community as a whole, the Labradoodle no longer completely fits within the crossbred (designer) dog category.

6 Month Old Labradoodle
Source: Searctempo [CC BY-SA 3.0 (https://creativecommons.org/licenses/by-sa/3.0)]

Since the Australian Labradoodle breeder's association desires to consistently breed true to type, have their dogs adhere to a detailed standard, remain registered and maintained solely by one breed club, ALAA, the Australian Labradoodle has completely shifted from being a crossbreed to a different type of breed altogether. Not quite a purebred dog breed since it continues to allow regular crossbreeding, a few key elements will dictate whether this breed ultimately shifts toward the purebred or strongbred dog breed category in the years ahead. If the ALAA eventually decides to close their studbook and breed only among their own breed without any further admixture from any of the founding breeds, they will shift toward the idea of a purebred dog. If they continue to keep their studbook open to allow the founding purebred dogs to continue to enter the Labradoodle at strategic times of need within the population of the breed in order to periodically increase genetic diversity for the overall health of their breed, this will shift them into the realm of the strongbred dog category. As long as they keep a firm grasp on their breed's inherited temperament, are able to clearly define it and are able to strive to work toward it, then they will definitely be on the road to strongbred dog status. Keeping the integrity of the breed by remaining within their own breeder's association instead of striving to have the breed officially recognized by the FCI, AKC or other such all-breed registry will be an advantage for their breed toward a strongbred dog. If they do seek AKC, FCI, UKC, ARBA, etc registration, that will definitely pull them toward the purebred dog and out of the strongbred dog breed category. It will be interesting to watch this forming breed's growth in the coming years and ultimately what path they will choose.

Stable Instability

In order to organize a space, there must first be disorder. When one strives to be better than one was before, some pain must first accompany the growth. Through great trials come great joy. Throughout all of life there is a balance between opposing forces. The Chinese call this the yin and the yang. These concepts are not experienced as dichotomy, but instead they are forces residing within one another. In other words, one cannot exist without the other. Metastability is such a concept. In a definitional research study compiled by Armin Kibele, et. al. on the applications of human movement, we can see these necessary forces at work.

"Although stable instability may seem like an oxymoron, individuals are often in a state of flux, which allows them to transfer smoothly from relatively stable to relatively unstable conditions (change from stance to flight phase during running). Without some degree of instability, it would be impossible to move; however, without some degree of stability, it would be impossible to maintain equilibrium or to remain upright. Hence, a degree of stable instability or relative instability is aptly described by the term 'metastability'.

"Thus, the state of relatively stable or metastable equilibrium is defined as the state in which a system remains for a long period of time, and any slight disturbance causing the system to deviate from the metastable state does not result in the system passing into another state. As soon as the external disturbance is removed, the system will return into the initial metastable state."[16]

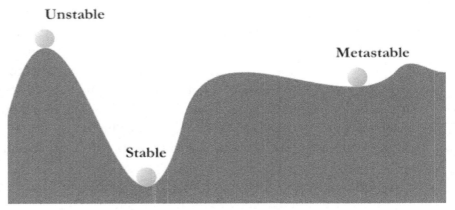

Inbreeding and outbreeding work in the same way as these examples. They do not cancel each other, but instead, they enhance one another. One cannot exist for long without the other. When they are used interchangeably in a balanced way, they stabilize a population over time. As the Livestock Conservancy notes, "Without pure breeds, crossbreeding quickly fails."[17] By focusing on a balanced approach to breeding dogs while working toward improved health and longevity, the strongbred dog is born.

With the advent of the strongbred dog there is a new way of looking at a dog breed. Where before we recognized purity through superior pedigree breeding, now we recognize strength through balanced pedigree breeding; a pedigree that reflects a healthy diversity as well as a stable conformity. Strong in health. Strong in lifespan. Strong in temperament consistency. Strong in ideals. Strong in persistence. Strong in integrity. Strong in standing up for what one knows is right, instead of conforming to what people of authority tell us should be. Standing strong against oppression and group think. Standing strong for individuality and innovation. With the advent of a well-defined, healthy, and sustainable way of breeding for the strength and viability of a dog breed, we can renew our commitment to the genetic health of our beloved pets.

Eleven Things Strongbred Breeders Know

1. Superior health and longevity can be accomplished in all dog breeds, without excuses for size. Therefore, all dogs can and should be bred for superior health and longevity before any other need.

2. Regular and systematic crossbreeding increases genetic diversity, improving overall breed health.

3. Thoughtful inbreeding is necessary to solidify traits common to a dog breed and to eliminate devastating genetic diseases.

4. Breeding for extreme looks is harmful to all dog breeds and should never be practiced or endorsed.

5. Dog breeds should be bred toward specific and thoroughly written standards and not altered to fit the ever-changing whims of human desire.

6. The responsible creation of new breeds of dogs that fit a new human need is a healthy and viable evolution of the dog species.

7. Temperament is genetic and can be significantly altered through breeding; therefore, temperament should be included in all dog breed standards.

8. Genetic temperament tests can and should be performed on very young dogs in order to show their true genetic nature without environmental influence.

9. Time is short; therefore, health and temperament improvements to the breed should occur without delay.

10. There is no need to waste time waiting for formal health testing results that are not common diseases within a particular breed. Therefore, formal health testing is only necessary for diseases that are common to the breed. Informal health testing in as many areas as possible is a necessity.

11. All breeders within a dog breed have an obligation to improve their breed toward its standards and should work together, not be in competition with one another.

Purebred Dog breeds adhere to the following:

1. Published pedigrees include only dogs of the same breed all the way back to the beginning of the breed.
2. Standards of the breed are written in broad terms to be interpreted by the breed club.
3. Dogs within a specific breed are outwardly measured against other dogs in a show ring by a judge.
4. Dogs adhering to the ideal for the breed are rewarded with show titles and prizes.
5. A particular dog breed can develop extreme examples based upon public or judge opinion.
6. Champion stud dogs and dams within the breed can appear many times throughout the pedigree. Breeding on one or two high ranking dogs within the breed is common and encouraged.
7. Certain pedigrees coming from specific lines within the breed are revered as more prestigious.
8. An overall uniform look is required to become a breed.
9. Temperament is assessed in the show ring when the judge approaches the dog during the few moments they are together in the ring.
10. Dogs can be disqualified by the judge for defecating in the show ring, snapping at the judge, or acting aggressive toward other dogs or people.
11. Purebred dogs are specifically trained for show ring etiquette.
12. Specific clips and cuts are a part of the look of the dog and a dog breed that is not clipped or cut properly, despite being clean and brushed, can be disqualified from the show. Furthermore, specific clips can emphasize or de-emphasize a certain dog's features.
13. Dogs come with a pedigree from a recognized all-breed registry. There are many of them including: AKC, UKC, CKC, ARBA, FCI, KC, etc.
14. Dogs are said to be "recognized" when they are officially registered through one of the all-breed registries.
15. Crossbreeding is generally not allowed, although some leniency exists in specific cases.
16. Great health is generally up to the individual breeder to prove their dogs are free from genetic health issues, as much as possible.
17. Many breeds have extremely unnatural features, such as very short snouts to the point of breathing difficulties or short legs and long bodies which cause back issues, etc.

Strongbred dog breeds adhere to the following:

1. Published pedigrees include all dogs bred, no matter the breed, going all the way back to the beginning of the breed.
2. Standards of the breed are written in exact terms to dissuade anyone from altering or deviating from the founder's ideals.
3. Each dog within a specific breed is measured only according to the ideal by the founder or certified judge, and never against any other dog within the breed. Points are generally awarded to the dog for its closeness toward the standards. Thus, only three judges in agreement [or the founder alone] determine the championship status of the dog.
4. Dogs closely adhering to the standards of the breed are awarded titles and prizes.
5. Extreme examples of the breed are discouraged at all times, as the point is to adhere to the exact standards of the breed as they are written and interpreted by the founder.
6. Champion stud dogs and dams can be as numerous as the dogs that adhere to the standards, or as few as the crossbred dogs that do not adhere to the standards. Dogs are bred based on the need of the breed, not because they have reached championship status.
7. Certain pedigrees are not revered as prestigious. Pedigrees only help the breeder know with which genetics he/she has to work to continue to improve the breed and always breed better than the parents.
8. A uniform look is not required as regular and systematic crossbreeding dictates that certain dogs will not adhere to the standards. We recognize a dog's status within a breed based on how many generations they are from the most recent crossbreed.
9. Temperament is assessed throughout the lifetime of the dog, beginning at birth. Genetically inherited temperament is included in the standards and each breeder must prove through formal standardized temperament testing that their dogs adhere to the temperament standards. If a dog's temperament does no adhere to the standards, the breeder is obligated to say why and how they are different.
10. Dogs can be disqualified from breeding, but never from showing. Every dog within the breed is worthy of being assessed toward the standards. However, aggressive dogs or dogs that have other temperament or health issues will be disqualified from breeding within the breed.
11. Each dog is assessed on their genetically inherited temperament, health and overall conformation. Training will not be considered in the assessment. This is because we want the natural genetic nature of the dog to be assessed, not how much training has impacted the dog's ability to show itself.

12. The dog's natural look is the ideal and is what should be assessed. Strongbred dogs are not specially clipped, but shown in their natural state in order to assess the genetically inherited look of the dog and not mask any flaws that may be present.

13. Dogs come with a pedigree directly from those people who care about the dog breed the most, the breed club itself.

14. Dogs are recognized by the breed club and its members. No need to go elsewhere.

15. Crossbreeding is not only allowed, but encouraged at specific times for specific improvements to the breed: genetic diversity, increased size, elimination of specific health issues, etc. Crossbreeding is regulated by breed club members.

16. Great health is up to the entire unified breed club with all breeders working toward a common goal.

17. Breeds possess a natural appearance, with no extreme features that detract from the overall health of the dog.

Chapter 9
Canine Health

I woke up one morning to an unexpected email from Lois stating that she had designated me as a co-owner for a male puppy named Huck that she had just sold to a young man in Denver. Thus, I unknowingly acquired partial ownership of a mystery puppy. "Was it a gift from the heavens or a curse from below?" I worried, but with optimism.

Since my breeding program was in its initial stages and I did not have much choice in what to breed, especially being in Colorado and two long days drive from Lois, I did need variety to lessen my breeding limitations. This was a very generous gift from Lois and definitely a chance to further separate my lines from Lois's and increase diversity in the breed, thereby establishing my own individual role as a new breeder. But, was this male puppy an ideal match for my breeding program or would he prove to be a misfit? "What is the catch?" I secretly asked myself, waiting for the other shoe to drop.

The only thing I knew about Huck were his parents, Storm and Princess. Storm had been born at my place and later transferred to Lois, so I knew he was a goofy, but extremely lovable, extra-large boy with a silver wolf gray coat and light eyes. Princess, however, was an unknown crossbreed, said to be a Labrador Retriever and Alaskan Malamute mix. Having met her once, I knew she was sweet, calm, smart and compliant. Her inherited temperament possibilities definitely presented themselves in a positive light, so I held out for a picture of Huck to see just what treasure I had acquired. After all, we were now adding Labrador Retriever into the mix of breeds used. As a fairly new breeder to a breed that regularly incorporates crossbreeding to increase genetic diversity as well as add additional genetic material to propel the dogs closer toward the end goals of the breed, I had to wonder just what sort of crazy new traits might present themselves from a breeding with Labrador Retriever imbedded in the ancestry.

Huck (Storm/Princess) at 10 months old.

Unfortunately for me, Huck's new owner was not very forthcoming with pictures. After a year, the only adult picture I had received was blurry and taken far away, but it suggested an amazing looking dog beyond my wildest dreams. Had my mother really given me such a gift? I analyzed that picture endlessly, blowing it up as much as I could before it became so pixilated that I couldn't make out any further details. What I thought I saw was a dog with a mask that looked that the wolf. Could it be? An American Alsatian dog without a black mask or a white-spotted mask... the first of its kind in the breed! I marveled at the breeding possibilities for hours, knowing that the look of the wolf's muzzle was recessive in nature to the black mask, which was most prevalent in our breed. I analyzed his pedigree which was a nice mixture of genes to increase genetic diversity and further decrease the overall inbreeding in the next generations. He truly seemed ideal.

Working with the co-owner's veterinarian in Denver, I scheduled a vet appointment to secure hip and elbow x-rays to make sure that Huck was clear of any joint issues. As usual, the veterinarian automatically sent all registration information and x-rays to OFA for review. When the OFA report came back showing mild hip dysplasia I was crestfallen. But, then, I saw that the registration number was not correct on his paperwork. This peaked my curiosity, so I went back to the veterinarian and asked for a copy of Huck's x-rays. When the pictures arrived in my inbox, I eagerly opened the attachment. After analyzing the identifying information on the x-ray, it suddenly became clear to me that they were not Huck's. After discussing the situation with the veterinarian's office, they finally determined that the x-rays had been switched accidentally with another dog that had completed its x-rays that very same day. The veterinarian's office apologized and immediately sent in the correct x-rays to OFA with the correct information. After several nervous months passed, Huck's x-rays returned from OFA with good hips scores and clear of elbow dysplasia. Relief washed over me as the crisis ended.

Sprinkle, the female I chose as Huck's match, was a silver wolf gray with striking yellow eyes and a loving, calm, gentle, smart and confident disposition. She, too, passed her OFA preliminary x-rays with a good hip score rating and showed negative for elbow dysplasia. The more I thought about the match and their genetic backgrounds, the more I convinced myself that I had walked into an extraordinary chance to improve the breed by decreasing inbreeding, increasing genetic diversity, and solidifying a confident, stable and secure inherited temperament. But, the most exciting aspect of this match-up was being able to finally knock at the door to the wolf mask, thereby adding to the breed's available list of desired wolfish outward appearance traits. My enthusiasm and excitement grew as Sprinkle finally came into her second heat. The time had come. Now, all that was left was to drive to Denver, retrieve Huck and bring him back to meet his match.

Huck rushed out of his high-rise apartment in the middle of Denver pulling heavily on his leash. He moved to jump on me as he strained to come closer to me in an enthusiastic greeting. Just what had I gotten myself into? He jumped into the back of my SUV as if he owned the world and we parted for home. It wasn't until we were some distance away from the bustling traffic of Denver that I was able to breath and truly look at Huck. He was beautiful. Simply stunning to behold. He did, indeed, have a wolf mask without white spotting to turn his skin pink. On the long six hour drive back to the southwest corner of Colorado where we lived, I was able to see Huck's true mind and his submissive spirit. His new owner had never owned a dog before, so Huck was a bit unruly, but his gentle, calm, compliant, and smart soul presented itself to me as I was easily able to get him under control while on the leash during potty breaks.

From the moment Huck stepped foot in our backyard, Sprinkle was quite enamored with him. She skipped, jumped, hid, chased, and flirted like a giddy school girl. Huck and Sprinkle bred successfully a few days later and in no time, my hope for the future of the breed rose to its highest level. If this litter was as good as my mind expected it to be, I would most likely want to keep a number of the puppies in the program to add their greatest to the lines. My eyes blurred as my mind began to think of the many ways we would be improving the breed from this one litter alone.

Huck returned to Denver and sixty-three days later, as if on cue, Sprinkle birthed her first litter of puppies. A large beautiful litter of twelve puppies, one of the largest litters ever birthed through the Dire Wolf Project. But, the best part for me was knowing that every single one of those puppies carried the wolf mask gene and I knew that I could continue its wolfish look in future generations. I sold three puppies on co-ownership contracts, two males and one female, and kept the nicest female for myself. The two male puppies actually showed the wolf mask and one of them, Sir Galahad, was a beautiful silver wolf gray color with medium length coat, erect ears, and the nicest most mellow, easy-going attitude. Imagine my excitement as I temperament tested the other puppies and realized that all of them were varying degrees of sweet, loving, confident, and smart; one of the nicest litters I have had the privilege of breeding.

Sir Galahad at 7 weeks old.

I had a very difficult time convincing myself to sell Sir Galahad. As a young six week old puppy, he calmly and gently came up to me, lay down beside me, and rested his head on my lap. He was content to fall asleep right by my side as long as he could be near. He was alert and aware of his surroundings and watched others for how to react to any changes in his environment. He did not have to be taught to calm down or not jump, but just seemed to know exactly how to act in order to remain polite. He enjoyed calm, gentle affection and would look deep into my eyes. He was consistent in these behaviors each time I visited the puppies. I wanted to keep him for the close connection I had made with him, but in Vallecito Lake, where we lived at the time, we simply did not have the room to keep too many dogs, so I opted to keep a female and co-own this amazing male pup, instead.

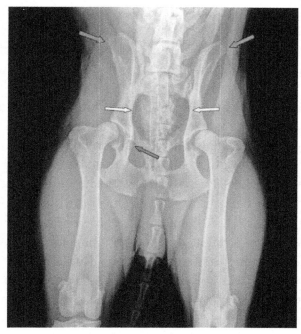

Sir Galahad hip x-rays
Arrows highlight uneven positioning.

Sir Galahad's new owner agreed to comply with all of the health testing requirements I wanted in order to be sure that Galahad was breed worthy. I anticipated that he would be the healthiest dog, considering that both of his parents were healthy and vibrant examples of the breed. It wasn't until OFA preliminary hip results came back with the horrible news that Sir Galahad received a moderate hip dysplasia rating that my heart sank so low in my chest that my pulse rate must have been almost undetectable. It was the first officially reported incidence of hip dysplasia in the breed in over twenty-five years of breeding.

The owner was equally devastated. He noted that Sir Galahad was happy and healthy, having no trouble moving, jumping, hiking, or swimming. He seemed like the healthiest dog. But not long after these results, the young owner became so terrified of the potential later effects of hip dysplasia that he sold his beloved furry companion to a friend and I never heard news of Sir Galahad again. My heart still aches for the terrible genetic loss of this great pup and the lack of knowledge about what became of him.

I had accepted, without question, the sole authority of OFA to make an informed decision regarding the hip health of a great dog based on one x-ray. Licensed OFA officials never saw the dog, knew any of his medical background, or experienced how he moved. The certified collaborative three veterinarian team was not there to take the x-ray or know how the dog has been positioned on the table. Is any of this information even necessary outside of analyzing one x-ray, a snapshot of Galahad's hips on one day at one time? Can one x-ray show all there is to know about a dog's hip health or is there more to this insidious deteriorating joint disease in dogs? Should we give the sole subjective authority to an organization such as OFA to make or break a dog's entire reputation based on one x-ray, especially if the x-ray turns out to not have been positioned as accurately as possible? In other words, did I do the right thing, or did I lose a great dog based on one organization's subjective interpretation of one veterinarian's abilities to clearly x-ray a dog's hips with correct positioning?

If we take the position that so many so-called dog breeding experts take, there is no doubt. Formal, third party analyzed x-rays should always be taken for every single dog to be bred and the final two year full scale OFA hip report the sole judge of a dog's hip worth. But, surprisingly, not everyone agrees. Fred Lanting, an all-breed judge writes, "The 'standard' view (positioning of dog for X-ray pictures of hips) is not the best... it is not the most accurate way to determine the real quality of hips. OFA, SV, and other registries have the dog stretched out on its back with legs straight out on the table, for the X-ray picture. While this is good for showing joint deterioration at the time, it is not accurate in showing true looseness, and it is not good for predicting what the hips will look like in a few years, when perhaps the dog has already produced puppies that inherit its hip quality."[1]

Furthermore, Dr. Anthony Cambridge, a board certified veterinary surgeon, clearly states that "Laxity is the key finding in dogs with hip dysplasia. There is a test for laxity we refer to as the otolarny sign... If we confirm this, this is hip dysplasia regardless of what we see on an x-ray."[2]

Barbara J Andrews, a prominent AKC Master Breeder and columnist for numerous dog magazines for over fifty years, reveals that "[o]ne of the original OFA board members was Dr. Gerry Schnelle, who in 1937 published the first paper on what we now call canine hip dysplasia. A pioneer in the field, his *Bilateral Congenital Sublixation of the Coxofemeral Joints of a Dog* was the first definitive study of CHD [canine hip displasia]. Dr. Schnelle publicly resigned from the board of OFA due to unresolved ethical concerns, stating he could not certify an x-ray on a dog whose muscular condition, overall health, and other factors could not be evaluated."[3] To be sure, Dr. Gerry Schnelle DVM wrote over 100 scientific articles, served on the editorial boards of Merck Veterinary Manual, North American Veterinarian, Journal of Small Animal Practice, Journal of the American Veterinary Radiology Society, and was editor of Veterinary Excerpts. He was the founder and emeritus member of the American College of Veterinary Radiology among many other accomplishments. His public resignation would not have been taken lightly.

The history of x-raying canine hips is an interesting one. Not only did one of the founding OFA veterinarian's resign in opposition to how hip certification was determined, but thirty years after Dr. Schnelle's discovery, the fulcrum x-ray coupled with palpation became a popular means of determining whether a dog showed clinical signs of the disease or not. As Barbara J Andrews recalls,

> "Fulcrum X-ray meant 'gently' forcing the fulcrum out of the hip socket to determine maximum joint laxity during radiographs. Fulcrum x-ray and palpation were a big deal back in the seventies. Promoted by Dr. Bardens, both were finally exposed as ineffective and dangerous methods of diagnosing or predicting canine hip dysplasia. Many breeders allege the procedures actually caused joint damage. Inarguably, both procedures resulted in the death of thousands of puppies and adult dogs that may have been sound. The reality of so many baby dogs killed before vets gave up on the value of palpitation is heartbreaking. Palpation was so inaccurate that many vets insisted on reported *hip socket manipulations*... That defies logic but it was the protocol of the time. Palpation finally earned condemnation in nineteen ninety-nine but it took over 20 years."[4]

More recently, the original German Shepherd Dog breed club in Germany, the SV, sponsored a significant genetic analysis of hip and elbow dysplasia in the German Shepherd Dog. This research study reviewed the hip radiographs of 47,730 breeding candidate German Shepherd Dogs born between 2001 and 2007 to determine the genetic heritability of canine hip dysplasia (CHD). Overall, researchers found that CHD within the study cohort had a 25% heritability. Prominent German Shepherd Dog breeder of over forty years, Ed Frawley, puts it this way, "[t]he SV in Germany has proven that genetics is only responsible for about 25% of the bad hips in dogs. This means that 70% to 75% of the bad hips are caused by environmental issues." A study using Labrador Retrievers further suggests this statement to be true. These researchers found a high correlation between increased CHD and dogs that were fed an unlimited diet which caused excess weight gain. "Using the OFA method, 7 of the 24 limit-fed dogs and 16 of the 24 ad libitum-fed dogs were diagnosed as having hip dysplasia. Similarly, using the Swedish method, 5 of the 24 limit-fed dogs and 18 of the 24 ad libitum-fed dogs were diagnosed as having hip dysplasia." They determined that, "[a]ccuracy of OFA-criteria scoring was poor: 55% of dogs scored 'normal' at 2 years of age became radiographically dysplastic by the end of life." They ultimately concluded that, "OFA-criteria score was profoundly influenced by environmental factors, such as diet restriction and age, reducing its value as a selection criterion."[5]

Furthermore, this study is the first of its kind to separate borderline rated dogs from unaffected dogs, as all previous studies lumped borderline rated dogs into the unaffected category. The research revealed, as with more significant CHD ratings, that borderline hip dysplasia is passed on to offspring and, therefore, should also not be bred. It was also determined that dogs with high CHD disposition would more likely also develop canine elbow dysplasia (CED). "Multivariate genetic analyses with separate consideration of borderline findings revealed moderate heritability's of 0.2-0.3 for the quasi-continuous traits with positive additive genetic correlation of 0.3 between CHD and both CED and CED-ARTH. For FCP, heritability of 0.6 and additive genetic correlations of +0.1 to CHD and -0.1 to CED-ARTH were estimated. Results supported the relevant genetic determination of CHD and CED, argued for both diseases against interpretation of borderline findings as health and implied genetic heterogeneity of CED."[6]

As it turned out, the other male I co-owned from this same litter did not successfully breed and the female I kept died in a tragic barn fire. The only dog from this highly anticipated litter that was able to be kept for further breeding was a small gold wolf gray co-owned female with a black mask. This set me back a great deal in my future plans for the breed as I reflected on the possibility that I very well may have lost the ability to produce the wolf mask in the breed in the future.

As Sir Galahad's co-owner clearly revealed to me, no one seeks to own a pet that must constantly go to the veterinarian for major health concerns. No one desires to pay thousands of dollars on veterinarian costs to find out their dog has a degenerative genetic disease that will progressively cause more and more suffering for their dog as it ages. No one wants to have to say good-bye to a great dog much too early because of health issues that could have been prevented through breeding. That is a large reason why many people choose to purchase a dog that has a clear pedigree from a breeder instead of acquiring a dog of unknown origin from the shelter. But, even though health is the most important concern for most people looking to purchase a new puppy, we each take a risk every time we choose a breeder. Has that breeder done everything in his/her power to eliminate as many genetic health issues as possible before breeding? Are the mother and father of a potential puppy clear of any genetic diseases? Can I trust the breeder to tell me the truth? Can we absolutely know the truth? These questions are important ones to ask, but very difficult to answer because not all breeders are alike. The public can easily become confused about the best way to solidly know if a breeder willingly exposes any ill health in their dogs.

The first thing to ask is what is truth and how does one know with certainty if something is true. Can we even know the truth about anything? Is there absolute truth in which to know? As we saw in the first chapter of this book, absolute truth does exist simply because if absolute truth did not exist that statement would have to be absolutely true in order to stand on its own premise, which refutes its original claim. Therefore, if there is an absolute truth about the overall health of a dog, a person could seek to learn the full reality of that dog's health, not simply some arbitrary set of rules to follow that proclaim a dog to be healthy, but the real truth behind a dog's healthfulness. Let's look at some concrete ways in which we might be able to determine whether a dog, and consequently an entire dog breed, is truly healthy.

Formal Testing

Formal health testing is defined as a certifying third party testing facility that accurately determines whether a dog has or has not developed a specific negative canine health issue. Generally, local general practicing veterinarians do not fall into this category because they may be biased or not specifically schooled in the fine art of preventative measures of canine diseases. They can vary greatly in their abilities, one from another, and thus the reason why the third party testing facility must be able to formally certify. These certifying facilities are generally accepted across the country as a way of identifying specific canine diseases and being able to predict whether they will ever manifest themselves or not throughout a dog's lifetime. The following are currently accepted formal testing facilities: Orthopedic Foundation for Animals

[OFA], Canine Eye Registration Foundation [CERF], AKC's Canine Good Citizen [CGC] test, genetic testing facilities such as Embark Veterinary Services, University of Pennsylvania Hip Improvement Program [PENNhip], and many others.

Informal Testing

Informal health testing is defined as any health test that has not been performed by a certifying third party testing facility. Tests performed by general practice veterinarians are one relevant example, but, any type of internal test performed by the breed club or breeder him/herself would be an example of an informal health test. In general, informal health testing is not seen as legitimate because the tests rely upon the accuracy and trustworthiness of the individual administering the test. Since there is no way of certifying the tester, the test is seen as invalid by any skeptic.

Prevention vs Elimination

There are two different kinds of approaches to breeding for superior canine health and longevity. Those who work to prevent as many health issues from occurring in their breeding stock as possible and those who work to eliminate as many health issues from occurring in their breeding stock as possible. Although they appear very similar on the surface, these two types are worlds apart from each other and approach canine health in vastly different ways.

The first type of breeder is the most accepted type in our day. In fact, many do not even realize that there is any other way than this way. Breeders conforming to the prevention breeding model are propped up on a pedestal and given accolades and credentials to match their glowing golden crowns. A breeder working diligently to prevent illness sees disease prevention solely as a breeder's responsibility; the almighty formal battery of canine health tests that should a breeder fail to accomplish would be punishable by severe ridicule and lifelong shunning is essential and must accompany each and every dog to be bred. At the very least, a breeder believing in this road to breeding glory would purposely test each breeding dog through OFA for canine hip and elbow dysplasia, CERF for formal eye certification, Embark Veterinary Services for official DNA results, regularly updated blood tests to provide continual evidence of healthy internal structure, endurance tests to prove healthy stamina, and Canine Good Citizen [CGC] testing to prove stable temperaments. Breeders of this type proudly wave their dog's scores all around for proof that they have obtained a superior level of disease prevention than most. If one of their dogs should happen to not pass any of the prevention tests, it would be neutered and stricken from the breeding program. No other illnesses are ever mentioned and no collective health data is required to be kept. Therefore, the prevention breeder never has to take the blame, having done everything in his/her power beforehand to prevent disease. If disease does occur, it is not the breeder's fault as he/she did everything one could to prevent disease from occurring. Furthermore, he/she does not know how such a health issue could have occurred. Most breeders fall into this category, as it is the only accepted means of dog breeding in our day.

However, there is a different approach. The road less traveled. One that exists in many other animal breeding programs, but that is expressly shunned in dog breeding; the health elimination breeder. A breeder working diligently to eradicate all disease from his/her breeding stock sees disease prevention as unattainable because disease is understood to be complex and hidden much of the time. A breeder adhering to this philosophy only tests for diseases that are currently prevalent in the breed. The tests used may be formal or informal, no matter, as long as the disease is correctly identified and targeted. These tests can shift and change depending on the needs of the breed at the time. The breeder in this category diligently keeps all health data in a recorded public database and actively encourages owners to share any negative health information with the breeder. This type may perform any of the formal tests above on an as needed basis, but may also periodically monitor their dogs randomly using formal testing to make sure the breeding program remains on track. If a genetic disease begins to surface, they work diligently to completely eliminate it from the lines, believing that only when a negative health issue is seen can it be eliminated, otherwise there is not enough data to determine where the disease lurks within the shadowy recessives of their dogs' lines. This type of breeder believes that canine diseases can never be perfectly prevented. They know and are able to state with clarity which dogs from which lines have developed which disease and can even venture how such a thing could have occurred in the breed. Very few breeders fall into this category, as it is highly unacceptable to the mainstream breeding world.

The key to health prevention breeding is the ability to know exactly when and how a negative health issue will arise. Many professionals work around the clock to find the genes associated with these persistent diseases. Unfortunately, as of this writing only one hundred sixty five or so single gene diseases are known at this time. This is very good, but not good enough to prevent all canine genetic diseases. One of the most important health prevention tests, the hip and elbow x-ray, does not have the privilege of being genetically mapped, so one must rely on expert interpretation on a more subjective level for hip and elbow accuracy, such as the Orthopedic Foundation for Animals [OFA]. Unfortunately, hip and elbow x-rays can return from OFA with a good or excellent rating for both parents while their offspring still develop hip dysplasia. In this case, and many other cases of canine ill-health, something else is going on here. Why did the formal test fail to prevent dogs from having hip dysplasia? When the inevitable happens and a health, temperament, or conformation issue arises in a dog, the unfortunate breeder hears a distant rumble carried on the wind, "You should have done more to prevent the issue from occurring in the first place." And, sadly, it doesn't matter how much the breeder did work to prevent health issues from their stock. The problem is that successful prevention means a breeder never sees the polygenic deleterious health issues that may lie dormant waiting the right combination... so if one does experience it in the dogs one breeds, it was never really prevented in the first place, but merely shoved aside for someone else.

But, the advocates for health prevention methods of breeding conveniently ignore, or do not understand, a fundamental truth - No one can prevent all health, temperament or conformation issues from occurring in animals; we can only work to eliminate them once they are known to exist. There are a few known health issues that are able to be seen through DNA. Those are the only known health issues that can be completely eliminated by a bit of formal testing. All others, including hip and elbow dysplasia, cannot be prevented by formal testing because the health issues are polygenic in nature. In other words, there are too many factors involved to wave the magic formal testing wand and stand on the words, "I have done all I can to prevent health issues in my dogs." This is because prevention rides on the idea that if we never see it then the breeder is dubbed "responsible" due to his/her proper planning and careful breeding. When instead, if one never sees the problem, there is no way to go about fixing it because a recessive polygenic disease can lurk just under the surface of a dog's genetics for years until it pops up in one of its offspring generations later. It is only then, when the issue manifests itself, that we can truly work to eliminate it from the breed.

So, the elimination breeding model works just as it does in the wild. When a health issue arises, the animal is eliminated from the gene pool and never bred. The more you eliminate animals with ill health, the less ill health you experience in a breed. Elimination means, though, that you must see a genetic disease in order to eliminate it. There amount of formal testing can prevent all genetic disease from encroaching on our dog breeding program. This type of breeder stands on the words, "I am not God and I can never know or do enough to prevent health issues in my dogs." This is because elimination rides on the idea that health issues may show themselves when we least expect it and so we must always be diligent observers of truth.

The prevention model breeder breeds for perfection as if an ideal can eventually be obtained. All ill health must be prevented so that no dog experiences trauma due to illness. If a dog is genetically ill, the prevention model dictates that it is the breeder's fault and blame lies squarely with the human. Perfection is the ideal and is seen to be able to be reached by man's own knowledge alone. The prevention model breeder does not anticipate that flaws will always need to be eliminated and believes that with enough prevention on the breeder's part, they will. There is a theoretical finite end to the work of eliminating weakness from the breed.

The elimination model breeds against imperfection as if there is no end to the toll and strife of life. It adheres to the notion that all creatures are flawed in health, temperament, and conformation. If a dog is genetically ill, the elimination model dictates that it is the animal's genetics at fault and the blame lies squarely on the genetic background of the dog, which the breeder must then eradicate from the line. No animal is seen to ever be perfect, and certainly no dog breed is perfect no matter how much humans select for the right traits to fit the desired standard. The elimination model breeder anticipates that flaws will always need to be eradicated. There is no end to the work of eliminating weakness from the breed.

The prevention model works in a clean and sterile environment where one must analyze, individually search for each disease one by one, and eventually amass a myriad of tests that can sort them all out. Any test that can be performed to find the genetic flaw and prevent it is applauded and used, no matter how successful the new test is at actually eradicating the disease. Anyone not using the test is vilified as a non-conformist.

The elimination model works in a messy and soiled environment where disease stains already exist. Genetic diseases are eradicated en masse as the soiled area housing genetic disease is cleansed. An individual must develop the keen eyes to see the manifestation of the tiniest fault lying dormant. It is only by knowing what a disease actually looks like when it is seen that it can be eradicated.

Dire Wolf Project breeders use some formal preventative tests that have been proven to have found simple genetic diseases lying dormant in a recessive state because the point of the elimination model is to eradicate disease whenever it is seen. DNA testing is one way of actually seeing the genes responsible for unigenic diseases. Although we can, through trial mating, eliminate recessive genes from our dogs, DNA testing speeds up the process needed to eliminate the disease. That being said, we do not rely on tests that are not solid indicators of disease. OFA hip and elbow x-rays are one such example. When a test can assess both parents as good or excellent in hip score, but still produce offspring showing hip dysplasia, such a test is not reliably predictive and should not be used as the means of prevention. Hip and elbow tests can and should be used as a means of showing hip and elbow dysplasia, but can never be said to prevent it. It is then more reliable to eliminate hip dysplasia through actual manifested observance of a dog's skeletal structure and laxity. The elimination method breeder, while eliminating skeletal issues, such as cow hock, down in the pasterns, thin hips, roached back, etc. will automatically address the looseness of a dog's hips.

When one blindly chooses to rely solely upon formal health tests designed at preventing ill health and genetic disease from a dog breed, one becomes steeped in the false belief that healthy dogs are the direct result of human intervention. When one deliberately refuses to rely blindly on health tests, but instead look at the actual dog in all of its weaknesses, one understands that we humans are simply care-takers of the animals we serve. We are not gods unto ourselves with the power to prevent illness from ever occurring, but we serve God by continually seeking perfection by eradicating health issues as they are manifested.

Individual or Collective Breeding
There are two ways of thinking about breeding dogs for health:
1. Each breeder individually works as much as humanly possible to breed full litters of 100% healthy dogs.
2. A collective group of breeders, preferably every breeder throughout the entire breed, cumulatively breeds litters in order to openly increase the overall health of the breed as a whole.

Each of these ways of breeding is admirable. They both seek to decrease genetic disease and produce healthy, long-lived dogs. But, which type of breeding can be seen to be more beneficial for our dog breeds as a whole?

Should we each work separately, but diligently to increase overall canine health or should we find a way to work together within our breed clubs to increase overall canine health, while at the same time improving our own breeding stock?

To be sure, it is an extremely worthy goal of the individual breeder to produce perfect health in each dog in every litter bred. When the responsible breeder produces litter after litter of sound dogs, the accumulation of responsible breeders around the world all working individually should automatically decrease the overall occurrence of ill health within the entire dog population. That is the theory, anyway.

However, a fundamental problem arises when individual breeders work by themselves to combat genetic disease. By working individually, as breeders have done for hundreds of years, it has typically been the case that breeders keep genetic disease to themselves. George A. Padgett, DVM, professor of pathology at Michigan State University, one of the world's most celebrated researchers, writers and lecturers on the entire subject of canine genetic diseases, states, "Almost no one talks openly about genetic disease in purebred dogs... That's why genetic disease is common... Since nobody talks about genetic disease, it is difficult to get a reasonable idea of how much disease is around-- how many dogs are involved."[7]

And why would the individual breeder talk about the genetic diseases plaguing their lines, especially when to do so would cast an ugly shadow over their facility? Those breeders who never disclose the health issues with which they battle have a distinct advantage over the breeder who dares to speak out about the issues. Unsuspecting buyers gravitate toward the breeder who hides behind the ribbons and notoriety acquired from winning easily in the show ring. Even if an individual breeder performs and publicly lists all of the most common formal health tests including: hip/elbow dysplasia, genetic eye disease, and DNA testing results for every single dog in their facility, it benefits them not to disclose the untold war they are fighting with the other 350 potential diseases that do not yet have formal health testing. After all, the individual breeder has his/her own responsibility to eliminate them and disclosing them could mean ruin for their very prestigious breeding program. As a result, individual breeders only talk about the good dogs. This unwillingness to disclose the true occurrence rates of genetic diseases within the purebred dog population has unknowingly increased the ill health of the purebred dog and today, genetic disease is commonly found among them. As George A. Padgett, DVM, further points out, "Since nobody talks about genetic disease, it is difficult to get a reasonable idea of how much disease is around – how many dogs are involved... Nobody talks about dogs with defect. You don't see dogs with defects. It's not hard to pick up the idea that nearly all dogs are normal... The reality is that there are lots of dogs with genetic diseases of one kind or another... If you don't see that there is a problem or you don't know there is a problem, it is easy to think that there is not a problem."[7a]

Today, scientists, veterinarians, owners and a select few brave breeders openly advocating and speaking out about the ill health that occurs in our beloved tail-wagging friends have begun to reveal an immense overwhelming dilemma that, left unchecked, will most likely lead to the genetic extinction of many of our most cherished breeds. As reported by Jason Copping writing for the Telegraph in the United Kingdom in 2008, "Many of Britain's most popular dog breeds could be extinct within 50 years because they are so inbred, vets have warned. Some pedigrees are suffering from a range of worsening health problems because they are being bred from a shrinking gene pool in an effort to create the most sought-after physical characteristics. Many breeds will die out as a result of hereditary diseases..."[7b]

Truly, if we care about the dog as a species, something drastic must change. We cannot continue to allow individual breeders to flounder by themselves without the knowledge that they need in order to breed for health. We can first start by opening up a safe dialogue with breeders where they will not be ridiculed, cast out, or reputations harmed by finally speaking out about the health issues they have been so diligently working on through the years. A collective database of the health issues should begin to emerge as more and more breeders feel safe to share what they know. And, if information needed to make informed decisions is lacking, the collective group of breeders, working together, can find answers to the tough questions about dogs that are carriers for certain diseases that plague their breed.

Generally, breeders working together have gathered in breed clubs. Breed clubs put on local shows, sponsor speakers to come to the locale, and provide a place to learn about the changes in dog showing and breeding. Breed clubs, although not officially associated with AKC or other all-breed registries, sponsor sanctioned AKC matches, which bring people from other parts of the country and world to a location to share their dogs. This openness to introduce one breeder to another would normally be applauded, but deep in the recesses of the breed club bowels lurks an insidious darkness. Backstabbing, gossip, finger wagging, and tattle-tailing run rampant as breeders compete in shows for the top prices and winnings. Some breed clubs may now be beginning to eliminate these dividing practices, but as director of veterinary medicine, George Padgett notes, "[h]istorically, control of genetic disease was never part of the responsibilities of a breed club, so the vast majority has never done anything about genetic disease."[8]

Andromeda (Harpo.Shennara) at 7 months old 2019

Chapter 10
Inherited Dog Temperament

Here lies DASH, the Favourite Spaniel of Queen Victoria
By whose command this Memorial was erected.
He died on the 20 December, 1840 in his 9th year.
His attachment was without selfishness,
His playfulness without malice,
His fidelity without deceit.
READER, if you would live beloved and die regretted, profit by the
example of DASH.
- Queen Victoria, epitaph on the gravestone of Dash, who was buried in
the castle's garden

From the moment his head poked out into the world, he made no noise and was completely motionless; so unmoving, in fact, that I had to make sure he was breathing. As I gently lifted his still warm, wet body into my arms, his tiny frame molded to the contours of my cupped hands. His yellow-eyed mother, Shennara, looked up at me with dilated pupils full of concern for her precious gift. When she realized I was not about to give him to her, she began vigorously licking her two other puppies to distract herself while I attended to her newest baby.

My mind shifted into overdrive as I tried to remember all of the steps to revive a stillborn puppy. I willed my mind to calm down so that I could think. I began softly rubbing its delicate side in the hopes of stimulating a verbal response before going into more drastic measures. No sound came and my heart skipped a beat. Then, just as I was going to begin steps toward clearing his airway and stimulating his heart, to my huge relief, he ever so slowly moved his head closer to my hand and drew in a lingering breath of air and I knew he was alive. I gratefully placed this large white ball of wet fur back down near his mom and he immediately moved his pink-nosed head to a nipple and began suckling heartily, as if he had known exactly where it had been all along and exactly what it was for. As mom licked him, he did not move to another position or unlock his grasp from his mother until he was full and his fur was dry. Then, he lie right where he was next to his mom, snuggled his head into her fur and lay still in a peaceful sleep.

Over the next hours as Shennara's body expelled her last five puppies and her tummy shrank back to its normal size, the white male pup never made a sound. As usual, I sat in constant vigil on my black director's chair overseeing the miraculous birthing events. A pad of paper and a pencil lay on the table to my right so that I could record measurements and notes of the puppies in their first moments in this world. When all of the commotion of the birthing process had ended, I replaced the towels with fresh clean ones and prepared the soiled ones for the wash.

Shennara curled her body around her babies and then shifted her body closer to them like a walrus scoots across the ice. In that bit of disturbance, all of her tiny, soft bundles of joy woke up and moved about, crawling over this one or under that one or around in a circle... all of them that is, except for that curious white male. He did not move quickly as the others did, but instead he moved with easy-going resolve as if time did not exist for him. He did not become desperate to find mom by anxiously moving this way and that. He never struggled or became agitated as his littermates did. There was definitely something different about him.

As the first hours passed from this litter's arrival, I decided on the names each puppy would receive. Since the white male was the only male in the litter, I gave him a majestic name to go with the Greek Mythology theme of the litter. I wrote Triton, Messenger of the Deep next to his section on my notes. "That would definitely be a name to live up to," I thought.

Triton laid his head on his mom's back leg and draped his front paws over her as she slept. He did not look at all comfortable, but there he lay breathing deep and slow after a particularly nourishing meal. My heart fluttered at the gift of such a precious site. Then his mother moved her leg to reposition it, knocking Triton off of her and pushing him out to the other edge of the den, quite a distance away from her and the pack. He was suddenly isolated and alone, but Shennara did not seem to notice and he did not make any noise.

Instead of coming to his aid, I watched him specifically to see how he would react to this potentially disorienting placement in which he now found himself. Would he cry out for help? Would he turn in circles sniffing in desperation hoping to find a scent that could draw him back to safety? Would he crawl in a random direction hoping to save himself by touching a piece of his mother that he could recognize? Would his heart beat faster and his movements quicken? Or would he remain calm and collected despite his predicament? This was a real chance for me to get a glimpse into the inner workings of the mind of a one day old puppy and I relished the opportunity to witness his reaction and find out how he would solve the dilemma in which he had been placed so unwittingly.

Triton lay still for a quiet moment exactly where he had come to a skidding halt. Then without any noise, he effortlessly rolled himself over onto his stomach, turned himself completely around to directly face his mother and quietly, softly, gently, but steadily, scooted directly back to her. After that initial two second pause, he did not hesitate, wander, change direction, move his head from side to side as if searching, cry out or in any way show fear, disorientation, displeasure, or panic. Instead, he simply crawled right back to his mother without fuss or distraction. When he felt her warm and inviting fur, he crawled right back onto her leg and immediately went back to sleep as if nothing had happened.

Triton (Harpo/Shennara) one day old.

My mouth dropped open slightly and I rubbed my eyes with the backs of my hands to clear them. Did I just see what I just saw? Never, in my ten years of observing one to three day old puppies, have I ever witnessed a displaced newborn puppy that has been completely turned around show such an easily successful end to this task.

Some puppies do not ever try to find mom and immediately cry out right where they find themselves lost. Most puppies will initially bob their head in a seeming effort to locate a familiar scent or detect some warmth. They will tend to move in a circular fashion until they find mom or become distressed and cry out. Others will move in a straight, but random, direction until they find mom or hit a barrier, at which point they will scoot along the barrier until they either find mom or become distressed and cry out. Some take longer than others. Some hesitate and change directions.

But never have I ever seen a pup take a moment as if thinking and then nonchalantly and casually locate the correct direction and confidently crawl back to mom without hesitation or fuss. I suspected that this puppy had taken those few moments right after finding itself lost because it had been processing his situation. At this point, it was mere speculation, but I continued to observe him closely in order to see if a situation would arise that would solidify my hypothesis.

These are the exact words I wrote about Triton on July 23, 2019 before he was even twelve hours old: "Puppy 3: large all white male, very mellow, quiet, lots of pink skin, long tail, was born without sack/head first, easy and quiet birth, no fussing, very slow and thinking."

A few hours later, as the puppies chowed down at the milk bar, Shennara began licking the brood to stimulate their bowels and clean them. As she nudged Triton's rear up and over her muzzle to get to him, his relaxed body tumbled forward and away from the pack and her reach. Shennara then moved on to fuss with another pup within her muzzle's range and I had a second opportunity to observe how Triton would react to being lost. Triton did not even appear to mind where he was. He did not cry out, sigh, move in circles, move forward, bob his head or seem stiff or agitated. Instead, his body relaxed completely and he went right to sleep where he had rolled, on his back with his paws in the air. This boy could definitely drift off to sleep easily, but he was either completely oblivious that he had found himself in an unknown area of the den or he just did not care. I made another note to myself about this unusual response.

Now, up until this time, all of my observations about each puppy in this litter have been anecdotal, but as all American Alsatian dog breeders are trained to do, I prepared for a formal, standardized temperament test in which every puppy is tested in the same exact way. Each puppy's reactions to each part of the test are recorded and scored according to the established temperament testing rubric used with every single puppy bred into the Dire Wolf Project from the very first litter birthed in 1988. All scores have been meticulously recorded in binders throughout the years and now online on each litter's respective webpage. I set aside the scoring chart for reference.

I placed the puppy scale in position and changed the towels to eliminate familiar scent. The notepad and pencil still rested next to my chair, but I added a timer to complete the set. With excited anticipation, I chose the first puppy and recorded its reaction to the specific tasks specially designed to observe changes in reaction to different stimuli in newborn puppies within the American Alsatian dog breed. I was very curious how Triton would perform.

Part of this first formal test is to give an average score for the vocalization observed from each puppy. Triton had never been heard grunting, crying out, or whining in any manner. He received a high score for this section. Another section of this first temperament test requires the scorer to average the energy level observed for each puppy. After two days, Triton had shown no excessive movement, but in fact, rarely moved about unless he was moving to go from eating to sleeping. He received the highest score for this section.

My hand moved down into the puppy pile as I began the first task, which is to pet the puppy, firmly and with some strength. Most puppies will immediately move their feet and attempt to crawl away. Some will cry out or startle or stiffen. Triton did none of these behaviors, but instead actually sniffed my hand as it moved from his nose and down his back. As a result, he received the highest score for this section.

I then picked up his white pudgy frame and placed him on the cold, smooth surface of the plastic puppy scale. Most puppies will either move around the scale, move off the scale, cry out, or some combination. Triton did not move on the scale at all, but instead slowly shifted his head from side to side as if investigating. He received the highest score for this section.

Next, I gently lifted Triton off of the scale, stood straight up with him in my arms and turned Triton over on his back in one decisive and practiced motion, keeping his head slightly higher than his rear. Most puppies will show some reaction to this completely unfamiliar position; initially stiffen their legs, cry out, try to right themselves, struggle, fuss, whine, scream, become stiff as a board and unmoving or any combination of these behaviors. Triton did not exhibit any of these. His tiny paws had a slight stiffness to them, but his back evenly molded into my hands. He did not yawn or make a sound. He also received the highest score for this section.

The last task in this first formalized temperament test is to place the puppy back into the den away from the other puppies. This time Triton did not immediately move toward the pile. He lay still where he was placed for four seconds. He did not cry out, whine or stiffen, but slowly moved out in a straight, forward motion. After going halfway to the puppy pile, he ended his exploratory travels to stop for a nap. This relaxed approach in an otherwise stressful situation is very unusual. He received the highest score for this last section as well.

The following are the exact notes I wrote on July 24, 2018, one and a half days after birth, regarding Triton's first formal temperament testing results:

First Temperament Test
Puppy #3:
How does this puppy come into the world?
This puppy was very mellow and quiet. This puppy was born without a sack and head first. His was an easy, quiet birth with no fussing. This puppy is a methodical thinker. This puppy receives a score of 9 for this section.
Noises this puppy makes during the first hours.
This puppy is quiet for the most part with some grunting at times. This puppy receives a score of 9 for this section.
What is the energy level of this pup?
This puppy is mellow and calm. This puppy receives a score of 10 for this section.
What is the reaction of this pup to the first medical examination?
This puppy quietly and slowly moved his head around the scale. It appeared that it wasn't so much moving, but investigating. This puppy receives a score of 10 for this section.
What is the reaction of this pup when turned over on its back?
This puppy did not struggle and did not fuss, cry or whine. This puppy did not completely relax, but he was not stiff and certainly did not have an elevated heart rate. This puppy receives a score of 10 for this section.
What is the reaction of this pup when placed back with its mother?
This puppy was slow and methodical in his search. He did not find mom and instead lie where he ended. He did not appear upset about not finding her, but was relaxed and easy. He then went to sleep. This puppy receives a score of 10+ for this section.
What is the reaction of this pup when touched by a human?
This puppy was very quiet and did not move with the pet, but sniffed the human's hand. This puppy receives a score of 10 for this section.
This puppy receives an overall score of 9.85 for this test.

My hands shook with excitement as I wrote down the final average score for Triton's first formal test. I could barely contain my disbelief and amazement. Not only was Triton a large male with what looked to be a gentle slope to his stop and medium length hair, but his temperament test and all anecdotal observations pointed to a pup that appeared to be exceptional. He initially thought about any new situation in which he found himself. He did not react with any behaviors suggesting uneasiness, discomfort or distress. He was extremely quiet and did not show excessive movement or activity. Because of these findings, Triton was awarded the prestigious "black collar" award, rarely given and reserved for only those top male puppies in both conformation and temperament. Only three of these black collars have been awarded in the history of the breed. I could hardly wait to announce my findings with the greater American Alsatian dog community on our Facebook page and share my joy.

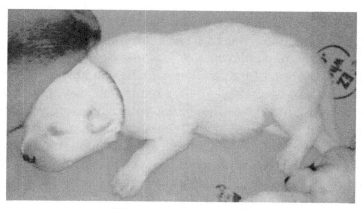

Triton at twelve days old.

DireWolf Dogs of Vallecito
Published by Jennifer Stoeckl [?] · July 24, 2018 · 🌐 ···

Let's talk about this pup named Triton. It is very rare, indeed, that I bestow a black collar on a pup in a litter, but this pup has been awarded this prestigious honor. Not only is he solid, heavy, great in proportion, and large in size, but he is also superb in temperament. This puppy wowed me today during the standardized temperament test which is not easy to do. This puppy is mellow, even-tempered, calm, collected and intelligent. He thinks easily and will likely have an easy time learning as a result. He is super quiet and does not get excited or upset by anything. He was not phased by being turned over and easily submit to the testing in each category. But, I could see his mind working the entire time. Not only is he great in temperament, but he will be a very large dog with a beautiful white coat coloring. If he ends up with yellow eyes and his ears stand as an adult, I imagine this puppy will be one of the very best dogs in the breed. Congratulations goes to this amazing boy. Something glorious this way comes.

Original post from DireWolf Dogs of Vallecito Facebook page, July 24,

To my delight, within minutes of posting the special announcement, fans of DireWolf Dogs began sharing their excitement for the breed. My heart swelled with joy to be the caretaker of this great gift from above. I bred Harpo, Triton's father, two other times and none of his puppies showed this special combination of responses. I could not wait to watch him develop and see if he would indeed progress as I suspected.

Then, as sometimes happens, a woman with an obvious passion for dogs and a bit of experience posted a good question, but reinforced it with a snarky comment revealing her strong bias. "How do you properly temperament test a two day old puppy? They show no personality at this age. It's like saying an infant will grow up to be a president because he has a nice hairline."

I could feel my heart skip a beat as it always does when I receive a direct challenge to something I share. Then, my mind's initial response joined in, *What if you are wrong and you have no clue what you are doing?* I took a deep breath in anticipation of the familiar demons that have haunted me since I was a girl. *You are not good enough,* they remind me. My pulse quickens. *Nobody cares what you have to say,* they insist with rising force. Another deep breath and I can feel my shoulders relax. *You have no credentials. Who do you think you are?* their voices linger on, but now not as powerful. One more inhale and my mind clears enough for me to reason with myself. *Stand up for yourself. You have just as much right to speak as they do. And besides, you know you are right. You were there and she was not. Be proud of what you know.*

Before I could answer her question, though, Lois replied. She is not known for candy-coating her responses, but Lois was particularly kind and took the time to share with this woman some very important aspects of what defines our work.

> "Oh, but you are so wrong about a pup not having a personality. If you watch from birth, you will see so many things. I see pups with brains that think. I see pups that cannot find the way back to their mom and others that know instinctively how to return. I see pups that run into walls and try to keep going (into the wall). I see pups that give up and cry. I see pups that stop and wait and feel the vibrations on the floor. If you just but look, you will see so much going on.
>
> "This all comes from observation and the teaching that I gave the breeders that breed my dogs. To pay attention and to observe without touching the pups - we call this the 'raw pup™' and one can only tell the genetic temperament of a dog/pup this way. Once a breeder begins handling and the mom begins teaching, the pup begins to adjust to the world and the stimuli around it.
>
> "The older the pup gets, the more the world around it influences and masks the innate character that we as breeders need to see. After a pup is trained, then who is the pup? A canine takes on the training and is molded and shaped. By then, you might get a glimpse of who the pup was from time to time, but it is much more difficult. However, when first born, we can see the raw genetics of who the pup is. Understanding this is how we breed for true inherited temperament."
>
> - Lois Schwarz, DireWolf Dogs of Vallecito Facebook page, July 28, 2018.

Well, Lois beat me to it with a very informative reply. I figured that explained things well enough for the woman to understand, so I did not venture a response. The woman rebutted with a declaration that all puppies do at this stage is eat and poop, so temperament cannot possibly be assessed. She shared, too, that puppies change so vastly in eight weeks that we cannot possibly be 100% correct. At that point, she tagged a few friends and several other skeptics arrived to share their thoughts.

One argument ran along the lines of, *This temperament test is a joke. If a breeder of a dog I was interested in claimed this, I'd run. Calling this temperament testing is deceitful.* Another person chimed in with, *Everything this breeder described is exactly what I would expect from every healthy puppy.* The original poster then shared that she knows lots of breeders and they all agree with her that temperament testing young pups like this is impossible. And the last argument made went something like, *The only thing I want from a pup at this age is attentiveness to mom and healthy feeding.* The woman who began the debate then declared her open distaste for Triton's claim and that she was no longer going to follow my page or this breed. Several others left with her.

By this time, I had a moment in my task-filled day and I felt quite empowered to speak my mind, so I sat down on the couch, put the laptop on my lap, and shared the following,

"Just because other breeders and dog trainers, even if it were all breeders and dog trainers in the entire world, do not agree with collecting temperament testing data at two days old does not mean that it cannot be done. Using the argument that 'the majority view is the right view' is not an argument. It is a logical fallacy and does not prove your point.

"Also, just because something hasn't been done, does not mean it can't be done. Believing so is also a logical fallacy. 'We've always done it this way'... or in this case... 'no one's ever done it this way'... is the logical fallacy of appeal to tradition. It is also not a valid argument and does not prove your point.

"You may disagree with collecting temperament data this young. That is your right. But, ridiculing me, and the project, for something you obviously know nothing about is dishonest. If you do not want to learn, but instead want to ridicule and spread hate about our project to others, that is also your right. Again, also dishonest, but it is a right you have.

"Here is a proposal for you... instead of posting with disdain about how wrong it is, it would have been much more productive to actually ask about the practice and find out what truly goes on. What is it that we actually see in a puppy this young? How can we see what we see in a puppy this young? What if... just what if... it were possible to see differing temperament traits in puppies this young? Would that be a bad thing... so wrong that one would stop following a breeder because they said it could be done?

"But again, as others have pointed out... it is one piece of information collected that is placed with two other standardized points of data that go along with a bunch of anecdotal evidence through constant observation that will give us a very well defined ability to know the innate, genetically inherited temperament in our dogs. We pride ourselves on this process. And... we do not force anyone to agree or purchase our dogs. So, you are free to do whatever you wish. We will continue to be honest, share our information openly, and breed great dogs."

- Jennifer Stoeckl, DireWolf Dogs of Vallecito Facebook page, July 28, 2018

I suppose I can be straightforward, too, when it is warranted. But, even though the skeptics did not have any solid evidence to support their views, are they, in fact, correct that a two day old puppy has no discernible temperament and simply eats and poops? Is it true that a puppy changes so drastically from two days to eight weeks that anything measured early would later be invalid? Let's delve into the science behind it and explore whether our claims are as outrageous as they may appear.

Different Types of Dog Behavior

For thousands of years dogs have enjoyed the position of man's best friend. There is some debate by scientists at the exact date that the wolf began its path toward domestication. Mark Derr explains in his book, How the Dog Became the Dog, "Genetic analyses conducted since the late 1990s have placed the origins of the dog as early as 135,000 years ago. That remains a tantalizing date, but most researchers into dog evolution have chosen to ignore it as too early. Scientists have divided into two camps, one placing dog origins around 40,000 to 50,000 years ago; the other, around 12,000 to 16,000 years ago. An additional proposed date of 27,000 years ago, based on nuclear DNA, came out of the completed sequencing of the dog genome."[1]

Regardless of when our domesticated partnership officially formed, through our close relationship with each other it seems that dogs have evolved to reveal a special kind of intelligence. Dr. Juliane Kaminski from Max Planck Institute in Germany found that our loyal companions can perform tasks that not even chimps could do.[2] Dogs have also been shown to effectively read our emotions and have adapted to closely watch and interpret our movements and body language.[3] According to recent scientific evidence, dogs have the equivalent ability to understand up to the level of a 2 year old child. As Science News magazine puts it in their article on dog intelligence, "Although you wouldn't want one to balance your checkbook, dogs can count. They can also understand more than 150 words, and intentionally deceive other dogs and people to get treats, according to a psychologist and leading canine researcher."[4] Some dogs can learn as many as 1000 different words and even interpret those words from graphic representations. Eighty-six-year-old retired psychology professor, John Pilley, demonstrates that his Border Collie, Chaser, knows the unique names of 800 cloth animals, 116 different balls, and more than a hundred plastic toys for a total of 1022 toys in all.[5]

However, in order to understand a dog's ability to communicate with us, it is necessary to understand how a dog's temperament varies depending on which tasks it was bred to perform. Some scientists believe that dogs were essential to our survival as a species. Until the beginning of the industrial revolution, dogs were bred to work together with us to find food and ward off enemies. Dogs helped us hunt, locate, and protect the things we needed. In return, they continued to thrive. As Greger Larson from Durham University in England concludes "Without dog domestication, civilization just would not have been possible."[6]

Different dog breeds show quite a wide range of adaptability to mold themselves in a human partnership. Some are excellent hunters, fearlessly attacking wild boar or other game. Others readily stay with sheep and goats as protectors from would-be predators. There are dogs that are bred to run extremely fast using their superior sight to chase down smaller fleeing prey. Still others use their soft bite to retrieve a delicate bird that has been flushed out in all types of terrain. Some breeds are superior diggers able to use their small bodies to enter fox or rabbit holes. Sled dogs have the stamina and independence to make split-second life-or-death decisions while traveling in very harsh weather conditions.

With the aid of human selection over thousands of years, these diverse abilities in dogs form our most cherished breeds, suggesting a large portion of any one dog's behavior is inherited. As geneticists Elaine Ostrander and Wayne Robert suggested in a discussion regarding the reasons behind why geneticists were interested in beginning genetic mapping with the dog, "the range of behavioral traits that appeared strongly associated with individual breeds suggested a mechanism to decipher the basic genetic vocabulary of behavior."[7]

Unfortunately, even the word "behavior" is not uniformly defined in the field of behavioral biology. Daniel Levitis, William Lidicker, and Glenn Freund co-authored a review article in 2009 regarding the definition of behavior as it is used in scientific publications. Their work illustrates just how diverse the definition for behavior is throughout the scientific community. The authors found absolutely no consensus after surveying 174 members of three behavior-focused scientific societies. In fact, there was widespread disagreement between those surveyed. The authors noted that respondents contradicted themselves, each other, and published definitions more than half of the time. The writers ultimately proposed a new definition, based on an overview of their findings that they hope other researchers will consistently adopt. "[B]ehaviour is the internally coordinated responses (actions and inactions) of whole living organisms (individuals and groups) to internal and/or external stimuli, excluding responses more easily understood as developmental changes."[7a] The researchers further excluded cognition as a component of behavior, stating that, "[w]hile behaviours necessarily rely upon internal information processing by the individual (e.g. cognition and endocrine signaling), we do not consider the processing alone to be a response, and therefore do not include it as a behaviour… In behaviour, we include the action, but deem the processing as necessary but not sufficient." They further reveal that this line of thinking is contrary to 80% of their respondents, but ultimately believe it to be illogical to include some internal processing and not others.

One aspect of the researcher's new approach to work toward a unified definition for behavior is that it allows for only outward or internal responses by the individual that can be controlled. Therefore, internal responses such as the secretion of digestive enzymes by the stomach in response to the presence of ingested food would not be considered a behavior under this definition. Furthermore, inaction that would need to be orchestrated by the animal as a response would also be reported as a behavior. They share the example of a guard dog that does not bark when it recognizes its owner. The dog must take in and process outside sensory information in order to determine how it will outwardly react. Because the dog must coordinate a number of different body systems in order to generate a response, the dog's non-verbal response should also be recorded as a behavior.

Types of Behavior

Instinctual - Inherited by all animals in the species

Innate - Inherited by some animals in the species with a degree of intensity

Learned - Positive/negative environmental experiences
- Observation
- Habituation
- Classical Conditioning
- Operant Conditioning

208

There are three types of behavior that an individual can exhibit: instinctive, innate, and learned. Instinctive behavior is a response to stimuli in the environment that occurs in all animals within a species. An example of an instinct would be when an unaltered dog marks territory. It is also instinct that drives a mother dog to dig during the birthing process. In contrast, although innate behaviors are also inherited, they can be altered through selection and not all dogs within the species respond in the same way to the same stimulus. An example of an innate behavior is the strong herding tendency in the Border Collie. Not all dogs possess an inherited herding ability, but some dog breeds, like the Border Collie, naturally collect animals into groups without ever being taught. Guarding is also another inherited behavior in the dog. Again, because not all dogs show the behavior equally, a guarding tendency is not considered instinctual, but innate.

The third type of behavior in dogs is not inherited, but instead is learned through positive or negative environmental experiences. These experiences can be learned through four different means: observation, habituation, classical conditioning, and operant conditioning. When a young puppy watches a morsel of ground beef drop to the floor and an older dog excitedly runs over to gobble it up, the watchful puppy will mimic the older dog's behavior the next time. In this example, the puppy learned through observation. When a young puppy experiences initial fear when passing by a barking dog on the other side of a fence, but then walks past that dog day after day until it no longer shows fear behaviors, the puppy learned through habituation. (A common word for habitual learning in dogs is socialization.) A dog can also learn through associated experiences. If the first few times a dog rides in a car to go to the vet and has negative experiences, the dog might end up fearing the car, even when it is later used to go to fun places. This would be an example of classical conditioning. Classical conditioning If a person signals a dog to sit and when it does is given a piece of chicken, this would be an example of operant conditioning. Operant conditioning is when an animal learns to perform a behavior more or less frequently through a reward or punishment that follows the behavior.[7b]

Personality vs Temperament

Oftentimes, differentiating between these three types of behavior can pose quite a challenge and, just as we explored with the definition of behavior, the three types of behavior are quite frequently used interchangeably, mixed up, and contradicted. The main focus of this chapter, however, is the innate behavior in the dog. This is because the Dire Wolf Project aims to continue to advance the domestication of the dog by reducing further working dog behaviors in order to more easily fit within our fast-paced and technology-based modern society. In light of this, there are two ways some choose to describe a dog's inherent behavior. Some use the term personality, while others use the word temperament. But, what is meant when one uses one term over the other? As above, these words are rarely consistently defined or used in a uniform manner.

Here are a few examples of the different definitions for the term temperament that are in current use:

1. Norma Bennet Woolf (Dog Owner's Guide), "Temperament is the general attitude a dog has towards other animals and people. Temperament is inherited but can be modified or enhanced by the environment."[8]

2. Amber Drake writing for "The Dog People" at Rover.com, "A dog's temperament is essentially the dog's general attitude toward people or other animals, and is a result of both inherited and environmental factors."[9]

3. Linda Cole writing for Canidae, "Temperament is defined as the physical and mental reaction to a stimulus." She continues, "A dog's temperament is largely based on instincts, but his environment also influences behavior."[10]

4. The American Temperament Testing Society, Inc, along with many others, uses the definition proposed by W. Handel, a German Police Dog Trainer, in his article, "The Psychological Basis of Temperament Testing" which reads, "the sum total of all inborn and acquired physical and mental traits and talents which determines, forms and regulates behavior in the environment"[11]

5. "Fisher & Volhard (1985, p.36) define temperament as 'the dog's suitability for a specific task or function.'"[12]

The first and second examples above pose a broad view of a dog's general attitude, which naturally leads one to a highly subjective interpretation of temperament. A general attitude of a happy, energetic Cattle Dog with possessive tendencies toward other animals might mean something completely different to a rancher wanting a herd protection dog than to a family living in an apartment in New York City.

The third and fourth examples share a combined view of both the inherited and the environmental aspects of a dog's entire behavioral make-up. While it is nice to have a sum total description of all that a dog is, this type of description conveniently fails to differentiate between these two very important aspects of a dog's behavior. Being able to discern exactly what is an innate response and what has been learned is a powerful distinction for both the breeder and the owner. Clearly, there are aspects of a dog's behavior that have been inherited, or the typical differences within breed function would not exist. Purposefully failing to determine between the two is a convenient way to approach a complex concept.

The last example seems to imply a particular ability toward completing various tasks instead of its innate qualities. What a dog can or cannot do may suggest an inherited origin, but may also suggest a learned response. Furthermore, the term "suitability" is also vague and can be varied in definition depending on the understanding of the person interpreting a dog's responses.

All of the above examples wrote in general terms to describe both an innate response as well as a learned response. According to personality psychologists, Philip J. Corr and Gerald Matthews, from Cambridge University, personality is generally defined as a set of behaviors, cognitions, and emotional patterns that evolve from biological and environmental factors.[12a] This definition of personality, which involves both innate and learned responses, seems to encompass what the examples above portray. Furthermore, each of the ideas presented above agrees that there are different types of personalities, but vastly disagrees on the definition for what those types would be.

Researchers who study canine behavior show quite a range of understanding between the use of the two terms temperament and personality. A comprehensive research review on the temperament and personality in dogs, compiled by Amanda Jones and Samuel Gosling from the Department of Psychology at the University of Texas in Austin observe, "One seemingly trivial, yet pervasive, basis for distinguishing between temperament and personality is the disciplinary affiliation of the researchers associated with each term. Research [between] animal and human has tended to use the term temperament and research [between] human children and adults has tended to use the term personality. However, this distinction is not maintained consistently and the terms are often used interchangeably."[13]

Without a solid definition of what exactly establishes a dog's temperament, we cannot hope to describe the different aspects it entails. It is for this reason that the Dire Wolf Project has chosen to maintain a specific differentiation between how a dog generally acts (personality) and its inherited natural response to stimuli (temperament). Dr. Radciffe Robins at the Cornell University College of Veterinary Medicine clearly explains the Dire Wolf Project's idea of temperament,

"Characteristics of Temperament
- Temperament is primarily a function of the dog's neurological makeup

- Temperament is 100% genetic; it is inherited, and fixed at the moment of the dog's fertilization/conception/birth
- Temperament in the dog cannot be eliminated nor transformed from one type to another. It cannot change during a dog's lifetime. It is the permanent mental/neurological characteristic of the individual dog. But there may be an overlap of different temperament [traits] in the same dog. For example sharpness may be seen with over aggression or submissiveness with being temperamental.
- Environment, Socialization or Training can modify the expression of an individual dog's temperament, but they cannot transform it nor eliminate it. The dog will die with the temperament with which it was born."[14]

We propose the following succinct definition for temperament to incorporate the concepts embedded within Dr. Radcliffe's characteristics of temperament above. This definition for temperament was first presented by Wayne Davis of the West Virginia K9 College in the 1980s. "The physical and mental characteristics of an individual dog, made evident through its reaction to stimuli in its environment."[15] Many others hold to this definition as well. Therefore, temperament can be viewed as a person or animal's nature or genetic predisposition, while personality or character can be said to contain the configuration of habits or one's disposition.

A Pretty Face

Before we move on, it is important to pause a moment and make sure of one thing. When assessing temperament in dogs, it is essential to choose for temperament before outward appearance. As Lois Schwarz is fond of saying, "It doesn't matter if a dog is pink with purple polka dots, temperament always comes first." This concept is one of the most difficult aspects for many breeders to adhere. When a beautiful dog comes along, it is so hard to look past that pretty face to truly assess a dog's inner beauty without bias. When its temperament is ultimately not ideal, letting that dog go from the breeding program is a very difficult, but a necessary choice to make.

I was faced with this very decision early on in my breeding career and I am very grateful that I had Lois as my breeding mentor to show me the way forward. I bred my female, Sooner, out of Packer and Ricotta to a lovely white shepherd/malamute crossbreed named Don Juan. Sooner had five puppies: a beautiful black sable male, a gold sable male, two silver sable females, and a black and tan female. The black sable male was hands down the most gorgeous puppy and had a truly amazing black wolf look with yellow eyes. There was only one problem. He was extremely vocal. He whined, barked, howled, and cried out all of the time. This was the very first litter I had ever experienced from beginning to end and I knew nothing at all about inherited dog temperament.

Don Juan/Sooner puppies (2010)

When I called Lois to talk with her about the litter, she specifically asked me to tell her which puppy was the quietest, calmest, and most easy-going. Now, I had no real background on how to assess these traits, but I could generally give a good idea of those three in comparison to only the puppies in this one litter. When I was honest with myself and only looked at the behaviors of the puppies themselves compared to one another, I knew that the black and tan puppy embodied all of those traits Lois had asked about. How my heart yearned to keep that beautiful black wolf-looking puppy, though. The prestige I would receive walking him downtown. The notoriety he would have online with the amazing pictures I could produce. The advancements in the look of the wild wolf that we could achieve within the breed. I really wanted to keep him, but Lois assured me that he was not the puppy for us. I reluctantly sold him, following Lois's mentorship, which then launched me into a serious investigation on the subject of a dog's inherited temperament.

Nature vs Nurture

When one begins any discussion of inherited temperament, one invariably runs into the nature versus nurture argument. Is a dog exhibiting a certain behavior because it was born that way, because its environment and surroundings lead it to react that way, or a combination of both with no way of discerning between them? How can someone know for certain whether a behavior is motivated by inheritance or by influence? This is especially important for a breeder, but owners may also want to know the inherited aspects of a dog's behavioral predisposition in order to guide them through specific and targeted training to counter any negative behaviors that may manifest.

Breeding for a specifically inherited temperament is extremely difficult, though, because before a breeder can do this effectively, that person must be able to differentiate between a dog's learned behavior (or environmental conditioning) and its inherited temperament (the actual genetic traits that will be passed on to the offspring). Unfortunately, science has not yet revealed any individual genes that contribute to the behavioral traits on which we hope to select. So, the only option for breeders is to use phenotype (the outward expression of a genetic trait) as a means of selection. The most difficult thing for an individual, however, is to be able to select the behavior that is associated with the actual genetic trait and not mistakenly select for a behavior that is not actually associated with inheritance.

Here is a clear example of when someone mistakes a dog's outward behavior for its inherited temperament. A couple, interested in a Labrador Retriever puppy, notice a particularly lovely chocolate male Labrador Retriever. This dog sits patiently in the back of a pickup waiting for his owner to return from the store. He is beautiful and majestic with a peaceful attitude toward them as they talk to him in the adjacent parking space. The owner returns shortly thereafter and the couple speak to the owner about his beautiful dog. The couple learn that the owner occasionally breeds him, so they exchange numbers. The couple go to see the beautiful chocolate Labrador Retriever at his home and the owner shows them how the Lab obeys every command. "I want a puppy just like him," the couple exclaim as they drive away from the exciting visit, unaware that the owner professionally trains his Labrador Retrievers for competition and this particular example was the most trained of the dogs the owner kept. When the couple return to choose their puppy and bring it home, they are surprised that this puppy is not as calm and well-mannered as the father. Their puppy barks and chases everything in the backyard, shows off its much increased energy level. But worst of all, he does not come when called.

Essentially, there are only two ways to obtain a good dog: acquire a dog with a stable inherited temperament that fits with one's unique lifestyle or train a dog to fit into one's unique lifestyle. Good dog trainers can work with each dog's different reactions to various stimuli and shape or mold the dog through experience and consistent training methods. Even if a dog shows problem behaviors, a good trainer can counter those so that a dog begins to respond appropriately and consistently. But, not all owners are great dog trainers or have access to a trainer that will be able to instruct the owner on how to modify a dog's behavior. It is for this reason that more and more owners are increasingly interested in acquiring a puppy that has all of the basic building blocks they need to eliminate the necessity of having to counter any unwanted inherited instincts that a beloved dog may exhibit. At the same time, when a person looks to choose a puppy for a particularly highly-skilled environment, such as military, police, or guide dog work, it becomes increasingly important to begin with the raw material that will show the most likely success within the program. If not, one can end up wasting valuable time and resources on a dog that simply did not have the best potential in the first place. The more a breeder or working dog program developer can successfully identify the dogs that have the best potential for passing on desirable temperament to their offspring, the better.

Heritability

But, how can a person determine how much of the environment plays a role in the reported behavioral differences in dogs? Behavioral geneticists have developed a way to answer this question and describe whether the probability of the behavior differences within a test group may be attributed to the environment or to genetic differences. It is called heritability. Heritability is defined by Encyclopedia Britannica as the "amount of phenotypic (observable) variation in a population that is attributable to individual genetic differences. Heritability, in a general sense, is the ratio of variation due to differences between genotypes to the total phenotypic variation for a character or trait in a population."[16]

So, if the environment can be shown to play a larger role in the observed behavior differences within a group, there is a lower heritability percentage. If the environment can be shown to play a smaller role in the observed behavior differences within a group, there is a higher heritability percentage. Therefore, within a given population, heritability would be the proportion of variation, or percentage of variation, between individuals that one could attribute to genes.

Suppose we state that the heritability of dog intelligence is 50%. This statement does not mean that the intelligence of a dog is 50% genetic. To clarify, imagine a litter of eight Basenji puppies. Four of the puppies are placed in loving homes with regular training as a control group. Each of the other four puppies are placed in separate 10x10 foot concrete spaces away from any stimulus from people or other dogs for a period of sixteen months. The exact same food automatically cascades down a tube each day at the same time and water comes from an automatic waterer. The bottom of the cage is wire mesh so waste can fall below, which is manually removed once a day through a hole. In this scenario, the four isolated puppy environments would be 100% controlled; quite sadistically controlled in fact, but completely controlled nonetheless. By sixteen months, the four isolated puppies' problem solving abilities would likely be quite low compared to the other littermates that were raised and trained in homes. Imagine now that each isolated dog is placed into a maze in which the amount of completion time as well as how many mistakes are made is tracked. Even though their environments have been 100% controlled, likely their abilities to successfully complete the maze would be different from one another. These differences could then be described as 100% heritable because none of the observed differences in their performance could be attributed to differences in environment.

It is extremely important for a breeder to understand the concept of heritability because altering the inherited temperament in dogs must involve selecting the genetic components of a dog's outward behavior and not simply what one perceives to be a dog's temperament. If the heritability of a trait is high, then the outward manifestation of a dog's behavior will be a good indication of its genetics. Choosing puppies with the best behaviors (phenotype) will also then be choosing puppies with the best genes (genotype). Conversely, if the heritability of a trait is low, then the outward manifestation of a dog's behavior will be a poor indication of its genetics. In other words, a dog that acts calm and collected may not actually possess the genes to pass on calm and collected to its offspring. Perhaps it was simply well trained, as was the case with the Labrador Retriever example above.

Dog shows are also good examples of how dogs can be trained to act a certain way in a controlled environment, but then act completely differently in another. On February 12, 2019, just after the AKC announced the Best in Show winner at the Westminster Dog Show, the top winning dogs' owners were interviewed about their dog's natural behaviors when out of the show ring. A Dachshund named Burns was described this way, "With his sausage of a body, short legs and big personality, Burns the longhaired dachshund looks guileless in the ring. His chestnut locks sweep the ground with every step. But at home … 'He's an escape artist,' said Carlos Puig, Burns's handler. There was the time he shimmied up a tree trunk next to a fence. Or the day he pulled a Ferris Bueller and went missing for four hours. He was later found on a construction site, eating lunch with the workers. While his ancestors in Germany were bred to hunt badgers, Burns prefers babies. 'He adores babies,' Puig said. 'If he sees a stroller, he dives his head right in there and then all of a sudden the baby goes, 'Wahhhhhh!'' If Burns finds an empty stroller, his instinct goes into overdrive. 'He starts digging around through the stroller, through everything, as if to say, 'Where's the baby?'' All of those instincts were kept in check when Burns won the hound group on Monday."[17]

Burns certainly gave no indication of his escapist, baby-loving ways while trotting around the show ring. If a person mistakenly bought one of Burns's puppies on the sole basis of his show ring performance, that person might be surprised at the behavior their new puppy exhibited. Furthermore, when one compares this Dachshund's behavior to other Dachshunds all over the world, how much of this pooch's behavior in the show ring could be attributed to its inherited temperament versus what this dog displayed in its home environment? Could Burns's tendency to dig into baby strollers be compared to the Dachshund's badger hunting instincts? In order to better answer these questions, one must take environment out of the equation in order to determine the highest possible heritability. Without an ability to remove environmental differences altogether finding the true genetic components of a dog's temperament can be very tricky. Let us now explore the two ways in which a person can eliminate environment in order to reveal what lies within a dog's inherited temperament.

Purebred Dog Breeds Help Show Inherited Temperament

Another way to sort out the genetic components of a dog's behavior compared to its environment is to compare the behavior of purebred dogs within completely different environments. Any behaviors held in common throughout much of the purebred population despite the large variability of environment could then be said to have a higher degree of heritability.

Achieving High Heritability

If high heritability is the ideal in order to make sure that a breeder or program director is choosing the actual genetic traits needed to produce the best potential inherited temperament in a group of dogs, how does one go about making sure to obtain it on a regular basis? As we hypothetically explored in the heritability section above, if a researcher were to be able to control every aspect of a dog's environment, the resulting differences between the dogs within such a study would reveal the genetic components of a dog's behavior. There are two possible ways to eliminate the environment from becoming a factor: control 100% of an experimental environment as we explored previously or observe behavior variations in newborns.

Although we were only speaking hypothetically at the time, actually, there have been extensive investigations seeking to completely eliminate any environmental effects so that heredity acting through behavior can be exposed. One experiment, in particular, remains the most comprehensive study done on the inherited temperament in dogs to date. We will explore its findings in a moment. But in general, controlling every aspect of a dog's environment and then replicating that exact environment for groups of dogs in order to compare their reactions to specific testing situations is very time-consuming, expensive, and in our modern minds today may even be deemed unethical.

When breeding dogs for a specific purpose it can be expensive and time-consuming to raise multiple dogs into adulthood raising them in exactly the same way to eliminate any environmental aspects before determining if a specific dog would make a good candidate for the work. It is much more economical and efficient if a breeding organization could determine the inherited temperament of a puppy as early as possible. Another added benefit to testing a young puppy is that the environment has not had time to become a significant factor. Therefore, the other way to make sure that environment is not a factor in any aspect of a dog's reaction to standardized tests is to test very young puppies. This latter idea, however, has not been significantly validated by researchers which we will also explore below.

Controlled Experiments and the Neonatal Period

A prominent long term series of experiments begun in 1945 conducted by John Paul Scott and John L. Fuller over a twenty year period remains the most comprehensive study on inherited dog temperament to date. As they explain, "Our over-all experimental design was to systematically vary the genetic constitution of the dogs while keeping all other factors as constant as possible.[18] They selected five diverse breeds for their intensive study: Basenjis, Beagles, American Cocker Spaniels, Shetland Sheep Dogs, and Wire-haired Fox Terriers. These five breeds represented most of the major groups of dogs recognized by dog breeders at the time; excluding toy and non-sporting dogs.

They separated their work into two phases: 1) establishing the similarities and differences among the different purebred breeds when raised in the same environment and 2) creating Mendelian crosses between two highly diverse breeds, namely the Basenji and the American Cocker Spaniel. The study extensively measured both of the ways for eliminating environment from the equation of inherited dog temperament by testing neonate behaviors between each breed as well as controlling all aspects of the dogs' environment as they grew in order to then measure their reactions as youth and adults. A total of 470 dogs and 102 litters were tested in a number of ways, including switching mothers at birth in order to analyze the effects a mother had on teaching her young.

From the very first moments after birth, the researchers acknowledged that it was obvious the puppies changed drastically from day to day and week to week. They knew that the heredity within a single puppy had to remain constant over time, but they quickly realized that the vast changes in growth meant that each puppy's inherited temperament had to manifest itself through a very different animal at birth than it did only a few weeks later. They devised a systematic observation schedule starting at birth and continuing up to sixteen weeks of age in the hopes of seeing the earliest manifestations of hereditary differences. The puppies were not touched by humans until five weeks old and the trained observers wrote down everything that occurred each day within a ten minute window. The researchers conclude that "[d]uring the very early stages of development there was so little behavior observed that there was little opportunity for genetic differences to be expressed. When the complex patterns of behavior did appear, they did not show pure and uncontaminated effects of heredity."[19] This clearly indicates that the period between birth and when complex patterns of behavior appear would normally be ideal for showing neonatal inherited temperament. The problem they faced, however, was that the researchers were able to observe measurable behavior during this time.

Test	Social	Emotional	Forced Training	Reward Training	Problem Solving	Physical or Physiological	Age (weeks)
Daily observation	x						0–16
Weekly observation, weighing			x			x	0–16
Maternal behavior	x						1, 7
Response to handling	x						5, 7, 9, 11, 13, 15, 52
Dominance							
Group	x						2, 3, 4, 6, 7, 8, 9, 10
Paired	x						5, 11, 15, 52
First barrier (detour)					x		6
Response to veterinary care		x					8, 10, 12, 14
Goal orientation or habit formation				x			9
Manipulation					x		10
Second barrier (maze)					x		14–15
(Transferred to outside runs)							17
Bi-weekly inspection, catching time			x				17–52
Somatotype, weighing						x	17, 34, 51
Reactivity		x					17, 34, 51
Following				x			18
Leash control and stair climbing			x				19–20
Motivation, T-maze				x			22
Discrimination, T-maze					x		23
Delayed response, T-maze					x		24–26
Trailing					x		27
Motor skill				x			29
Obedience			x				30
Retrieving				x			32
Spatial orientation					x		33–36
Physiological assessment						x	51
Response to confinement		x					51

Schedule of Observations, Training, and Testing
Scott and Fuller. Genetics and the Social Behavior of the Dog. University of Chicago Press. 1965. Table: 1.3. Kindle Edition.

Once the puppies reached five weeks old, they tested the puppies in various ways every two weeks until they were fifteen weeks old. The first performance test began at six weeks, in which the puppies had to navigate a barrier in order to find food. Mazes and social tests were also incorporated. The following is a table of the various tests performed at different developmental stages over the lifetime of the experiment.

During the neonate period (newborn to two weeks), the team developed several theories which still exist today. First of all, they recognized that puppies have a sense of touch and a sense of taste. The researchers reasoned that a puppy does not seem to have a sense of smell, although a study since this time by Peter G. Hepper and Deborah L. Wells strongly suggests that a newborn puppy does, indeed, have a sense of smell. "Perinatal exposure [to aniseed] resulted in a significantly greater preference for the aniseed food than the other types of exposure."[20] The Scott and Fuller study also noticed that newborn puppies did not seem to learn by experience. "A puppy would crawl to the edge of the scale platform, fall off, and begin to yelp in distress. When placed in the middle of the platform, it would do the same thing over again."[21] They also acknowledged that although motor capacities were limited, a neonatal puppy's vocalizations consist mainly of distress vocalization in a series of rapid whines and yelps. They ultimately concluded that "[t]he [neonatal] puppy can be greatly disturbed physiologically by averse condition, but there are few ways in which it can be affected psychologically."[22] They further conclude that "all behavior at this age is adapted to infantile life and that the characteristic patterns of adult behavior are completely missing. In fact, if one had only behavior to go by, one might assume that the neonatal puppy belonged to an entirely different species from adult dogs."[23]

One significant aspect that the Scott and Fuller experiments revealed was the distinct difference in the rate of vocalizations categorized by breed. Although they mention the finding only in passing, it is significant that the Beagle was reported to have far fewer vocalizations as a neonate than was seen in the later periods. It is also interesting to note that the Basenji showed a more prolonged incidence of vocalizations in the neonate period than the puppies did once their eyes and ears began to open. The fact that puppies use their vocal abilities as neonates to signal their distress is also significant. The researchers attributed these differences to the scale stating, "These reactions were obtained while the pups were weighed and probably measure discomfort resulting from contact with the cold metal scale platform."[24]

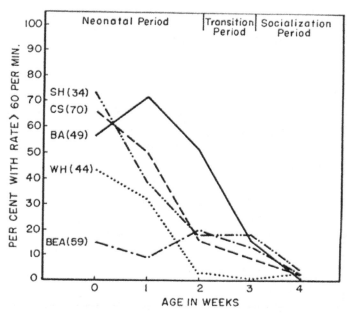

Distress vocalization decline rate - first 4 wks
Scott and Fuller. Genetics and the Social Behavior of
the Dog. University of Chicago Press. 1965. Fig. 4.1.

But the mere fact that each breed reacted so differently during weekly weigh/measure time for four weeks allows a glimpse into each breed's inherent differences that cannot be attributed to environment or learned response. Although we cannot know why each puppy became distressed at this time, it is important to note that it did occur. Unfortunately, the Scott and Fuller experiments did not notice very many behaviors in neonates on which they could assess, so only one observation during this time, the distress vocalizations, was tracked.

Another significant study completed in 1997 tested 630 eight week old German Shepherd puppies in several areas including: sociability, independence, fearfulness, competitiveness, general activity and explorative behavior. These scores were then compared to scores gathered at 450-600 days of age using the Swedish Dog Training Centre's protocol for selecting dogs for different kind of work, including breeding. The researchers noted that "individual variation in behaviour observed among puppies to a large extent can be explained both by hereditary factors and by effects of common litter environment. The results also implies [sic] that adult behaviour cannot be predicted as early as at eight weeks of age. Breeding programs aimed to improve behaviour in dogs may not be based on information collected on tests performed as early as at eight weeks of age."[25] In this study, it appears that high heritability was seen at eight weeks among the puppies with significant differences reported among them, but these differences were not seen to be predictive of adult behavior.

A more recent inherited temperament study done specifically with Border Collies in 2014 by Stefanie Riemer et al attempted to compare neonatal reactions to six week old puppies and again to adults between one and a half to two years old. Ninety-nine puppies from eighteen litters raised in separate breeder homes were tested using standardized measures. Each two to ten day old puppy was separated from its mother for an average of fifty-five minutes prior to each test. They were first laid on a blanket which had been visually divided into a grid of sixteen squares. The distance each puppy traveled and the degree of vocalization within two minutes was then recorded. After the two minutes, the experimenter picked up the puppy and measured sucking force based on an objective scale. The puppies were then also tested at six weeks and again as adults. The researchers ultimately "found little correspondence between individuals' behaviour in neonate, puppy and adult test. Exploratory activity was the only behaviour that was significantly correlated between the puppy and the adult test. We conclude that the predictive validity of early tests for predicting specific behavioural traits in adult pet dogs is limited."[26]

Many other studies have been performed especially to determine suitability for guide and service dog programs. Most research does not attempt to test during the neonate or transitional periods and those that do clearly show very little correlation for predictive adult behaviors. It is interesting, however, that the studies report significant differences among same age puppies. Dire Wolf Project breeders also regularly report significant differences in the observable behavior of same age puppies. These differences are exactly what Dire Wolf Project breeders focus on to make selective breeding decisions for each litter bred into the project since the beginning of the breed. Because environment and experience play a larger and larger role and inherited traits diminish as time passes, it is unwise to expect neonate, transitional, and puppy testing results to successfully predict adult behavior. Early temperament testing establishes the best chance for obtaining dogs who have the greatest potential, but it can never predict what actual observable behavior will result.

- True: Early temperament testing cannot predict adult behavior.
- True: Early temperament testing eliminates environmental influence and therefore reveals inherited temperament.
- True: Early temperament testing indicates puppies with the greatest potential for preferred adult character.

What can be achieved through standardized temperament testing, as well, is a way to categorize the inherited temperament observed within a litter.

Through testing, both standardized testing and regular observational reporting, it is possible to show which puppies do not possess the skills at that point in their development to go on in the breed. If a breeder can quickly identify the puppies who show unwanted negative behaviors, such as excess vocalization, fear-based reactions, heightened distress when isolated, significant struggle when confined, etc., he/she can further assess the puppies that have not yet shown a significantly identifiable innate response to the early testing. With each standardized test and anecdotal observation the likelihood that the breed's overall inherited temperament will begin to shift, regardless of how the puppies actually react as adults. <u>This is because adult behavior can be greatly shaped and molded through both experience and training and is much less likely to be reflective of inherited temperament.</u>

Let me be clear. The Dire Wolf Project does not utilize neonate and transitional temperament testing to predict adult behavior. We use temperament tests to compare the puppies against themselves in a standardized way. We report significant differences in temperament, especially in puppies of lower generational value (first or second generations) within the project, which guides us in determining the puppies that should and should not continue to shape the breed.

What is a "RAW Pup™?"

A "RAW pup" is a term coined by Lois Schwarz to describe a young puppy that has not been handled by humans, socialized, or trained in any way. This testing is important as it makes sure that the breeder assesses the genetic principle in each puppy's temperament and not a puppy that has been conditioned through touch or manipulation since birth. This test is especially important to do with crossbred litters, but must be performed on all American Alsatian dog litters in order to form a basis and standard for breed-wide inherited temperament. These tests are not predictive of adult behavior, but merely a way to differentiate between the inherited temperaments of the puppies. These tests have been performed for each litter since the beginning first generation dogs in 1988 and each puppy has been scored according to the temperament testing scoring guide established by Lois Schwarz. Trained breeders within the Dire Wolf Project now have a solid basis on which to compare the American Alsatian pup to the purebred German Shepherd Dog, Alaskan Malamute, English Mastiff, Anatolian Shepherd Dog, and Great Pyrenees among others.

Certified American Alsatian Dog breeders formally temperament test each puppy bred into the Dire Wolf Project at the beginning of each puppy developmental period including: the neonatal period, the transitional period, and the social period identified by Fuller and Scott as discussed earlier. Each test is scored using the established rubric for the breed, which is included in the Appendix section of this book. The first standardized "RAW pup" test established specifically for the American Alsatian Dog breed is performed just after birth. A puppy must remain in its natural state until 2.5 to 3 weeks old when breeders perform the second standardized temperament test. This means that a breeder must not interfere with the puppies in any way other than necessary cleaning. However, the breeder must be a constant observer of any significant differences in each puppy's reactions to natural events during this time. Responses could show what a puppy does when separated from the litter, after the mother has been away for a specific amount of time, how verbal a particular pup is compared to others in the litter, etc. After the second standardized temperament test has been completed with all puppies in the litter, a breeder now begins to socialize and shape a puppy's personality based on the testing results. A puppy that scores poorly on the "RAW pup" testing will be socialized much more than the others. This will raise the puppy's scores on the third temperament test, which is not a "RAW pup" test, but a test to measure the success of the training and experience interventions performed by the breeder. This, then, prepares each puppy for the transition to its new home on average from eight to twelve weeks of age.

The Holy Grail of Inherited Temperament

The missing link for inherited dog temperament is how observed behavior in young puppies correlates to observed behaviors in adult dogs. Someone could literally revolutionize dog breeding forever if he/she could match early puppy reaction to stimuli with adult behavior at a high rate of heritability. Unfortunately for breeders, there is no easy answer and the quest to find the Holy Grail of inherited dog temperament must take into account the vast experiences and training that dogs undergo as a natural consequence of existence. As the Riemer study on early behavior in pet dogs concluded, "Future studies should investigate developmental trajectories by repeatedly assessing dogs between the age of 6 weeks and 1.5 years and by following them up until old age. This will yield further insights into the ontogeny of behaviour in dogs and the question from what age meaningful predictions about later behaviour can be made."[27]

It is interesting that so many researchers wish to pursue this line of thinking, as if developing observable measures in the young and comparing them to the adult is the only way forward. Dogs are extremely malleable, so without a consistent way to remove the environmental influences that shape and change one adult dog from another, it becomes almost an impossibility to accomplish a true definitive comparison between young puppies and adults. And yet, we know that certain aspects of a dog's temperament must be inherited, so perhaps a specific test can be devised.

One of the foundational aspects of a test for adult animals that could reveal inherited temperament traits is described by Dr. Temple Grandin, a well-known animal behaviorist working at the University of Denver, "In all animals, genetic factors influence reactions to situations which cause fear therefore, temperament is partially determined by an individual animal's fear response."[28] In other words, an important factor in assessing an adult animal's inherent responses is to elicit a fear response. Without causing stress for an adult animal in order to counter the effects of learning and experience, one cannot hope to observe an innate response to various stimuli. A sudden mysterious loud noise, an unexpected nearby movement, an intimidating approach by a stranger, etc may be some of the ways in which someone could observe the inherited response in grown dogs, if one can get passed the ethics committee.

However, another important aspect of an adult inherited temperament test is novelty, therefore, the test may not be shared in any way with the handler and ideally the dog has had no exposure to the test stimuli or environment over its lifetime. That is why the American Temperament Testing Society, Inc cannot possibly test the inherited temperament of a dog even though their protocols attempt to produce an inherited response. Each aspect of the test is clearly posted publicly so that anyone can expose their dog to the format of the test in advance, thereby invalidating the score. While the opening umbrella does potentially startle a dog, a person can still teach a dog to react to startling events like an umbrella opening quickly and without warning. This significantly skews any ability to test a dog's inherited temperament. But, as we explored at the beginning of this chapter, the American Temperament Testing Society, Inc does not hold to the same definition of temperament as the Dire Wolf Project.

Which Temperament Traits Should One Choose?

Every breeding program has a different need for the inherited temperament in their dogs. A K9 police unit may need a dog to exhibit high drive and willingness as well as a protective, tenacious nature. A guide dog program may look for a confident and calm dog with an innate ability to sustain a level of patient resolve instead of pushy determination. When working to differentiate a desired behavior from an inherited temperament trait, a person must break down a dog's outward abilities to its most fundamental levels. When a person can identify the actual inherited aspects of a dog's temperament, one is better able to select the right genetic temperament combination for the task.

Tervuren Hitting a Flyball Box

Credit: Elf, Nov 2004, Scottsdale, AZ.
Source: http://en.wikipedia.org/wiki/Image:Flyballbox_terv_wb.j
pg

As a fun example, let's dissect the abilities required for a dog to win at Flyball racing. If we break down the components to the most basic requirements of this fast-paced dog relay race perhaps we can arrive at an approximation of what may need to be inherited in order to outperform other teams. Suppose a person wanted to produce an entire breed of dog that would instinctively perform well in Flyball. The first thing the breeder would need to determine is what the actual aspects of a dog's genetically inherited temperament are that will produce a winning dog. Let's break down the task of Flyball into its most fundamental parts.

The sport of Flyball requires short bursts of speed, enough size to hit the spring-loaded ejection box coupled with a light enough weight that won't impede the dog's agility, a keen eye for fast ball retrieval, an ability to turn on a dime, and a heightened willingness to play the game. If we break these down into their fundamentals, we come to the following:

- Top sprinting speeds
- Agility
- Medium size/weight
- Athletic body type
- Ability to detect a distant object while sprinting
- Strong desire to chase
- Desire to perform

Luckily for us, there is already a breed of dog that has been bred for centuries to achieve top speeds over short distances, but also has the smaller size preference as an added benefit. The Whippet, known as the "Poor Man's Racehorse," can reach speeds of 35 miles an hour, stands 18 to 22 inches tall at the shoulders, and weighs 15-31 pounds.[29] Not only is its body shape ideal for accelerating quickly and running at top speeds, but the Whippet is a willing participant in racing sports. Obviously, all of these traits have been inherited in this breed as they are uniformly passed down to each offspring. Indeed, at the 2016 Crufts dog show, the Flyball team, Four Paws Flyers, that included the Whippet named Hustle, repeatedly made up for any lost gains in time the team may have acquired. As the announcer revealed, "Four Paws Flyers take the first leg and this [Hustle] is probably one of the quickest Flyball dogs I have ever seen. I would love to get a stopwatch on it. Wastes no time and it really does help out the Four Paws Flyers."[30] Although Four Paws Flyers did not ultimately win the final show down, the only dog to be identified by name for its superior speed and agility from the announcers was the Whippet.

Now, if a dog breed can be selectively bred for the specific body design that allows it to reach top speeds over land, the desire to chase objects moving away, the energy to sustain sprinting speeds, the keen eyesight to track fast-moving prey, and the agility to change direction on a dime, we could also assume that one could breed against these qualities. Perhaps instead of wanting a dog to fun the fastest, we want a dog breed to not have a tendency to run at all, but instead lope or walk; a slow dog instead of a fast one. How slow could we achieve? Perhaps instead of a dog that desires the chase, we could produce a dog that desires to remain stationary, even when prompted by an excited animal running away. Perhaps instead of an agile dog that could turn 180 degrees in a split second, we wanted a dog that lumbered and sauntered around the turns on a track. Even when coaxed and encouraged, its top speed was achieved by trotting at an easy pace. Assuming the health of the dog was intact and the structure of the dog was normal, if we can breed for certain specifically inherited traits, it would stand to reason that we could also breed against these same specifically inherited traits.

Luckily for us, there is a breed of dog that embodies the slow, methodical plodding of a lumbering canine. Reaching top speeds of only 15 miles an hour, the English Mastiff, with its large frame and easy-going attitude, has little desire to chase. As Karen B. London, PhD, a certified applied animal behaviorist, certified professional dog trainer, and author on dog training and behavior, wrote about an English Mastiff running through an Agility course, "This dog [English Mastiff] is more mellow and a great deal slower than a lot of other dogs, but his efforts are appreciated. His body is not perfectly suited to the sport, but he does it anyway, and that's what makes it so beautiful. It's a bit like watching a weight lifter compete in figure skating or a shot putter attempting to run a marathon. It's clearly not the perfect match between body

227

type and event, but just participating is admirable."[31] The English Mastiff is massive and heavy-boned reaching weights of 200 pounds, but as Dr. London further notes, "The dog continues at his pace, not looking overly exuberant, but showing no signs of reluctance either."

Body type seems to have a lot to do with a dog's speed capabilities. We can definitely place the confines of body type into our temperament equation, but desire and persistent dedication also play an inherited role in how willing a dog is to perform, despite its overall size. The easy-going Bloodhound, while also a thick-boned, heavy dog for its size (23-27in. tall), weighing up to 110 pounds is overall much smaller than the English Mastiff. According to AKC, the Bloodhound, "...has earned a reputation as a man-trailer without equal. Police departments around the world have relied on these muscular, single-minded hounds to follow the scent of humans-maybe a criminal, or a lost child, or a confused senior. An assignment might last all day and night, over hills and through swamps, but Bloodhounds won't give up until they follow the trail to the end. Even in these days of high-technology, no scenting device yet invented is as accurate as the Bloodhound nose."[32] Due to this breed's consistent ability to track scent with unyielding dedication, "[t]estimony of a Bloodhound's mantrailing results is acceptable in almost any court," the AKC reports.[33]

It appears that size is not the only equation in a dog if we want to develop slow and methodical dedication to task. If the Bloodhound can be bred for centuries for the ability and desire to search for lost people at such a superior level that their results are admissible in court, then it also stands to reason that these traits must be somehow inherited in the dog. As Deputy Williams shares, speaking about his search and rescue dog, Baxter the Bloodhound, "These dogs were bred to follow scent and basically hunt people."[34] The ability to selectively breed for highly specific inherited temperament traits is a very valuable adaptive quality of the domesticated dog.

Quantitative Genetics

Before we delve into the specific temperament traits that the Dire Wolf Project has identified through the years by breeding different crossbreeds, it is important to talk about polygenic inheritance, or when a specific phenotype is represented by several different genes. Back in 1988 when the breed began, Lois developed her sliding scale theory of polygenic inherited traits. After years of study on how genetic traits are acquired in the domesticated dog, she came to the conclusion that certain inherited traits are so complex that they cannot be explained by simple Mendelian inheritance. This led her to the view that certain aspects of a dog's inheritance were held by several chains of genes. These chains could then be manipulated through phenotypic selection which resulted in a dominant pull with a range of different phenotypic results between the dominant and the recessive. The more genes on the chain for a polygenic trait that showed dominant, the closer the phenotype would slide toward the dominant side of the scale. The fewer genes on the polygenic chain that showed dominant, the closer the phenotype would slide to the recessive side of the scale. However, the parts of the chain that held the dominant genes would show up in the outward manifestation of the individual.

An example of a trait that is held on Lois's idea of the sliding scale would be erect ears. She reasoned that erect ears were the norm for wild canids and that floppy ears were the direct result of domestication selection. As it happened, the exact same occurrence was also experienced by the researchers of the Russian Fox Farm Experiments in the 1950s and can be seen in many different families and orders of domesticated animals around the world. As the fox farm researchers state, "In the domesticated foxes, morphological aberrations such as floppy ears and curly tails occurred in addition to changes in standard coat color."[35] In Lois's work, she came to the conclusion that there was a dominant pull toward the erect ear phenotype seen in wild canids. She further speculated that the floppy ear of domesticated animals was the recessive, meaning that the ear of a dog would tend to rise depending on how much of the dominant genes within the chain that determined ear erectness. She further documented that two floppy-eared dogs could produce erect-eared puppies if the parents shared the genetic pull toward erect ears. She has recorded this many times in her crossbreeding over the years.

Unbeknownst to Lois, in the 1920s a particular branch of population genetics had begun combining statistics, Mendelian principles, and evolutionary biology; the exact same ideas that she had witnessed through her many breeding experiences. As Mary L. Marazita, Director of the Center for Craniofacial and Dental Genetics in the School of Dental Medicine among many other accomplishments, details, "By the 1920s, quantitative genetics – as we know it today – was developed by Fisher and Wright as a synthesis of statistics, mendelian principles, and evolutionary biology."[36] Quantitative genetics is particularly interested in phenotypic variation which cannot be explained by simply Mendelian inheritance. As geneticists writing for Oxford Bibliographies explain, "Quantitative genetics is the study of the genetic basis underlying phenotypic variation among individuals, with a focus primarily on traits that take a continuous range of values. Some familiar examples include height, weight, and longevity. However, traits that take discrete values (e.g., number of offspring) may also be analyzed within a quantitative genetics framework."[37]

While taking a completely different path, Lois was able to determine the complex world of genetic variation among individual dogs. She later expanded the idea of the sliding scale to include the complex polygenic inherited temperament traits that she began to uncover. Lois established an entire way of breeding for polygenic inherited traits by developing a uniform ten-point sliding scale to make it easy for the public who follow her work to understand. Likely, she has never even heard of quantitative genetics, but the concept of breeding for variant phenotypic traits revolutionized her breeding program. Following are the ten separately inherited temperament traits held on a sliding scale based on phenotypic variation that Lois uncovered. There may be others, but these are the ones that have so far been identified through her work.

On the scales below, the traits that have been established to possess a dominant pull are listed on the right and the recessive traits are listed on the left. It is believed that each box represents a separately inherited temperament trait. However, due to the high variance shown on each single phenotypic trait below, it is highly likely that each of the following individually inherited traits are polygenic in nature. Therefore, following Lois's idea, each of these traits is presented on a sliding scale. So, although a trait is dominant over another in the sense that in a heterozygous dog the dominant side of the scale carries both dominant and recessive traits, the dominant trait can be manifested in a degree of intensity. This may also mean that these phenotypic dominant traits may be incomplete, allowing the recessive traits of a heterozygous dog to show through in varying degrees. We present the following from what has been observed and recorded in standardized temperament testing environments on each dog bred throughout the lifetime of the Dire Wolf Project.

Ten Genetically Inherited Temperament Traits in Dogs

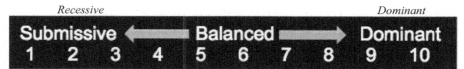

Highly submissive dogs are described as easily corrected and will drop down to the floor possibly releasing urine and/or rolling on its back. They bend to the will of another with ease. In contrast, fiercely dominant dogs are described as being strong-willed and assertive. They do not back down easily and maintain a level of assertiveness especially when confronted.

A friendly dog is outgoing and willing to meet and greet at any time. They can be seen wagging their tail and panting in seeming happiness to have another's attention. An indifferent (aloof) dog is uninterested in other people or dogs, but when approached will show a slight wag of tail or movement to be pet. Although uninterested, they are not afraid and will politely accept affection from others. In our experience, there are two types of aggression that are often used interchangeably; inherited and environmental. Dogs that inherit aggressive temperaments are completely uninterested in other people and dogs. An aggressive dog will first stare then raise its hackles if approached. If an approach continues it will bare its teeth and ultimately lunge forward in an effort to get another to back off. The best example of this type of aggression can be seen in the Russian Fox Farm Experiments where the opposite of the friendly foxes were those that were aggressive upon approach. This type of aggression is not to be confused with nervousness, although they can co-exist.

A confident dog is one that does not react to sudden, unexpected events. It is self-assured in almost any situation. It will readily investigate people or situations that are unfamiliar. A nervous (shy) dog, on the other hand, does not want to investigate. It will turn or hide its eyes from the unfamiliar situation and can sulk, pout, or want to hide when scolded. Nervous dogs hold their tails low or between their legs and pull back their ears as they lower their head. They are cautious of new things and can be seen as shy of dogs, people or environments, each of which can be inherited separately. In severe cases, nervousness can manifest itself as aggression, fear-biting, urination and uncontrollable shaking. Most dogs have some level of nervousness.

Many people believe that a confident dog is the dominant trait and therefore nervous is inherited only if both parents hold the nervous trait, but it is our experience that a genetic nervousness is much more complicated than that. In our experience, genetically nervous dogs can produce relatively confident puppies. Furthermore, a genetically confident RAW dog™ is rare and most puppies need some level of socialization training in order to bring out more confidence. Because of these two occurrences in the dog, we believe nervous to be the dominant trait.

Bonded dogs are those dogs that innately desire close territory as well as a desire to please and do what is asked by their owners. Some would replace the word bonded with loyal, although this trait is more than just loyalty, but also includes a genetic desire for a tight, close or familiar territory. Independent, in contrast, is a dog that has a very broad idea of territory such as a herd protection dog and a desire to do whatever is most beneficial to them at the moment. They do not mind being out of sight of their owners and can roam far and wide if allowed. They do not have a desire to please, but only tend to want to have their own way. When off leash, they are reluctant to return unless the reward is higher than their off leash interests.

Relaxed dogs spend the majority of the time sleeping and resting. They do not require much exercise. Hyperactive dogs are always on the move physically; digging, chewing, running, chasing, and exploring.

Dogs that are oblivious are unaware of their surroundings. They do not look around and take in the happenings in their environment very well. They are impulsive and can be seen as extremely goofy dogs. Some may bark constantly, seemingly for no reason. Alert dogs, in contrast, are aware of all that surrounds them. They can be described as a dog that pays attention. They hear the slightest noise and see the slightest movement even from afar. Alert dogs make good watch dogs.

This category holds both play and prey as they are closely related to one another. Play and prey drive may be inherited separately, but for now, we have no evidence to suggest a split. However, many do maintain that play and prey drives are not the same. In any case, we present them here together until evidence can be gathered to warrant a separation. A low drive dog does not initiate play on its own but has to be coaxed. It does not have a tendency to chase moving objects and playing fetch may seem uninteresting. The dominant trait of the high drive dog, on the other hand, chases moving objects readily. They pounce, grab, shake, and tug on toys. Fetch is a simple task that they perform with ease. They can stay focused on an object for an extended time and do not tire of play easily.

A hard dog can take a lot of pressure on the leash and a lot of force to its body without reacting. A dog of this type does not acknowledge soft touch and prefers to be handled with deep pressure and lots of manipulation such as lifting and rolling. Touch sensitive dogs do not need much pressure to react and respond to very light touch.

Dogs that are not sound sensitive are not bothered by loud noises of any kind. Sound sensitive dogs are bothered by loud noises and may become very agitated and/or fearful. Clawing, whining, barking, howling, running away, shaking, and hiding under beds, etc. are all signs of sound sensitiveness. Although nervousness is a part of this category, a confident dog can easily be sound sensitive and exhibit fear of thunderstorms, gun shots, and other sudden loud noises. This is different than a dog exhibiting nervousness in unknown situations.

Dogs that possess a high pain threshold do not seem to feel much pain. This type of dog may not exhibit any outward signs that it is hurt or sick. When shots are given, this dog does not yelp out or show any discomfort. In contrast, a dog with a low pain threshold will yelp and cry easily when in pain. After the cause of the pain has stopped, a dog with a low threshold for pain may continue to exhibit behaviors of continued pain. This inherited temperament trait should not be confused with a hard dog. A hard dog, although oblivious to light touch and pressure can easily yelp and/or whine when in real pain.

Ideal Large Breed Companion Dog Temperament

So, what temperament traits would one seek out if a person were to want to create a large breed of dog that exhibited a slow, methodical attitude, but was devoted to its humans and wanted nothing more than to be with them? What traits from the above would embody a dog that could inherently possess qualities that limit active working behaviors that may pose a significant challenge to families with little dog training experience and no need to work a dog in the field as in days gone by?

When we have a clear and consistent vocabulary to discuss dog temperament as a starting reference, we can more easily describe the temperament of the dogs being bred under the Dire Wolf Project. The National American Alsatian Breeder's Association that governs Dire Wolf Project breeding practices does not wish to recreate the wild Dire Wolf temperament, but a domesticated dog with the exact Dire Wolf body and bone structure as they are portrayed in skeletal remains. We must, then, establish a temperament in a large breed of dog that can live happily in our modern age. We, therefore, seek to genetically establish the first companion dog temperament in a large breed of dog. We wish to eliminate all large breed working behaviors such as barking, digging, jumping, chewing, chasing, and pacing. This is being accomplished through selective breeding using strict standardized temperament testing and constant observational analysis in puppies from birth to eight weeks old.

The following chart is a graphic representation of the ideal inherited temperament of the purebred American Alsatian in its RAW dog™ state in accordance to the American Alsatian standards of the breed.

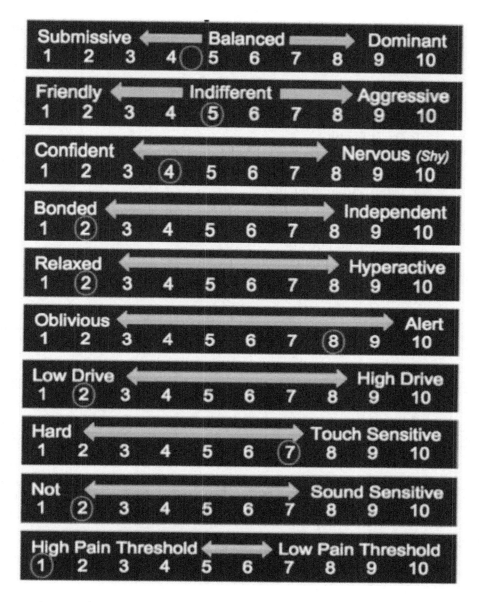

As noted, American Alsatian dogs have been established as the world's first large strongbred dog breed specifically designed and systematically bred as companion dogs. First the health of the American Alsatian breed must always be considered. Secondly, the inherited temperament of each pup is assessed in order to reveal the best dogs that should go on to shape the continuing lines of a strongbred companion dog breed. These temperament requirements must fit within the category of a companion dog breed. In 1987, the founder observed and recorded what owners wanted in a dog. Lois's findings from her customers were the catalyst that shaped the ideal traits of a companion dog. However, Lois wanted to truly change the inherited temperament, not just the behavior, in her dogs, so she devised a specific way to alter the genetics inherent in the temperament of her dogs in order to reach her goal. The following are the observable (phenotypic) character traits that she hoped to achieve in her dogs once she fundamentally altered the inherited temperament of the dogs she bred through selective breeding:

1. Great health
2. Minimal barking/whining/ jumping/ digging
3. Doesn't wander/keeps boundaries naturally
4. Calm and intelligent
5. Sensitive/easy to train
6. Playful, yet not hyper
7. Confident, not shy
8. Tolerant of others/dogs
9. Dedicated to their family
10. Low prey-drive

Why Breed a Large Companion Dog?

A typical question that is often asked when discussing a large breed companion dog is why breed a new breed of large companion dog. There are many reasons why a person might ask this question, which usually reveals the person's strong bias. Nonetheless, the question itself, without adding a hidden agenda onto it, is a legitimate question to ask and so a brief exploration of the reasons behind why the Dire Wolf Project seeks to breed the first large breed companion dog follows. Although the quote below was meant to address a concern over the creation of the Shiloh Shepherd dog, it applies equally to the American Alsatian dog and encapsulates this argument in all of its nuanced prejudices.

> "You also clearly state breeds of the modern day have diminished working ability due to the fact they are no longer used for there [sic] original intended purposes. I couldnt [sic] agree more and its [sic] a crying shame. However there are still a percentage in a multitude of breeds whom [sic] still work there [sic] dogs in [sic] gun dogs, retrievers, and multi purpose [sic] dogs. But far less than before im [sic] sure. However I feel that this is why it is our duty as working dog enthusiasts to maintain the working stock and not dilute it into something else for the soft political world we have today. IMO [In my opinion] if a person cannot handle the working ability, drive, energy level, mentality, etc...... of a certain breed they should look for another. Breeders shouldnt [sic] be indulging the desire for designer breeds. It

simply implies a person is out for $$$. There are many breeds out there- low drive non working [sic] /cull GSD's [sic] - whom [sic] need family and pet homes. As well as many other working breeds and non working [sic] can provide pet dogs. Why should we start mixing blood to obtain a pet when shelters are full and many other bred [sic] dogs(health certified) are not wanted dew [sic] too [sic] the dog lacking ability to work?"[38]

First of all, there are several different arguments embedded in the above quote, so let's break them down in order to address them one at a time.

1. Shelters are full and creating a new breed of dog only adds to the shelter population.
2. Creating a softer version of a large dog breed that already exists harms these working dog breeds. Look for a breed that already exists instead of watering down the working breeds with similar looks and altered temperaments.
3. Designer breed creation happens because the founders are out for money.
4. Many mellow, non-standard temperaments already exist within large working dog breeds and these dogs that should not be used for breeding need homes, too.

The first premise that the author makes is that shelters are full, so there is no need to create a new breed of dog. This implies that by creating a new breed of dog, more dogs are being bred which statistically will also end up in shelters. First of all, the idea that shelters are full is a myth that has been perpetuated by a number of people interested in the shelter trade. Many shelters are so "not full" that they have to obtain their dogs from other places. The "adopt don't shop" people rarely speak about just how many dogs are imported from other countries.

The National Animal Interest Alliance (NAIA) began collecting data on shelter populations in 2005 and the statistics are very revealing. In one of the shelters within Spokane County, Washington, near where I live, a total of 1,512 dogs were received at the SpokAnimal C.A.R.E center in 2017. Of those 71 were euthanized and 1,337 were placed. That sounds like a deficit of 104 dogs, but when the number of dogs transferred into the shelter facility are identified a much different picture comes into focus. According to data collected from the shelter's own public reporting, 73% of the dogs (1,101) that came into the SpokAnimal C.A.R.E center were transferred in from somewhere else, not brought in by the general public. Only 27% of the dogs (411) actually represent the number of dogs from the inland northwest that were either lost or surrendered to this shelter. Since the shelter was able to place or euthanize 1,408 dogs during the year, if the shelter had not brought in dogs from outside of the facility itself, the shelter would have experienced a 71% deficit and their facility would have been empty much of the year. Furthermore, the term "transferred in from outside of the area" is not defined and easily could mean that 997 families in the Spokane, WA area may have "rescued" dogs from areas all over the United States, but also quite possibly outside of country. The National Animal Interest Alliance reveals a chilling statistic to the press, "We [Americans] imported an estimated 1 million dogs annually from Turkey, several countries in the Middle East and as far away as China and Korea."[39]

Make no mistake, animal shelters are big business. Here is a link to NAIA Shelter Project compiling the data from animal shelters in order to combat the myths promulgated by "adopt don't shop" advocates:

http://shelterproject.naiaonline.org/

It might be fascinating to find out the statistics for your own county's animal shelter. That being said, there is growing evidence that breeders within the United States are not the issue with overcrowded shelters. Creating a new breed of dog has very little to do with the shelter population. Saying so is a misrepresentation of the facts.

The second argument places the blame of watered down purebred working dog temperaments on the existence of new breeds of dog. This is simply a "does not follow" (non-sequitur) issue, since creating a new breed of dog that has a different temperament than an already existent working dog actually eliminates the need for anyone to breed sub-standard temperaments within the working dog breed. For example, the German Shepherd Dog breed is bred specifically as a herding/protection dog with a high drive, determined, active character. When Lois created the American Alsatian dog, she did so for the expressed purpose of creating a separate breed so that she would not confuse or lie to the public by calling her dogs something they were not. This allows the German Shepherd Dog to keep its own breed character intact. There are breeders within the German Shepherd Dog community in the United States who breed mellow, calm, non-working temperaments within the German Shepherd Dog breed, though, and those breeders are the ones who may truly cause confusion and loss of working temperament within the breed.

There is a recent trend to breed dogs that do not fit the working standard for which they were originally bred. Unfortunately, this trend creates a highly unpredictable temperament within an otherwise uniform dog breed. Yes, I agree completely with the person above that it is a real shame that the working temperament of these breeds are not being preserved. But, it was not the fault of the breeders who choose to breed an entirely new breed to fit the needs of the public. Why have these working breeds begun to have soft temperaments that do not have the capability to work? Is it because the beauty contest for dogs, the dog show, created it in order to win? Or was it the general public, now transitioning from a mostly agricultural lifestyle to a more industrial one needed a different type of dog? Perhaps a little of both. But, the case is, and has been for a long time now, that the dog owner of today does not live on a farm, but in the city or suburbs where there is little tolerance for a barking dog, a prey driven dog, an aggressive dog, a guard dog, a high-energy herding dog, or a yippie dog. Many want a relatively easy going dog that does not bark, dig, chase, jump, or bite, but that loves to snuggle and remain close, devoting themselves to their owners... and small dogs do not always fit the bill. There is a void in this area. It is certainly up to those working dog enthusiasts to preserve the integrity of their chosen breeds, but it is also equally great to see legitimate, caring individuals breeding large dogs for a new era of dog ownership. In all reality, this practice of creating a new large breed of docile dog allows the working breeds to continue their long held and cherished traditions preserving their history and protecting their future. Without the new large companion breeds popping up, more and more breeders would begin to breed their large working dogs to go against their established standard behavior.

The next argument claiming that founders of new dog breeds are simply out to line their pockets with gold is a cheap shot, but unfortunately, it is also a frequent one. First of all, it is important to point out that it is not wrong to want to make a living and if a person can do so and also live their passion of helping others find happiness in a great dog, then all the better. Producing healthy dogs with great temperaments that fit perfectly within the lives of modern Americans and is strikingly unique in appearance is a worthy goal. If that goal also helps the founder live a good life, why should that matter? Unscrupulous breeders only interested in money do not devote their entire lives to the dream of developing a new breed with attention to health, temperament, and a unique look. They do not keep in contact with every owner, have lifetime genetic health guarantees, create a health foundation, refuse to go down the path of recognition from all-breed dog registries, and stand by ideas that seem controversial at first glance in our current era. As well, dog breeding is extremely costly. There are too many expenses for any of us DWP breeders to live anything but modest lives.

Lastly, the claim that the creation of new breeds of dog takes the customers away from legitimate, already-established purebred dog breeds is unfair. In a free market system, upon which the United States is built, consumers manage their own decisions. The founder of a new breed of dog does not force anyone to buy his/her animals. It is up to the consumer. When there is a void in the marketplace and a new product fills that vacuum, the person who successfully provides a viable option to the formerly popular item should be celebrated, not vilified. It is a natural consequence of a shift in consumer need that promotes one over another. Producing large genetically healthy and sound dogs with calm, mellow, easy-to-train inherited temperaments is what people demand in our modern age. The Dire Wolf Project aims to please.

Triton is now seven months old and a dream to train. At two months old he learned after one trial to kennel on command. He never had to be asked twice after being shown that one time. He was always willing to comply. Triton was never taught formal heel position, he naturally heels perfectly at my side wherever we go. He does not bark, whine, dig or jump. He learned easily that his toys were his to chew on, but nothing else. He communicates easily by body language and asks with his eyes and facial expressions to do things he wants. He is neither shy, fearful, nor overly outgoing or pushy. He is not excessive in energy and has the steady patience to remain calm and collected for hours at a time.

Triton (Harpo/Shennara) at 7 months old.

He has only ever complained one time when he needed to be let out to use the outdoor facilities, otherwise he always complies with every command. He is not aggressive nor dominant with either humans or other dogs. In fact, he has been known to give up his food if another dog insists, so sometimes I have to make sure the other dog does not eat his food, too. He does not wander or roam, but always stays close to home despite the fact that we are surrounded by miles of state land. He easily learned to sit, stand, down, and stay. He had some trouble learning to up into the car only because he looked to me to help lift him as a puppy instead of jumping up on his own and I did not insist until he became too heavy to lift. He literally has no flaws in temperament that can be noticed according to the ideals within the American Alsatian dog breed.

Now, either I am an exceptional dog trainer and I could train any dog to be as calm and collected as Triton or he possesses the fundamental innate characteristics which could be shaped easily to fit within my slower lifestyle. If it were not for the public skepticism I received when I presented Triton with the prestigious black collar as a one day old puppy, I may have even overlooked the significance of Triton's first temperament test scores. But, as it happened, there is no denying that I got it right. At one day old, without any environmental influence to mask his responses, I was able to correctly assess this dog's potential. Perhaps it was a fluke and I just got lucky this one time or just maybe there really is something to this whole notion of early temperament testing and the ability to fundamentally shift the genetic temperament of a dog.

Minerva (Merlin/Corona) 2016

Chapter 11
First Heat Breeding

"What can be asserted without evidence can be dismissed without evidence."
~ Christopher Hitchens

The air outside was calm with a chilly briskness, but inside the four foot by four foot space, it was measurably warmer. The hour was well after midnight, but my mind was wide awake with anticipation of the special event soon to come. White fluffy down covered the bottom of the den like a nest as Elwin, my white Alaskan Malamute, lay on her side panting softly. The heat mixed with heavy wetness from the moisture of her breath gathered all around me. Her belly was swollen, but soon I saw it harden briefly as Elwin's panting suddenly stopped and she began to push. Her soft straining grew more intense almost immediately. After sixty-three days of patient waiting, the time had finally come. Surprisingly, within minutes of her initial contractions, the first puppy arrived. There had been no grunting or straining and the puppy easily glided out of the birthing canal and into the world. Without hesitation, Elwin reached behind her and gently tore the protective sack so that her new puppy could take its first breath. The puppy wiggled and turned like an otter playing in the water on a hot summer's day as the mom licked and fussed to clean this new life. Elwin dutifully fawned over her new baby as it finally found its legs and scooted toward her warm body, the white downy fur reaching out to nestle the new pup in. The puppy, as if it had known about the world all along, found

243

a hardened protruding nipple and began suckling with gusto as Elwin caressed its body with her tongue.

No sooner did the commotion of a new birth subside when Elwin began actively pushing again. She did so without leaving her first puppy's side. She continued to nuzzle her baby as she pushed. The contractions seemed easy and without strain and Elwin's body was optimally loose and relaxed. The next puppy arrived without fuss as well and Elwin cleaned it without disturbing her first born. As with the first, the second puppy eventually gathered its legs underneath it and pushed its way toward mother's comforting side to take its first drink of the protective colostrum from mom's first milk.

For the next several hours, Elwin remained still, calm, and very relaxed. For the first time in her life, she was content and at ease. Typically, Elwin paced and whined to go for a walk or play with a toy or chase a butterfly. She never sat still for long and her mind always raced with thoughts of what to do next. Now, however, Elwin's entire demeanor was slow and calm and attentive. Her five beautiful newborns lined up in a row like birds on a wire. The only sound was the peaceful suckling of precious life beginning anew.

For the next three days, Elwin did not stray from her brood. The only time she moved at all was to switch sides. I provided her water and food at regular intervals so that she did not want for anything. She held her bathroom urges for the first seventy-two hours after her initial puppy arrived. I stayed by Elwin's side night and day for those entire three days, sleeping when I could on a cot next to her den. The large, plump, roly poly babies ate and slept, preferring to lie on their mother's warm body as Elwin softly breathed and rested.

Elwin's litter was the easiest puppy birth I had ever experienced. All of the puppies arrived in the world with ease, head first, and vibrantly confident of where to get what they needed. It was almost like clockwork. In fact, Elwin was such a great mother that within the next three days, she took over two orphaned puppies from another litter after their mother became ill. Some may speculate that Elwin must have been a well-seasoned mother with many previous litters behind her, but if you thought that, you would be wrong. In fact, Elwin was only eight months old at the time of this birthing experience, which means that she came into her first season and bred successfully at six months old.

First heat breeding is highly controversial and taboo in our civilized western culture. It has been since the Victorian age when purebred dogs began and the proper way to breed dogs was laid out by the aristocracy. To this day, many myths and fairytales surround the practice of first heat breeding. Breeders who dare to step out of line from the majority's accepted breeding practices will pay the price by being shunned, severely ridiculed, and deemed an unethical irresponsible breeder with no moral compass and a will only to make money off of the abused backs of puppies that haven't fully developed. The sordid rhetoric from the majority pressures breeders, who simply want to be accepted, into waiting until their dogs are at least two years old before breeding. As the story goes, a minimum level of health testing should be the natural inclination of any responsible breeder, so it is only right that an ethical breeder would want to wait, for the sake of the growing dog and the sake of the health of the puppies.

All of the above sounds so reasonable and caring, doesn't it? Who wants to harm dogs, after all? Who wants to breed unhealthy puppies? Only the worst breeders, to be sure. No one who wants to breed successfully challenges this notion and now many breeders are faced with increasing legislation regulating what is and is not abusive dog breeding. The problem is that none of the above majority think is based on any proof or solid science. Because the lies have been told and the taboo has been held for so long without being challenged, it is now illegal to breed a female dog on its first heat in the United Kingdom. "The local authority will require assurances that bitches: under the age of one will not be mated"[0] Losing the required license to breed is the punishment for the breeder who dares to defy this regulation.

But, what about the truth? Where does the truth come into this conversation? Is it true that breeding dogs on the first heat will statistically decrease that dog's physical and/or emotional health? Is it true that breeding dogs on the first heat will increase a puppy's chances of obtaining health issues? Is it true that breeders are increasing the health risk to the young mother or in any way harming the mother or her puppies by breeding on the first heat? Is it true that breeders cannot obtain enough health information about their young females when they do not take the first two years to observe and formally test for common canine diseases?

If these statements were to be proven true, I would be the first in line to prosecute any breeder who chose to deliberately harm their dogs in this way and I would never again breed a female on her first heat. The Dire Wolf Project does not advocate for animal abuse and adamantly opposes any breeding practice that deliberately disregards the physical or emotional health of any dog. But, as we shall see, this is not the case. First heat breeding is not a vile, evil breeding practice and there is absolutely no call for the rampant abuse perfectly respectful breeders endure who openly practice it. A review of dog breeding history, dog breeding research, a look at solid science and a thorough observation of feral street dogs and domesticated dogs that have returned to the wild reveal the truth.

First Heat Breeding History

Since the time man first domesticated the dog, first heat breeding has been the norm. In 1413, the Duke of York, Edward of Norwich, wrote a book entitled, <u>The Master of Game</u>, in which he describes in great detail how to breed hunting dogs. In this book, Sir Edward of Norwich clearly states that a female dog generally comes into her first heat at twelve months old at which time she can be bred. He never questions breeding her at that time and gives a lot of advice on how to perform it properly. He also clearly defines that his dogs come into heat twice a year, as is experienced by all domesticated dog breeds. Furthermore, this conscientious and highly literate master hunting dog breeder fully admits that breeding females at twelve months is singularly determined by the dogs themselves that are in better condition than others.

> "The bitches by jolly in their love commonly twice a year, but they have no term of their heat, for every time of the year some by jolly. When they be a twelve month old, they become jolly, and be jolly while they await the hounds without any defence, twelve days or less, and sometimes fifteen days, according as to whether they be of hot nature or of cold, the one more than another, or whether some be in better condition than others."[1]

If one counts all of the years that man has been selectively breeding dogs literally over 11,000 years or more have gone by without tragically dire consequences to our beloved furry companions. It has only been in our most recent times, over the last 100 years, that first heat breeding has become offensive to some and grossly irresponsible to others.

First Heat Breeding Controversy Development

As mentioned earlier, the first heat breeding controversy is nothing new. In fact, it surfaced as a taboo sometime at the turn of the twentieth century when dog breeding and showing became a highly popularized sport. Leon Whitney, DVM in the 1930s addressed this very topic in depth in his book Breeding Better Dogs. In fact, he was very scientific about it, recording everything that occurred, including pictures and measurements to the finest detail. He took the time to mark down each dog, how old she was, how many puppies she had and how easy the whelp was. After breeding hundreds of dogs, mostly hounds, he concluded that there was no significant difference in whelping statistics whether a dog was bred on its first heat or if one waited for the 2nd or 3rd heats to breed.

In his day, it was also said that breeding a female on her first heat would stunt her growth. He also clearly refuted this through his experiments. Dr. Whitney's book has been branded highly unethical and deeply controversial because of the very detailed way in which he scientifically took puppies out of the womb before they were fully developed in able to dissect them to learn more about his field of veterinary science. However, it is only through having done this work that we now know so much more about the breeding, whelping and growth process of the domesticated dog. "There seems to be no reason for not breeding a bitch the first time she is ready, and often many good reasons for doing so…I have made very many of these first-season matings and have never seen a bitch harmed in any way by it."[2]

Another well-known author writing in the 1940s and 50s, Dr. Kyle Onstott, also addresses this with a bit more diplomacy in his book, The New Art of Breeding Dogs. He states, "The matter of the age of breeding stock is one about which there is gross misapprehension. That it is desirable to mate aging bitches to young dogs, or vice versa, is a firmly fixed belief, but without scientific foundation. That they be sexually mature and vigorous is the only consideration necessary to be given to the age of animals to be mated."[3]

Lois has literally bred around 400 litters over the course of her lifetime, breeding dogs many different types of dogs from Rottweilers to Peekapoos. It is mind-boggling to think about. Lois's sister once told her that she should not say that too loudly since it is a statistic that horrifies many people, but, Lois has devoted her entire life to breeding dogs and when one does, one can amass a good amount of experience over the years. When Lois says that no dog that she has ever bred on its first heat has ever had complications due to being young, I take a step back a bit in reverence to the power of that statement.

Furthermore, it is interesting to me that the breeders that are the most upset about breeding a female on her first heat have never once tried it. Oh... they wouldn't dare because, "That's disgusting!" The time it takes to look up the truth of whether it really is disgusting or not is never taken and as a result the lie continues to this day as strongly as ever.

Natural Breeding Cycles after Domestication

First of all, it is important to build a clear understanding of the natural breeding practices of the domesticated dog. The process of domestication for man's best friend began 11,000 to 30,000 years ago. "Wolf domestication was initiated late in the Mesolithic when humans were nomadic hunter-gatherers."[4] Dogs are seen helping cavemen hunt on the walls of Lascaux in France. Ancient Egyptian writing and art show sleek Saluki type dogs standing guard over temples. The first mention of a specific dog breed or type in written literature comes from Homer's Iliad in 800ac where "In vain loud mastiffs bay him from afar, And shepherds gall him with an iron war;"[5]

The domestication process has now been studied quite in depth in our modern time and even reproduced recently with the Silver Fox Farm Experiments in Russia. The Silver Fox began its domestication process not too long ago sometime around 1948 by a Russian geneticist, Dmitri Belyaev. The now domesticated fox looks to have a domesticated temperament that is as independent as a cat, but as loyal as a dog. Curiously, though, "[f]oxes reach sexual maturity at the age of 10 months,"[6] whereas in just fifty years of deliberate domestication, the domesticated fox now reaches sexual maturity at 7-8 months of age.[7] As the Russian Fox Farm experimenters state, "The shifts in the timing of development brought about by selection of foxes for tameability have a neotenic-like tendency; the development of individual somantic traits is decelerated, while sexual maturation is accelerated. Higher levels of sexual hormones in the plasma and increased gonadal weight during prepubertal period are indicators of earlier sexual maturation of tame foxes."[8]

This shift to a lower age of sexual maturity is also seen in domesticated buffalo. To be sure, domesticated buffalo have had a much shorter evolutionary timeframe than the dog, but nonetheless they also have been shown to differ in their sexual maturity ages. Anjali Aggarwal, a Senior Scientist at the National Dairy Research Institute in Karnal, India explains, "Wild or feral female buffalo reaches sexual maturity at 2-3 years of age. Domesticated buffalo that is cared for and fed properly is likely to reach puberty early."[9]

The formation of lower ages of sexual maturity over time as wild animals become more and more domesticated is a very interesting observation. It points to the very real idea that with domestication, the natural maturity level of an animal shifts downward until the very ability to breed becomes earlier and earlier. Speaking about the changes that occur due to the process of domestication, an evolutionary view of domestication study concludes, "Reproductive cycle changes such as polyestrousness... are typical."[10]

248

We can further clarify the natural breeding nature of domesticated animals by looking toward their habits when they are allowed to breed freely. Homeless animals roam the streets of large cities all around the world. Spay and neuter programs especially target feral cats and dogs at early ages because they will not hesitate to breed at the earliest possible time. FixNation, a non-profit organization in Los Angeles dedicated to rounding up feral cats for free neutering services writes, "If you ignore the cats they will continue to breed. Rapidly and prolifically. Cats will start having litters when they're only five months old."[11] Furthermore, veterinarians for VCA explain, "Cats have their first estrous (reproductive) cycle when they reach puberty… On average, puberty, or sexual maturity, first occurs in cats at about six months of age, but this can vary slightly by time of year."[12]

The natural state of a domesticated dog's reproductive timeframe reaches sexual maturity earlier than it had in its wild state. This fact is part of a dog's make-up and apart from systematically undoing the thousands of years of dog evolution, it cannot be changed or altered through human means… at least that has never yet been accomplished.

When Domestication Reverts Back to the Wild State

Conversely, domesticated dogs that return to their wild roots and begin to breed amongst themselves may keep some of their domestic ways, but they also take on many of the traits of their wild cousins. Dr. Curt Stager of Paul Smith's College in the Adirondacks explains, "They're [feral animals] former domestics that have gone back into the wild, but it turns out, the animal itself is a mosaic of the original domestic, and the original wild type. It's a creature onto itself. So in the wild, they go back to their old way of having a breeding season… although they changed how they breed, they keep the fast growth that they were selected for, and the big reproduction. They make lots of babies when they reproduce, so it's an amazing mix. So what we've got now is an entirely new critter that's the same species, but new forms of these formerly wild animals that are here because of human contact to the legacy of having been domestic now in an entirely new setting"[13]

Eventually, domestic animals gone wild show longer and longer timeframes before coming into their first season and are ready to breed. The Australian Dingo is one such example. "Most female dingoes become sexually mature by 2 years of age while male dingoes will be sexually mature by the time they are a year old. Only the most dominant members of an established

Dingo pack will breed leaving the other members to help with the feeding of the pups."[14] The breeding habits of the Dingo are now very similar to that of the wild wolf.

Indeed, according to Merriam-Webster, the very definition of a feral organism is one that has escaped from domestication and returned, partly or wholly, to its wild state. This definitely makes sense. The domesticated dog is something different. It is not a wild creature and is not naturally selected, so should not be expected to adhere to wild reproductive behaviors. Although Dire Wolf Project breeders strive to mimic natural selection as closely as possible for the sake of the health and longevity in our beloved animals, we should accept the domestic dog's natural state.

Nature's Way

So then, what are the specific reasons why the Dire Wolf Project chooses to breed dogs on their first heat? First of all, as presented in the chapter on "God's Breeding Plan," breeders within the Dire Wolf Project subscribe to mimic nature's way of breeding as closely as possible. We practice this way of breeding because nature has the best health and longevity record man has ever seen in the years man has been selectively breeding animals. It is admirable to look toward and hope to mimic a breeding regimen that produces the best results.

In light of this, some critics will then quickly point out that wolves do not tend to breed until they are two years old, therefore, if we wish to mimic the wolf, the Dire Wolf Project, too, should wait to breed dogs until two years old. Certainly, the wild wolf has much to teach us. On the surface, this argument seems sound, but when one looks at the facts surrounding nature's way of breeding, it simply does not hold the same merit.

The reason this argument seems logical at first glance is because it is true that the typical age that wolves begin to breed is around twenty-two months, or just shy of two years old. As a significant 1979 study combining the efforts of four prominent medical and behavioral biology foundations clearly indicates regarding wild wolf reproduction, "No female wolves have been known to breed before 22 months of age in the wild."[15] Since most people have no true understanding about wolf reproduction cycles, the person posing this argument may feel the excitement of easy victory and prematurely high-five the others watching from their easy-chairs. But when we take a closer look at the reasons behind this fact, a much more complex picture of wolf reproduction begins to emerge.

Just for the sake of clarity, the study explains the observations in more depth, "… it has been stated that reproduction in wolves usually does not commence before the 22 month of postnatal life. Reproductive activity of wolves in the first year of life has, however, been reported [in captivity], but seems to occur only occasionally. An extremely late onset of reproduction (five to six years) is also known to occur." A clearer picture begins to emerge as the fog begins to lift. Although it has never been witnessed in the wild, wolves in captivity do occasionally breed in the first year. Again, citing the same 1979 study above, the researchers also explain, "In contrast to dogs, 10 month-old wolf females that have reached 80-100% of adult weight commonly do not enter estrus and, hence, are delayed for their first cycle until 22 months of age." The fog lifts completely as we now understand that wolves do not actually enter into estrus at the same time as dogs; domestication has significantly altered the dog's reproductive cycle.

Not only do wolves breed once a year, unlike dogs, but many female wolves do not even enter first estrus until twenty-two months old. Since wolves also only breed during a specific time of the year, the age at which a young female wolf has the opportunity to breed may get pushed back. In other words, her age at first mating depends on when she was born in relation to the mating season. For example, if a female Red Wolf was born at the very beginning of the mating season in late February, four or even six weeks earlier than other Red Wolf pups being born at the end of March, she may come into estrus at twenty-three or even twenty-four months as her body readies itself for the coming mating season. In any case, regardless of the exact age of the female wolf at the first mating, she still copulates on her first heat.

Ultimately, though, it is hard to directly compare the wild wolf's breeding age to the domesticated dog simply because man has significantly altered this part of wolf's close cousin and now the domesticated dog comes into its first heat at 8 to 11 months of age. It still holds true that the natural breeding practices of the domesticated dog when left to its own devices are to breed on the first heat, just as with the wolf. We can take a look at domesticated dogs who have since gone back to the wild and are breeding amongst themselves. They do, indeed, breed on their first heat. Many spay/neuter programs exist for these wild dogs so that they will not continue to breed and overpopulate. The street dogs in India are one example.

So, how do wolves deal with health issues if they breed on their first heat? Health is naturally maintained because any health issues that arise are automatically completely eliminated from the gene pool. What happens to dogs gone wild? They also do not show up at the local veterinarian's office for x-rays at two years old. It is the same as the wolf. Any health issue that arises completely takes the dog from the gene pool... no questions asked. End of story. Survival of the fittest at its finest.

This is what God's Breeding Plan means. We breed as closely as possible to this approach. If a health issue debilitates a dog, we do not breed it, potentially even eliminating entire lines from the breed. Lois has done this many times. A person must leave emotions out of the decision and look to just what would eliminate the dog from breeding if it were in the wild. We are very serious about this endeavor and do not compromise. It is too serious a matter to make excuses for ill health.

In Cayo Santiago, Puerto Rico, a collaborative study between the University of Missouri and the University of Puerto Rico of the mating behavior in rhesus monkeys revealed, "The periodicity of estrus in the 34 mature females of one social group was studied during the 1960 breeding season. Among the 28 which gave birth, 20 apparently conceived during the first estrous period, 6 did not conceive until the second and the time when 2 conceived was uncertain."[16]

According to MountainNature.com, "Female black bears usually become sexually mature by their fourth summer…"[17]
The Get Bear Smart Society further reveals that "[t]he average breeding age for female black bears if 3.5 years and for female grizzlies is 4.5 years."[18]
It appears that in the wild bears breed on their first heat.

A Need to Wait for Formal Health Testing

Another aspect to the equation is that there is no clear correct answer to what is the best number of years to wait to make sure that every health issue is cleared before breeding. People will have as many answers to this question as there are people to answer it. The reasons for any arbitrary number will be just as differentiated. Many people (possibly even a majority?) subscribe to the idea that it is best to wait at least two years to breed a dog. Someone came up with it, perhaps someone with clout (really not sure), and others followed until a group of people were all saying the same thing.

Did anyone stop to think about why two years? The reason most will state is because the Orthopedic Foundation for Animals (OFA) will not officially score for hips and elbows until a dog is two years old. However, what waiting-to-breed advocates do not ever reveal is that there is a preliminary hip and elbow scoring procedure that gives a breeder a very high rate of accuracy (98 percent) when a dog is thirteen months old, as we saw in the health chapter.

Hopefully everyone knows that bad hips and elbows aren't the only health issue that can come along and ruin a breed. Take hypothyroidism, we could add that to the mix and we know that in the American Alsatian dog breed the symptoms for hypothyroidism begin at two and a half years old. So, let's at least wait until all of our dogs are two and a half years old before we breed them. Surely that will eliminate all instances of hypothyroidism and catch hips and elbows, as well. So, there's three biggies that would for certain not be bred into the lines, right? Nope... wrong. A breeder could wait for two and a half years to breed his/her dogs but then hypothyroidism shows up at three years old. Well, shoot.

Let's take a look at cancer. That can show up at seven or eight years old. Golden Retrievers have a pretty high percentage of cancer in their breed, suggesting that there is a genetic component to it. Should we then wait until seven or eight years old to breed? And what's more, I have heard impassioned arguments for waiting until a dog is ten years old to breed. As the person suggests, then the breeder will be perfectly clear to only be breeding dogs that prove longevity.

You see, there is no end to this discussion. There is no right answer. Any answer you give will be what a human makes up for reasons that the person sees as most important. However, the most important piece is not how long to wait to breed... the most important piece is what will you do when a health issue does come up?... because it will, no matter how diligent you are. Health issues will appear. It is the nature of breeding animals.

But, at least we'd be able to say we've done everything we can, right? Don't believe the rhetoric because it is not always true that a breeder who waits for some accepted amount of time to breed their dogs in order to perform a few health tests is therefore breeding healthier dogs. If it is all about the image of being a responsible breeder, then one will get an image, but the truth can still be concealed. One cannot test for epilepsy, panosteitis, and any other number of health issues that could come up. One still does not have proof of those because no proof can be had. You still have to rely on the word of the person breeding. What is that word worth to you? You will have to get to know the person, plain and simple, and have a relationship with your breeder to make sure he/she has the morals and honesty you desire that will tell you if you can trust them to do everything they possibly can to prevent as many health issues from occurring as possible.

So, let's look to the statistics of the health in the American Alsatian dog breed. Truthfully, the health of our breed is exceptional when compared to many other breeds of dog. We have tracked all reported health issues coming from our breed since its inception in 1988. The most prominent health issue in our breed is currently hypothyroidism at 2.6% when comparing dogs born for the last four years. (This equates to five dogs in the last four years, btw) So... 97.4% of the dogs that have been born in the last four years have not been reported as developing hypothyroidism. Let's look at the next highest percentage, cryptorchidism, at 2.1%. We have never bred a dog with cryptorchidism into the lines, ever. Yet, still there is a 2.1% occurrence rate for this issue in the last four years... almost as high as hypothyroidism. It is probably hiding among the females and being passed that way, but there is no real way to know since it is a sex-linked issue. So, we continue to breed it out as we go along, which is what we will do with hypothyroidism, as well.

When we look at the statistics of the breed's health, we see that even the most prominent health issue results in an extremely high percentage of dogs that do not ever develop the health issue. When there is such a high rate of dogs without the health issue, why wait to see if it arises? The odds of it occurring is seriously very low, especially since when it does occur we openly report and monitor the dogs from that line, potentially eliminating an entire line if it comes to it. The statistics suggest that we would be waiting for something to arise that amounted to nothing, which would again be a huge waste of time for no reason at all.

The Need to Wait for Maturity's Sake

Another argument from waiting-to-breed advocates is the "wait until your dog is mature and its bones have solidified" argument. It goes like this, dogs "should not be bred too early because they are still maturing mentally and won't make good mothers."[19] If you do not wait to breed, you will harm your dog because birth is too strenuous on a dog that has not had their growth plates closed completely. This is a very similar argument to the "you will stunt your dog's growth" argument.

Actually, there are many ranchers who adamantly contradict this statement. Several ranchers working at the University of Melbourne in Australia report, "Calving difficulty was commonly believed to result from mating heifers at too young an age. However, calving difficulty is now known to be a problem of first-calf heifers, whether they calve first at two years or three years."[20]

To be sure, any female can have birthing complications no matter at which time she is bred. Take three examples from the Dire Wolf Project. Bonnie Lee (first bred on her third heat), Lady Igraine (first bred on her second heat), and Sprinkle (first bred on her third heat) all had complications for their first whelp. Birthing difficulties certainly do happen. But, in these three cases, it did not occur because of being immature. Two of the dogs were two years old and the other was one year and a half.

In fact, using the same logic as the initial premise, since I have experienced the most number of birthing complications after the first heat, I could make the argue that waiting to breed is more dangerous for the mother and her puppies. Unfortunately, just like the initial premise, there is a serious lack of evidence, other than my own experience breeding twenty litters, that this statement is true. I would need to obtain much more information before claiming this as absolute truth. And, so does the original premise. Ultimately, one cannot know if dogs require mental maturity to be good mothers without further evidence. Is it because of the first heat, because of the first whelp (regardless of when), or because of the genetic make-up of the dog itself which causes difficult births? One should not simply assume the issue is first heat breeding without the evidence to back it up.

Another argument in this category is that breeding a young female will stunt her growth or cause her delayed adult weight achievement since she must not only provide for her young, but also continue to grow, herself. Again, ranchers find this same argument in their field and easily address the concern. "It is commonly believed that early calving can seriously retard the growth of heifers. However... calving at two years has practically no effect on the mature bodyweight of cows. More detailed experiments have shown that early calving may delay body development for up to 12 months, but almost the same mature size is reached. This effect can be minimised if the heifers are fed well after calving."[21] Most canine mothers, regardless of age, lose weight and look skinnier during lactation. Just like the ranchers above, it is important for the breeder to counter that effect as much as possible by properly nourishing her throughout this time.

Since cattle have a gestation period of 283 days, calving at 2 years means that the heifer would have bred just after one year old. Speaking about what age it is safe to breed a heifer, the Institute of Agriculture and Natural Resources at the University of Nebraska – Lincoln states, "Breeding should occur when the heifer reaches puberty. Puberty is a function of breed, age, and weight. Most heifers will reach puberty and be bred by 12 to 14 months of age and will be between 55% and 65% of their mature weight when they first begin to exhibit estrous cycles."[23]

Susan Schoenian, Sheep and Goat Specialist for University of Maryland Extension, answers the following question: "Should ewe lambs and doelings be bred to produce their first offspring when they are approximately one year of age? Or should you wait until they are yearlings to breed them for the first time? The answer depends. There are many factors to consider and pros and cons to each breeding decision.

"Breeding ewe lambs and doe kids allows you to exploit their reproductive and genetic potential. It is well-documented that ewes that are mated as lambs will have a higher lifetime production than ewes that are mated for the first time as yearlings.

"One of the most compelling reasons to consider breeding ewe lambs and doe kids is genetic improvement. Your lambs and kids should have the best genetics on your farm. Breeding them early will reduce the generation interval and accelerate genetic improvement.

"At the same time, ewe lambs and doe kids have lower conception rates, give birth to fewer offspring, produce less milk, and are more likely to experience problems during the periparturient period. In addition, there may be sacrifices in growth. Ewes and does that are bred early may not catch up (in weight) until their second or third mating. For this reason, producers who show yearlings often delay breeding."[24]

As Debbie James reports for Farmer's Weekly, "With good management and nutrition, ewe lambs can successfully produce offspring at 12 months old, says independent sheep specialist Kate Phillips."[25]

In a study conducted in 1962 by the U.S. Department of Agriculture, a total of 173 ewes were observed continuously for one estrous period. It was determined, among other conclusions, that "[a]ge was positively related to the number of lambs born, but had no significant effect on any of the other variables studied."[26]

In a study conducted in 1990 by the Department of Animal and Poultry Science from the University of Guelph in Ontario, Canada, researchers separated 187 gilts (female pigs under the age of one) into four groups. The researchers then bred the first group at the first estrus, the second group at the second estrus, etc., in order to evaluate any differences in reproductive performance. The study concluded that no discernable distinction between matings was experienced. "Overall, reproductive performance after four parities was similar for gilts mated at first, second or third observed estrus."[27]

In 2002, a study that reviewed growth plate closure compared with age at sexual maturity for several different species of laboratory animal conducted by researchers at the University of Guelph in Ontario, Canada, found that "[s]pecies showing synchrony between sexual maturity and age at cessation of bone growth included the cat, dog [Greyhound], rabbit, horse, and cow."[28] This is significant because this study clearly illustrates that bone growth closure in the dog, and other domesticated species, is fairly close to its age at sexual maturity. In fact, the dog was just above rabbits on the scale as being the closest to a 1:1 ratio between the two features studied. When a person indicates that issues with growth or lack of dog development at the time of sexual maturity is an issue with breeding on a dog's first heat, this argument does not take into account the relative closeness of a dog's sexual maturity to its full skeletal development.

Time is of the Essence

When a person is out to accomplish something, time is of the essence. The creation of an entire new breed using only domesticated dogs and breeding backwards to a wild look is extremely difficult. It has taken 15,000 to 30,000 years of domestication to undo the wolfish appearance of the first dog. We continue to alter our man-made perfections and breed more and more away from this natural look. But, health has a lot to do with structure, so we breed toward the natural look because it is not only interesting to breed a domesticated dog that has the same bone and body structure as an extinct wild animal, but it is also the most healthy body type. No stub noses to make breathing difficult. No double merles. No excessive sloping or roached backs. No mangled teeth. No unnatural breeding procedures. No skulls that are too small for the brain... and on and on. It takes time to accomplish this and it may possibly not even be able to be accomplished in any one person's lifetime, let alone merely thirty years, especially when we insist on never using any recent wolf blood to jump ahead in the wolfish appearance. In our current pace, we are at around twenty generations from the beginning of the breed. That's an average of about one and a half years for each generation. Now, lengthen the amount of time it would take to get where we are now if we had to wait, say... five years, to breed each dog. If Lois had done this from the beginning of the breed, we'd still be at around six generations, which is approximately back at around the year 1998 give or take; just after the first English Mastiff was introduced.

The number of puppies would also be significantly reduced. It would stand to reason that we would need to wait for years before a single litter from one dog could be bred. I suppose it might even out if Lois had been able to keep a certain number of dogs, but she would have had to keep a much higher number of dogs in order to create the same number of puppies for everyone. You see, there would need to be puppies kept who were five years old and ready to breed, as well as four years old and three years old and two years old and one year old and just born in order for her to continue breeding each consecutive year. That is four more dogs for each breedable dog in order for her to maintain her current amount of puppies. As it is now, she can breed the best pups in the litter and they are still relatively young enough to allow them to go to good homes for the duration of their lives.

Kyle Onstott, dog breeder and judge for regional dog shows in the mid-1900s, sums this argument up nicely when he concludes that it would be silly to wait for a dog's complete maturity, as it wastes time that is not necessary to waste. "Some breeders, especially German Breeders of German Shepherd dogs, are insistent that bitches should not be bred until full and complete maturity – not before the second, better not before the third, menstruation. In the case of a bitch with an abnormally long back or loin, or one with a tendency to a sway of the spine, or where the food supply is inadequate as it concerns quantity, quality, or balance, this delay is certainly justified; but the using of such a bitch for breeding, or any bitch not properly nourished, at any time is a very dubious experiment. There is, however, much unnecessary loss of time in the awaiting of full physical maturity of normal and well developed dogs before utilizing them for breeding."[29]

But, wait-to-breed advocates may ultimately want to lessen the number of dogs bred. There is a growing movement of people who believe that dogs should not be kept as pets and that humans are the cause of all the great evils in this world. If humans were to stop breeding dogs, cats, fish, birds, etc. then the world would be better off. People who believe the above easily infiltrate themselves into dog forums and loudly proclaim how breeding regulations are necessary. If one took the advice of those who advocate for breeders to wait-to-breed, there would certainly be a lot fewer dogs in this world. This would be so because breeders would have to keep many more dogs in order to maintain the same level of litters. If they could not increase their population size to keep dogs for years and still breed the same number of litters, then fewer litters would automatically be the result.

That brings me to the question, what does one do with a six year old dog who no longer needs to breed for the program? It is exceedingly more difficult to place a dog at six years old than it is to place a dog at one year old. Five years of its life have been spent sitting in a kennel awaiting its turn to breed. Five years, when it could be receiving one on one attention and the love and affection it truly deserves. We do not keep our breeding dogs for longer than we have to for their own benefit. It is selfish to keep dogs for years solely to breed them. We love our dogs and want them all to have that individual family life they deserve. What kind of life would it be for a dog to sit in a kennel for five years waiting to make sure that it was completely healthy, when the odds are it was always completely healthy?

Money Isn't Everything

Lastly, the least important factor that nonetheless makes an impact on the business behind breeding dogs, is the monetary significance of waiting to breed dogs until they are five years old. Dog food alone would be around $3000 per dog for that amount of time without any litters from that dog to offset the cost. Say we have one litter for that one dog (as we often do) that would be more than 1/5 of the price of the litter. Not to mention all of the health tests associated with the reasons why we waited. Tack on another $1000 for those. Then, if there were any complications associated with the birth of a litter, we could easily be increasing costs by another $500 or more. Now, we are at $4500 to $5000, which is roughly two puppies from an average five puppy litter. It does not make much business sense to keep a dog that long for the sole purpose of waiting to see if any health issues arise, especially when the chances are extremely low that they will.

Stanley (Boss/Shenanigan) 2019

Chapter 12
"Who's Afraid of the Big Bad Wolf?"

"It doesn't matter if a dog is pink with purple polka dots, health and temperament always come first." - Lois Schwarz

The only light in the room emanated from the small lamp on the bedside table that glowed through a white tissue neatly propped up in its box in just such a way where a faint shadow formed on the wall that looked eerily like a wolf's snarling frame. The young girl's mother reclined on the edge of the bed with an old weathered copy of Grimm's fairytales as the darkness of the forest began to grow all around. The young girl slid deeper into the covers, her eyes widening as she glimpsed an unexpected movement from the shadow on the wall. She heard a distant owl hoot in the recesses of her mind as the low hanging branches of the trees in the woods slowly began to surround the innocent girl and her basket. Yellow eyes drew nearer as the penetrating silence of the damp darkness withdrew in fear. A low growl could be heard as the narrow path began to disappear in front of her. The shadow advanced with stealthy precision, but the girl hadn't a care as she drew her red cape closer to stave off the encroaching cold.

Years later, when the little girl with her innocent wide-eyed fear of a large menacing creature of the night became an adult, she turned a corner in the road safe behind the wheel of her yellow station wagon driving home from a weekend's camping trip at the ranch. In the dim light of the coming dawn, a movement among the trees caught her eye and she happened to turn her head in time to see a small, pathetic-looking creature stare out from the undergrowth. Its tall ears and thin body reminded her more of a coyote than a wolf. Her disappointment at seeing the reality of the monster that she feared all those years before grew as she thought about how much more real the big bad wolf had been in her imagination as a child.

The small wolf turned its head to slink back into the darkness as she sped up to merge into the increasing traffic at the start of rush hour. Leaving the real wolf behind her, she thought how grand it would be to walk through the forest with a big bad wolf at her side. Her mind's eye pictured an overwhelming presence standing with confident strength and penetrating command. What if her childhood fear could be harnessed into a special kind of beast; a golden-eyed lover that could form a special sort of bond with its people? She knew the health of her ideal dog would need to be impeccable and the temperament of her ideal dog would need to be mellow, calm, and sweet, but just what would it look like? Could a large, imposing scary beast combine with the innocent personality of the little girl walking confidently to grandma's house?

When Lois first envisioned her idea of a lamb in wolf's clothing in 1987 she did not want her breed to resemble the lithe gray wolves of today, but the powerful wolves that filled the scary children's stories of old; the big bad wolf of her imagination. This imagined wolf had to be strong, powerful, and impeding with a bit of secrecy in its yellow-eyed stare. No modern wolf could embody that kind of appearance. She turned into the parking lot where her shop was located and put the beat up heap of a car into park. Gathering her things and punching the lock on the door, she unlocked the front door, turned the sign to "open," and walked into the back where her grooming station waited for a brand-new day.

As she attended to her morning routine, she continued her vision until she laid out a comprehensive standard for what her ideal dog would encompass. The more she thought about the perfect combination between beauty and strength, the more the big bad wolf took shape in her mind. She saw its massive paws spread out with each quiet step. She entangled her fingers into the savageness of the stiff, black-tipped, agouti-colored coat. She caressed its broad head and large sloping muzzle as her eyes met the bright yellow eyes of her imaginary companion. Throughout the day when no one needed her attention

262

and she had time to think, her mind turned again to her dream.

Lois thought it would only take three generations to secure the look of the big bad wolf of her imagination. As it turned out, that original notion was much too ambitious. Crossing with such diverse breeds to obtain the genetic diversity she needed to secure a mellow companion dog temperament proved to need much more time and attention. In the midst of working toward her ideal temperament, certain health issues arose that further pushed her appearance ideals to the back of the line. Still, she refused to compromise on great health and temperament in order to focus on a stunning wild appearance. It did not take long for her to decide between producing a wolf-looking dog with temperament and health issues or a mix-looking dog with great temperament and health.

Twelve years after the plans for her new breed first took shape, Lois had a new batch of puppies resting in the room next to her bed. As she often did, she climbed into the den to sit with the three week old puppies just beginning to gather their feet under them and waddle around. Her hands reached down and lifted one of the plump males to cuddle it in her arms. Lois's soft voice blended into kisses as she brushed her face against the fuzzy one's muzzle. He blinked at her as the light from overhead illuminated his crystal blue irises. Lois sat up in surprise. She held him up again to exam them more closely. Sure enough. She had seen correctly. This pup's eyes were a bright azure blue like a cloudless sky just before the sun begins to start its descent.

What a curious finding. She searched back through her memory scanning the pedigree on how this pup could have possibly received blue eyes. She had never see bright eyes like this in all of her years breeding dogs. Could one of her dogs have had Australian Shepherd or Siberian Husky in their background? No, she knew that the Siberian Husky litter she bred long ago was never used because of the excessive independence and overwhelming energy all of the pups exhibited. Her brows furrowed as she strained to recall just where this pup's eyes could have originated.

The blue-eyed pup licked her nose just before she gently placed him back with his littermates. She named him Packer and she made a note in the litter's binder about this curious phenomenon. Then, she went on with her day cleaning pens and brushing out the undercoat from her dogs as another winter turned to spring.

Four weeks later, as the puppies played in the yard under the lilac bushes, Lois sat near them on a bench nearby. The puppies immediately rushed over to her, licking her feet and playing with her shoe laces; all accept one. Packer sat down behind the pack of puppies and looked up at Lois cocking his head to the side as she spoke to him. But instead of bright blue eyes looking back at her, they had turned into a bright golden yellow. Lois cupped her hands to her mouth with glee and marveled at the wonders of God's creation, silently thanking Him for this fabulous gift.

Thirty Years of Breeding with No Results

Recently, some particularly upset individuals severely ridiculed the Dire Wolf Project on one of the breeder's Facebook pages. Most of the disagreement was about the biased belief that Dire Wolf Project dogs do not look anything like the wild wolf after thirty years of breeding and so the Dire Wolf Project cannot be breeding properly and must be solely out for money based on the Dire Wolf name.

Due to the heightened nature of the ridicule from the opposition, we were not able to have a decent conversation, but the question posed was still a good one. Perhaps a more rational and logical thought process can shed some light on the answer to why, after thirty years of breeding, do Dire Wolf Project dogs still not resemble the Dire Wolf.

First of all, it is important to remember that a "wolfie-looking dog" and a "dog that looks like a wolf" are two different things. There are many breeds already in existence that have a superficial wolfie look to them. Here are a few: Siberian Husky, Alaskan Malamute, silver German Shepherd Dog, Samoyed. To be absolutely clear, these breeds have a somewhat wolfish look but they are easily identified as not being a wolf or a wolfdog because they have fundamental physical tells, such as: white toenails, white spotting, curled tails, small feet, rounder features, dark eyes, smaller teeth and skulls, etc.

In contrast, a dog that looks like a wolf would not only look wolfie as the above breeds do, but would also have the fundamental wild traits that wolves possess, such as: yellow eyes, small round ears, large feet, straight tails, large teeth, large skulls, agouti colored coats, no white spotting, etc.

Before we go any further, let's agree to eliminate any wolfdog breeds as the entire point of creating a dog breed that looks like a wolf is to not include any wolf content, which fundamentally alters the temperament in a

264

domesticated dog. The following breeds have all been identified as having significant wolf content: Czech Vicak, Saarloos Wolfdog, Blue Bay Shepherd, Northern Inuit Dog, Utonogan, Tamaskan Dog, North American Indian Dog, Noble Alaskan Companion Dog, and Tundra Shepherd. These breeds are wolfdogs of varying degrees according to DNA evidence. Of course they would look like wolves, since they actually possess recent wolf content.

To my knowledge, at this time, there is no other breed of dog in existence that is determined to create a domesticated dog that looks like a wolf without resorting to adding wolf content. That means that no one has ever been able to produce a dog, let alone an entire breed, that looks like a wolf without adding wolf content. Furthermore, because no one has accomplished this task, no one knows just how long such an endeavor will take.

Imagine the time it would take to consistently produce just one of the wolf traits described above. Let's take yellow eyes as an example, not even the slanted aspect, just the color alone. It is important to note that domesticated dogs have be bred for hundreds, if not thousands, of years to have dark brown or blue eyes. (Note: The yellow eyes of the Weimaraner are due to the diluted color, not the wolf trait.) One would need to consistently choose puppies that have the lightest eyes in the litter, over and over, throughout each generation, disregarding all else, in order to achieve this in the least time possible. That, by itself, would take years and years to accomplish. We might be able to achieve one yellow-eyed dog in about five generations, if we consistently worked on that trait alone, but then you would have to populate the breed with the trait to consistently produce yellow eyes in every dog bred, so let's say ten years for this one trait.

Now, think about eliminating the white spotting that occurs in many domesticated dogs. Thankfully, the German Shepherd Dog, as an entire breed, has been dedicated to this for hundreds of years. So, that can hopefully take some time off of our count. But, when crossbreeding to the Alaskan Malamute, white spotting enters the picture again. If one worked exclusively on eliminating white spotting from the lines, it would take several generations, and several years, to consistently eliminate white spotting. Let's say half the time it takes to produce yellow eyes, so five years. Now, add those years to the years needed to consistently attain yellow eyes. So far, we are at fifteen years.

What about large feet. Almost all domesticated dogs have small, compact feet compared to their size. This is because the standards for these breeds require it. Again, the minimal years it would take of concentrating solely on increasing the overall foot size of the dogs bred into the program would mean many more years added to our tally above. Let's add another ten years to our tally.

Now, add on the number of years for the other wolf traits, such as a large skull size, large teeth, small-rounded ears, a very gently sloped stop, slanted eyes, correct coat type, agouti coloring, etc. Let's add ten years for each of these traits... that's seventy more years... It looks like we are now at just under one hundred years.

But, the Dire Wolf Project isn't just out to achieve a dog that looks like a wolf. Dire Wolf Project breeders hope to achieve, or come close to achieving, a dog that exactly replicates the bone and body structure of the extinct prehistoric Dire Wolf; the largest wolf ever to roam our planet. So, we must also allow time to actually increase the bone structure of the domesticated dog to mimic the thick bones of the Dire Wolf as well as the increased skull size, etc. that makes the Dire Wolf so distinctive from the Gray Wolf. Many believe that we cannot ultimately achieve this goal, so let's add on a bunch of time for this. Admittedly, it is way easier to produce the thin bones of the Gray Wolf than it is to consistently produce the larger bones of the Dire Wolf. Let's give twenty years for this, although the jury is still out on whether we can or cannot achieve this at all. So, we are at around one hundred fifteen years.

Now, put all that time aside for a moment because the Dire Wolf Project is committed, above all else, to a calm, gentle, intelligent companion dog temperament. By starting with energetic working breeds, Lois spent twelve years, with constant monitoring, solely working on changing the temperament from a hyper working dog to a mellow companion dog before even beginning on any of the cosmetic traits above. We are not at around one hundred twenty-seven years.

But, wait. A health issue crept into the lines. We must now stop all production of any of the above traits and spend time eliminating the health issue. Let's allot eighteen years to work on any and all health issues that could creep in, all the while continuing to monitor health in our dogs. We are now at one hundred fifty years.

Now, most modern dog breeds began around one hundred fifty years ago by mixing already established dog types, achieving a separate dog breed within a few generations. However, most dog breeds are not working to de-domesticate the outward appearance of the domestic dog without adding any wolf content. Turning a ten to thirty-thousand year old domesticated dog back into its wolf ancestry in appearance is no easy task. Again, no one has ever attempted it successfully and most resort to adding wolf content to cut time and achieve a dog that looks like a wolf at a much quicker pace.

But, with all of that said, we feel that our current dogs do have many wolfish traits already. Many of our dogs have yellow eyes, thick bone structure, agouti coat color, slanted eyes, no white spotting, short straight tails, etc. The dog on the front cover of this book, Skipper, even has overall look, although his overall height is lacking and his muzzle is dark. So, perhaps the goals within the Dire Wolf Project cannot be completed in one lifetime, but we strive to achieve them as quickly as we can without compromising on health, temperament or adding wolf content. It takes a much greater amount of time than even Lois ever imagined.

Why No Wolf Content?

Many dog breeds have recently sprung up around the world claiming to have achieved the wolf look without using any wolf content. Some of these breeds even admit their recent wolfish roots, but claim to no longer be breeding in wolf content of any degree. All of these breeds have claimed to achieve a domesticated dog-like temperament, downplaying any wolf-like temperament issues that one might experience. Several wolf look-alike dog breeds have even been placed into the foundation stock service of the American Kennel Club (AKC) and others have achieved recognition through the American Rare Breed Association (ARBA). However, with recent DNA testing advancements and the new ability to tease out the genetic components of the breeds within a dog, all of these so-called wolf look-alike breeds have been shown to range from low to high wolf percentage within their genetic make-up except one, the American Alsatian dog. Almost forty dogs within the Dire Wolf Project have now been DNA tested with no wolf percentage of any kind. To be sure, the Dire Wolf Project could possibly achieve many of its appearance goals if we were to utilize recent wolf blood. For what reason does the Dire Wolf Project maintain a strong aversion to breeding wolf to any degree?

Lois decided to begin her breed in a different way. Instead of concentrating on the look of the dog breed first, Lois chose to perfect the health and temperament before working on the wolfish outward appearance of her breed. All others began with the goal of creating a dog that looked like a wolf first. Or, in the case of the Czechoslovakian Vlcak, the breed was begun as an experiment for increased aggressive tendencies when patrolling the border, which turned out not to work due to the wolf's timid disposition. Because it is not an easy task and takes a great deal of dedication and time to revert a domesticated dog back to a wild appearance without adding wolf content, the term project best describes our work.

More importantly, however, Lois fundamentally understood that wolves are wild animals and have a strong shy demeanor with many temperament issues that can be extremely difficult to breed out after they have entered. Her entire beginning goal was to produce a mellow, gentle companion dog temperament which would be easy to train and fit within the modern lifestyle of busy city life. This specific large breed companion dog temperament defines the breed and without the gentle, sweet, loving, mellow, non-working temperament of the American Alsatian dog, the entire reason for the breed's establishment would be lost.

As I have never bred a wolf or wolfdog of any content, I have limited knowledge in this area. David Cunningham, a well-known breeder from Vermont, wrote the following to describe his current feelings about his experiences breeding wolfdogs:

"After breeding wolf-dogs (descended from mixed breed dogs I had been breeding since 1967) for more than 20 years, I finally stopped breeding them for two reasons: 1. There were more and more people raising wolf-dogs, and I didn't feel there were enough adequate homes to take all that were being produced, and 2. I came to the conclusion that what we've come to consider the normal trainability of the average dog is really alien to wolves. It is not a natural element of wolf behavior, and has been selected for during the tens of thousands of years (or more) of selective breeding that developed the dog from the wild wolf (I believe there is a bigger difference between the mind of a wolf and the average dog than there is between the body of a wolf and a toy poodle). So whenever you cross dog with wolf you lose hundreds of generations [sic] worth of selective breeding for the 'Man-Made' trainability we value. Though my wolf-dogs gained remarkably in health and vigor over the average dog (my mixed breed dogs were already superior to registered purebreds in that area), I missed the trainability I valued so highly in my mixed breed, but no wolf line. I once thought I could produce a 'dog' that was a wolf physically, but a good dog mentally, but I was wrong, and I failed, and since I put so much value on the trainability of a good dog, I stopped breeding my wolf-dogs, which at 125 to 150 lbs. were still averaging a 14 year lifespan, and had no genetic health issues at all. The wolf in some of my current wolfhound crosses is unrelated to my old line, and comes from malamute - wolf crosses I bred to be weight-pulling dogs for competition, with little expectation of them being trainable pets. After evaluating the first crosses of one of my 5/8 malamute - 3/8 wolf males onto an Irish wolfhound bitch for five years, I came to the conclusion that that small amount of wolf had little, if any deleterious effect on the trainability of the resulting pups, so made a similar cross two more times for the genetic diversity it gave my line of wolfhound crosses. I don't consider my present wolfhound, malamute and wolf crosses with only 3/16 wolf in them to be 'wolf-dogs'."[1]

Domesticated Dogs Evolved from Ancient Wolves

Our most beloved pets, so diverse in their outward appearance, have now been shown to have come solely from the gray wolf. Darwin once famously speculated whether the domesticated dog could have also derived from the jackal or the coyote, but with new advancements in DNA, these ideas have now been put to rest. But, this split between dog and wolf occurred such a long time ago that many reason that the domesticated dog now holds the DNA of extinct ancient wolves and can be said to only be distantly related to the modern gray wolf. As geneticist, Adam Freedman, explains, "A sharp bottleneck in wolves occurred soon after their divergence from dogs, implying that the pool of diversity from which dogs arose was substantially larger than represented by modern wolf populations."[2]

Furthermore, it appears that wolves today do not share the same genetic features that domesticated dogs share. Adam Freedman's research also suggests a much narrower timeframe from when dogs began their selective evolutionary beginnings, "We find that none of the wolf lineages from the hypothesized domestication centers is supported as the source lineage for dogs, and that dogs and wolves diverged 11,000–16,000 years ago in a process involving extensive admixture and that was followed by a bottleneck in wolves. In addition, we investigate the amylase (*AMY2B*) gene family

269

expansion in dogs, which has recently been suggested as being critical to domestication in response to increased dietary starch. "[3]

Not only that, but further research suggests that dogs have adapted in the years they have been isolated from breeding among their wolf cousins to be able to ingest higher starch amounts. The genetics also may reveal significant changes to the nervous system in domesticated dogs compared to wolves. Researchers performing whole gene sequencing of dogs and wolves revealed the following, "Here we conduct whole-genome resequencing of dogs and wolves to identify 3.8 million genetic variants used to identify 36 genomic regions that probably represent targets for selection during dog domestication. Nineteen of these regions contain genes important in brain function, eight of which belong to nervous system development pathways and potentially underlie behavioural changes central to dog domestication. Ten genes with key roles in starch digestion and fat metabolism also show signals of selection. We identify candidate mutations in key genes and provide functional support for an increased starch digestion in dogs relative to wolves. Our results indicate that novel adaptations allowing the early ancestors of modern dogs to thrive on a diet rich in starch, relative to the carnivorous diet of wolves, constituted a crucial step in the early domestication of dogs."[4]

The domesticated dog that we know today, represented in so many of the different types all around the world, do not share as much in common with Gray Wolves as they might have thousands of years ago. In a study conducted in 2016, the population subdivisions, demography, and genetic relationships of gray wolves were investigated compared to dogs. The study indicated that the dog was a divergent subspecies of the gray wolf and was derived from a now-extinct "ghost population" of Late Pleistocene wolves. The researchers assembled and analyzed a data set of thirty-four canine genomes. Their research supports the hypothesis that dogs were derived from an extinct wolf population. Furthermore, the study found that up to 25% of Eurasian wolf genomes showed signs of dog ancestry. This suggests recent admixture of dog DNA within the wolf.[5]

It appears that literally over ten to fifteen thousand years have passed without what looks like any significant admixture of wolf blood in the domesticated dogs we know today. It has taken significant time to develop and evolve the domesticated dog temperament in our most beloved breeds. What a marvelous long-term evolution experiment it has turned out to be.

Not only that, but it has been proposed that the Gray Wolf and the Dire Wolf split into separate evolutionary lines over three hundred thousand years ago when canis lupus diverged from canis chihliensis. Creating a wolf look that mimics the bone and body structure of the extinct prehistoric Dire Wolf using only domesticated dogs, which have been in the process of domestication for over 13,000 years takes some time. Not only must be continue the domestication process of the temperament within the dog, but at the same time we must work to reverse the outward appearance of the dog to revert back to an extinct form of ancient wolf.

David Cunningham eloquently compiled the information between dog and wolf in this post he wrote on a Facebook group on April 20, 2017. It clearly explains the evolution of man's best friend and how the genetics in our beloved dog breeds just may have been the superior qualities of the ancient wolves that fit perfectly with their ability to adapt to humankind. It is with sincere appreciation for David Cunningham's knowledge and work that I quote the following:

"Another problem with crossing dogs with the wolves we now know is that the dog itself may well have been developed from a subspecies of wolf that is now extinct, and might well have had some anomaly (such as much more trainability than the average wild wolf) that made it just a better 'dog'. Primitive Man didn't need anything but what all wild wolves bring to the table in a hunting companion. All he needed were animals that would run down and hold a large ungulate (such as a moose or aurochs) at bay until the men could run in and drive their stone-tipped spears into it. Then all the tame wolves had to do after cleaning up the gut pile and other parts not wanted by their human 'partners', and coming back to the camp with them, was not kill the human children running around to qualify as "dogs". The neighbors had no sheep or chickens to worry about them killing, they could run free and do as they pleased, and by sleeping in camp they protected the people from cave bears and other beast of prey that might sneak in under the cover of darkness. During hard times the majority of the pack would be killed off and eaten, and you can bet that the ones who were the tamest, the friendliest and obeyed commands the best were the last to be eaten, and often survived until spring. This resulted in selective breeding for tameness and the ability to obey commands even if the

271

Humans didn't realize they were doing so. I'm sure Humans all over the northern hemisphere were taming the local wolves in their area and using them for hunting, but as the people keeping the wolf-dogs descended from that special subspecies migrated around, when they introduced their 'better dogs' to an area they quickly superseded the local 'dogs' (as happened within recorded history when Europeans colonized the Americas. When Caitlin and other painters were recording the tribes of the west, all their paintings showed wolf-like dogs in the Native villages, but within a short time, all those wolf-derived native dogs had all but disappeared, and been replaced by European dogs, as recorded by the first photographers to take pictures of the last of the Natives living their natural way. I believe this was because the European dogs were just 'better dogs' than the dogs derived from North American wolves). I believe this wolf subspecies that went on to be the ancestor of the majority of todays [sic] domestic dogs was a small, dingo-like, possibly desert dwelling animal from the Mideast or Asia, and that's why whenever dogs are left to their own devices they revert to the common, dingo-like pariah dog seen practically everywhere in the world. As a matter of fact, I believe the Dingo in Australia is the perfect example of atavism; of a domestic animal reverting back to the original form of its wild ancestor if left without human interference for a long enough period of time. So when we cross dogs with wolves today, we are not just crossing wild and domestic specimens of the same species, but are using wolves that already have proved unsuccessful in the production of the domestic dog. They just don't have the anomaly that original odd subspecies had."[6]

Dire Wolf Appearance

Paleontologists only feel certain about the bone and body structure of the Dire Wolf's appearance as they uncover thousands of Dire Wolf Skeletons encased in our Earth's own historical museum. These complete and well-preserved skeletons can tell us definitively about the size, weight, and overall shape of the Dire Wolf but cannot determine ear height, typical coat coloring, length and texture of fur, or eye color. What we know regarding those physical traits we can only speculate based upon a thorough examination of what scientists know about carnivore survival through Mother Nature's natural selection. However, through Isotopic Analysis we can learn about the Dire Wolf's eating habits which directly affected how the Dire Wolf could use its massive body to effectively hunt and thus acquire the build needed to maintain such a diet. By also analyzing the diverse body structure of domesticated dog breeds, we can speculate with some degree of certainty about other habits that may have had an effect on the Dire Wolf's appearance compared to its close cousin, the Gray Wolf.

The Dire Wolf stood just over two feet and a half feet tall, thirty inches, and weighed on average one hundred ten pounds with a maximum weight of one hundred fifty pounds, although some sources indicate slightly heavier. The larger bone set of the Dire Wolf compared to Gray Wolves living today would have created a much broader, stockier, and denser animal. The feet of the Dire Wolf were larger with a notable splay enough to carry the heavy frame. The Dire Wolf's head is most significantly unique in that it was much broader, larger in size, and heavier than the typical Gray Wolf. Despite this increase in skull size, the Dire Wolf shows a smaller brain cavity. The length of the Dire Wolf from head to tail was around five to size feet.

Mackenzie Valley Wolf
Photo credit: Santiago Atienza

The Yukon Wolf or the Mackenzie Valley Wolf could be said to be the closest modern wolf to possess a similar size compared to the measurements of the Dire Wolf.

Scientists have developed two theories for coat color in the Dire Wolf depending on where the Dire Wolf may have originated. During the Ice Age, the watery passage between the northern Siberian coastline and Alaska's closest shores was completely covered in a thick layer of ice. This would have allowed migrating animals free passage across the Bering Land Bridge. Researchers maintain that the Gray Wolf crossed this icy passageway, arriving after the Dire Wolf already dominated the North American landscape. It is entirely possible that the Dire Wolf also took this convenient route earlier and set up residence long before the Gray Wolf emerged onto the scene.

Another intriguing theory exists, however. Since the Dire Wolf population dominated the Gray Wolf ten to one, we could come to the conclusion that the Dire Wolf emerged from a completely different location. Some researchers speculate that the Dire Wolf came from South America, migrating north until reaching the chilly tundra surroundings of North America. As Dire Wolf skeletons have also been found in parts of South America, this is entirely possible, although most scientists have now rejected it in favor of the land bridge theory.

These two migration theories pose an intriguing mystery and two coat color hypotheses begin to emerge. It is generally believed that the Dire wolf was the direct descendent of the Armbruster's Wolf, *Canis armbrusteri*, while the modern Gray Wolf is descended from the Hare-eating Wolf, *C. lepophagus*. Thus, the Dire Wolf is a completely different species from the Gray Wolf, much like the coyote or jackal. The diversity of these two wolf species would allow for a greater variety of coat texture and coloring. With the possibility that the Dire Wolf migrated north from South American, this prehistoric mammal could have possessed more of the reverse colored look of the South American maned Wolf. The legs of the Dire Wolf would then have been darker than the body, which would have had a more subtle banded coloration.

On the other hand, if the Dire Wolf traveled along the Bering Land Bridge as did the Gray Wolf afterwards, then the Dire Wolf could have more closely resembled the Gray Wolf in color.

Most paleontologists believe the light silver agouti coloring of the Gray

Wolf is the more plausible argument. Paleontologist Caitlin Brown, speaking to journalist Karen Brulliard at the Washington Post, "thinks white is 'feasible,' gray is likely, and only black is impossible, because [as she states] 'we know for sure that black coats showed up in modern wolves from breeding with Native American dogs.' Brown, who had not heard of Schwarz's project, deemed it 'cool,' when told about it. 'They have that big, bulky body, which is what I would have imagined,' she said of the dogs in photos on Schwarz's website."[7]

Can the Dire Wolf Actually Be Recreated?

There are certainly many dogs that achieve taller and heavier weights than the Dire Wolf is said to have had. Some English Mastiffs achieve weights upwards of two hundred pounds. The Irish Wolfhound and the giant Alaskan Malamute easily stand thirty-eight inches tall at the shoulders. All three of these breeds have given their genes to the dogs being bred within the Dire Wolf Project. So, it would definitely be possible to achieve the overall size and weight expectations of the Dire Wolf using only domesticated dogs, but the difficulty arises when talking about the exact bone and body structure of the Dire Wolf compared to a domestic dog version. That may be a different story completely. The reason is that the Dire Wolf shows an overall thicker bone structure than the modern Gray Wolf. Again, dog breeds like the English Mastiff or bandogge types show a thicker build to their legs than other dogs, but do they actually have increased bone thickness or simply more musculature? To this author's knowledge, it has yet to be studied scientifically.

One thing that has been interesting for the breed, however, is that keeping the phenotypic look of a thick bone structure is very difficult to maintain over time in the breed. Quite often the thickness in leg structure diminishes greatly as we turn the generations. It may be due to the fact that breeders must continue to include dogs with thinner bone structure for other needs within the breed, but it also may be that altering dogs that come from ancient Gray Wolf ancestry may not result easily in the thick bone structure that appears in the Dire Wolf. If the Dire Wolf Project ever actually is able to achieve it with any consistency in the future, it will one amazing find.

Another impossibility may be achieving a larger tooth size that will be able to match the canines of the Dire Wolf. We know that larger skull sizes automatically show large tooth sizes, but even the Gray Wolf shows larger canine tooth measurements than the domesticated dog. That may be one of the last physical aspects we work on within the breed, if we ever come to it. Currently, we have enough difficulty keeping an erect ear due to the most recent crossbreeding that has been necessary within the breed. So, until some other physical appearance traits become solidified, an exactly measured canine tooth may be a long, long way off.

Currently, we have achieved the following traits with some consistency within the American Alsatian dog breed. The main issue has been, though, producing them all together in one dog.

- substantially larger paws compared to the body frame
- highly slanted yellow eyes
- deep black pigmentation
- correct height and weight as predicted for the Dire Wolf
- correct length from head to tail as predicted for the Dire Wolf
- medium length agouti colored coat with longer mane and tail hair
- all black toenails and minimal to non-existent residual white spotting
- small erect ears
- short tail
- thicker looking legs and broad heavy overall build
- light wolf muzzle, as opposed to the black mask

Wolfie-looking dogs have manifested in the breed from time to time. We will continue to work on health and temperament above all as we also sneak in as many outward appearance traits toward the overall goal as we can. As many skeptics have noted, the Dire Wolf Project does continue to see quite a bit of diversity within the outward appearance in the breed. The newest crossbreed, the second English Mastiff, has now entered a line and so Lois Schwarz is currently working to incorporate the selective temperament and appearance traits from this line that the breed needs going forward, including: thicker bone structure, mellower overall temperament, larger skull size, and larger overall height and weight. As usual, it will be a process to weed out the traits that are not needed within the line such as: hanging skin, round eyes, dark brown eyes, short muzzle with a deep stop, short coat and thin undercoat, long floppy ears, and yellow coat coloring.

Conclusion

It certainly does take time to move from a domesticated dog to a wild wolf look. Above that, the Dire Wolf has some features that may or may not be able to be achieved using only domesticated dog breeds. Not only that, but the Dire Wolf Project hopes to further evolve dog domestication by creating the first large breed companion dog bred solely for our modern lives. It is not an easy process and takes a great deal of effort and time. We cannot rush the process and only take the next right step in the direction that will improve the breed toward our goals while always monitoring health and longevity. It may not be able to be accomplished in any one person's lifetime. As one person replied to a picture posted on the Dire Wolf Project Facebook page, "I hope you all are able to recreate just one dog that resembles the Dire Wolf before I die." It would be an honor and we will certainly continue to try.

Zorro (Trucker/Sooner) around 2003

Chapter 13
The Dog's Future

"So many of our dreams at first seem impossible, then they seem improbable, and then, when we summon the will, they soon become inevitable."
– Christopher Reeve

Just like the ebb and flow of the rhythmic tide of life, dreams must be realized one breath at a time. They cannot be rushed or hurried. They should arrive at the optimal moment when their fulfillment can do the most good for the most people. The best dreams last beyond one's lifetime; a mantle to be taken up by those who follow after.

There are days when I envision the future so clearly in front of me. With a steaming cup of coffee, my mother emerges on some crisp, early morning, from her small rustic cabin set back in the tall pines, to see what her daughter is up to. With the peacefulness of nature's beauty all around, the crunch of a pine needle carpet underneath, and the promise of a new day, we meet on a metal bench just off the weathered trail in the middle of the property to enjoy a moment together watching the sun rise over Huckleberry Mountain to the east. Time is the most precious gift humans share with one another and so we sit and dream together.

We look straight ahead and I envision the tall, enclosed barn where the whelping rooms, the grooming room, the health clinic, the office, the temporary indoor kennels, the office, and the large arena is laid out. We imagine where our offices, front store and feeding room might be located. We talk about the outdoor swimming pool next to the barn for the dogs to play and exercise. We add a fenced and manicured outdoor training space where the jumps and tunnels will go. We further discuss the parking lot and the barn's entrance where visitors can enter for training, shows, and conventions.

Then, I point slightly to the right down the hill where the pull through camping spaces will be located, each one set up with a fire ring and hook-ups for those interested in spending time with the founder and her dogs at the Dire Wolf Project headquarters. Perhaps a few cabins, too, for any interns that have been assigned to work at our facility. The trail to the Lake Roosevelt overlook just down the hill and out the gate to the south.

Our eyes pan farther south as we imagine the natural rock-lined caves buried into the side of the hill; warm in the winter and cool in the summer as the earth's loving embrace envelopes the space. We share the dream of the dens opening right out into the forest where a natural stream flows downhill for the beautiful dogs to drink freely as the sun climbs higher into the sky. What a beautiful natural enclosure we project as we talk about the observatory above the dens where people can sit and watch the large dogs play in their calm and gentle way.

I shift on the bench to look behind me to the west past the trees where I point toward the meadow behind. This space is meant for the other animals that represent an age long past away. The Heck Horse herd grazes peacefully in our minds as we walk past the Musk Ox enclosures to the Aurochs paddocks. A small prehistoric paradise for visitors to imagine what life would have been like in North America at the end of the last Ice Age.

I turn again on the bench to look toward the north where the greenhouse is scheduled to be built. We talk about the root cellar, the raised-bed garden and the fruit trees that line the edge of the forest soaking up the brightness of the southern sun. Lois imagines the shorter fall days when we meet to pick the last of the summer harvest and place the bushels of food into the root cellar to prepare for the coming winter.

I remind her of our plans to beautify the land with paved roads, flowers, old world street lamps, and Dire Wolf statues made of bronze. Inside the garage two project vans sit awaiting their use transporting puppies to their new homes. Or perhaps a private jet sits ideally in a hangar at the private airport an hour away so that the puppies can travel to their new homes without distress. I smile at her as she laughs at my private jet dream.

"Aha!" I hear a distant rumble exclaim as a sudden wind brushes my face lifting my hair in a brief wavy swarm. "It IS all about the money!" No. It is about a dream to provide the very best lives for the animals in our care and giving back something of great worth to the loving families who need what so few others provide. We reach for a better way. A sustainable way. A way in which we honor every precious life and bring renewal and reform to a broken breeding system. We hope for lasting change for the care and protection of man's best friend. To finally promote great health and longevity above all else without apology or compromise. To form a unified breeding community that always works in conjunction with one another for the benefit of all dogs within the breed instead of in competition with one another for the benefit of one's own promotion. This, in turn, lifts every breeder up together as one.

Lois and I embrace as she stands to return to her little cabin at the edge of the forest to get ready for her day. I meander to where the dogs look out through their pens with their bright yellow eyes and I marvel at how much effort and sacrifice it has taken to continue the project while at the same time enduring the exhausting ridicule that comes from those who regularly hope for our failure.

I recall when Lois first announced that she purchased a purebred Irish Wolfhound to breed into the lines. Oh, how the Irish Wolfhound community berated Lois consistently for months and months after they found out. "You will ruin the Irish Wolfhound breed!" one breeder jeered. "Don't you know the Irish Wolfhound has an extremely low longevity? You will ruin YOUR breed!" another unimpressed observer weighed in. Letters and emails poured in from the concerned Irish Wolfhound community. As Lois recalls on her website regarding the constant ridicule at the time, "This was a major decision and she [Ahwna] cost me a lot of money plus a lot more than just money."[1]

Oh, the uproar Lois caused by purchasing an Irish Wolfhound for the breed. And yet, what Lois did by breeding a purebred Irish Wolfhound to a purebred M'loot type Alaskan Malamute would have been of great value to the Irish Wolfhound community had they only understood the nature of crossbreeding for genetic diversity and then back breeding to get back to standards. My mind traveled back to the awkward moment I sat on the couch at my grandmother's home between my mother on the left and my aunt on the right. I remember the empty silence that followed my mother's statement that the Irish Wolfhound's health could be improved if only the breed club would consider crossbreeding with a M'loot Alaska Malamute, her horrifying comment hanging limp in the air.

Little did any of us know at the time as we sat in that awkward moment that a prominent breeder on the other side of the country, David Cunningham, has been working on just this very thing with his M'loot Alaskan Malamute and Irish Wolfhound crosses. Many of his latest generations already look so similar to purebred Irish Wolfhounds with much better health and longevity that it might be hard for a professional AKC judge to tell them apart. But there is so much stigma surrounding crossbreeding, who knows how long it will be before David Cunningham's dogs might be recognized as a viable option to help secure a better future for the Irish Wolfhound. For the sake of the Irish Wolfhounds, themselves, I hope it is sooner rather than later.

But then again, our willingness to use inbreeding as a tool to eradicate disease and solidify necessary traits can be just as controversial. The hysteria that is caused by openly speaking out for ideas that are currently out of favor

As I sit here putting the final touches to this book, I find a series of posts on reddit.com from last year that simply breaks my heart. The ridicule, hatred, disgust, hurtful jeers, personal attacks, and misinterpretations that spill forth from the black, oozing tar pits of the Internet lying in wait to devour an entire pack of unsuspecting Dire Wolves should they enter to defend our ideas is extremely disheartening. "'God's Breeding Plan' cannot be sustainable simply because it is trademarked and mentions God," I read. The evil of gossip and lies spread about for the seeming sole purpose of leading others away from the Dire Wolf Project; constantly portraying our values and breeding practices as "a grab bag of really weird science" or worse naming the founder a fantastical zealot making money off of a great marketing scheme. The saddest part is that all of it is so far from reality and truth, but, one cannot change someone's mind if they choose to ignore the existence of reason. A person can only educate and inform as openly as one can, but no one can force someone to agree when they are stuck behind the dogma.

Society should renew its commitment to treat our most loyal animal companions as the invaluable assets they are. Breeders should maintain these unique breeds as well as improve their lives by working together to eliminate the genetic health and conformation issues they face and strive to increase their lives to match their captive held wild cousins. They deserve no less from those they depend on. As Richard Frankham et. al. in his masterful text, Introduction to Conservation Genetics, concludes, "While maintenance of 90% of genetic diversity for 100 years is a reasonable practical compromise, it is unlikely that all the species requiring captive breeding can be accommodated. Species are being maintained with lesser goals (and smaller sizes) as a consequence of shortage of resources."[2]

With practical breed-wide conservation goals for the preservation of their breed, breed clubs can sustain their beloved breeds over time. In addition, breed clubs should create and develop breed-wide health and temperament monitoring in open forums to be held accountable for their work. Unified breed clubs should require certification programs for breeders within their breed to insist that breeders adhere to careful selection for health, temperament, and viable conformation before outward appearance and the sake of purity.

Genetic management for breed preservation should be the hallmark of the members of the breed club so that significant loss of genetic diversity does not continue to occur. Breeders should work together to manage genetic rehabilitation and restoration of severely inbred, isolated, and rare breeds. Those breeders who out-perform the goals within the breed club should be rewarded for their efforts and allowed to become recognized mentors for other breeders who may need support.

We must not be too filled with pride regarding our own knowledge that we fail to take direction from nature's example all around us. We can and should learn from the superior health and longevity in wolves. When inbreeding, we must also substantially increase population size so that inbreeding can be minimized as the breed develops. Then, just like the wolf, when the population size has increased enough to allow for significant crossbreeding, we should strive to keep as much genetic diversity as possible in the breed in order to minimize the effects of any inbreeding depression that would occur at the point we were inbreeding. When inbreeding is coupled with increased population size and outcrossing is matched with decreased population size, an ebb and flow balance between the two opposing forces naturally exists.

American Alsatian puppies 2018

Appendix A
List of Logical Fallacies

Here we present several different errors in logic that a person might experience when speaking to others regarding the Dire Wolf Project. Indeed this author has personally encountered all of the claims below when speaking about the project in the midst of other dog enthusiasts. It should be noted that each claim used in this section has been either paraphrased or reworded for clarity. Throughout the last fifteen years, each of these claims has, in some way, been presented to this author as a valid argument meant to dismiss, ridicule, or discredit the Dire Wolf Project and its strongbred dog breeding practices.

Fallacies of Relevance

Relevance Claim #1: Appeal to Force
It is illegal in England to breed a female dog on its first heat.

This argument uses force or even the threat of force to make the audience accept a conclusion. Within this argument is a threat that if the breeder lived in England, the authorities would be called and the breeder would be shut down. Unfortunately, this is not an argument that will convince anyone that their choice is the best one. This is because it is completely irrelevant what is and is not legal in another country. Since Dire Wolf Project breeders do not breed in England, it is irrelevant. This argument is meant to discredit the Dire Wolf Project for supposedly doing something illegal, and therefore suggestively harmful requiring punishment by law. However, whether or not it is indeed illegal to breed a female dog on its first heat in England does not in any way answer the question of whether it is harmful or unethical to do so. Therefore, an entire chapter on breeding a female dog on its first heat is devoted to the real discussion on this topic.

A mutt with yellow eyes? You should be ashamed of breeding this dog intentionally and then giving it the name it has! Fraud to say the least. Someone should report you.

Threatening an opponent with fraud and sending a report to the authorities is not at all helpful to an argument. The sheer level of intolerance and disrespect presented here does nothing to support any claim, except to perhaps elicit a reaction from the audience and to give the impression that the Dire Wolf Project is engaging in criminal activity by its mere existence. The above statement shows a true lack of logical thought as well as a profound twisting of truths by using foul and hurtful language. It would not be surprising if this type of comment was also meant to anger the opposition so that they speak out of turn and shout back. It is important in debate to remain neutral in one's emotional state and continue to speak calmly and rationally; countering this type of verbal aggression by quietly correcting any mistakes presented in the rebuttal, such as the mistake of calling the dogs within the Dire Wolf Project mutts. A mutt or mongrel is a mixed dog of unknown origin, so the fact that the Dire Wolf Project can trace the lineage of each dog bred into the project to its foundational sources would automatically cease to identify it as a mutt. In truth, the dogs bred into the Dire Wolf Project are a new type of breed altogether. The breed cannot be considered purebred, since we regularly and systematically crossbreed for overall health and genetic diversity, but neither can the dogs be considered mutts or even mixed breeds because many American Alsatian dogs do indeed breed true to type. Instead, we propose a new term, the strongbred dog, to identify this type of dog breed; one in which the dogs are not held in a closed stud book, but instead a perpetually open one. This concept is so new and revolutionary that we have devoted an entire chapter to the idea of the strongbred dog breed concept, but also this book, in and of itself, is a review of this new way of breeding dogs that harkens back to the way humans have bred domesticated dogs since the dog evolved from its wild ancestors.

Relevance Claim #2: Genetic Fallacy
American Alsatians are just mutts with a high price tag and we all know that mutts are a shot in the dark as far as health is concerned.

It is a genetic fallacy to claim that an idea, person, or thing is wrong because of its racial, geographic, or ethnic origin. In this case, the person is arguing that it doesn't matter what the Dire Wolf Project is really about because it all boils down to the simple fact that these dogs are mutts and as a result of their mixed genetic make-up are to be disliked and dishonored for their diversity. Unfortunately, this statement does not make any solid points as to why a mix of genetic components would be undesirable and assumes a great deal about the dogs within the Dire Wolf Project. That is why we have devoted Chapter 7 to the project's understanding of crossbreeding and why it is necessary to always have an open studbook where regular and systematic crossbreeding can be practiced at any time the breed needs to introduce new genetic material.

Relevance Claim #3: Personal Attack (abusive)

Lois is a Christian and therefore breeds outside of well-established science. OR God's Breeding Plan is a joke.

There are a lot of assumptions made in the above statements. First of all, Christians throughout the religion's existence have been at the forefront of many scientific discoveries. One relevant example, genetics, was discovered by a Catholic Augustinian monk named Gregor Mendel. That being said, Lois does understand her world through the lens of her religion. However, it is completely intolerable to have absolutely no idea of the nature of her claims and at the same time state, on the basis of her religion alone, that what she proposes is a joke. Perhaps, after a thorough review, one may come to the conclusion that it is indeed a joke, but without considering the idea itself and the results of her work, one cannot possibly claim anything solely because of her religious affiliation. Not only is this approach dishonest, it is shameful. Chapter 5 is devoted to unraveling the understanding of the term the founder coined as "God's Breeding Plan."

Relevance Claim #3: Personal Attack (circumstantial)

Why should we care about the Dire Wolf Project? We all know that the Dire Wolf Project is founded by an uneducated woman who has been divorced and remarried three times. She can't even decide what her last name will be let alone how to breed dogs.

While it is correct that Lois Schwarz, the founder of the Dire Wolf Project, did not attend college or achieve any degrees in any field of study and has no official recognition of any kind from any renowned organization as well as the fact that she has been divorced and remarried three times, those facts are completely irrelevant to whether the founder's breeding practices actually have any merit. Lois Schwarz is who she is, but the very fact that she did sacrifice a formal education to passionately pursue her dreams disregarding all else should not be sneered at, but looked at with admiration. While others took the time and money necessary to attain legitimacy through degrees from reputable colleges and universities, Lois used her time on this earth to do the work behind what books and classes explain and also what books and classes do not explain. She was not arbitrary in her methods and so Chapter 4 is devoted to discussing the very real person behind the founding of this new breed of dog. As Christine Vara, lead editor of the blog, "Shot of Prevention," argues, "*ad hominem* attacks are acts of desperation by those who believe they have some absolute truth; but are incapable of supporting it through scholarship, science, logic and common sense."[1]

Relevance Claim #4: Argument to the People (Bandwagon Approach)
We all know that hind movement cannot predict whether the hips are good or bad.

Do we, indeed, all know that? Appealing to the understanding of the majority listening does not, in any way, prove that one cannot predict with any accuracy if hips are good or bad by assessing hind movement. Just because a group of people think differently from one another does not mean that those in agreement are correct. If someone does argue that breeding differently than others automatically means our dogs are unhealthy and/or unsound in temperament they are using the bandwagon approach. For example, many thought the world was flat, but in fact, as we now know, that idea was incorrect. A vast number of scientists once believed that a human being would never be able to withstand traveling at fifty miles per hour or faster. We now also know this to be false. Health is of utmost importance to our breeding practices and so we take an in-depth look at the health of the dogs within the Dire Wolf Project in this book.

Relevance Claim #5: Argument to the People (Snob Approach)

Responsible breeders know that every breeding dog must have cleared hip and elbow scores before breeding, which cannot be done until two years old.

In this claim, only the best breeders are the responsible kind and their practices should tell the rest of us know-nothings what is morally and ethically best to do when breeding dogs. It is very similar to the bandwagon approach except not just everyone, but only the best of everyone, has the authority to properly dictate what should be. It is kind of like saying, only AKC registered pedigreed dogs are worthy of a higher price tag because they have superior ancestries. However, it does not matter what superior backgrounds the group of people have that state a certain claim. What matters are the actual practices themselves and whether these practices can be proved to harm the dog or the puppies in any way thus causing the dog or the puppies to suffer. Breeding female dogs on their first heat is such a controversial topic in our modern age that we discuss in depth the history, research, science, and experiences behind these practices.

Relevance Claim #6: Appeal to Tradition

The Dire Wolf Project's goals are not possible to achieve. No one has ever shown that you can take only domesticated dogs and return to a wild type, let alone increase bone thickness in order to mimic an extinct prehistoric predator.

The mere idea that something has never been done before does not, in and of itself, mean that it cannot be accomplished. Certainly, the reason why the Dire Wolf Project causes some unrest within the dog breeding community is because much of what we claim has not been done before. Whether or not the Dire Wolf Project can truly reach its goals will have to be seen. We are dedicated to finding out if it is possible to attain and will continue toward our goals until we cannot achieve further progress. But, to quickly dismiss the project outright as unattainable is faulty thinking and prohibitive to the discussion.

Relevance Claim #7: Appeal to Novelty

We have known for years now that inbreeding is not needed to secure type. New advancements in genetics have clearly shown this. You are living in the distant past, my friend.

It is so easy to become caught up in the fallacy that modern ideas must automatically be better than traditional ones. It is all the rage at this time in our modern dog breeding world to blame increasing health problems solely on high degrees of inbreeding, whereas, only one hundred years ago it was all the rage to proclaim that inbreeding was the best way to go about securing good health, proper breeding and superior temperament conformity. In contrast between both perspectives, the Dire Wolf Project chooses to remain in the middle between these two extremes. We believe that crossbreeding and inbreeding are necessary components of any healthy dog breed. As you will see with the latest genetic testing in the chapter on inbreeding, the very idea of setting traits <u>must</u> include a certain degree of inbreeding by its very nature and the more genetic traits the parents have in common, the more inbred the offspring, regardless of the parents' relationship to one another.

Relevance Claim #8: Appeal to Improper Authority

The first temperament test is forty-eight hours after birth? Are you aware of multiple peer-reviewed papers on the subject, none of which indicate reliable temperament testing in puppies under six weeks? Even guide dog facilities have protocols for evaluation at later ages and they have an immense degree of pedigree information and a rich population to study.

It is always a good practice to share relevant information from authorities that have studied the topic in depth. Sometimes, however, people working to discredit another will bring to the forefront authorities that simply have no relevancy to the topic being discussed. First of all, we must recognize that in the above argument the opponent states "multiple peer-reviewed papers, none of which indicate reliable temperament testing in puppies under six weeks." They may not <u>indicate</u> any reliable temperament testing under six weeks, but perhaps the articles in question, which were never specifically cited, did not even test puppies under six weeks old and therefore did not have the data to present one way or the other. If they did not, then these articles cannot be considered proper authorities on the subject of temperament testing puppies under six weeks old. Secondly, appealing to guide dog programs to prove that temperament cannot be evaluated at young ages is irrelevant to the subject at hand. Just because other breeding programs do not have temperament tests at young ages does not in the least prove that temperament tests on newborn puppies cannot be accurate. There are very real and very important reasons why we perform temperament tests at such young ages. We discuss these at length in this book.

Breeding females on their first heat is not particularly recommended by popular geneticists.

Geneticists have knowledge regarding DNA, deleterious alleles, phenotype vs genotype and experience in the science lab separating the tiniest forms of matter, but what does the study of genetics know about the morality of breeding female dogs on their first heat? Appealing to an authority is important, but the authority must have the particular knowledge about the issue at hand being argued. Unless the geneticist or scientist has done research specifically identifying key components associated with the argument, the authority is useless to the discussion at hand and simply misdirects the conversation adding no value to the points presented one way or the other. Also, the person arguing has not provided any real researched support for the claim. A genetic appeal to science by simply adding the term geneticists or scientists to bolster the argument is fundamentally dishonest.

Relevance Claim #9: Appeal to Biased Authority
The Humane Society of the United States says that a responsible breeder only sells puppies to people he/she has met in person and must have a spay/neuter contract. Since you sell dogs without ever laying your eyes on the family and you allow the owners to keep their dog intact, you cannot be a responsible breeder.

The Humane Society of the United State (HSUS) is a non-profit organization that portrays itself as working tirelessly to eradicate all animal abuse. However, in an interview with Ted Kerasote in 1992, Wayne Pacelle, the CEO of HSUS (2004 - present), stated the following in answer to the question of if he would envision a future with no pets in the world, "If I had my personal view perhaps that might take hold. In fact, I don't want to see another cat or dog born. It's not something I strive for, though. If people were very responsible, and didn't do manipulative breeding, and cared for animals in all senses, and accounted for their nutritional needs as well as their social and psychological needs, then I think it could be an appropriate thing. I'm not sure. I think it's one of those things that we'll decide later in society. I think we're still far from it."[2] Furthermore, the president of the official lobbying arm at the HSUS as well as the chairman of HSUS's "Humane USA" political action committee, Michael Markarian, stated in his essay in the journal, *The Abolitionist*, in 1997, "Activists purposely breaking laws that are unjust, such as hunter harassment laws, or committing acts of civil disobedience to help animals, are effective rebels because they tie the movement's issues together with First Amendment, freedom of speech, and civil liberties issues. A perfect example of effective rebellion is an Animal Liberation Front raid on a laboratory that frees puppies from its confines and exposes video footage of the researchers torturing the animals. Sure, the activists broke the law, but all of their activities focused directly on saving animals and exposing cruelty."[3] If Mr. Pacelle, who ran the HSUS from 2004 to 2018 and ten years prior was the organization's chief lobbyist and spokesperson, expects to eventually eliminate all dog breeding, and Mr. Markarian, who has held high office at HSUS since 2005, believes that breaking the law is justified to expose what he perceives as cruelty to animals, then the HSUS would be expected to have the most comprehensive list of what a responsible breeder should be so that very few, if any, breeders would be able to be seen as responsible. This authority is then essentially biased toward dog breeders because it may have an open agenda against dog breeding. For this reason, they should not be used to bolster an argument about responsible breeding.

Relevance Claim #10: Appeal to Emotion
Breeding dogs on their first heat is like having your twelve year old daughter get pregnant. That's disgusting and wrong.

When someone chooses to point out an example that is seemingly related, but looks to bring about an emotional response from the audience, it is dishonest logic. It does not prove, one way or another, that breeding dogs on the first heat is harmful to the dog. It merely brings about negative emotions, which sway the audience without having to discuss the actual issues specifically related to the topic of first heat breeding. This is why we devote an entire chapter to explaining this practice within the Dire Wolf Project.

I disagree with how this project is run. The high inbreeding is disgusting.

Again, this person is working to bring about an emotional response from the audience by generalizing that high inbreeding is disgusting. This statement does not help the conversation in any way by proving that high inbreeding is detrimental to dog breeding. He/she simply makes a blanket emotional statement in order to elicit a response from others to agree with him/her. Needless to say that the person did not even take into account that we actually do not practice high inbreeding to the same degree as other purebred dog breeds with closed stud books. Again, an entire chapter will discuss inbreeding in depth and how it relates to the Dire Wolf Project's breeding practices.

Relevance Claim #11: Argument from Adverse Consequences

I disagree with breeding on the first heat. I could never see my sweet six month old puppy giving birth, she would never be emotionally ready.

A person using this type of logical fallacy asserts that the opponent's argument must be false because of how much the person dislikes the outcome if the argument were to be true. The person arguing in this way inadvertently anthropomorphized his/her precious dog in order to retain the belief that the dog possesses sensitive emotions that would be damaged by giving birth to puppies at a younger age. Whether it is true or not that the dog would experience emotional duress by birthing puppies at six months old is never considered. The mere perception of it being true is enough to convince this person that it would be a horrible outcome. Furthermore, if the person is suggesting that his/her dog would come into her first heat at four months old in order to give birth at six months old, which would be a very rare situation indeed. Arguments using an exception as an example are logically dishonest in and of themselves. Many dogs do not come into the first heat until they are nine or ten months old, then giving birth at eleven or twelve months of age. But, perhaps the person arguing somehow hyperbolized the argument by placing the first heat at the same point in time as a dog giving birth. If a small dog did come into its first heat at six months old, successfully bred and was able to bring puppies to term and birth them, the bitch would be eight months old at the time of birthing, not six months old. The person arguing never outright stated that his/her dog did come into its first heat at four or six months old, so we cannot be sure of what is reality and what is not. Furthermore he/she has presented no proof, whatsoever, that sensitive emotional consequences would likely take place. The argument is based solely on the person's own projected feelings about the situation, whether flawed or not. This example is simply an argument with ammunition run amok.

Relevance Claim #12: Argument for Personal Incredulity

I just don't see how you can have a dog the size of a Dire Wolf, with the heavy bone structure which comes with heavy muscling, and make it essentially a couch potato in any successful way.

The person posing this argument believes that because he/she cannot understand how it can be done that it ultimately cannot be done, or more accurately should not be done. However, it is irrelevant whether the person knows the intricacies of how it happens. The personal knowledge of someone working to disprove the legitimacy of Dire Wolf Project breeding practices is not the issue. The issue is whether it can be done. Just because a person does not understand the intricacies of how a car runs, does not mean that it does not run.

Component Fallacies

Component Claim #1: Begging the Question

People who want a dog that only acts to accessorize their selfish needs without having to do anything or build any kind of relationship would indeed be better off with a stuffed, robotic dog.

How does this person conclude that an American Alsatian dog and a robotic dog are the same thing? This person comes to the conclusion without any evidence that these dogs are no better than a robotic dog bought out of a box and that a person cannot develop any relationship with an American Alsatian dog just the same as one could never do with a mechanical toy. How did they assume that these dogs are lifeless and non-responsive? Without ever experiencing an American Alsatian dog for him/herself, this person has come to a conclusion that is not only illogical, but ignorantly faulty and badly mistaken. Comparing one thing to a completely unrelated and irrelevant other thing is not an argument of meaning or substance. The inherited temperament of the American Alsatian dog is such an important topic that we have devoted Chapter 10 to delving deeply into this new idea of knowing the inherited temperament from newborn to three week old puppies and altering the inherited temperament in our dogs by selectively breeding over time to fit perfectly within our modern societal needs.

Component Claim #2: Circular Reasoning

God did not create a breeding plan. (Why should I believe that?) Because God does not exist. (Why should I believe God does not exist?) God has nothing to do with it.

Circular reasoning starts out with a premise and ends with the same premise without citing any proof. When the beginning idea is also the concluding idea, all that is happening is that the conversation is going around in circles. When a person argues in this manner, he/she likely does not understand how the argument they pose does not have solid evidence to back up the claims. Only through solid evidence as seen through research and/or duplicable experience can an argument be logically sound. The truth is, those breeding under the Dire Wolf Project have solid logical arguments for believing in God's Breeding Plan, which is why we dedicate Chapter 5 to understanding this concept as it applies to strongbred breeding. God's breeding plan does not exist because God does not exist therefore God's breeding plan does not exist because God does not exist...

Component Claim #3: Hasty Generalization

Perhaps if they stop with the Dire Wolf nonsense, lower the prices of puppies to a reasonable figure, and get several more people and dogs involved in their breeding program, they'll end up with a recognizable breed with the attributes they're aiming for, although the King Shepherd people seem to have gotten there already.

There are so many generalizations in this example. Each concept presented can be an entire topic of debate, but this argument suggest that very easy fixes to what is assumed to be fundamental issues with the breed can automatically conform the breed to a more appropriate way of doing things. Unfortunately, many of the fixes are external issues that have nothing whatsoever to do with the actual breeding practices of the Dire Wolf Project and whether they have merit of not. The final statement is meant to be a jab as well; comparing the Dire Wolf Project to the King Shepherd, with which it has nothing at all in common. The Dire Wolf Project cannot simply be waved away as trivial and childish in scope, hence the need for the length of this book. In fact, the research and experience behind this new breeding concept called the strongbred dog is as vast as a human lifetime, which Lois has spent perfecting her message for a dog breeding world. By deviating from the purebred dog scene as well as the designer dog scene, the Dire Wolf Project has redefined the very nature of dog breeding in our modern age. We dare to look toward nature and mimic, as closely as possible, the natural occurrences we see in the wild wolf. Hopefully, this book will help readers to see the vast scope of the Dire Wolf Project's breeding practices and how it cannot just be waved away with a bit of verbal magic. Attaining the perfect dog could never be done within a few generations by combining different components in the way suggested above. Every dog also has many imperfections which need to be bred out and the process is much more in depth than the arguer suggests. That is why it is important to more fully understand the fundamentals of the Dire Wolf Project's breeding practices through an entire book full of references, research and clear examples of breeding experiences.

Too much inbreeding, not enough science.

This little gem of a sentence sums up the hasty generalization perfectly. In a fun soundbite, the entirety of the Dire Wolf Project is dismissed without care. However short and sweet this argument is, it does not come close to understanding the intricate details behind the Dire Wolf Project's breeding practices and certainly does not use evidence or research to explain his/her position. We have devoted a chapter to inbreeding for true clarity of the research and experience to build up the logical thinking behind our inbreeding policies. Furthermore, science and research have been thoroughly cited throughout this book, with extensive citations in the bibliography section for the reader's convenience.

You began with all working dog breeds, which do not possess mellow, companion dog temperaments. There is no way the dogs within the Dire Wolf Project are companion dogs.

This argument jumps to a conclusion and judges the Dire Wolf Project without knowing all the facts. The reality is that we systematically choose puppies based on organized and standardized temperament tests since the beginning of the breed. Through selective breeding we have been able to significantly alter the original working temperament in our dogs. That is why this book outlines the intensive temperament work within the breed in Chapter 10.

Component Claim # 4: False Cause
False Cause A: Not the Cause of the Cause
All of the foundation breeds used within the Dire Wolf Project are known to have high instances of hip dysplasia, so it would be rather foolish to not even hip score. Your breed must be riddled with health issues if you do not even test for them.

False Cause is seen in formal arguments when one asserts incorrectly that one thing causes another thing when in fact they may not be related to one another at all. Not testing for an issue does not cause the issue to arise. Furthermore, this person has come to the erroneous conclusion that the Dire Wolf Project does not test for any health issues within the breed and therefore has no knowledge of what health concerns are present. On the contrary, we do test our dogs as well as eliminate dogs or lines of dogs from the breed which produce a consistent incidence of health issues. The person above who posed this argument assumed that formal standardized health testing can be the only authority to provide any understanding that an entire dog breed has or has not inherited a degree of hip dysplasia. Asserting that the Dire Wolf Project's dogs must be teeming with innumerable incidences of health issues simply because the project does not formally health test using the tests that satisfy their own beliefs does not cause health issues to arise. It could easily be that a breeder tests for all of the formal health tests to which this person subscribes and their dogs are not healthy or long-lived. It can just as easily be true that a breeder who does not use any formal health tests breeds superior health and longevity. The formal testing, itself, does not cause or cease to cause great health and longevity. Breeding healthy dogs and refusing to breed unhealthy dogs is the direct cause of a dog breed being healthy and long-lived. If one claims that our dogs are unhealthy and die young, one must prove that we breed unhealthy specimens. Great health is so important to Dire Wolf Project breeders that Chapter 9 is devoted to understanding just how we accomplish superior health and longevity in our large breed dogs.

False Cause B: After This, Therefore Because of This
Given the breeds involved, it is quite unbelievable that there is no incidence of hip dysplasia.

Traditionally, the German Shepherd Dog has a sullied history of severe hip dysplasia, causing extreme pain when walking and ultimately severe bone fragmenting in the hip joint area. It is devastating to watch the dysplastic dog walk and more heartbreaking when the decision to end the dog's drastic suffering by humanely euthanizing the dog is the final result. To be sure, hip dysplasia can range from mild to severe and there has been a strongly suggested genetic component due to the fact that certain dog breeds are more prone to the disease than others. However, not all dog breeds possess hip dysplasia to any significant degree. Looking to other breeds that have been a part of the American Alsatian dog's foundation does not mean that any dog bred from those foundation breeds had hip dysplasia. Claiming it does solely based on the other breeds that do show a significant rate of hip dysplasia is not proof that we do indeed have the same rate of hip dysplasia.

Component Claim #5: Red Herring

Strongbred breeding is a great catch phrase and the Dire Wolf Project certainly has a good story, but lots of breeders spin good stories about how great their breeding programs are and are later found out to be criminals hiding all sorts of lies.

The Red Herring is a deliberate attempt to change the subject or divert the argument from the discussion at hand. A person with a keen sense of understanding logical fallacies can easily spot this type of false thinking in online public debate because the conversation suddenly takes a sharp turn and those engaging in the discussion are no longer speaking on the same topic, but instead have launched into a whole different discussion that may not even be related to the original post. In the example above, instead of continuing to speak about strongbred breeding and the Dire Wolf Project, it is likely that the conversation will begin to take off in the direction of breeders who have lied and then been convicted of horrible crimes against the animals in their care. The Red Herring not only changes the conversation's focus, but also can suggest without stating it outright that the second topic is somehow related to first, which it most certainly is not. It is absolutely preposterous to assume that other breeders who have established themselves as criminals are in any way related to Dire Wolf Project's breeders or the way in which we have established our breeding practices.

Component Claim #6: Straw Man Argument

It sounds like these irresponsible [Dire Wolf Project] *breeders are not interested in the health of their dogs at all, but only want to play around with different breeds.*

The straw man argument attempts to shut down any opposing views by overstating, exaggerating or over-simplifying the arguments with which the person disagrees. This type of fallacy ignores the real and subtle points offered, diverting the conversation away from the important issues to be debated and discussed. In the example above, the person oversimplifies the Dire Wolf Project's use of a very intricate and detailed idea of regular and systematic crossbreeding by instead describing crossbreeding as "playing around with different breeds." This oversimplification aims to create a mere cartoonish caricature of Dire Wolf Project breeders doing the real work of improving dog breeds. To be sure, the laughing stock of the dog breeding world would be a much easier target to squelch than a viable new dog breeding program that produced superior health and longevity from one's own purebred dog breed. One can dismiss the entire strongbred dog breeding idea with one broad sweeping brush of the hand and upturn of the nose, but, the Dire Wolf Project will not be easily defeated when the health and longevity of the breed tells the tale. If the person is honest, one must confront the pages in this book with equally compelling ideas backed by science in order to bring us down as irresponsible. Substituting an easy target for the actual opponent does not address the real ideas involved.

Component Claim #7: Non Sequitur

The Dire Wolf Project. The name alone makes anything they're offering ridiculous.

A non sequitur is seen when one's mind skips a crucial step in the logical progression of their argument. They may start out with a premise, but then move too quickly to the conclusion of their argument without fully developing the middle terms. In the example above, the person posing this argument has left out an entire train of thought in the middle of their argument. We cannot truly know what the person's middle terms may have been, because it was never stated, but we can reconstruct a possible logical thought process to see if we can find out what might have been missing in this person's mind. Here's one way the person could have taken us through their entire thought process:

"The Dire Wolf Project. This sounds like an archeological study of the wild canid using real DNA, but, that would be impossible, considering there is no live Dire Wolf DNA available to scientists. Because the Dire Wolf Project is not about an archeological study and does not use Dire Wolf DNA, the name does not fit with recreating a Dire Wolf using only domesticated dogs. If the Dire Wolf Project can't even be trusted to be logical about their name, how can anyone trust them on anything else they say? The name alone makes anything they're offering ridiculous."

Now, this expanded argument is also not logical and now fits within the Begging the Question fallacy or possibly even the Complex Question fallacy, but at least it is a well thought out point.

Component Claim #8: Slippery Slope
If you are breeding stock young, with very close generations, you are skewing the "issues and concerns" in the breed you fix to those that are apparent by average breeding age. Depending on the issues and concerns you have, that might be okay, but the younger the average breeding age is, the narrower a lens you've got. It has in the past driven people to focus on cosmetic traits as they are more readily apparent early on.

When using the slippery slope fallacy, a person may begin the makings of a solid argument, but then end with a general statement that many others have gone the wrong way, implying that the Dire Wolf Project will also go the same way. One cannot know the future of the Dire Wolf Project and so to assume that we will fall into the same traps as others because of a practice we are performing is dishonest thinking and has nothing to do with whether what we are doing is right or wrong. In defending a position, it is important to stick to the facts and present those facts clearly and concisely, which we work to do in each chapter and concept developed in this book.

Component Claim #9: Either/Or
Either the Dire Wolf Project performs every formal health test available on every single dog in their program or their project is doomed.

300

When one claims that there are only two choices, completely denying the existence of other, perhaps even more desirable, choices, one uses the component fallacy of either/or. In the above example, it is assumed that formal health testing is the only option to succeed and without it there is no other possibility but to fail. Unfortunately, this line of thinking completely eliminates the ideas of test mating or informal health testing, which actually help to determine the health of dogs used in the program. We will take a very in-depth look at health as it relates to the Dire Wolf Project in this book.

Component Claim #10: Faulty Analogy

I personally admire the Donovan Pinscher program. They have been breeding for about the same amount of time as the Dire Wolf Project. They have really achieved a dog that breeds true, is instantly recognizable, and works like a maniac. They are tightly inbred, but unlike the American Alsatian, they have the appearance and temperament they were looking for.

The author of this example has decided that the Donovan Pinscher program and the American Alsatian dog began with a similar breeding pattern, to create a new breed of dog using a combination of other breeds of dog to form the new one, as well as have been breeding for a similar amount of time and therefore can be compared to one another. The Donovan Pinscher dog began with all bully breeds, very similar in look. Also, all of the breeds with which he began had some working ability which he sought to enhance. It is not the same thing in the least to use several completely different breeds, which look and act very differently from one another, and to breed back to a wild type with the thickness of bone of an extinct animal, all the while moving the temperament from a working type to a completely non-working type. The components of the two programs do not remotely match and so this analogy would be completely faulty in thinking. We go into much more detail regarding the idea of selective breeding for health, temperament and conformation throughout this book.

Component Claim #11: Undistributed Middle Term

German Shepherd Dogs have hip dysplasia. American Alsatians are made up of German Shepherd Dogs. Therefore, American Alsatians have hip dysplasia.

Dire Wolves are extinct prehistoric animals. American Alsatians are not extinct. Therefore, American Alsatians cannot possibly be bred back to resemble Dire Wolves.

The undistributed middle term is like saying "all snails are cold-blooded. All snakes are cold-blooded. Therefore, all snails are snakes." The middle term does not fit with the first term and therefore the last term is untrue. Just because American Alsatian dogs have derived from German Shepherd Dog lines does not mean that any of the German Shepherd Dogs used had hip dysplasia nor does it necessarily follow that American Alsatian dogs have the same degree of hip dysplasia that German Shepherd Dogs within their breed. We review the health of the dogs within the Dire Wolf Project in much more depth in the chapter on health.

Component Claim #12: Contradictory Premises
The Dire Wolf Project regularly mixes dog breeds, but the Dire Wolf Project considers their dogs to be a breed. This is illogical.

If one premise is true yet contradicts the other premise, then one or the other may be true but not both. In other words, both parts of the statement cannot be true. Therefore they are contradictory and there is no logical answer to the question or argument for the thought. In this particular example, the person posing the arguments suggests that the Dire Wolf Project uses the logical fallacy of contradictory premises to describe the dogs within the project as a breed. Since the late 1800s, the definition of a breed has been strictly defined as one having no admixture of any other breed as far back as the pedigree will go. The statement that regular crossbreeding naturally results in a mixed dog or mutt and cannot be said to be a breed is only true if one holds to a narrow view of what a breed is and is not. If one believes that a breed must breed true or it cannot be said to be a breed, then the statement would indeed be something that the Dire Wolf Project could never reconcile.

However, we propose that this narrow definition of a breed needs to be altered to include periodic specifically defined crossbreeding for genetic and overall health improvement. When most of the dogs within the breed produce like progeny, then even with some variation we can still claim them to be within a specific breed. A small example would be the Labrador Retriever. Within this breed we see quite a lot of physical variation in the bone and body structure of the dogs, yet people associate the breed based on color (black, brown, or yellow) and temperament. The same is true for the Chinook dog breed, which also formally presents a crossbreeding program in order to improve the breed and increase genetic diversity. Yet, because those two breeds are "recognized" by AKC, no one has much difficulty speaking of them as a breed. Because it is such a new idea, we will go into a deeper understanding of the Dire Wolf Project's crossbreeding program in chapter 7.

Component Claim #13: Special Pleading
Inbreeding is terrible and should never be practiced, except for the Donovan Pincher program. His dogs are nice.

Special pleading appears in illogical thought when exceptions are granted to special individuals in which the person arguing has an interest. One can make an exception for the inbreeding from the Donovan Pincher program since the person happens to like the dogs within the accepting breeder's program. Lavish praise is then heaped on the exception, despite the fact that the exception also presents a negative that has not been refuted by the person posing the argument. Notice that inbreeding being terrible was never backed up with any evidence. In this book, this author works to present a very detailed view of inbreeding and why it is practiced within the Dire Wolf Project without remorse.

Component Claim #14: Appeal to the Stone
The Dire Wolf Project is a ridiculous idea.

This fallacy occurs every time a person simply denounces an argument as absurd without stating why. It is the most frequently used logical fallacy and basically it uses no logic whatsoever to make a point. There are no facts or examples to back up any of the claims.

Fallacies of Ambiguity

Ambiguity Claim #1: Equivocation
Lois freely admits that she views dog breeding as slavery and yet she continues to bring more and more dogs into the world. Quote from "The Breeds That

Have Gone Into Our Dogs" page at the Schwarz Dogs website, "The pup did not understand this slavery and demand on it and did not like it one bit."

When the logical fallacy of equivocation is used, a dishonest thinker deliberately quotes an ambiguous statement purposefully misinterpreting the statement's original meaning in order to claim that it means something completely different. Sometimes, a particularly vulnerable statement may be true if read one way, but not true if one disregards the original meaning to interpret it a different way. Lois uses ambiguous statements all over her website because she writes using her dyslexic mind. We go into depth on the subject of dyslexia and how it shapes the person Lois is today in the chapter on the Dire Wolf Project founder. It is always wise to work to find out what the original intent was when reading through Lois's website, especially when she is being quoted out of context. However, more generally, it is always wise to go to the source of any quote on any subject to make sure the original intent remains intact.

Ambiguity Claim #2: Amphiboly
Lois believes that Dire wolves may still exist in some other form! Here is a quote from her website. "Dire Wolves are no longer on the face of the Earth as they once were." This lady is crazy!

When someone misinterprets someone's writing because of a misunderstanding that involves grammar, it is considered amphiboly. Lots of official signs have often been mocked because of this. Take for example the "Slow Children at Play" sign. Grammatically speaking, the sign should read, "Slow, children at play." But the punctuation is missing, therefore, many make the joke that "slow children" are at play.

In the example above, the writer has misinterpreted Lois because of a missing comma to separate her two thoughts. The meaning is therefore skewed because of the grammatical error. The sentence should read, "Dire Wolves are no longer on the face of the Earth, as they once were." Lois means that although Dire Wolves once roamed our planet, they are now extinct. If the person would have quoted the entirety of her statement, this would have been clear, but a deliberate attempt was made to mark Lois as a crazy person.

304

Ambiguity Claim #3: Composition

I have heard that one of their dogs is aggressive and a very close friend of mine has two American Alsatians that are seriously shy. It appears that they are not breeding stable temperaments. How sad.

In the above example, three American Alsatian dogs dictate the temperament profile of an entire breed. However, there have been over two thousand dogs bred throughout the thirty years that the Dire Wolf Project has been in existence. Therefore, three dogs can never adequately represent the breed as a whole. It may be that this person happened to hear about the three dogs that do not have secure temperaments. It may also be the case that this person has a biased opinion of the dogs she personally met or that she is outright lying about knowing them. There is no way of determining for certain without checking into which dogs she claims to have been introduced. Furthermore, not all dog behavior is inherited. Training and experience certainly can play a large part in dog behavior. That being said, the person arguing this claim has definitely heard a rumor regarding the first aggressive dog example. She did not see the work and dedication from Dire Wolf Project breeders that went into helping this new dog owner with his American Alsatian dog. The last two examples are unknown to us and so we cannot comment on the validity of the information presented. However, genetic temperament is extremely important to the Dire Wolf Project and through our work, we have been able to establish ten separately inherited temperament traits. Temperament is paramount and so the work that has been accomplished in the breed regarding inherited temperament of the dog is fully addressed and discussed in this book.

Ambiguity Claim #4: Division

The Dire Wolf Project claims to breed Dire Wolf looking dogs, but many of their dogs do not look like wolves at all. They should just stop breeding before they ruin more lives with their nonsense.

In this assertion, the person tries to make the claim that because the whole of the Dire Wolf Project claims to be breeding Dire Wolf looking dogs, but because some of the dogs do not fit with the claim, the entire project must be dismissed as unjustified. First of all, the very reason we call our breeding program a project is because it is an ongoing endeavor that takes time to achieve. We should not be ridiculed and vilified simply because we do not produce wolfie-looking dogs 100% of the time. Also, the outward appearance goal of the project is the last aspect of the entire breed on which we work, so it will take more time to accomplish. But most importantly, "many" of our dogs may not look like wolves, but others do have lots of wolf-like features, all the while persisting on not adding any wolf content.

Ambiguity Claim #5: Misplaced Concreteness

The founder of the Dire Wolf Project allows God to breed her dogs so she does not have any plan for the future of the breed.

People making this error in thinking have not taken the time to understand the idea behind the comment from the founder that she allows God to breed her dogs. They have assumed that she does no planning or thinking about which dogs will breed with others. In fact, some people have gone so far as to claim that the dogs must breed in a free-for-all fashion without regard to health and/or temperament concerns and it is, therefore, obvious that she is a wacko without any understanding of what she's doing, and therefore the entire dog breed must be dismissed. This is far from reality. The founder does indeed believe that God is the ultimate breeder of the Dire Wolf Project; however, she does not allow her dogs to breed any way they choose. We have devoted a chapter to dispelling the myths surrounding the founder of the breed as well as defining "God's Breeding Plan" in depth.

Fallacies of Omission

Omission Claim #1: Stacking the Deck

If the Dire Wolf Project had started with a larger foundational base, maybe a few dozen crosses using the same breeds of dogs, but dogs as distantly related to one another as possible, and then selected from among the offspring of those first crossbreeds, to come forward with their breeding program, outcrossing as necessary to add traits they wanted, then they might have what could be called a recognizable breed by now, one with a reasonable COI [coefficient of inbreeding] and true genetic diversity. But these dogs are all over the place, as well as being inbred.

This is often seen in an argument when someone spends a great deal of time listing out all of the things that are based on their own opinion and completely ignoring the evidence from the other person. One person's opinion of how to change things is not an argument based on any solid evidence.

Omission Claim #2: No True Scotsman
No reputable breeder would ever breed their female on its first heat. OR Reputable breeders always hip and elbow score their stock before breeding, so breeding on the first heat is just wrong.

By whose definition is this the case? Who gets to define what is and is not a reputable breeder? When people claim this, they have a preconceived notion of what someone ought to be like, which may or may not be what is true. Every breeder is different and if a breeder can back up their practices with reasons for breeding a certain way, even though it is different from another's way, then who is to say that that breeder is not also reputable? This type of claim is a way of defining terms in such a narrow and unrealistic manner that it excludes or omits valid alternatives. Defining a reputable breeder in such a narrow way does not allow for anyone with opposing viewpoints to be classified among them. It does not account for different types of breeders and certainly does not contain the breeder who has full knowledge of every dog bred into the breed going all the way back to the beginning of the breed. We have devoted an entire chapter to understanding why the Dire Wolf Project allows females to be bred on their first heat, despite the rhetoric that it is unethical.

Omission Claim #3: Argument from the Negative
Because you do not formally health test your dogs before you breed them, you do not know if they are healthy or not.

Performing formal health tests does not automatically mean a dog is healthy. So called "health" tests, in actuality, only really prove that a particular dog does or does not have a certain disease. There are numerous other diseases that do not have health tests associated with them. A dog can pass all of the formal health tests out there and still be unhealthy. However, as a matter of fact, there are many different ways that a person can know their dog is healthy or not without the use of formal health tests. The reasons behind this are explained in detail in this book. It's kind of like, I'm not a meteorologist so who am I to say it is raining outside.

Omission Claim #4: Appeal to Lack of Evidence
You only have a few dogs tested through the Orthopedic Foundation of Animals (OFA) and the ones listed are only preliminary results with one case being a

fair score, so you have no proof that you are not breeding dogs with hip problems. Therefore, it only stands to reason that you must be hiding something.

When someone claims that there is a lack of evidence it does not automatically stand that one's preferred interpretation must therefore be correct. Lack of evidence, itself, is not automatically evidence of ill-intent or misconduct. However, the person making this claim is actually dismissing the real evidence in existence because this person does not, in fact, believe that the existing evidence has any merit. So, in order to correct this logical thinking error, the person would need to first prove that the existing evidence is incorrect or incomplete and that the lack of OFA evidence is indeed somehow hiding something. Assuming the evidence that does exist is incorrect or incomplete is not enough and simply stating that the lack of evidence is therefore an indication that the Dire Wolf Project is hiding something does not, in fact, prove that breeders are indeed hiding something. However, if we were out to hide something why would we care to write an extensive book on the subject of deeply and openly examining our breeding practices as well as publicly maintaining an extensive health database sharing all reported health issues within the breed?

The American Alsatian health database is complete fantasy because there is no link to public health evaluations.

The American Alsatian health database can absolutely be completely accurate despite the fact that they are not linked to public health evaluations. First of all, not all health can be linked to public health evaluations. Epilepsy, panosteitis, cryptorchidism, and many other health issues that have been seen in the American Alsatian dog have no public health evaluations to which they can be linked. Even so, the accuracy of the health database cannot be assumed solely by linkage to public health evaluations. It may be more appealing for some skeptics to have unrelated authorities prove that what we claim on the health database is accurate, but not having them does not mean they are inaccurate.

Omission Claim #5: Hypothesis Contrary to Fact
Just because a vet says that one's dog doesn't have hip dysplasia then it doesn't? That's a joke. General practicing veterinarians cannot be trusted to know anything about hip dysplasia.

In this example, the opponent completely disregards all general veterinarians. To be sure, veterinarians have a broad overview of many different health issues in dogs and most do not have a deep, narrow focus on specific ones, but that does not mean that all veterinarians possess no authority to be used in argumentation. The years of extensive study in graduate school as well as the multiple years of internship do give many general practicing veterinarians some credibility. Furthermore, a particular veterinarian may have extensive knowledge regarding a certain health issue in dogs, especially if that person not only has a veterinarian medicine degree, but has also performed specific research surrounding the topic being discussed. It would, therefore, be unwise to eliminate all veterinarians regardless of their knowledge. I agree, however, that to stake an entire argument solely on one general practicing veterinarian's word would be a serious lack of evidence. Therefore, health and how we eliminate ill health from the breed is discussed at length in this book.

Calling their program the Dire Wolf Project is either pure hype, or pure fantasy. Based on the going rate for the puppies, I'm guessing the former.

The Dire Wolf "hype" has only been going on since the Game of Thrones series on HBO and recent fantasy video games, but the fact is that the Dire Wolf Project has been in existence since 1988, much earlier than Game of Thrones or World of Warcraft. Also, this person does not consider that the Dire Wolf Project, in its own standards, has a desire to reproduce the exact bone and body structure of the extinct prehistoric Dire Wolf as seen in well researched fossil remains; much different than the fantastically large Dire Wolves recently portrayed in the media. The Dire Wolf Project has never claimed to be creating a six hundred pound beast, such as myths, folklore, and a recent popular TV series suggest. The person arguing this point comes to a conclusion despite that the facts point to a completely different end.

Omission Claim #6: Complex Question
Here's a question for the people who think that creating a wolfish looking dog that is low energy and dumb is a good project if it's done with better practices than in this "Dire Wolf" scheme: How do you want to fixate a unified type without inbreeding?

In this question, there are a lot of assumptions made that are untrue, but the author never suggests proof that the false statements are indeed accurately stated. Instead, the person posing the question assumes they are true, proceeding with a question that could be totally unrelated to the assumptions beforehand. In order to answer this type of question, it is necessary to state what is assumed to be true in the question and discuss how they are untrue and/or misleading. The question posed can actually be ignored until the assumptions are cleared up. But, we do talk extensively on the Dire Wolf Project's temperament ideals and how we get closer to them. Indeed, this entire book is devoted to establishing the very real breeding practices to which the Dire Wolf Project adheres.

How is it possible to have been developing a breed for thirty years and still have almost no consistency in the look of the dog? Not to mention like five or so litters every year and relying on heavy inbreeding to lock down a desired look, yet still you are far from your goal. And because you are inbreeding at such a high degree, you are just like and no better than the purebred dog breeders and their terrible increase in health issues. The Dire Wolf Project should be a breed by now, not just a "breed in development." Your dogs do not even look like wolves after all this time. There are many breeds that started around this same time and are already recognized breeds.

The person using this argument does not understand what the Dire Wolf Project fundamentally is. The person who made the statement above obviously understands only one way of defining a breed and is assuming that a breed only needs to be recognized by a similar look in order to be said to be a breed. The person also assumes that attaining this look should be a quick process and since it has been thirty years and we do not have a uniform look, we must be breeding incorrectly. Again, not fully grasping the goals of the Dire wolf Project or comprehending the nuances of breed development is not relevant to the truth of the matter. This book hopes to address the very deep level of knowledge that has gone into strongbred breeding and why it is that thirty years can go by without achieving a consistent look that defines the breed. The answer lies with the concept of strongbred breeding itself, which is a completely new concept and obviously unknown to the person submitting the false claim.

Appendix B
Definitions of Terms

When speaking in depth on any topic it is essential to first agree upon certain terms. Within each chapter, I have worked to help the reader understand precisely what the most important terms are, however, I thought it might be useful to have them all in one place so that the reader may first look down this list if he/she so desired in order to have a complete understanding of the ideas I convey behind each term.

Backcrossing

Backcrossing is a breeding strategy where one first breeds a cross or hybrid and then breeds back to one of the parents in an effort to minimize the genetics of one parent and increase the genetic material passed to the offspring from the other parent. This strategy was used in 1999 when the breed experienced a bottleneck.

Backyard Breeder

The term backyard breeder generally refers to a relatively inexperienced person who has one or two dogs in their home and choses to occasionally breed them. When the term first appeared, most backyard breeders bred purebred dogs, but now it has become more popular to breed known mixed breed dogs as well, if the owner believes them to have superior temperaments and/or looks. Backyard breeders usually sell their dogs at very inexpensive prices since they only have litters once in a while as a means of enjoying a little extra income. Backyard breeders can have the mentality that because their beloved pet is perfect to them it would be wonderful for others to enjoy such a great dog, too. They generally believe that the puppies will look and act just like their well-loved dog. They do not anticipate any negatives to breeding and generally sell their puppies to other people in the area through advertisements in the local paper. Backyard breeders can have AKC registration papers for their puppies. Backyard breeders were all the rage not long ago and many people were breeding their family pets on occasion. However, with the wide-spread advertising for spay and neuter agendas, most people no longer adhere to this practice or purchase puppies from people who do practice. As a result, the backyard breeder is a rare find. However, the term has remained and many now use it in a derogatory way to describe a person breeding dogs who is not knowledgeable, regardless of how or what they breed.

Character
The configuration of one's habits, disposition

Close Crossbreeding
Close Crossbreeding refers to breeding different breeds of dog that are genetically similar. An example would be the Irish Wolfhound and the Deerhound.

Coefficient of Inbreeding
The probability that two genes at any locus in an individual are identical by descent from the common ancestor(s) of the two parents. The coefficient of inbreeding can either be calculated by pedigree or shown through DNA analysis.

Crossbred Dog
A crossbred dog is a dog that originates from two purebred parents of different breeds. It can result from a first generation mating or any subsequent generations as long as there are only two purebred dogs within its ancestry. It is usual that the crossbred dog has a known pedigree. Another term often used in lieu of crossbred dog is designer dog.

Crossbreeding
Crossbreeding refers to breeding two dissimilar dog breeds that have been separately maintained for extended periods of time. An example would be the English Mastiff and the Fox Terrier.

Cur
A mongrel of unknown mixed descent. The term has a negative connotation based on its origins.

Deleterious Alleles

Deleterious means causing harm or damage, so a deleterious allele, which is usually recessive, is an allele that causes harm to the individual. Recessive genetic diseases are generally described as deleterious.

Designer Dog

A designer dog is another term that is usually used interchangeably with the term crossbred dog. It generally describes a mix between two purebred dog breeds, however, some use the term as a way to describe a dog breed that has been specifically designed for monetary gain. Although inaccurate, the American Alsatian dog is sometimes described as a designer dog.

Extinction

Extinction occurs when there are no more individuals of that species alive anywhere in the world. Extinction is a natural part of evolution. Small, isolated populations tend to plummet toward extinction at a faster rate, but extinction can also occur due to a particularly impactful devastating event that drastically reduces population size.

Extinction Vortex

If populations become small for any reason, they become more inbred and less demographically stable, further reducing population size and increasing inbreeding. When inbreeding rates increase dramatically, but population size remains small, due to increased infant mortality, early deaths due to genetic disease, devastating natural disasters, etc. then a breed cannot sustain an ongoing favorable population size and eventual extinction may be the result.

Feral

A feral animal is one that has escaped domestication and returned to the wild state.

Filial

Filial denotes the generation or generations after the parent or founding generation. In the Dire Wolf Project, we use the filial number to show the number of generations away from a most recent crossbreed. It depicted in short by using the letter "f." The generational number is then placed after the abbreviated filial. Therefore, an f2 would show that a particular dog was two generations away from the most recent crossbreed, regardless of how many other crosses were further into the pedigree.

Genetic Diversity
Genetic diversity refers to the total number of genetic characteristics in the genetic make-up of a species or breed. It serves as a way for populations to adapt to changing environments. It is distinguished from genetic variability, which describes the tendency of a particular genetic characteristic to vary. The Dire Wolf Project works to maintain a high degree of genetic diversity within the breed, while also working to solidify overall breed-wide similarity in appearance and temperament.

Genetic Drift
Variation in the relative frequency of different genotypes in a small population, owing to the chance disappearance of particular genes as individuals die or do not reproduce. Not all individuals within a group will go on to breed. Genes held only within the individuals that do not go on to breed may become lost over the lifetime of the group.

Health Test
On the surface, this term does not appear to have much need for definition and most would understand it to mean any test given or performed that determined an aspect of a dog's health. However, some among the dog breeding community define this term much more narrowly and it is worth mentioning how it can be used and how it is used throughout this book. Certain people believe that formal health testing completed solely by authorized third party organizations are the only "health tests" required to be performed and that any other health testing is illegitimate and irrelevant. Some of the authorities that would be recognized as legitimate third party health testing facilities include: the Orthopedic Foundation for Animals [OFA), Canine Eye Registration Foundation [CERF), genetic testing [EMBARK is one that is generally accepted), Brainstem Auditory Evoked Response test [BAER), DAVCO, and PENNhip. In order to distinguish between them, we will use formal health testing to refer to third-party health testing clinics recognized by the more narrow definition and informal health testing to refer to all other health testing which can be performed to determine an aspect of a dog's health.

Heterosis
The tendency of a first generation crossbreed to show qualities superior to those of both parents. It is often used interchangeably with hybrid vigor.

Homogeneous
Homogeneous refers to having all of the same parts of the same kind and is mostly used with respect to matter, gases, etc., but it can also be use while discussing a population.

Homozygous
This term refers to having to identical alleles of the same gene or genes.

Hybridization
The process of an animal or plant breeding with an individual of another species or variety.

Hybrid Vigor
The improvement or increased function of any biological quality in a hybrid offspring. It is often used interchangeably with heterosis.

Identical by Descent
This term is used in genetic genealogy to describe a matching segment of DNA shared by two or more people that has been inherited from a common ancestor without an intervening recombination.

Inbreeding
Breeding close relatives such as father/daughter, mother/son, or sister/brother.

Inbreeding Depression
Inbreeding depression is by a lack of fitness due directly to inbreeding levels. Inbreeding depression is shown on a continuum and can range from minimal to severe symptoms. Inbreeding depression can cause a higher infant mortality rate, lower birth rates, shorter lifespans, and increased incidence of genetic disease.

Linebreeding
Linebreeding is an inbreeding breeding strategy using loosely related individuals from one line. An example would be to breed a female back to her grandfather or uncle.

Linecrossing
Crossing two inbred lines within a breed that have been separately maintained for a significant period of time.

Mongrel
A mutt of unknown descent, a cur; usually depicted with a negative connotation.

Mutt
A dog of mixed unknown origin.

Outbreeding Depression
Reduced fitness within a population due to significant outbreeding.

Outcrossing
A strategy of breeding those that are unrelated within the same breed or species.

Polyestrous
Having more than one period of estrus within a year. Horses and sheep are polyestrous because they can have other estrus cycles if they do not become pregnant. Wolves are monestrous because they have one estrus cycle per year based on the season regardless if they become pregnant or not.

Polygenic
A trait controlled by two or more genes (usually by many different genes) at different loci on different chromosomes, such as height, weight, erect or floppy ears, etc.

Puppy Mill
The puppy mill used to be called the puppy farm in the late fifties. Snoopy, a popular cartoon drawn by Charles Schultz, was said to be born on a puppy farm. Puppy mills were generally places out in the country where commercial breeders produced several litters of puppies each year as a means of serious income for the family. Puppy mills went out of style when it was revealed that some puppy mills unethically housed their dogs in small cages off of the ground like other farm animals. Many times, horrific conditions applied and breeding dogs could be undernourished and diseased. Now, puppy mill is a very derogatory word to describe anyone who breeds dogs commercially, regardless of the conditions in which their dogs are kept. It is a way to diminish the credibility of a commercial dog breeding facility, especially if the breeder can

be seen to not have the best conditions for their dogs. What those best conditions are, however, is rarely defined and sometimes people can go overboard with the use of this term if they disagree with a breeder's breeding practices. Lois has oftentimes been accused of being a puppy mill despite the fact that her facilities are clean and the dogs are not diseased. Generally when this term is applied to Lois it is because the person disagrees with her way of breeding. A person breeding dogs for profit is now called a commercial breeder.

Purebred Dog
A dog of a modern breed with a documented pedigree in a closed stud book in which no other different breeds are included.

Reproductive Fitness
The number of fertile offspring contributed by an individual that survives to reproductive age.

Selective Pressure
Any phenomena that alters the behavior and fitness of living organisms within a given environment.

Strongbred Dog
A new type of modern dog breed with a documented pedigree held in a permanently open studbook that is regulated by a unified breed club in which all breeders work together toward a common standard.

Specious
A term to describe something that is superficially plausible, but actually wrong.

Temperament
A person or animal's nature or genetic predisposition.

Appendix C
Dire Wolf Project Health Foundation

The Dire Wolf Project's first priority is to the overall health of the dogs within the project. We are committed to doing whatever it takes to solidify the superior health and longevity within our breed. As such, the Dire Wolf Project has established a health foundation within its regulatory breed club in order to make sure that as we grow in breeders and all those that come after will have a solid foundation with which to rest their own work. The following are the most fundamental aspects of the health foundation that helps hold every certified breeder accountable for the health and longevity of the dogs they breed.

Health Database

We have a list of genetic defects that have affected the breed. It is complete to the best of our knowledge going back to the beginning of the breed, open to the public, and houses all known genetic diseases, as well as some diseases that may or may be potentially genetic in nature. This database helps breeders understand the reported incidence of genetic ill health within the breed and determine which defects should be attacked on a breed-wide basis.

Health Committees

Breeders and breed enthusiasts work together to overcome health issues within the breed. Currently, within the breed there are a group of people working together to root out information in the breed regarding hypothyroidism. Testing is being encouraged for all dogs regardless of symptoms in order to have a large collection of data with which to work. DNA testing has also begun throughout the breed.

Open Health Discussions

The DireWolf Dog Health group consists of breeders, owners and others interested in the health of American Alsatian dogs. It is a forum where all can speak openly regarding the health in the breed. Any information shared in this group is collected and placed in the health database.

Restricted Registrations

Lois Schwarz has devised a registration system in which certain dogs, who should not be bred, receive restricted registration paperwork. It is a color-coded system and lists both temperament scores, any known health information as well as the official pedigree.

Strong Support

The National American Alsatian Breeder's Association is a strong supporter of honest breeders. There are rules and regulations that can prevent a breeder from continuing to breed based on if they do not breed for health first, according to our rules. If breeders are found misrepresenting the health or pedigrees of their dogs, they can be stripped of their permission to use the trademarked names strictly held by the National American Alsatian Breeder's Association. This was established by Lois Schwarz before any other breeders were a part of the breed.

Apprentice and Intern Breeders

Each breeder must go through a series of phases to come into full certified status. The apprentice breeder must understand how to breed for health first above all else. They must understand that temperament is second to health and only after those two more important aspects are correct should they breed for the outward appearance aspects of the breed. The NAABA remains in control of breeders, which is one of the reasons why the breed strictly remains free of all-breed registry control, such as the AKC or UKC. We cannot allow another entity to sway us from our goals or allow them to include just anyone to breed the American Alsatian dog without first coming into full knowledge of our strict adherence to our breeding practices. The time has come for breed clubs to take back their breeds and lose the gripping hold that AKC has on its members.

Test Mating

Before the advent of genetic testing, there was no way of knowing which dogs carried genetic disease without mating to find out what genetic diseases a particular dog had lurking underneath its genetic surface. Now, geneticists are able to identify just over 200 genetic diseases in dogs tested. With some degree of certainty (not all tests are 100% accurate yet), breeders can DNA test their dogs to find out which dogs are affected and/or are carriers for these diseases. That being said, (according to George A. Padgett, DVM) there are over 500 diseases that have been identified as genetic in the dog. This being the case, some 300 diseases still have no test associated with them, therefore, test mating is still the most effective means of knowing with certainty if a particular dog is a carrier for a genetic disease or not. American Alsatian dog breeders perform these test matings, in full view of the public and complete disclosure to the buyer surrounding the risks associated with a particular dog acquiring the disease, in order to know what lies dormant in wait of the perfect opportunity to rise to the surface and show its loathsome face.

Appendix D
How to Debate Purists and Activists

I can remember early on in my quest for knowledge regarding the ideas to which my mother clung so passionately that I would spend hours reading books, articles and websites on each subject. My mother rarely gave me any strong arguments for her way of thinking about dog breeding. Instead, the conversation went something like this:

"I heard from someone on a dog chat group that a responsible breeder should never breed a female on her first heat."

"There is no evidence of that," Lois would counter with strong, but quiet, certitude. "There is no problem breeding a female on her first heat. Look it up for yourself."

With a disappointed, but determined attitude, I began my review of the research. Initially, I had to weed through a lot of opinion and group think, but It wasn't long before I found books where veterinarians and scientists who had bred a significant number of dogs on their first heat in order to learn if the rhetoric was true or false pointed out that no significant complications arose, emotionally or physically, when breeding a dog on its first heat. In fact, many found that a female became more mature and had easier future births by employing this practice. I began to realize that the myriad of dissenters were those who had never bred a dog on its first heat, or others who performed it one time with a bad experience. Literally no one had any solid scientific evidence that breeding dogs on their first heat was detrimental to their emotional or physical state.

Controversial topic after controversial topic would arise and I would ask Lois for her thoughts. She inevitably pointed me back to the research and told me to look it up for myself. I suppose she just did not want to spend any necessary time with someone to explain her years of knowledge if that person was not willing to do the work to find out for themselves. So, off I went to read some more. Time after time, I could not find fault in her work after weeding through the diatribe and coming to the research itself from the breeders and scientists themselves. Yet, time and time again, I would encounter people online in chat rooms who confidently argued how ludicrous and wrong Lois was; calling her all kinds of names and such.

At that time, I had no skills of debate and I was greatly conflicted. Should I believe someone who has done the work behind her statements or should I believe someone else who passionately states the opposite and outwardly ridicules those who do not follow the established breeding rules of the sophisticated breeding elite? It wasn't until years later that I finally felt much more confident and had amassed piles of books, scientific articles, and solid references for these ideas. Now, when I do encounter someone shouting how irresponsible it is to breed a certain way that differs from their own conception of responsible breeding practices, I can counter them with confidence. Perhaps after reading this book, you, too, may have more confidence to debate those spewing long, steaming lava flows of nonsensical rhetoric.

How to Debate Dog Breeding Purists and Animal Right's Activists

It must be awfully comfortable to be an outspoken dog breeding purist or animal right's activist. Oh, to have that unearned sense of moral superiority upon which rest self-inflated narcissistic tendencies. I say unearned because those purists and activists who speak out fervently against backyard breeders and puppy mills typically have not actually accomplished anything positive for dog breeding. In fact, they may not even be breeders at all. The majority certainly have minimal experience and many of them have only bred one or two litters from their family dog. Heck, some purists may not have even bred a litter at all and one can be sure that the activist would never do so, but they sure have a lot to say about how it should be done.

Certainly, the majority of them have never bred their own stock for over three generations, let alone more than that. It is super convenient to buy one dog from this kennel and another dog from that kennel and call the match "your" breeding when, in fact, the so-called "breeder" is merely combining the genetics from the kennels where he/she bought the dogs. The dogs do not become "your" masterpiece until one actually does the work involved to weed out health issues, improve temperament and conformation by breeding multiple generations of one's own stock. That is where the rubber meets the road. That is where the reality of true dog breeding occurs.

But, speaking about what should or should not be a dog breeding practice all the while condemning those who breed differently by calling them "backyard breeders" or worse "puppy mills" makes a purist or activist look and feel good. Even if they do not breed dogs themselves, have never dealt with a health issue, or have any evidence to back up their claims, just speaking out about their perceived atrocities of dog breeding and dog breeders is enough to make them become good and, by default, all others, who breed outside their high moral agenda, bad. In other words, in order for them to be morally superior, their target must be morally inferior. Calling a breeder a backyard breeder or a puppy mill gives them a sense of satisfaction with their status in the universe, even if it never helps a single human or dog live a better life.

This is the basic tactic. When someone calls a breeder a puppy mill or a backyard breeder because that person happens to disagree with them about inbreeding or crossbreeding or creating a new breed, they are using tyranny to win their argument. Plain and simple. When someone slanders a particular breeder because that person happens to disagree with them about breeding females on the first heat or not obtaining innumerable formal health tests before breeding, that should be seen as bullying. When someone labels another person as a bad human being because they disagree with that person's viewpoint, they are attacking one's character without justification. That is not okay. In fact, it makes them tyrants and it is okay to call them out on that point.

Dog breeding purists on the one hand and animal right's activists on the other have literally taken over the majority of American belief about dog breeders in the United States. Either one is in the activist camp that hates dog breeders all together because one believes breeders are simply out for profit in order to line their pockets with gold or a person is in the camp that hates crossbreeding and designer breeders because they are destroying dog breeds as we know them. Many times, these two extreme views ban together to call out anyone who claims to be different, especially if that person has solid arguments to back up their claims. Both types of cynics can be incessant bullies and it is easy to become bombarded by them, getting hit from both sides simultaneously because they both have the same agenda; to make sure the targeted breeder stops breeding dogs. And if they can drag that breeder's name through the mud and make others believe he/she is a despicable human being, all the better, because they come out smelling like a rose.

There are times when it is necessary to call out a breeder. When dogs are being abused and/or the breeder commits egregious crimes against animals, then absolutely that person should be held accountable. Each state specifically defines abusive dog breeding practices and those breeding within the state are bound to adhere to them. A breeder who fails to maintain a necessary level of care for their animals should not be allowed to breed. Plain and simple.

But, one's definition of abusive behavior cannot be "any breeding practice that goes against my own superior understanding of dog breeding." That is a recipe for disaster, which indeed is what we have going on right now with dog breeding in our beloved land of the free. True abuse should be clearly defined and mitigated. No question. But, lobbying for stricter breeding regulations because of an irrational bias against dog breeding, breeders, and overall pet ownership will only harm our beloved pets in the end.

If a breeder is no longer allowed to manage their animals appropriately in order to weed out disease and breed for health and longevity because a few activists believe that all inbreeding is abusive, then not only do the dogs suffer because of increased regulation, but people who own the dogs suffer as well. As we saw in the inbreeding chapter, only inbreeding allows one to see the deleterious alleles hiding underneath the surface of a dog's genetics so that it can be bred out. Crossbreeding can only mask it, never eliminate it. Any legislation banning the use of inbreeding is a serious intrusion of one's freedom to breed for superior health. Passing legislation to stop the practice of first heat breeding without any arguments rooted in fact, simply ties a breeder's hands and unnecessarily wastes time for a breeder to make real and lasting change for their dog breed's health.

When a legitimate breeder uses research and science to back up their work for the long-term overall improved health and longevity in his/her dogs, legislation should allow a breeder to proceed unhindered. Abusive practices harm dogs, but vilifying a breeder simply because that person believes differently is tyranny and oppression. Animal activists with their agenda to eventually end all pet ownership should not be allowed to gain the upper hand in our country.

At the same time, dog breeding purists maintain that breeding their way is the only way. Crossbreeding or creating a new breed of dog for a new need should not be assumed to be adding more dogs to shelters and rescues. Certainly, the dogs being bred in these new programs should not automatically be pegged as unhealthy dysplastic monsters simply because the informed breeder understands the limitations of formal health tests and chooses to follow a different path. Increased restrictions and legislation for breeders that force them to conform to standardized health tests tightens the noose around the breeder who cares more for the health of their dogs than for the prestige of false credentials.

Why Should We Debate Dog Breeding Purists or Animal Rights Wackos?

Before we get into exactly how to debate a purist or activist, it is important to ask why debate them in the first place. To be sure, not every fight is worth having. One does not want to end up regretting the interaction as well as the time spent wasting it on trivial people and their trivial ideas when they could care less about you or the conversation you have. No one wants to become frustrated by a debate when it is obvious that the other person merely enjoys causing confusion and are not taking you or your thoughts seriously. When this occurs, no one wins. Therefore, it is necessary to choose your fights carefully.

There are only three situations in which debating a purist or activist is beneficial.

First, it becomes necessary to begin a debate if someone threatens to take away your dogs if you do not properly explain to them why inbreeding, etc. is beneficial to dog breeding.

Second, you miraculously found someone who honestly wants to know your position and seek to understand why crossbreeding can help a purebred dog breed without fundamentally changing it. This person is rational in bringing forth their evidence, just as you are with the evidence you have. Everyone wins with a debate of this sort.

Third, you should debate a purist or activist if there is an audience, not for the sake of the purist or activist, but because the audience members who are listening but not participating may be influenced by your arguments. It is worth getting into a debate because you will give the audience a different perspective that otherwise would have been tossed aside without evidence. You may actually help someone see that the notions they have been following actually aren't the truth of the matter after all.

Nine rules for debating others with an agenda against creating a new breed of dog.

1. *Deliberately head into the firing squad.*

Debates with others who are out to promote an agenda are like a battle. You should be prepared to be hit with mortar fire from all sides. Once you understand that a debate is like a battle and expect the blows to come, you can begin to deflect them. In contrast, you can keep your head in the sand and pretend the shots are not whizzing by all around you, think that the bullies will just see the error of their ways and eventually stop their incessant lies, or believe that others will somehow come to your aid during the debate, but you would be wrong. People with an agenda and a sense of moral superiority do not stop and most sensible people do not know how to help, even if they could discern right from wrong in a debate. So, when engaging in a debate with someone, be brave and expect the big guns to appear.

2. *Strike first.*

When you expect a firing squad, you can be prepared to fire the first shot. Hit them where it counts to throw them back on their heels in order to put them on the defense. When a debate ensues, you have one chance and only one chance to strike first. If you can do it successfully, the debate will be over quickly. This takes research and time spent understanding your opponent. You have to know what he/she will say, how he/she will react to you, what his/her favorite tactics are, and what positions he/she might take. You will need to fully learn the opposition's arguments. There is no substitute for preparation. Know your opponents' tendencies, particularly if he/she has a tendency to lower his/her hands. That's where you punch.

3. *Frame your opponent.*

Some have argued that an activist's entire repertoire consists of only one tactic: to show their opponent as incompetent and unworthy of debate. If someone can successfully label you as immoral, then they win. But, the same is true on your end. When you can shift from a debate where you are rational, kind and collected and they are irrational and emotional to a debate where you, too, also point out their immoral and illogical thinking, you can shift the debate in your favor. People do not think rationally, but instead think emotionally. They will not always remember your arguments, no matter how compelling they were, but they will always remember the emotional tone.

Two examples of framing the opponent and shifting the tone of the debate could go something like this.

Opponent, *"Breeding female dogs on the first heat is disgusting."*

328

Rebuttal, *"Wasting two or more years waiting for a few test results that can easily be faked and may not even be an issue for the breed instead of actually breeding to eliminate the negative health that does plague the breed is absolutely inhuman."*

Opponent, *"The high levels of inbreeding in your breed are appalling."*
Rebuttal, *"Not eliminating serious health issues within a breed because you are scared of inbreeding is an extreme example of cowardice."*

4. *Keep your own emotions out of the exchange*

If you remain calm, all the while throwing verbal daggers at your opponent, it is very likely that their own arguing with you will resort to illogical personal attacks. When this happens, you know you have them on the run.

5. *Discuss, don't attack (no ad hominem - personal attacks)*

Think of it this way; the first one to throw out a personal attack loses. An ad hominem attack only arises when all of the logical arguments fail. So, keep your arguments logical and do not make any personal comments regarding your opponent at all. That includes pointing out any spelling mistakes, stating how ugly their dogs are, falsely labeling them as racist, etc. It is okay, however, to point out that their arguments are tyrannical and oppressive, if they are.

6. *Listen carefully and try to articulate the other position accurately*

The point is to accurately portray their argument in a way that falsifies their claim, but make sure you do not misrepresent what they are saying. That only makes you look shady and out to win at all costs. Give them the floor and allow them enough time to show their weaknesses. Then, you can pounce.

7. *Show respect*

Remember that your opponents are people and should be treated with respect as all people should, no matter what they believe. They may have some very harmful ideas, but they usually hold so strongly to these mistaken ideas because they strongly believe it is best for the animals they love. They usually care passionately for animals and their bias comes from that place of fierce loyalty to what they perceive is beneficial, right and good. So, keep that in mind even if they do not seem to be the most loving or kind-hearted individual at the moment.

8. *Acknowledge that you understand why someone might hold that opinion*

It is okay to admit that on the surface it might seem like these practices are harmful, after all, it is the majority's message and hardly anyone is speaking out against these falsities. But, then, hold them accountable to the truth. Do not allow them to continue to remain in their comfortable complacency. Give them something that pokes them out of that easy-chair and helps them think through their biases to find reality. They, themselves, may never come to see the truth behind your arguments, but someone reading or listening nearby may.

9. *Changing facts does not necessarily mean changing world views*

You are now armed with lots of facts and maybe even some new ideas, but bombarding someone with facts is not the catalyst for changing someone's mind. It is ever so difficult to shift someone who holds to steadfastly to a particular world view. As a renowned rocket scientist turned award-winning law professor and author explains, "As a result of the well-documented confirmation bias, we tend to undervalue evidence that contradicts our beliefs and overvalue evidence that confirms them. We filter out inconvenient truths an arguments on the opposing side. As a result, our opinions solidify, and it becomes increasingly harder to disrupt established patterns of thinking."[1]

If you can frame the idea in such a way that allows the other person to keep their world view, but also accept a new idea, then there is a better chance of shifting someone's mindset to a better way. The thought process goes something like this, "Hey, I know you are passionate about great health for dogs. I am, too. You can still hold to your strong belief that superior health and longevity is the answer to the many health issues plaguing our most-cherished pets. Here is the reason why I believe that this idea means better health and longevity for dogs. Let's work together toward our shared goal of longer and better lives for our beloved animals."

Appendix E

Dire Wolf Project Temperament Tests

Expectations of the American Alsatian Dog Breed

1-2	A puppy who scores here is NOT a purebred American Alsatian dog. We do NOT have puppies who score here. Plain and simple. With the first generations we did, hence the numbers remain in order to compare the outcross and the purebred American Alsatian dog to a base.
3-4	Purebred American Alsatian dog never score this low. Some outcrosses score here. We are not impressed at this score, but will keep notes and see what they do in further testing.
5-6	A score of 5 is the average for puppies of an outcross breeding. If the pup is an F-1 and scores here, ok. F-2's scoring here is ok. F-3's scoring here is not as good. We expect them to rise with the temperament test #3. This is a lower score for a purebred American Alsatian dog.
7-8	This is a pretty good score for first, second, and third generation outcross dogs. This is an ok score for a purebred American Alsatian dog. Some of our purebred American Alsatian puppies may score here. We will note the reasons and socialize and guide the pup accordingly.
9-10	This is an exceptional score for an outcross. We expect our purebred American Alsatian puppies to score here.
10+	This is the ultimate score for the American Alsatian dog breed.

All truebred (F5 - F18) American Alsatian dogs have a consistent temperament and each puppy born above the 5th generation possesses a very similar inherited temperament to the above with a slight range in variation of one point on either side.

However, this breed remains under development and crossbreeding is a regular occurrence within the Dire Wolf Project. Because we believe in crossbreeding to keep our dogs healthy and eliminate inbreeding depression that can occur after years of breeding related dogs, our customers must be aware of how crossbreeding may affect the temperament of puppies in a particular litter. Though many first (f1) through fourth (f4) generation crossbred litters make great companion dogs, they do not necessarily perfectly conform to the standards of the breed in either temperament or conformation until the fifth generation. Therefore, the temperaments in these crossbred litters will fluctuate much more broadly.

Standardized Temperament Testing Procedures

The National American Alsatian Breeder's Association has established its own temperament testing procedure performed on each puppy in each litter since the beginning of the project in 1988 in order to systematically and fundamentally change the inherited temperament of the foundation dog breeds to match the ideals established by Lois to fit with a specifically inherited large breed companion dog. Each breeder temperament tests puppies before they are shaped through their environment by experiences or training as revealed earlier. After solid health, a unique large breed companion dog temperament is the most important feature of this breed and has been the sole focus, apart from health, for the first twenty four years of the project.

Each test is standardized for the specific purpose of assessing the inherited temperament that would be necessary in a large breed companion dog breed so that every puppy has the same opportunity as the other puppies in the exact same environment. In addition, each breeder within the Dire Wolf Project must be trained and certified to give the temperament tests in a standardized manner. The only difference, then, is the puppy's response to the test's stimuli and not a change in the way the test is administered. A copy of the standardized temperament testing procedures and scoring rubrics have been placed in Appendix F. Please note that these tests should not be used without the training that must accompany them in order to make sure test administration has also been standardized. Furthermore, these tests have been specifically designed to assess a companion dog temperament and should not be used to claim a general overall ideal dog temperament.

Temperament Test #1
Birth - 3 Days Old
(ears and eyes are closed, crawling, sense of smell developing, no teeth)

1. How does this pup come into the world?

1-2	3-4	5-6	7-8	9-10	10+
Came out very energetic and crying nonstop.	Extremely energetic. Cries and struggles when mom licks and moves it. This pup is strong and determined. May get upset and bark or growl.	Very energetic, pushed his/her way into the world. Lots of movement such as bobbing head, moving feet back and forth. Some grunting, but not very loud or noisy.	Does not mind mom licking, picking up or holding him. May squirm somewhat and grunt but not much.	May grunt a tad but not much. Is more of a thinker. Some movement, but not much. Lies still when mom licks or moves it.	Does not care about any licking or movement. Breaths, and thinks. This pup is quiet and muscular and goes straight for milk when all of the excitement is over

2. Noises this pup makes during the first 8 hours of life.

1-2	3-4	5-6	7-8	9-10	10+
Cries, whimpers, grunts, and screams nonstop. Has a high-pitched voice.	Whimpers if pushed or prodded. Grunts while eating. May scream at times and/or has a high-pitched voice.	Is only quiet while eating. Otherwise, grunts and whimpers. No high-pitched screaming or crying.	Grunts when picked up or moved. Otherwise, not noisy.	Is quiet when suckling, and moved or touched. Rarely noisy. Very deep throaty growl or bark when heard.	Does not make any noises. This includes when suckling, being picked up or moved, pushed, or prodded.

3. What is the energy level of this pup?

1-2	3-4	5-6	7-8	9-10	10+
Very high energy level at all times. Goes from one place to another and cannot find the milk. This pup may stray away from the litter and not know where he is. Will cry for mom.	When touched this pup goes into action pushing and trying to go forward. Moves head all around looking for milk.	Will not lay still in your hands but otherwise is content when with mom or littermates.	Is always eating. Does not want to be taken from mom. Moves to get back. Otherwise, this pup is content and does not move much.	Pushes everyone out of the way whenever it wants to. Is content when suckling, eats and then sleeps. If there is not any milk he will push others away to find one.	Lays still in your hands and does not care about anything but food and sleep. More laid back and mellow about anything that happens to it.

4. What is the reaction of this pup to the first medical exam?

1-2	3-4	5-6	7-8	9-10	10+
This pup hates the exam and cries, yellow and squirms to get away. Continues to cry for no reason, will not stop crying until placed with mom and finds milk. Is full of energy. This pup may yawn in defiance. But mostly yells or screams.	This pup is noisy and dislikes the examination, but does not scream or yell. Tries to get off the scale. When placed on the floor next to mom this pup is still traumatized by the ordeal until mom nudges the pup who then forgets and finds milk.	This pup is quiet but yawns in defiance. Squirms when on its back and does not like your fingers in its mouth. Otherwise this pup is ok and is not traumatized. It does not have an elevated heart-rate and/or cries or screams.	This pup is quiet and mellow until turned on its back. At this point, the pup tries to turn back over then puts up a fight. Calms back down when put right side up. Lies still on the scale. Is happy to get back with mom and find milk. This pup is not traumatized by the ordeal.	This pup may yawn as instinct permits, but does not make any noises or movements during the exam. May grunt upon turning over, but does not fight or squirm. Is absolutely not traumatized by the ordeal.	This pup is very similar to 9-10 but yawns less or not at all. This pup may fall asleep in the cup of your hand. Is certainly not traumatized by the ordeal.

5. What is the reaction of this pup when turned over on its back?

1-2	3-4	5-6	7-8	9-10	10+
Stiff or will not be turned over. This pup is traumatized! Heartbeat is elevated. May scream in defiance. Very hyper and squirmy.	No struggle heartbeat elevated. Stiff. This pup is traumatized.	Heart beat slightly elevated. May cry out in protest. May try and trick you to get back up right. Gives in and is still. Not traumatized.	This pup struggles and/or whimpers slightly at first but then lays there. Not stiff and does not have feet tucked under. This pup is not traumatized in any way.	No struggle, but may yawn. This pup's body is completely relaxed. This pup is not traumatized in any way.	Lays there relaxed and does not care. Is in no way traumatized. Does not yawn. May fall asleep.

6. What is the reaction of this pup when placed back with its mother?

1-2	3-4	5-6	7-8	9-10	10+
Cries and or howls, moves around in a circle head bobbing every which way. Does not seem to know which way is the right way to go.	Cries and or howls but is not as loud. Finally starts to try and locate his mom and is quiet as he thinks and smells and moves in a circle.	Is strong and moves around in a circle, thinking sniffing, smelling and trying to locate some movement or feel of littermates or mom. May whimper slightly.	Is calm and is a thinker. Moves head back and forth trying to locate mom. Finally starts moving straight in the direction of mom and littermates.	Knows exactly where he is in relationship to mom and littermates, can sense it. Takes his time and is sure of the direction. May go off in wrong direction but fixes it without incident. No noise is made.	Does not really care. Just lays there. Finally feels mom or littermates or senses them. Then moves straight towards them. May wait until mom touches him. He knows his direction then and is sure of himself.

7. What is the reaction of this pup when touched by a human?

1-2	3-4	5-6	7-8	9-10	10+
Freezes and/or screams. Wants to get its head under something.	Startles and cries and tries to get away. Jerks his head or body away from your touch. Not stiff.	Immediately yawns and may take his head back away from human.	Yawns and is alert, but not stiff.	Thinks about it may yawn. Not stiff.	Thinks about it, is alert, but does not really care.

Temperament Test #2
2.5 to 3 Weeks
(Eyes and ears are open. Hearing and sight is weak. Early walking, mobile.)

1. Drop an object into the den away from the pups.

1-2	3-4	5-6	7-8	9-10	10+
Yelps or screams with a high-pitched tone. Draws immediately back away from the noisy object. Continues to cry and scream.	Whimpers or cries, may scream briefly. Draws back away from the noisy object. May continue to softly whimper.	Stiffens then draws back or flinches. Remains quiet. May sniff and move slightly in direction of object, but remains stiff.	Slightly startled at first, but does not draw back. Gets up on all fours or sits intently.	Not startled and does not draw back. Remains quiet and may look towards object.	Does not care. Is not startled and does not draw back. Is not stiff or nervous. May sniff in direction of noisy object, but does not go to investigate. Remains in place. May place head down and close eyes.

2. Using your whole hand, roughly pet the pup from muzzle to tail.

1-2	3-4	5-6	7-8	9-10	10+
Stiffens and complains loudly with a high-pitched yell or scream. Moves briskly to leave. Does not know which way he is moving. Flinches and yawns each time you touch its head	Stiffens slightly and whimpers, but not loudly. Will yawn. Stiff and scared in place.	Remains quiet. Moves head down and stiffens tail, but then moves toward littermates	Remains quiet. May lower head slightly with the touch. Does not move, but is alert and aware of your hand.	Is relaxed and quiet. Is not stiff in any way.	Initially lifts up head to push into the pet. Is very relaxed and quiet. Closes eyes and relaxes into your petting.

3. Pick up the pup from its den using your whole hand to simulate mother dog's mouth.

1-2	3-4	5-6	7-8	9-10	10+
Pup stiffens at first then struggles and cries violently and loudly to get down. Continues to cry throughout the test. Is not aware of surroundings. This pup may flinch with the touch.	Stiffens and cries out. May be some movement at the initial lifting. Draws up legs and tail goes underneath. Crying may stop during the test, but pup remains quite stiff.	Remains quiet, but may be stiff, drawing up legs and tail underneath. Pup does not move in anyway. Very rigid.	Pup may whimper softly or grunt, but is not stiff. Tail is loose and legs hang down freely.	Pup remains quiet throughout. Pup is not stiff and legs and tail hang freely. Pup is alert and confident.	Pup is quiet and relaxed. Pup's legs and tail hang freely. Back is loose. Pup may close eyes and fall asleep.

4. Turn the pup over on its back securely supported.

1-2	3-4	5-6	7-8	9-10	10+
Struggles and fights being turned over. This pup is continually screaming. This pup is VERY traumatized and flinches with any touch.	Whimpers slightly or cries softly. Struggles at first, then remains stiff with legs and tail drawn up. May cease to cry or whimper, but body remains stiff throughout. Might try to right itself.	Remains quiet throughout. Struggles initially, then remains stiff with legs and tail drawn up.	Remains quiet. Stiffens at first with legs draw up and tail turned in, but then relaxes. Does not struggle.	Remains quiet. Does not stiffen. Legs and tail are loose. Alert and confident.	Remains quiet. Does not seem to care. Rolls with hand and every muscle is loose. May close eyes and fall asleep in your hands

5. Place the pup in a high-sided wicker basket by itself. How does this pup act when separated from litter mates?

1-2	3-4	5-6	7-8	9-10	10+
This pup immediately moves for the side of the basket. Pup cries and screams in a high-pitched tone. This pup struggles and tries to hide in the corner. Continually screams throughout the test. Elevated heart rate, traumatized and distressed. If you touch this pup he will flinch.	Pup whimpers and cries and may howl because he's alone. This pup moves around looking for others. Uncomfortable. Wants his mom. May howl and whimper and whine. If you pick him up he will stop crying.	Whimpers for litter mates. Looks around, gets up smelling and sniffing and wants to find somebody to be with. Misses everyone and wants to be warm. Does not lie down or sit, but continues to move around the basket. May whimper, but not as much as 3-4.	Whimpers a little, then grows quiet and sits. Moves and searches around the bottom of the basket, but eventually lies down. Remains alert and might move again or follow the corner of the basket.	Remains quiet. Sits at first and looks around. You can see the dog thinking about its situation. May move around a tad, but not as much as 7-8. Then lays down in the crook of the basket. Looks around and watches. Alert and aware of surroundings.	Remains quiet. May look around slightly, move to the crook of the basket then lie head down and close eyes. This pup is confident and alert. It seemingly knows that there is no harm.

6. Replace the pup back near its siblings, but not with them. How does the pup react?

1-2	3-4	5-6	7-8	9-10	10+
Immediately scoots underneath the puppy pile. As long as his head is covered this pup is not yelling.	Might whimper a tad before moving to the pack. Has a tendency to go under pile.	May whimper, look around, smell your hand and go over to the pile.	Wants to stay with you and play. Biting at your feet. Is awake, alert, and energetic. May return to the pack and bite other pups or chew on them to play.	May meander back to the pack and may entice other pups to play, but softly. Not with energy. May stay with you and play with your toes or shoestrings. Will tire quickly and return to the pack.	Remains quiet and meanders over to the pile of pups and lays down at the edge of pups. May also stay close to you and sniff your foot. May curl up next to your foot or body.

338

Temperament Test #3
6 Weeks to 6.5 Weeks Old
(Baby teeth have come in. Hearing, sight, and smell are developed. Highly mobile. Wagging tail and vocal.)

1. Drop an object into the den away from the pups.

1-2	3-4	5-6	7-8	9-10	10+
Screams and runs to hide under his litter mates.	Whimpers or cries, may scream briefly. Draws back away from the noisy object. May continue to softly whimper.	Stiffens then draws back or flinches. Remains quiet. May sniff and move slightly in direction of object, but remains stiff.	Slightly startled at first, then looks at the object and stands up to investigate	Sits up to look at the object. May stand to investigate or sniff in the direction of the object.	Slowly looks up at the object then lays head back down and falls back asleep.

2. Using your whole hand, roughly pet the pup from muzzle to tail.

1-2	3-4	5-6	7-8	9-10	10+
This pup is stiff as a board and will scream and cry with a high-pitched yell.	Stiffens and whimpers, but not loudly. Stiff and scared in place.	Remains quiet. Moves head down and stiffens tail, but then moves toward litter mates.	Remains quiet, but may lower head slightly at first with the unexpected touch. Wags tail.	Moves with your hand. May look up at your when your hand starts down his back. May wag tail gently.	Moves head in the direction of the pet. May close its eyes in content. Does not move from is position. Looks up at hand when it moves away.

3. Pick up the pup from its den using your whole hand to simulate mother dog's mouth.

1-2	3-4	5-6	7-8	9-10	10+
This puppy is very stiff. Traumatized. Continues to yell and whine as if in pain.	Stiffens and cries out. May be some movement at the initial lifting. Draws up legs and tail goes underneath. Crying may stop during the test, but pup remains quite stiff.	Remains quiet, but may be stiff, drawing up legs and tail underneath. May wag tail stiffly and vigorously. Very rigid movements.	This puppy may grunt at first, but remains loose.	This puppy is quite loose and calm. It may wag his tail gently.	This puppy is very loose and calm. It makes no sound.

4. Turn the pup over on its back securely supported

1-2	3-4	5-6	7-8	9-10	10+
This puppy is very stiff. Extremely traumatized. Continues to yell and whine as if in pain.	Whimpers slightly or cries softly. Struggles at first, then remains stiff with legs and tail drawn up. May cease to cry or whimper, but body remains stiff throughout. Might try to right itself.	May wag tail vigorously in a stiff motion. Body is somewhat stiff, but not as much as 3-4.	Remains quiet. Stiffens at first with legs draw up and tail turned in, but then relaxes. Does not struggle.	Remains extremely quiet and loose. May lick or wag his tail gently, not fast.	Continues to remain loose and very calm. May close eyes and fall asleep.

5. Place the pup in a high-sided wicker basket by itself. How does this pup act when separated from litter mates?

1-2	3-4	5-6	7-8	9-10	10+
Whines and whimpers and goes to hide in the corner of the basket. May try to jump out, barks and whines at the fact that he cannot.	Pup whimpers and cries and may howl because he's alone. This pup moves around looking for others. Uncomfortable. Wants his mom. May howl and whimper and whine. If you pick him up he will stop crying.	Looks around, gets up smelling and sniffing and wants to find somebody to be with. Does not lie down or sit, but continues to move around the basket.	This pup will wag his tail with intensity and go toward you. May jump up on edge of basket wagging tail vigorously.	Looks up at you and gently wags his tail. May sit or go to the edge of the basket to be closer to you. Leans on the edge of the basket in hopes of getting a pet.	May look up at you and gently wag his tail. May sit or lie down and continue to look at you. When you do not return your hand, if he's not tired, he may either continue to gaze at you or if he is tired, he may close eyes and fall asleep.

340

6. Replace the pup back near its siblings, but not with them. How does the pup react?

1-2	3-4	5-6	7-8	9-10	10+
Goes immediately underneath the pack, whining the whole time.	Might whimper a tad before moving to the pack. Has a tendency to go under pile or bury his head.	May drop its head in stiffness initially. Then goes immediately over to the pack and may bark and wag tail strongly enticing the other pups to play with him. Is no longer interested in you.	Wants to stay with you and play. Biting at your feet. Is awake, alert, and energetic. May return to the pack and bite other pups or chew on them to play. Tail wags vigorously.	This puppy will remain with you and gently play with your shoes or hands. He may continue to wag his tail gently. He may also entice other puppies to come over to you and play	He may gently wag his tail and lean next to you. He may play with your shoes or hand if you remain. No noise or sound from the puppy.

References

Chapter 1

[1] *Rubin, Dave. So, You Think You're Tolerant? Prager University. July 9, 2018. Retrieved July thirteen, 2018. https://www.prageru.com/videos/so-you-think-youre-tolerant*

[2] *Gould, Stephen J. (1997), "The late birth of a flat earth", Dinosaur in a Haystack: Reflections in Natural History (PDF) (1st pbk. ed.), New York: Three Rivers Press, pp. 38–50, ISBN 0-517-88824-6*

Chapter 2

[1] *Whitney, Leon F. How to Breed Dogs. Howell Book House. 1971. Revised Edition. Page 53. Originally printed in 1937.*

[1a] *Wheeler, Kip. Logical Fallacies Handlist. Carson-Newman University. August 2002. Retrieved: January 5, 2018. https://web.cn.edu/kwheeler/fallacies_list.html*

[2] *Lord, Charles G; Lee Ross; & Mark Lepper. Biased Assimilation and Attitude Polarization: The Effects of Prior Theories on Subsequently Considered Evidence. Journal of Personality and Social Psychology 1979, Vol. 37, No. 11, 2098-2109. http://citeseerx.ist.psu.edu/viewdoc/download?doi=10.1.1.372.1743&rep=rep1&type=pdf*

[3] *Bacon, F. Novum organum. (original 1621). Oxford: Oxford University Press, 1889. pg. 46 Taken from: Mahoney, M.J. & DeMonbreun, B.G. Cogn Ther Res (1977) 1: 229. https://doi.org/10.1007/BF01186796*

[4] *Bellumori TP, TR Famula, DL Bannasch, JM Belanger, & AM Oberbauer. Prevalence of inherited disorders among mixed-breed and purebred dogs: 27,254 cases (1995-2010). J Am Vet Med Assoc. 2013 Jun 1;242(11):1549-55. doi: 10.2460/javma.242.11.1549. https://www.ncbi.nlm.nih.gov/pubmed/23683021*

[5] *Szeremy, Susi. Should You Choose a Purebred or a Mixed-Breed? American Kennel Club. January 5, 2016. https://www.akc.org/expert-advice/lifestyle/why-you-should-choose-a-purebred-instead-of-a-mix-breed-dog/*

[6] *Beuchat, Carol. Health of purebred vs mixed breed dogs: the actual data. Institute of Canine Biology. March 29, 2015. Retrieved: January 31, 2019.*

https://www.instituteofcaninebiology.org/blog/health-of-purebred-vs-mixed-breed-dogs-the-data

6a *http://wiki.c2.com/?IntellectualDishonesty Retrieved: June 15, 2018.*

7 *Szeremy, Susi. Should You Choose a Purebred or a Mixed-Breed? American Kennel Club. January 5, 2016. https://www.akc.org/expert-advice/lifestyle/why-you-should-choose-a-purebred-instead-of-a-mix-breed-dog/*

8 *Khuly, Patty. The Great Debate: Are Mutts Healthier Than Purebreds? January 6, 2012. VetStreet. Retrieved: January 31, 2019. http://www.vetstreet.com/our-pet-experts/the-great-debate-are-mutts-healthier-than-purebreds*

Chapter 3

1 *ASPCA. Position Statement on Criteria for Responsible Breeding. https://www.aspca.org/about-us/aspca-policy-and-position-statements/position-statement-criteria-responsible-breeding Retrieved: November 20, 2018*

2 *AKC. AKC's Guide to Responsible Breeding. https://www.akc.org/breeder-programs/breeder-education/akcs-guide-responsible-dog-breeding/ Retrieved: November 20, 2018.*

3 *The Kennel Club. The Kennel Club Assured Breeder Scheme Standard. March 2018. https://www.thekennelclub.org.uk/media/726864/abs_standard.pdf Retrieved: November 20, 2018.*

4 *WikiHow. https://www.wikihow.com/Create-a-Responsible-Dog-Breeding-Program Retrieved: November 20, 2018.*

5 *Ellis, Shaun. The Man Who Lives with Wolves. Harmony Books. 2009. pg. 226. Retrieved on August 15, 2017.*

Chapter 4

1 *AKC. Mission Statement. Retrieved: January 4, 2019 https://www.akc.org/about/mission/*

2 *Lois Schwarz. The American Alsatian. L.E. Schwarz. 2011. Page 9*

3 *Shaun Ellis. The Man Who Lives With Wolves. Harmony Books. New York. 2009. Author's Note.*

4 *International Dyslexia Association. Dyslexia Definition. https://dyslexiaida.org/definition-of-dyslexia/ retrieved: June 8, 2017 Adopted by the IDA Board of Directors, Nov. 12, 2002.*

5 *International Dyslexia Association. Dyslexia at a Glance. https://dyslexiaida.org/dyslexia-at-a-glance/ retrieved: June 8, 2017*

[6] *Rokos, Jim. Dyslexics Think Differently. Dyslexic Design. September 9, 2016. Retrieved: June 8, 2017. https://www.thersa.org/discover/publications-and-articles/rsa-blogs/2016/09/dyslexics-think-differently*

[7] *Davis, Ray; Suzanne Hailey. Davis Dyslexia Correction Center. 2001. Retrieved: June 8, 2017. https://www.davisdyslexia.com/big_picture.html*

[8] *Eide, Fernette. Q&A: The Unappreciated Benefits of Dyslexia. Wired. September 20, 2011. Retrieved: June 8, 2017. https://www.wired.com/2011/09/dyslexic-advantage/ Interview with Danielle Venton*

[9] *National Association for Gifted Children. Twice-Exceptional Students. Retrieved: March1, 201 https://www.nagc.org/resources-parents/twice-exceptional-students*

[10] *International Dyslexia Association. Gifted and Dyslexic: Identifying and Instructing the Twice Exceptional Student Face Sheet. 2017. Retrieved June 8, 2017. https://dyslexiaida.org/gifted-and-dyslexic-identifying-and-instructing-the-twice-exceptional-student-fact-sheet/*

Chapter 5

[1] *https://www.kul.pl/files/57/nauka/Rowe_The_Problem_of_Evil.pdf*

[2] *Royal, Barbara E. DVM. A Wild Approach to Your Pet's Health. Huffpost. July 29, 2011. https://www.huffingtonpost.com/barbara-e-royal-dvm/integrative-pet-health_b_845538.html*

[4] *PBS. Gray Wolf Fact Sheet. April 13, 2012. http://www.pbs.org/wnet/nature/river-of-no-return-gray-wolf-fact-sheet/7659/ retrieved on: 09-11-2017.*

[5] *Bellumori TP, TR Famula, DL Bannasch, JM Belanger, & AM Oberbauer 2013 Prevalence of inherited disorders among mixed-breed and purebred dogs: 27,254 cases (1995-2010). J Am Vet Med Assoc 242: 1549-1555.*

[6] *https://www.ncbi.nlm.nih.gov/pubmed/23683021, https://www.instituteofcaninebiology.org/blog/health-of-purebred-vs-mixed-breed-dogs-the-data*

[7] *Maldarelli, Claire. "Although purebred dogs can be best in show, are they worst in health?" Scientific American. ScienceLine. 02/21/2014. Retrieved: 9/23/2018. https://www.scientificamerican.com/article/although-purebred-dogs-can-be-best-in-show-are-they-worst-in-health/*

[8] *Urfer SR, Gaillard C, Steiger, A (2007). "Lifespan and disease predispositions in the Irish wolfhound: a review" http://www.tierschutz.vetsuisse.unibe.ch/unibe/portal/fak_vetmedizin/c_dept_dcr-vph/e_inst_tierschutz/content/e191756/e224004/e224515/e239759/ Diss_Urfer_2007_ger_eng.pdf (PDF). Vet Q. 29 (3): 102–111.*

[8a] *Bernardi, Gretchen. Longevity and morbidity in the Irish Wolfhound in the United States 1966–1986. Irish Wolfhound Club of America. 2004. Retrieved: January 15, 2019. http://www.iwclubofamerica.org/longevityBernardi*

9 *Parker et al, 2011 https://www.ufaw.org.uk/dogs/cavalier-king-charles-spaniel-syringomyelia https://cgejournal.biomedcentral.com/articles/10.1186/s40575-015-0016-7*

10 *Ellis, Shaun. The Man Who Lives with Wolves. Harmony Books. New York. 2009 pg 184.*

11 *Guinness Book of World Records. 2018. http://www.guinnessworldrecords.com/world-records/oldest-dog.*

12 *Cassidy, Kelly M. "Breed Longevity Data." February 01, 2008. http://users.pullman.com/lostriver/breeddata.htm*

13 *Adams, V.J., et al., Methods and mortality results of a health survey of purebred dogs in the UK. Journal of Small Animal Practice, 2010. 51(10): p. 512-524.*

14 *VetCompass. VetCompass: Health surveillance for UK companion animals. 2011 [cited 2011 November 29]; Available from: http://www.rvc.ac.uk/Vetcompass/. http://www.venomcoding.org/venom/Research_files/Longevity%20of%20UK%20Dog%20Breeds.pdf*

15 *INDog. The Indian Pariah Dog: pure, ancient, indigenous. Retrieved: Jan 17, 2017. http://www.indog.co.in/.*

16 *Behrendorff, Linda and Benjamin L. Allen. From den to dust: longevity of three dingoes (Canis lupus dingo) on Fraser Island (K'gari). Australian Mammalogy. Vol 38(2). pgs. 256-260. https://doi.org/10.1071/AM16005. May 9, 2016. http://www.publish.csiro.au/am/am16005*

17 *https://www.marxists.org/reference/archive/spirkin/works/dialectical-materialism/ch02-s06.html*

18 *Rettner, Rachael. What Exactly Does It Mean to Die of 'Natural Causes'? LiveScience. October 27, 2017. Retrieved: February 28, 2019. https://www.livescience.com/60787-what-is-death-by-natural-causes.html*

Chapter 6

1 *https://isogg.org/wiki/Identical_by_descent*

2 *Robinson, Kate. EmbarkVet. Email Correspondence. Retrieved: July 17, 2018.*

3 *Dog Breed Health. A Beginner's Guide to COI. 2018. Retrieved: July 17, 2018. http://www.dogbreedhealth.com/a-beginners-guide-to-coi/*

4 *quoted from 1963 by W.V. Soman in his book "The Indian Dog" page 34 http://indog.co.in/the-indian-dog-by-w-v-soman/ retrieved July 17, 2018.*

5 *National Institutes of Health. Dog Genome Assembled. July 14, 2004. Retrieved: January 31, 2019. https://www.genome.gov/12511476/2004-advisory-dog-genome-assembled/*

[6] *Food and Agriculture Organization of the United Nations. Annex 2. Working Definitions for Use in Developing Country Reports and Providing Supporting Data. Retrieved: February 18, 2019. www.fao.org/3/y1100m/y1100m03.htm*

[7] *Budiansky, Stephen. The Truth About Dogs; an Inquiry into the Ancestry, Social Conventions, Mental Habits, and Moral Fiber of Canis familiaris. Viking Penguin. New York. 2000. p. 33-35.*

[8] *Dreger DL, et. al. Whole genome sequence, SNP chips and pedigree structure: building demographic profiles in domestic dog breeds to optimize genetic trait mapping. Disease Models and Mechanisms. 2016 Dec 1; 9(12): 1445–1460. http//dmm.biologists.org/lookup/doi/10.1242/dmm.02737 Retrieved: 01/15/2019.*

[9] *Wright, Sewall. Coefficients of Inbreeding and Relationship. The American Naturalist. Vol. 56, No. 645 (Jul. – Aug., 1922), pp. 330-338. http:www.jstor.org/stable/2456273*

[10] *Beuchat, Carol. How many generations of pedigree data should you use to estimate inbreeding? Institute of Canine Biology. 08-20-2014. Retrieved: 02/20/2019. https://www.instituteofcaninebiology.org/blog/how-many-generations-of-pedigree-data-should-you-use-to-estimate-inbreeding*

[11] *Melina, Remy. The Incredible Explosion of Dog Breeds. Live Science. August 5, 2010. Retrieved: January 24, 2019. https://www.livescience.com/8420-incredible-explosion-dog-breeds.html*

[12] *Sponenberg, D. Phillip; Beranger, Jeannette; Martin, Alison. Managing Breeds for a Secure Future: Strategies for Breeders and Breed Associations (Second Edition) (p. 98). 5m Publishing. Kindle Edition.*

[13] *https://www.instituteofcaninebiology.org/blog/comparing-inbreeding-of-dogs-and-horses*

[14] *The Kennel Club. Inbreeding - Using COIs. 2019. Retrieved: January 22, 2019. https://www.thekennelclub.org.uk/health/for-breeders/inbreeding/*

[15] *Darwin, Charles. The Effects of Cross and Self Fertilization in the Vegetable Kingdom. 1876. page 438.*

[16] *Dog Breed Health. A Beginner's Guide to COI. 2018. Retrieved: July 17, 2018. http://www.dogbreedhealth.com/a-beginners-guide-to-coi/*

[17] *Frankham, Richard; Ballou, Jonathan D. Introduction to Conservation Genetics. Second Edition. Page*

[18] *Frankham, Richard; Ballou, Jonathan D. Introduction to Conservation Genetics. Second Edition. Cambridge University Press. Page 293.*

[19] *Frankham, Richard; Ballou, Jonathan D. Introduction to Conservation Genetics. Second Edition. Cambridge University Press. Page 290.*

[20] *Charles Scribner's Sons. King, Helen Dean. Encyclopedia.com https://www.encyclopedia.com/science/dictionaries-thesauruses-pictures-and-press-releases/king-helen-dean*

21 *Nakanishi, Satoshi; Tadao Serikawa; Takashi Kuramoto. Slc:Wistar outbred rats show close genetic similarity with F344 inbred rats.Exp Anim. 2015; 64(1): 25–29. Published online 2014 Sep 8. doi: 10.1538/expanim.14-0051 https://www.ncbi.nlm.nih.gov/pmc/articles/PMC4329512/*

22 *Whitney, Leon F. How to Breed Dogs. Howell Book House. 1971. page 160.*

23 *Frankham, Richard. Inbreeding and Extinction: a Threshold Effect. Conservation Biology. August 1995. https://doi.org/10.1046/j.1523-1739.1995.09040792.x Frankham, Richard; Ballou, Jonathan D. Introduction to Conservation Genetics. Second Edition. Cambridge University Press. Page 341.*

24 *G. J. Ubbink, B. W. Knol & J. Bouw (1992) The relationship between homozygosity and the occurrence of specific diseases in Bouvier Belge des Flandres dogs in the Netherlands, Veterinary Quarterly, 14:4, 137-140, DOI: 10.1080/01652176.1992.9694350, https://www.tandfonline.com/doi/abs/10.1080/01652176.1992.9694350*

25 *Kettunen, Anne et. al. Cross-Breeding Is Inevitable to Conserve the Highly Inbred Population of Puffin Hunter: The Norwegian Lundehund. PLOS One. Published: January 20, 2017 https://doi.org/10.1371/journal.pone.0170039*

26 *Gr´egoire Leroy, Florence Phocas, Benoit Hedan, Etienne Verrier, Xavier Rognon. Inbreeding impact on litter size and survival in selected canine breeds. The Internet Journal of Veterinary Medicine, Internet Scientific Publications, LLC, 2015, 203 (1), pp.74-78. <10.1016/j.tvjl.2014.11.008>. file:///Users/admin/ Downloads/Inbreeding%20impact%20on%20litter%20size_accepted.pdf*

27 *Armstrong, John B. Longevity in Standard Poodles. University of Ottawa. 1999. https://www.dogenes.com/poodle/lifespan.html*

28 *Crnokrak P, Roff DA. Inbreeding Depression in the Wild. Heredity Edinb. 1999 Sept; 83 pgs 260-70. https://www.ncbi.nlm.nih.gov/pubmed/10504423*

29 *Frankham, Richard; Ballou, Jonathan D. Introduction to Conservation Genetics. Page*

30 *Spiering, Penny A; et al. Inbreeding, heterozygosity and fitness in a reintroduced population of endangered African wild dogs (Lycaon pictus). Conservation Genetics. (2010) 12:401–412 DOI 10.1007/s10592-010-0147-z https://repository.si.edu/bitstream/handle/10088/13790/Spiering%20et%20al%2020 11.pdf?sequence=1&isAllowed=y*

31 *Becker, Penny A et. al. Inbreeding Avoidance Influences the Viability of Reintroduced Populations of African Wild Dogs (Lycaon pictus). PLoS One. 7(5):e37181 May 2012. https://www.researchgate.net/publication/225030176_Inbreeding_Avoidance_Influe nces_the_Viability_of_Reintroduced_Populations_of_African_Wild_Dogs_Lycaon_p ictus*

32 *Mech, David L; Luigi Boitani. Wolves: Behavior, Ecology, and Conservation University of Chicago Press. 2003. (Kindle Locations 1176-1178). Kindle Edition.*

[33] Mech, David L; Luigi Boitani. *Wolves: Behavior, Ecology, and Conservation* University of Chicago Press. 2003. (Kindle Locations 1183-1185). Kindle Edition.

[34] Geffen, Eli, et. al. *Kin encounter rate and inbreeding avoidance in canids.* Blackwell Publishing. 2011. https://www.wolf.org/wp-content/uploads/2013/08/328kinencounter-rate.pdf

[35] Bensch, Staffan; et. al. *Selection for Heterozygosity Gives Hope to a Wild Population of Inbred Wolves.* PLoS One. December 2006. https://journals.plos.org/plosone/article?id=10.1371/journal.pone.0000072

[36] Crnokrak, Peter. and DA Roff. *Inbreeding depression in the wild.* Heredity (Edinb). 1999 Sep;83 (Pt 3):260-70. Retrieved: November 15, 2018. https://www.ncbi.nlm.nih.gov/pubmed/10504423

[37] Joly, Etienne. *The existence of species rests on a metastable equilibrium between inbreeding and outbreeding. An essay on the close relationship between speciation, inbreeding and recessive mutations.* Biology Direct. 2011 Dec 9. Retrieved: July 17, 2018. https://www.ncbi.nlm.nih.gov/pmc/articles/PMC3275546/

[38] Frankham, Richard et al. *Introduction to Conservation Genetics.* Cambridge University Press. 2014. pg. 331.

[39] Sponenberg, D. Phillip; Beranger, Jeannette; Martin, Alison. *Managing Breeds for a Secure Future: Strategies for Breeders and Breed Associations (Second Edition)* (p. 92). 5m Publishing. Kindle Edition.

[39a] Seath, Ian J. *Nearly 20 Years of DNA Testing – What Can We Learn?* Dog-Ed: Social Enterprise. February 17, 2019. Retrieved: March 6, 2019. https://dogeduk.wordpress.com/2019/02/17/nearly-20-years-of-dna-testing-what-can-we-learn

[40] Moses, Lisa; Steve Niemi; and Elinor Karlsson. *Pet genomics medicine runs wild.* Nature. July, 25, 2018. Retrieved: February 18, 2019. https://www.nature.com/articles/d41586-018-05771-0

[41] Kavin, Kim. *Don't use dog DNA tests to make life-or-death decisions for your pet, experts warm.* Washington Post. July 30, 2018. Retrieved: February 18, 2019. https://wwwwashingtonpost.com/news/animalia/wp/2018/07/30/dont-use-dog0dna-tests-to-make-life-or-death-decisions-for-your-pet-experts-warn/?noredirect=on&utm_term=.1cdd5954db79

[42] Moses, Lisa; Steve Niemi; and Elinor Karlsson. *Pet genomics medicine runs wild.* Nature. July, 25, 2018. Retrieved: February 18, 2019. https://www.nature.com/articles/d41586-018-05771-0

[43] Kavin, Kim. *Don't use dog DNA tests to make life-or-death decisions for your pet, experts warm.* Washington Post. July 30, 2018. Retrieved: February 18, 2019. https://wwwwashingtonpost.com/news/animalia/wp/2018/07/30/dont-use-dog0dna-tests-to-make-life-or-death-decisions-for-your-pet-experts-warn/?noredirect=on&utm_term=.1cdd5954db79

[44] *Padgett, George. Control of Canine Genetic Diseases. Howell Books. 1998. Page 141.*

[45] *Sponenberg, D. Phillip; Beranger, Jeannette; Martin, Alison. Managing Breeds for a Secure Future: Strategies for Breeders and Breed Associations (Second Edition) (p. 99). Kindle Edition.*

Chapter 7

[1] *Ross, Marlene. Wakon Giant Alaskan Malamutes. http://www.wakongiantalaskanmalamutes.com/.*

[2] *Pennisi, Elizabeth. Where did your dog come from? New tree of breeds may hold the answer. Science. Apr. 25, 2017. https://www.sciencemag.org/news/2017/04/where-did-your-dog-come-new-tree-breeds-may-hold-answer*

[2a] *Pennisi, Elizabeth. Where did your dog come from? New tree of breeds may hold the answer. Science. Apr. 25, 2017. https://www.sciencemag.org/news/2017/04/where-did-your-dog-come-new-tree-breeds-may-hold-answer?r3f_986=https://www.google.com/*

[3] *Melina, Remy. The Incredible Explosion of Dog Breeds. Live Science. August 5, 2010. https://www.livescience.com/8420-incredible-explosion-dog-breeds.html Retrieved: February 5, 2019.*

[4] *Caius, Johannes. Of English Dogges, the diversities, the names, the natures, and the properties. Abraham Fleming, trans. (1576; rat. ed. London: A. Bradley, 1880) quoted from: Ritvo, Harriet. Pride and Pedigree: The Evolution of the Victorian Dog Fancy. Victorian Studies. Indiana University Press. Vol. 29, No. 2 (Winter, 1986), pp. 227-253.*

[5] *A.S., The Husbandman, Farmer and Grasier's Compleat Instructor (London: Henry Nelme 1697), pp. 129-133. quoted from: Ritvo, Harriet. Pride and Pedigree: The Evolution of the Victorian Dog Fancy. Victorian Studies. Indiana University Press. Vol. 29, No. 2 (Winter, 1986), pp. 227-253.*

[6] *Frankham, Richard et al. Introduction to Conservation Genetics. Cambridge University Press. 2014. pg. 348.*

[7] *Ritvo, Harriet. Pride and Pedigree: The Evolution of the Victorian Dog Fancy. Victorian Studies. Indiana University Press. Vol. 29, No. 2 (Winter, 1986), pp. 227-253.*

[8] *Greger, Dayna L et al. Whole-genome sequence, SNP chips and pedigree structure: building demographic profiles in domestic dog breeds to optimize genetic-trait mapping. Disease Models and Mechanisms. 2016 Dec 1. Retrieved: 7/20/2018. https://www.ncbi.nlm.nih.gov/pmc/articles/PMC5200897/*

[9] *Matheny, Keith. Isle Royale likely down to 1 wolf — here's why it's a big problem. Detroit Free Press. December 4, 2017. https://www.freep.com/story/news/local/michigan/2017/12/04/one-wolf-isle-royale-pack/902023001/*

[10] *Flesher, John. Officials OK plan to rebuild Isle Royale wolf population. Associated Press. June 7, 2018. Retrieved: June 18, 2018.*

https://www.freep.com/story/news/local/michigan/2018/06/07/officials-ok-plan-rebuild-isle-royale-wolf-population/681565002/

[11] *Frankham, Richard et al. Introduction to Conservation Genetics. Cambridge University Press. 2014. pg. 199*

[12] *Frankham, Richard et al. Introduction to Conservation Genetics. Cambridge University Press. 2014. pg. 348.*

[13] *Crow, James F. Alternative Hypotheses of Hybrid Vigor. Dartmouth College. April 27, 1948. https://www.ncbi.nlm.nih.gov/pmc/articles/PMC1209419/pdf/477.pdf*

[14] *Conron, Wally. I Designed a Dog. My Story. Reader's Digest. July 10, 2007. https://web.archive.org/web/20120314061218/http://www.readersdigest.com.au/article/1 6022%26pageno%3D1*

[15] *Sue. All About Designer Dogs. fidosavvy.com. MyWay, LLC. 2019. Retrieved: February 7, 2019. https://www.fidosavvy.com/designer-dog-breeds.html*

[16] *AKC. AKC Announces New Program for Mixed Breeds. Press Release. April 14, 2009. https://www.akc.org/press-releases/akc-announces-new-program-for-mixed-breeds/*

[17] *The Kennel Club. Designer Dogs. https://www.thekennelclub.org.uk/our-resources/media-centre/issue-statements/designer-dogs/*

[18] *Humane Society Veterinary Medical Association. Guide to Congenital and Heritable Disorders in Dogs. May 2011.https://www.hsvma.org/assets/pdfs/guide-to-congenital-and-heritable-disorders.pdf*

[19] *Maldarelli, Claire. Best in Show, Are They Worst in Health? Scientific American. February 21, 2014 https://www.scientificamerican.com/article/although-purebred-dogs-can-be-best-in-show-are-they-worst-in-health/*

[20] *Powell, Denise. The Dalmatian/Pointer Backcross Project: Overcoming 20th Century Attitude about Crossbreeding. Tufts' Canine and Feline Breeding and Genetics Conference. 2011.https://www.vin.com/apputil/content/defaultadv1.aspx?id=5101841&pid=1134 0&print=1*

[21] *Zurflieh, Virginia. Underground News Flash!!! Reinventing the Box: The Fantastic Account of Dr Bruce Cattanach's Bobtail Boxers. 04/22/2000. Retrieved: February 8, 2019. http://www.nightrider.com/bu/1998%20issues/oct_bu_98/bobtail.htm*

[22] *Nichols, Anne; Kathy Berge; and Steve Dudley. Background: Why Pure-Bred Dogs Are in Trouble. Bernese Mountain Dog Vitality Project. 2017. Retrieved: February 8, 2019. https://www.bmdvitalityproject.org/background/*

[23] *Nichols, Anne; Kathy Berge; and Steve Dudley. Litters. Bernese Mountain Dog Vitality Project. 2017. Retrieved: February 8, 2019. https://www.bmdvitalityproject.org/litters*

[24] *Johannes, James E. Congo Trip 2010. Retrieved: February 8, 2019. https://web.archive.org/web/20160303172456/http://www.dibubasenjis.com/congo10.htm*

[25] *Basenji Club of America. Foundation Stock Sorted by Year of Import. 2017. https://www.basenji.org/index.php/sort-by-import-date*

[26] *Greger, Dayna L et al. Whole-genome sequence, SNP chips and pedigree structure: building demographic profiles in domestic dog breeds to optimize genetic-trait mapping. Disease Models and Mechanisms. 2016 Dec 1. Retrieved: 7/20/2018. https://www.ncbi.nlm.nih.gov/pmc/articles/PMC5200897/*

[27] *Chinook Club of America, Inc. A Brief History of the Chinook. Retrieved: February 8, 2019. http://www.chinookclubofamerica.org/chinook-history.html*

[28] *Chinook Owner's Association. Chinook Breed Conservation Program CBCP). Retrieved: 7/20/2018. https://chinook.org/chinook-conservation-program/*

[29] *Chinook Owner's Association. Chinook Breed Conservation Program CBCP). Retrieved: 7/20/2018. https://chinook.org/chinook-conservation-program/*

[30] *Kettunen, Anne; Marc Daverdin; Turid Helfjord, Peer Berg. Cross-Breeding Is Inevitable to Conserve the Highly Inbred Population of Puffin Hunter: The Norwegian Lundehund. PLoS One. January 20, 2017. https://journals.plos.org/plosone/article?id=10.1371/journal.pone.0170039*

[31] *Norwegian Lundehund Club. Questions and Answers on the Crossbreed Project. December 20, 2015. http://www.lundehund.no/index.php/english2/117-other-articles-in-english*

[32] *Stronen, Astrid V. et al. Genetic rescue of an endangered domestic animal through outcrossing with closely related breeds: A case study of the Norwegian Lundehund. PLoS One. June 1, 2017. Retrieved: 7/20/2018. http://journals.plos.org/plosone/article?id=10.1371/journal.pone.0177429*

[33] *Norse Kennel Club. The Norwegian Lundehund outcross project. 2015. Retrieved: February 8, 2019. file:///Users/admin/Downloads/The%20lundehund%20outcross%20-%20NKK.pdf*

[34] *Beuchat, Carol. Saving the Norwegian Lundehund: An Update from Milo. 1/18/2017. Retrieved: 7/20/2018. https://www.instituteofcaninebiology.org/blog/saving-the-lundehund-an-update-from-milo*

[35] *Van den Broek, Iris. Pedigree analysis and optimisation of the breeding program in the Irish Setter. Wageningen University. June 2017. http://www.jbuiten.nl/Ierse_setter/Eindversie%20thesis%20Ierse%20Setter%20-%20Iris%20van%20den%20Broek-1.pdf*

[36] *Ottesen, Merete and Thomas Ottesen. Outcross between irish setter and irish red and white setter 2018 – 5 puppies born 24. april – All puppies sold. 2017.https://alvertoppen.wordpress.com/2017/09/26/outcross-between-irish-setter-and-irish-red-and-white-setter-planned-autumn-of-2017/*

[37] *Irish Kennel Club. http://ikc-ie.access.secure-ssl-servers.info/international-outcross-programme-irish-red-and-white-setters-and-irish-red-setters*

[38] *Gubbels, Ed. J. The Conservation of the Wetterhoun. February 2012. https://www.nvsw.nl/uploads/downloads/Wetterfokbeleid/BehoudWetterhoun.pdf*

[39] *Dutch Association for Stabij and Wetterhoun. Outcross Breeding Policy. 2012.*

https://www.nvsw.nl/uploads/downloads/Wetterfokbeleid/FerliteitWetterhounen2005-2011.pdf

[40] *Roosendaal, Marjolein. March 13, 2012. Dutch Association for Stabij and Wetterhoun. Outcross Breeding Policy. 2012. https://www.nvsw.nl/index.php?sp=110*

[41] *Turcek, FJ (1951). "Effect of introductions on two game populations in Czechoslovakia". Journal of Wildlife Management. 15: 113–114.*

[42] *Steer, Gary. Wild Dog Dingo. Sky Visuals Pty Ltd. Video. Published 1986. https://www.youtube.com/watch?v=70vmFasMPHs&app=desktop*

[43] *Frankham, Richard; Ballou, Jonathan D. Introduction to Conservation Genetics. page look up*

Chapter 8

[1] *Sponenberg, D. Phillip; Beranger, Jeannette; Martin, Alison. Managing Breeds for a Secure Future: Strategies for Breeders and Breed Associations (Second Edition) (p. 97). 5m Publishing. Kindle Edition.*

[2] Sponenberg, D. Phillip; Beranger, Jeannette; Martin, Alison. Managing Breeds for a Secure Future: Strategies for Breeders and Breed Associations (Second Edition) (p. 98). 5m Publishing. Kindle Edition.

[3] *Mullen William. Extinction Came First, Then the Magic Egg. Chicago Tribune. October 3, 1999. Retrieved: February 8, 2019. https://www.chicagotribune.com/news/ct-xpm-1999-10-03-9910030250-story.html*

[4] *BBC News. BBC Drops Crufts from Schedule. December 12, 2008. Retrieved: February 12, 2019. http://news.bbc.co.uk/2/hi/uk/7779686.stm*

[5] *The Kennel Club Crufts. Crafts Broadcast Times and Presenters Announced. 02/26/2015. https://www.crufts.org.uk/content/news/crufts-broadcast-times-and-presenters-announced/*

[6] *Dog Breeding Reform Group. Welfare Reports: Introduction. Retrieved: February 12, 2009. http://www.dogbreedingreformgroup.uk/welfare-reports.html*

[7] *Irving, Ronnie. KC Chairman's Speech. Welsh Kennel Club Dinner. 2007. Retrieved: February 12, 2019. https://www.ourdogs.co.uk/News/2007/Aug2007/News240807/ronnie.htm*

[8] *AKC. Glossary. Retrieved: February 8, 2019. https://www.akc.org/about/glossary/*

[9] *AKC. Open Registration. Retrieved: February 9, 2019. https://www.akc.org/register/information/open-registration/*

[10] *EasyPetMD. Chinook. http://www.easypetmd.com/doginfo/chinook*

[11] *Chinook Club of America. A Brief History of the Chinook. 2016. Retrieved: February 9, 2019.http://www.chinookclubofamerica.org/chinook-history.html*

[12] *Amsden. Robert. The Most Famous Dog in the World. Laconia Daily Sun. December 29, 2016. Retrieved: February 9, 2019. https://www.laconiadailysun.com/news/local/the-most-famous-dog-in-the-world/article_cc354d9d-fe23-541f-8701-84561bf6c0f5.html*

[13] *Sponenberg, D. Phillip; Beranger, Jeannette; Martin, Alison. Managing Breeds for a Secure Future: Strategies for Breeders and Breed Associations (Second Edition) (p. 43). 5m Publishing. Kindle Edition.*

[14] *Australian Labradoodle Association of America. About Us. 2018. Retrieved: February 10, 2019. https://alaa-labradoodles.com/about-us.html*

[15] *Australian Labradoodle Association of America. About Us. 2018. Retrieved: February 10, 2019. https://alaa-labradoodles.com/about-us.html*

[16] *Kibele, Armin; Urs Granacher; Thomas Meuhlbauer; and David G Behm. Stable, Unstable and Metastable States of Equilibrium: Definitions and Applications to Human Movement. Journal of Sports Science and Medicine. November 24, 2015. https://www.ncbi.nlm.nih.gov/pmc/articles/PMC4657434/*

[17] *Sponenberg, D. Phillip; Beranger, Jeannette; Martin, Alison. Managing Breeds for a Secure Future: Strategies for Breeders and Breed Associations (Second Edition) (p. 93). 5m Publishing. Kindle Edition*

Chapter 9

[1] *Lanting, Fred. Hip X-ray Accuracy: Utility & Reliability: PennHIP vs. SV and OFA Hip-Extended Views. The Dog Place. Canine Genetics. November 2013. Retrieved: December 13, 2018. http://www.thedogplace.org/GENETICS/X-ray-Accuracy_Lanting-1312.asp* Dr.

[2] *Dr. Anthony Cambridge, board certified for veterinary surgeon. Recognizing Hip Dysplasia in Dogs - VetVid Episode 014. VetVid. www.thedogplace.org/Videos/Hip-Dysplasia.asp*

[3] *Health Certification. Barbara J Andrews. originally published in ShowSight Magazine. January 2001. The Dog Place. 2015 update. http://www.thedogplace.org/Genetics/Health-Certification1-0101_Andrews.asp*

[4] *Barbara J Andrews, Science Editor, SAAB, AKC Master Breeder www.thedogplace.org/Health/Xray-Risk-Shielded-1104_Andrews.asp*

[5] *https://pdfs.semanticscholar.org/7465/d2a1f574e7d0b76ef9de113be7ed6a7d67a6.pdf*

[6] *https://www.academia.edu/33562099/Genetic_analyses_of_elbow_and_hip_dysplasia_in_the_German_shepherd_dog*

[7] *Padgett, DVM. George A., Control of Canine Genetic Diseases. Howell Book House. New York. 1998. Page 10.*

7a *Padgett, George A., Control of Canine Genetic Diseases. Howell Book House. New York. 1998. Page 10.*

7b *Copping, Jason. Pedigree dogs face extinction due to inbreeding. The Daily Telegraph. May 11, 2008. Retrieved: March 2, 2019.*
https://www.telegraph.co.uk/news/earth/eathnews/3341924/Pedigree-dogs-face-extinction-due-to-inbreeding.html

8 *Padgett, George A. Control of Canine Genetic Diseases. Howell Book House. 1998. pg 8.*

Chapter 10

1 *Derr, Mark. How the Dog Became the Dog: From Wolves to Our Best Friends (p. 33). The Overlook Press. Kindle Edition.*

2 *PBS. Dogs Decoded. Nova. Transcript. November 9, 2010. Retrieved: June 06, 2011.*
https://www.pbs.org/wgbh/nova/nature/dogs-decoded.html

3 *PBS. Dogs Decoded. Nova. Transcript. November 9, 2010. Retrieved: June 06, 2011.*
https://www.pbs.org/wgbh/nova/nature/dogs-decoded.html

4 *Science News. Dogs' Intelligence On Par With Two-year-old Human, Canine Researcher Says. August 10, 2009. Retrieved: February 21, 2019.*
https://www.sciencedaily.com/releases/2009/08/090810025241.html

5 *Cooper, Anderson. The Smartest Dog in the World. 60 Minutes. CBS. October 5, 2014. Transcript. Retrieved: February 21, 2019. https://www.cbsnews.com/news/the-smartest-dog-in-the-world/*

6 *PBS. Dogs Decoded. Nova. Transcript. November 9, 2010. Retrieved: June 06, 2011.*
https://www.pbs.org/wgbh/nova/nature/dogs-decoded.html

7 *Ostrander, Elaine; Wayne, Robert. The canine genome. doi: 10.1101/gr.3736605 Genome Res. 2005. 15: 1706-1716 Cold Spring Harbor Laboratory Press*
https://genome.cshlp.org/content/15/12/1706.full.html

7a Levitis, Daniel A.; William Z Lidicker, Jr; and Glenn Freund. Behavioural biologists do not agree on what constitutes behaviour. Animal Behaviour. 78 (2009) 103-110. Retrieved: March 15, 2019.
https://www.reed.edu/biology/courses/bio342/2010_syllabus/2010_readings/levitis_etal_2009.pdf

7b Khan Academy. Learned Behaviors. Behavioral biology lessons. Retrieved March 15, 2019.
https://www.khanacademy.org/science/biology/behavioral-biology/animal-behavior/a/learned-behaviors?modal=1

8 *Woolf, Norma Bennet. Tough temperaments: Dominance, aggression viciousness – there is a difference. Dog Owner's Guide. 2019. Retrieved: February 21, 2019.*
http://www.canismajor.com/dog/behvterm.html

9 *Drake, Amber. Aggressive, Stable, Confident: How to Test Your Dog's Temperament. The Dog People. 2019. https://www.rover.com/blog/aggressive-stable-confident-test-dogs-*

temperament/

[10] Cole, Linda. *What Does "Dog Temperament" Really Mean? Canidae Blog. May 8, 2018.*
https://www.canidae.com/blog/2018/05/what-does-dog-temperament-really-mean/

[11] *American Temperament Testing Society, Inc. About Canine Temperament. 2019. Retrieved: February 21, 2019. https://atts.org/about-temperament*

[12] *Lopate, Cheryl. Management of Pregnant and Neonatal Dogs, Cats, an Exotic Pets. John Wiley & Sons Publishers. May 12, 2012. p 122.*

[12a] *Corr, Philip J.; Gerald Matthews. The Cambridge handbook of personality psychology. (1. publ. ed.) Cambridge: Cambridge University Press. 2009. ISBN 978-0-521-86218-9 Retrieved: March 15, 2019.*
https://www.researchgate.net/profile/Gerald_Matthews2/publication/228079787_The_Ca mbridge_Handbook_of_Personality_Psychology/links/0c96052c98c4802056000000.pdf

[13] *Jones, Amanda C and Samuel D. Gosling. Temperament and personality in dog (Canis familiaris): A review and evaluation of past research. Applied Animal Behaviour Science 95 (2005) 1-53. April 4, 2005.*
http://citeseerx.ist.psu.edu/viewdoc/download?doi=10.1.1.585.6800&rep1&type=pdf

[14] *Robins, Radcliffe. Understanding Dogs Temperament in Dogs – Its Role in Decision Making. Retrieved: February 19, 2019. www.hsi.org/assets/pddfs/temperament_dogs.pdf*

[15] *Robins, Radcliffe. Understanding Dogs Temperament in Dogs – Its Role in Decision Making. Retrieved: February 19, 2019. www.hsi.org/assets/pddfs/temperament_dogs.pdf*

[16] *Taylor, Cynthia and F. John Meaney. Heritability. Encyclopedia Britannica. January 28, 2014. Retrieved: February 14, 2019. https://www.britannica.com/science/heritability*

[17] *Whiteside, Kelly. Westminster Dog Show: When Good Dogs Behave Badly. New York Times. February 12, 2019. Retrieved: February 14, 2019.*
https://www.nytimes.com/2019/02/12/sports/best-in-show-westminster-bad-dogs.html?smid=nytcore-ios-share&fbclid=IwAR2pV0xSfpTMWWv2ixMb0D7nGtaeIKrZY4DtFJTrs4Z8bnUDMV bRrD9grTw

[18] *Scott, John Paul and John L Fuller. Genetics and the Social Behavior of the Dog. University of Chicago Press. 1965. Kindle Edition. Chapter 1: A School for Dogs; para 13*

[19] *Scott, John Paul and John L Fuller. Genetics and the Social Behavior of the Dog. University of Chicago Press. 1965. Kindle Edition. Ch 1: A School for Dogs; The Observation of Development, para 3.*

[20] *Hepper, Peter G. and Deborah L Wells. Perinatal Olfactory Learning in the Domestic Dog. Chemical Senses, Volume 31, Issue 3, March 1, 2006. Pages 207-212.*
https://doi.org/10.1093/chemse/bjj020.
https://academic.oup.com/chemse/article/31/3/207/342446

[21] *Scott, John Paul and John L Fuller. Genetics and the Social Behavior of the Dog. University of Chicago Press. 1965. Kindle Edition. Chapter 4: The Development of Behavior; The Neonatal Period; Capacities for organization of behavior, para 1.*

[22] *Scott, John Paul and John L Fuller. Genetics and the Social Behavior of the Dog. University of Chicago Press. 1965. Kindle Edition. Chapter 4: The Development of Behavior; The Neonatal Period; Summary, para 2.*

[23] *Scott, John Paul and John L Fuller. Genetics and the Social Behavior of the Dog. University of Chicago Press. 1965. Kindle Edition. Chapter 4: The Development of Behavior; The Neonatal Period; Social Behaviors, para 5.*

[24] *Scott, John Paul and John L Fuller. Genetics and the Social Behavior of the Dog. University of Chicago Press. 1965. Kindle Edition. Chapter 4: The Development of Behavior; The Neonatal Period; Motor capacities, fig. 4.1.*

[25] *Wilsson, Erik and Per-Erik Sundgren. Behaviour test for eight-week old puppies – heritabilities of tested behaviour traits and its correspondence to later behaviour. Applied Animal Behaviour Science. 58 (1997) 151-162. Retrieved: February 24, 2019. https://eurekamag.com/pf/008/008217168.pdf*

[26] *Riemer, Stefanie, Muller C, Viranyi Z, Huber L, Range F. The Predictive Value of Early Behavioural Assessments in Pet Dogs – A Longitudinal Study from Neonates to Adults. PLoS ONE. 9(7):3101237. 2014. Retrieved: February 24, 2019. https://doi.org/10.1371/journal.pone.0101237*

[27] *Riemer, Stefanie, Muller C, Viranyi Z, Huber L, Range F. The Predictive Value of Early Behavioural Assessments in Pet Dogs – A Longitudinal Study from Neonates to Adults. PLoS ONE. 9(7):3101237. 2014. Retrieved: February 24, 2019. https://doi.org/10.1371/journal.pone.0101237*

[28] *Grandin, Temple and Mark J. Deesing. Behavioral Genetics and Animal Science. Academic Press. April 21, 2017. Retrieved: February 23, 2019. http://www.grandin.com/references/genetics.html*

[29] *AKC. Whippet. 2019. https://www.akc.org/dog-breeds/whippet/*

[30] *Crufts. Flyball – Team Final. Crufts 2016. Youtube video. Retrieved: February 25, 2019. https://www.youtube.com/watch?v=Drp8Gu4lx5U*

[31] *London, Karen B. Mastiff on Agility Course. Bark magazine. December 2015. Updated July 2016. Retrieved: February 22, 2019. https://thebark.com/content/mastiff-agility-course*

[32] *AKC. Bloodhound. 2019. Retrieved: February 22, 2019. http://www.akc.org/dog-breeds/bloodhound/*

[33] *AKC. Bloodhound. 2019. Retrieved: February 22, 2019. http://www.akc.org/dog-breeds/bloodhound/*

[34] *Cross Adventuring. How Long Does It Take a Bloohound to Track and Locate a Missing Person? July 2, 2017. Youtube video. Retrieved: February 25, 2019. https://www.youtube.com/watch?v=y_LWofOdrws*

[35] *Trut, Lyudmila, Irina Oskina, and Anastasiya Kharlamova. Animal evolution during domestication: the domesticated fox as a model. Institute of Cytology and Genetics, Siberian Branch of Russian Academy of Sciences. Novosibirsk, Russia. March 3, 2009. Retrieved: February 25, 2019. https://doi.org/10.1002/bies.2008000070*

[36] *Marazita, Mary L., Quantitative genetics and the first golden age of genetics. Trends in Genetics. Volume 15, Issue 3, 120. March 01, 1999. Retrieved: February 25, 2019. https://www.cell.com/trends/genetics/pdf/S0168-9525(98)01657-6.pdf*

[37] *O'Brien, Eleanor, John Hunt, and Jason B Wolf. Quantitative Genetics. Oxford Bibliographies. April 29, 2015. Retrieved: February 25, 2019. http://www.oxfordbibliographies.com/view/document/obo-9780199941728/obo-9780199941728-0064.xml*

[38] *Yoshy on May 25, 2010 from the Shiloh Shepherd Dog discussion located on German Shepherd Dog Forum http://www.pedigreedatabase.com/community.read?post=391145-shiloh-shepherds&p=7*

[39] *Goffe, Sheila. The US has become a dumping ground for foreign 'puppy mill' and 'rescue' dog. Here's what needs to change" FOX News. June 30, 2018. Retrieved: February 25, 2019. https://www.foxnews.com/opinion/the-us-has-become-a-dumping-ground-for-foreign-puppy-mill-and-rescue-dogs-heres-what-needs-to-change.*

Chapter 11

[0] *In Brief. Do I need a licence for breeding and selling dogs? Animal Law. Retrieved: February 11, 2019. https://www.inbrief.co.uk/animal-law/licences-for-the-breeding-and-sale-of-dogs/*

[1] *Norwich, Edward of, The Master of the Game, pgs: 82-83*

[2] *Whitney, Leon F. How to Breed Dogs. Howell Book House. New York. 1971. Revised Edition. Pages 53-54.*

[3] *Onstott, Kyle. The New Art of Breeding Better Dogs. Howell Book House. 1962. Second Edition. Page 201.*

[4] *Driscoll, Carlos, David MacDonald, and Stephen J. O'Brien. From Wild Animals to Domestic Pets, an Evolutionary View of Domestication. National Academy of Sciences. National Academy Press. 2009. Retrieved: February 26, 2019. https://www.ncbi.nlm.nih.gov/books/NBK219727*

[5] *Homer. The Iliad of Homer. Gutenberg Project. Retrieved: ebruary 26, 2019. https://www.gutenberg.org/files/6130/6130-pdf.pdf*

[6] *Discovery. Facts about the Red Fox. Nature Encyclopedia. Humanima Portal. Retrieved: February 26, 2019. http://www.humanima.com/decouverte/en/article/red-fox*

[7] *Goldman, Jason. Monday Pets: The Russian Fox Study. Scientific American. The Thoughtful Animal. June 14, 2010. Retrieved: February 26, 2019. https://blogs.scientificamerican.com/thought-animal/monday-pets-the-russian-fox-study*

[8] *Trut, Lyudmila, Irina Oskina, and Anastasiya Kharlamova. Animal evolution during domestication: the domesticated fox as a model. Institute of Cytology and Genetics, Siberia Branch of Russian Academy of Sciences. BioEssays 31:349-360. 2009. Doi: 10.1002/bies.200800070.Retrieved: February 26, 2019. https://onlinelibrary.wiley.com/doi/epdf/10.1002/bies.200800070*

[9] *Anjali Aggarwal, Ramesh Upadhyay. Heat Stress and Animal Productivity. Dairy Cattle Physiology Department, National Dairy Research Institute in India. Springer India. 2013.*

[10] *Driscoll, Carlos, David MacDonald, and Stephen J. O'Brien. From Wild Animals to Domestic Pets, an Evolutionary View of Domestication. National Academy of Sciences. National Academy Press. 2009. Retrieved: February 26, 2019. https://www.ncbi.nlm.nih.gov/books/NBK219727*

[11] *FixNation. Feral Cat FAQ's. Retrieved: February 26, 2019. http://www.fixnation.org/about-tnr/faqs /#Q9*

[12] *Llera, Ryan and Cheryl Yuill. Estrous Cycles in Cats. VCA Animal Hospitals. Retrieved: February 26, 2019. https://vcshospitals.com/know-your-pet/estrus-cycles-in-cats*

[13] *Stager, Curt. When domesticated animals return to the wild. Natural Selection. Canton, New York. February 25, 2016. Retrieved: February 26, 2019. https://www.northcountrypublicradio.org/news/story/31104/20160225/when-domesticated-animals-return-to-the-wild*

[14] *Burrell, Sue. Dingo. Australian Museum. Animal Species. November 29, 2018. Retrieved: July 16, 2018. https://australianmuseum.net.au/learn/animals/mammals/dingo*

[15] *Seal, U.S., E.D. Plotka, J.M. Packard, and L.D. Mech. Endocrine Correlates of Reproduction in the Wolf. I. Serum Progesterone, Estradiol LH during the Estrous Cycle. Biology of Reproduction 21, pp. 1057-2066. 1979. Retrieved: February 26, 2019.*

[16] *Conaway, Clinton H. and Carl B. Koford. Estrous Cycles and Mating Behavior in a Free-Ranging Band of Rhesus Monkeys. Journal of Mammalogy, Volume 45, Issue 4, January 1965. Pages 577-588. https://doi.org/10.2307/1377329*

[17] *MountainNature.com. Bear Reproduction. Retrieved: February 26, 2019. http://www.mountainnature.com/wildlife/bears/bearreproduction.htm*

[18] *Get Bear Smart Society. Reproduction. Retrieved: February 26, 2019. http://www.bearsmart.com/about-bears/reproduction*

[19] *Smart, Sylvia. Dog Breeders Professional Secrets. Dogwise Publishing. 2009. Pg. 55.*

[20] *Kroker, Geoff, Bendigo and Lisa Clarke, Hamilton. Age of beef heifers at first mating. Agriculture Victoria. June 2000. Retrieved: February 26, 2019. http://agriculture.vicgov.au/agriculture/livesstock/beef/breeding/age-of-beef-heifers-at-first-mating*

[21] *Kroker, Geoff, Bendigo and Lisa Clarke, Hamilton. Age of beef heifers at first mating. Agriculture Victoria. June 2000. Retrieved: February 26, 2019. http://agriculture.vicgov.au/agriculture/livesstock/beef/breeding/age-of-beef-heifers-at-first-mating*

[22] *Whitney, Leon F. How to Breed Dogs. Howell Book House. New York. 1971. Page 53*

[23] *UNL Beef. At what age I it safe to breed a heifer? Institute of Agriculture and Natural Resources. October 6, 2009. https://beef.unl.edu/faq-2009breedingage*

[24] Schoenian, Susan. *To breed or not to breed: Breeding ewe lambs and doelings.* Maryland Small Ruminant Page. 2010. Updated: 2015. Retrieved: February 26, 2019. https://www.sheepandgoat.com/breedingewelambs

[25] James, Debbie. *Guide to breeding from ewe lambs.* Farmers Weekly. July 27, 2017. Retrieved: February 26, 2019. https://www.fwico.uk/livestock/livestock-breeding/guide-to-breeding-from-ewe-lambs

[26] Hulet, C.V., R.L. Blackwell, S.K. Ercanbrack, D.A. Price, L.O. Wilson. *Mating Behavior of the Eye.* Journal of Animal Science. Volume 21, Issue 4. November 1, 1962. Pages 870-874. https://doi.org/10.2527/jas1962.214870x

[27] Young, L.G., et al. *Reproductive performance over four parities of gilts stimulated to early estrus and mated at first, second or third observed estrus.* Canadian Journal of Animal Science. 1990 70(2): 483-492. Retrieved: February 26, 2019. https://doi.org/10.4141/cjas90-060, http://www.nrcreasearchpress.com/doi/pdf/10.4141/cjas90-060

[28] Kilborn, Susan H., Guy Trudel, Hans Uhthoff. *Review of Growth Plate Closure Compared with Age at Sexual Maturity and Lifespan in Laboratory Animals.* Journal of the American Association for Laboratory Animal Science. Volume 41, Number 5, pp. 21-26(6). September 2002. Retrieved: February 26, 2019. https://www.ingentaconnect.com/content/aalas/jaalas/2002/00000041/00000005/are00005#

[29] Onstott, Kyle. *The New Art of Breeding Better Dogs.* Howell Book House. 1962. Second Edition. Page 33-34.

Chapter 12

[1] Cunningham, David. *Friends of Pedigree Dogs Exposed Group.* Facebook. April 20, 2017. Used with permission.

[2] Freedman, Adam H. et al. *Genome Sequencing Highlights the Dynamic Early History of Dogs.* PLOS Genetics. January 16, 2014. http://journals.plos.org/plosgenetics/article?id=10.1371/journal.pgen.1004016

[3] Freedman, Adam H. et al. *Genome Sequencing Highlights the Dynamic Early History of Dogs.* PLOS Genetics. January 16, 2014. http://journals.plos.org/plosgenetics/article?id=10.1371/journal.pgen.1004016

[4] Axelsson E, Ratnakumar A, Arendt M-J, Maqbool K, Webster MT, et al. (2013) *The genomic signature of dog domestication reveals adaptation to a starch-rich diet.* Nature 495: 360–364.

[5] Zhenxin, Fan. et.al. *Worldwide patterns of genomic variation and admixture in gray wolves.* Advance. Cold Spring Harbor Laboratory Press. Genome Research. 2016. 26: 163-173

[6] Cunningham, David. *Friends of Pedigree Dogs Exposed Group.* Facebook. April 20, 2017. Used with permission.

[7] Brulliard, Karen. *Dire wolves were real. Now someone is trying to resurrect them.*

Washington Post. July 31, 2017.
https://www.washingtonpost.com/news/animalia/wp/2017/07/31/dire-wolves-were-real-now-someone-is-trying-to-resurrect-them/?utm_term=.e7db594b9121

[2] *London, Karen. The Eyes Have It – What Can Be Seen In a Dog's Eyes. Dog Behavior Blog. May 12, 2008. https://www.dogbehaviorblog.com/2008/05/the-eyes-have-i.html*

Chapter 13

[1] *Schwarz, Lois. Outcrossing to the Irish Wolfhound. 2011.*
www.schwarzdogs.com/outcrossing-to-the-irish-wolfhound

[2] *Frankham, Richard et al. Introduction to Conservation Genetics. Cambridge University Press. 2014. pg. 352*

Appendix A

[1] *Christine Vara, December 14, 2016, Shot of Prevention (Blog), Attacks on Journalist Brian Deer on Poor Scholarship and Unethical Behavior.*
https://shotofprevention.com/2016/12/14/attacks-on-journalist-brian-deer-based-on-poor-scholarship-unethical-behavior/#more-14916

[2] *Kerasote, Ted, Bloodties: Nature, Culture, and the Hunt. Kodansha Globe. 1994. Page 266.*

[3] *HumaneWatch.org. Wayback Machine 1, Markarian 0. HumaneWatch.org. August 9, 2010. Received: July 15, 2018.*
https://www.humanewatch.org/wayback_machine_1_markerian_0/

Appendix D

[1] *Varel, Ozan. Facts Don't Change People's Minds. Here's What Does. Next Big Idea Club. September 8, 2017. Retrieved: February 27, 2019. https://heleo.com/facts-dont-change-peoples-minds-heres/16242/*

About the Author

Jennifer Stoeckl and Odessa (Packer/Ricotta)

Jennifer Stoeckl is the co-founder of the Dire Wolf Project working closely with her mother, Lois Schwarz, to bring about a new hope of healthier, long-lived lives for our most beloved furry companions. She spent over ten years in apprenticeship learning the benefits of some of the most misunderstood ideas in dog breeding. She has come to know just what it takes to speak up with steadfast purpose for what is right when it comes to fighting for a better life for those creatures that cannot speak for themselves. In the midst of the highly-charged dog breeding and showing world where high-stakes prizes, prestige, and money blind those from seeing the desperate cry of pain and suffering that comes with strictly breeding within an archaic and outdated eugenics-based system, she stands with the Dire Wolf Project in firm opposition. Surrounded by equally outspoken animal activists who ultimately claim irresponsible and harmful dog breeding rhetoric and shame those who dare to speak out against them, she rises up with the Dire Wolf Project to bravely proclaim the truth behind responsible dog breeding She understands that the animals in our care deserve to be protected from tyrannical and oppressive breeding practices that ultimately harm their futures. With a strong belief that our cherished dogs deserve to live long and happy lives free of any pain that could have been prevented by breeding for superior health above all else, she brings together scientific research and logical reasoning to present a better way of breeding man's best friend.

In 2008, Jennifer Stoeckl began DireWolf Dogs of Vallecito raising healthy, loving, large-breed family companion dogs. She works tirelessly each day to increase awareness of and bring about lasting hope for the future of the dogs in her care. She works with families all around the world to help them find their next tail-wagging best friend, whether it is from her or someone else. Her main interest is in helping to match the best families with the best dogs.

In 2010, Jennifer co-founded DireWolf Guardians American Alsatian Dog Training Program in order to help those who cannot otherwise own a dog unless it is highly and specifically trained for a special need. She trains many different types of service dogs, but is also interested in expanding into courthouse facility therapy dogs where the wild look of a DireWolf Dog may provide comfort and emotional protection for victims of violent crime, especially children.

Jennifer received her Bachelor of Arts degree in French language from Oregon State University. She studied French language and culture at the University of Poitiers, France in 1997. After graduating, she then traveled to Namibia in Africa as a teacher trainer in 1999 where she lived in a mud hut working at local schools to improve the educational experience for children living in the rural savanna. Upon returning to the United States, Jennifer received a Master's degree in Education from George Fox University in Oregon and became a special education teacher where she helped young children navigate school systems with limited resources. She eventually left teaching in 2015 to pursue advocating for increased health and stable temperaments for our four-legged friends through the Dire Wolf Project's unique breeding practices

She lives with her husband, Jay, in the beautiful inland northwest on 28 acres of Ponderosa forest surrounded by state and federal land only a few hundred yards from the glorious Columbia River. In keeping with her humanitarian heart, she became a professed member of the Secular Franciscan Order in 2005 and continuously seeks to live a meager life without the trappings of most societal must-haves, while devoting her life to helping others through her generous support of families in need. She currently lives in a forty-year old 300 square foot motor home where she writes on a solar-powered computer that rests on a small RV dinette booth. She loves nature and animals, believing that all of life is precious from the moment it is formed in the womb to the moment it departs this earth seeking peaceful rest.

In the years to come, Jennifer hopes to continue helping others through her love of dogs. She hopes that all of her life's experiences will guide her to always take the next right step each moment of every day.

Other Dire Wolf Project Books

The American Alsatian
By: Lois Schwarz

Handbook for New Puppy Owners
By: Lois Schwarz

Want a really beautiful and healthy breed of dog? If you are thinking about bringing a new puppy into your family, then check out this breed! And before you commit, do the work! Research the breed. Buy this book to help you understand the total breed. Educate thoroughly before you buy your new puppy.

An easy to understand care and training guide. The founder of the Dire Wolf Project, Lois Schwarz, takes you step-by-step, foot-by-foot, through a teaching process that is so simple you will wonder why no one ever told you about this before! This is a MUST have for any dog lover who wants a happy, well-mannered, loving dog.

eBook: $19.00
Paperback: $39.00

eBook: $19.00
Paperback: $39.00

Send check or money order to:
Lois Schwarz
4175 Winnetka Road
White City, OR 97503

Made in the USA
Coppell, TX
18 November 2021

65986788R00214